THE CO

A book in the series

Latin America Otherwise: Languages, Empires, Nations

Series editors:

Walter D. Mignolo, Duke University

Irene Silverblatt, Duke University

Sonia Saldívar-Hull, University of California at Los Angeles

THE CORD KEEPERS

Khipus and Cultural Life in a Peruvian Village

Frank Salomon

DUKE UNIVERSITY PRESS Durham and London 2004

© 2004 Duke University Press
All rights reserved
Printed in the United States of America on acid-free paper ∞
Typeset in Minion by Tseng Information Systems, Inc.
Library of Congress Cataloging-in-Publication Data appear
on the last printed page of this book.

CONTENTS

ILLUSTRATIONS AND MAPS

Figures

Maps

TABLES

Latin America Otherwise: Languages, Empires, Nations is a critical series. It aims to explore the emergence and consequences of concepts used to define "Latin America" while at the same time exploring the broad interplay of political, economic, and cultural practices that have shaped Latin American worlds. Latin America, at the crossroads of competing imperial designs and local responses, has been construed as a geocultural and geopolitical entity since the nineteenth century. This series provides a starting point to redefine Latin America as a configuration of political, linguistic, cultural, and economic intersections that demands a continuous reappraisal of the role of the Americas in history, and of the ongoing process of globalization and the relocation of people and cultures that have characterized Latin America's experience. *Latin America Otherwise: Languages, Empires, Nations* is a forum that confronts established geocultural constructions, that rethinks area studies and disciplinary boundaries, that assesses convictions of the academy and of public policy, and that, correspondingly, demands that the practices through which we produce knowledge and understanding about and from Latin America be subject to rigorous and critical scrutiny.

The Incas were a great mystery—at least according to many Western pundits who could not understand how a complex, highly stratified empire, stretching from southern Colombia to northwest Argentina, with a road system larger than Rome's and a political organization that incorporated millions—could have existed without a "true" or European-like system of writing and accounting. The Incas' closest instrument was the *khipu*—a set of knotted cords that served, in ways we hardly understand, as the nerve system of an empire.

One frontier of Andean scholarship today is trying to making sense of the khipu, and Frank Salomon's exciting book is a pioneering contribution to the field. Salomon's curiosity was piqued when he noted that village leaders in Tupicocha, a community in the central Peruvian Andes, proudly wore khipus as a badge of civic authority. While these men couldn't decipher their khipus' meanings, they did offer Salomon their historical knowledge. The result of this exchange, along with an exploration into other khipu legacies, is an intriguing investigation into these knotted cords and their contexts of use over a period of four centuries. Significantly, Salomon, in the process, challenges us to reexamine our own assumptions about the relation between writing and "civilization" as well as about the nature of "writing" itself.

A T THE START, newcomers to Inka studies always ask, "Could they write?" Chalk in hand, I falter. The answers don't sound reasonable: "Yes, but not in any way we can explain." Or, "No, but they behaved like a literate society anyway."

This puzzlement is as old as contact itself. Hardly had Spanish soldiers hit the beach of what is now northern Peru, when Hernando Pizarro himself (1920 [1533]:175) was startled to see "Indians" recording in knots what seemed like double-entry accounts for things the invaders had taken away. Yet the technique for keeping records on knotted cords, called *khipus*, is one aspect of America that Europe never really discovered. Later, when half a colonial century had gone by, Spaniards seemed almost resigned to just not "getting" the Andean way of recording. No early Spanish colonist is known to have made a concerted effort at learning it, even though experience had taught Spanish judges to respect the accuracy of Inka-style records.

"Could they write?" was also an interesting issue to Andean natives who grew up in the age of conquest. A lifetime after Pizarro saw his first khipu, an unknown Quechua-speaking native of central Peru wrote the only known book which preserves a pre-Christian religious system in an Andean language. It starts with these words:

> If the ancestors of the people called Indians had known writing in former
> times,
> Then the lives they lived would not have faded from view until now.

As the mighty past of the Spanish Vira Cochas is visible until now,
So too would theirs be.
But since things are as they are,
And since nothing has been written until now,
I set forth here the lives of the ancient forebears of the Huaro Cheri people,
Who all descend from one common forefather.

What faith they held,
How they live up until now,
Those things and more.
Village by village it will all be written down:

How they lived from their dawning age onward.
(Salomon and Urioste 1991:41–42, 157).

This anonymous writer himself knew about khipus and mentioned them twice (Salomon and Urioste 1991:112, 211, 142, 242). But if khipus were among his sources, he kept that fact to himself. After all, he was writing at a time—circa 1608—when "extirpators of idolatry" were under orders to burn khipus. As it happens, villagers of his own home today hold a set of khipus which offer a tantalizing clue to the unknown system. That set is the subject of this book.

To the set's owners, too, "Could they write?" is still an interesting problem. Troubled with their relationship to a sacred but no longer intelligible legacy, which they see as crucial to their cultural self-image, they were kind enough to let me delve into it.

But why is "Could they write?" such a compelling question? What's so important about this question anyway? What do we mean when we ask? Is there a better way to ask? These doubts, too, were among the reasons for undertaking the book.

For several years I was devoted to studying the anonymous Huarochirano's words (Salomon and Urioste 1991). At first, in John V. Murra's Cornell classroom in the 1970s, the names of the Huarochirí *ayllus* (corporate descent groups) such as Sat Pasca or Caca Sica had sounded to my novice ear as fabulous as the names of Gilgamesh and Utnapishtim the Faraway. Much later, in 1989, I began traveling around Huarochirí to learn the ecological, political, and land-tenure facts mythicized by stories of the ancient divinities (*huacas*). It turned out that the ancient ayllus were still very much in business, carrying on the ancient and heroic task of wringing an agropastoral living from the semiarid heights. Satafasca, Cacasica, and Allauca were names on soccer jerseys.

As it happens, my acquaintance with the cord records of Tupicocha village (1994) coincided with the beginnings of a period of renewed interest in Inka khipus. I hope the results will add something—much less than a decipherment, but more than a speculation—to the perennially baffling task of recapturing a code seemingly different from all other "lost scripts."

I also hope that it will in some measure repay the generosity of the many who supported this study.

The institutions that supported research were the Instituto de Estudios Peruanos in Lima, the John Simon Guggenheim Memorial Foundation, the National Science Foundation under grant 144-FW88, the School of American Research under its National Endowment for the Humanities Resident Fellowship, the University of Wisconsin Graduate School Research Committee, and the Wenner-Gren Foundation for Anthropological Research. Their support is deeply appreciated.

Just as crucial were institutions in Huarochirí: the *parcialidades* (sectors) of Tupicocha, which own the *quipocamayos*, the Comunidad Campesina of San Andrés de Tupicocha, and the Municipality. The parcialidad of Segunda Satafasca and the Peasant Community are thanked with special warmth for granting me honorary membership.

Several museums kindly helped me view pre-Hispanic khipus: the American Museum of Natural History in New York, the Musée de l'Homme in Paris, the Museo Nacional de Antropología y Arqueología in Lima, and the Ethnologisches Museum of the Preussischer Kulturbesitz in Berlin. The staff of the Archivo Nacional de Historia in Lima, and especially Director of Lima's Archivo Arzobispal, Laura Gutiérrez Arbulú, together with her cataloger Melecio Tineo Morón, were of great help. Father Thomas Huckemann of the Prelatura de Cañete, Yauyos, and Huarochirí helped with the problem of lost parish archives. Susan Lee Bruce of Harvard's Peabody Museum is thanked for her clarifications about the Tello-Hrdlička holdings.

Gary Urton, the anthropologist who has done the most to advance khipu studies in recent years, has proven a clear-sighted and generous colleague at every turn and an able convener of the community of khipu enthusiasts, which includes William Conklin, Regina Harrison, Tristan Platt, and many others. There is a special connection among ethnographers who share a terrain, and among these Hilda Araujo, then of Peru's Universidad Nacional Agraria de la Molina, stands out. To see her at work in the field is to know the gold standard of ethnography. I am glad I had a chance to learn from Marcia Ascher and Robert Ascher, who created the modern foundations of khipu study and whose courses I foolishly missed in Ithaca. The scholars who helped me along with dialogue, critique, hospitality, or a practical leg up are innumerable. I would like to thank especially Tom Abercrombie, Francisco Boluarte together with Teresa Guillén de B., Duccio Bonavia, Tom Cummins, John Earls, Marie Gaida, Patricia Hilts, Kitty Julien, Daniel Levine, Carmen Beatriz Loza, Pat Lyon, Carol Mackey, Bruce Mannheim, Regis Miller, Patricia Oliart, Juan Ossio, Elena Phipps, Jeffrey Quilter, Joanne Rappaport, María Rostworowski, Vera Roussakis, the late John Rowe, Gerald Taylor, Luis Eduardo Vergara Lipinsky, Nathan Wachtel, and Tom Zuidema. It was a pleasure and an honor to work with Karen Spalding, who helped make Huarochirí a canonical name among Latin Americanist historians. (What Karen and I did together forms two sections of chapter 5: "A Late-Colonial Episode of Rebellion, Ethnicity, and Media Pluralism" and "The Implications of a Campaign of Corded Letters.") Many turns back in the winding road, this all began with George Urioste's Cornell seminar on the Huarochirí Quechua manuscript.

At the University of Wisconsin, Madison, wonderful students helped with various parts of the project: Melania Alvarez-Adem, Mark Goodale, Jason K. McIntire, and Steve Wernke, who helped create the project Web site (http://www. anthropology.wisc.edu/chaysimire/index.htm). Department Administrator Maggie Brandenburg kept work on track with her almost magical knack for problem solving. David McJunkin provided radiocarbon expertise, Richard Bisbing of McCrone Associates Laboratory provided fiber expertise, and Onno and Marika Brouwer did the cartography. Kildo Choi and Robert Bryson drew the diagrams.

This book grew under the glittering aspens of Santa Fe at the School of American Research (SAR), where Doug Schwartz, Nancy Owen-Lewis, and an able staff helped it along. Thanks especially to Sally Wagner, for donating a dream house, which is the kind of house writers need. Thanks to my homey Ana Celia Zentella for showing what kind of human being an anthropologist ought to be. For good times and good thoughts, I thank my other SAR "classmates," especially Dave Edwards. Edith Salomon L. Rosenblatt and Wilhelm Rosenblatt, of Albuquerque, helped distill a drop of the ancient scholarly stuff from other times and places.

In Peru, the people who sustained this job are beyond counting. Among the residents of Huarochirí (provincial capital), Abelardo Santisteban Tello provided insight into the regional inheritance. In Tupicocha, I owe special thanks to Celso Alberco and his family, including the colony which his sister Maritza founded in Elmhurst, Queens, New York — right around the corner from where my then-immigrant mother, Mathilde Loewen, went to high school half a century before. León Modesto Rojas Alberco and his family taught me a world of village history. Margareto Romero generously opened Mújica's archive. Don Alberto Vilcayauri and his daughter Elba Vilcayauri were faithful guides and helpers to me, as they are to all "Tutecos." I am especially grateful to young Nery Javier and to his family. Alejandro Martínez Chuquizana and Tueda A. Villaruel, schoolteachers and friends of local culture, helped find some vital links to the tradition. With Wilfredo Urquiza of Tuna, Roberto Sacramento of Concha, and Martín Camilo of Tupicocha, all philosophically minded men, I passed hours of discussion on the mountain path or in the patio. Mayor Roy A. Vilcayauri provided help including work space in the Municipal Hall. Aurelio Ramos, who brought the computer age to Tupicocha, provided cartographic assistance. The people consulted on specialized cultural matters are mentioned by their real names in the chapters, and to each of them I am grateful. The staffs of the NGO Instituto de Desarrollo y Medio Ambiente and of the public health post, as well as the storekeeper Lidia Ramos, helped keep life cheerful during the murky months of fog.

I would like to thank the Guevara-Gil family, Oscar and María Benavides, the Bronstein family, and the Flint-Baer family, all of Lima, for their many acts of kindness toward Laurel Mark, my kids, and me. The Mayer family, especially the late Lisbeth Mayer, and the family of Liduvina Vásquez became dear to us in those years for more than scholarly reasons. I thank my kids, Mollie and Abe, for their patience and awakening sympathy with Peru. As for the joy that carries one through the days, nobody really knows where it comes from, but I think mine comes from Mercedes Niño-Murcia.

THE CORD KEEPERS

FIGURE 1   Villagers looking at quipocamayo on author's
work table. From personal collection of author.

THE UNREAD LEGACY:

AN INTRODUCTION TO TUPICOCHA'S KHIPU

PROBLEM, AND ANTHROPOLOGY'S

I N 1994, a fluke of ethnographic luck brought me face to face with the officers of Tupicocha village, Peru, as they draped themselves in skeins of knotted cords which constitute the most sacred of their community's many traditional regalia. Villagers call these *quipocamayos*, a cognate of the ancient Quechua word for a khipu master, *khipukamayuq*. The core Quechua sense of *khipu* is 'knot.' They also call the cords *equipos*, or *caytus* (the latter deriving from a Quechua term meaning "wool thread, spool of wool, ball of wool, piece of cloth, string, cord, etc." according to Jorge Lira (1982 [1941]:127).

Khipus are usually associated with Inka archaeology. Although "ethnographic" khipus for herding or confessing are known, historians treat the political role of khipus as a chapter that closed early in the colonial era. Tupicocha's cords represented an unsuspected continuity and, with it, an unexpected chance to see how this pristine graphic tradition functioned in political context. That lucky encounter provides an entry into a central problem of Andean studies: the management of complex information in a state-level society lacking "writing" as usually understood.

Tupicocha provides no Rosetta stone. But it does open an ethnographic and ethnohistorical window on how the cord system articulated political life as organized by corporate kinship groups. It also provides some clues about specific details of the code. In following them up, I will suggest how an "ethnography of writing" — Keith Basso's term (1974) — must be extended to put systems grossly different from alphabetic "writing" onto an even heuristic footing with more familiar ones.

A Glimpse of Equipos and a Glance at Semiological Pluralism

In 1994 I was seeking early-colonial indigenous writing related to a 1608 Quechua text. I sought it where the source originated: around the mountain village of San Damián near the center of Huarochirí Province in Peru's Department of Lima (see map 1; Salomon 1995, 1998a, 2002b). San Damián de los Checa is a name with ethnohistorical charisma.[1] It was here, in what the Inkas called the "Thousand of Checa" (Huaranga de Checa in Hispano-Quechua),[2] that an anonymous native scribe around 1608 wrote the only known book recording the lore of the pre- or non-Christian deities in an Andean language (Salomon and Urioste 1991; Taylor 1997). The unknown compiler wrote in Quechua, the political language of the Inka state and later the "general language" of early Spanish rule. He used the alphabet and many scribal conventions.

In San Damián Milton Rojas, a schoolteacher who grew up in a Huarochirí peasant home, kept a tiny part-time store. I liked to kill a twilight half hour there because he had made a cheerful little museum of it. He painted the walls glossy green, and decorated them with a changing array of oddments gathered from magazines and NGO brochures. Teacher's college had given him some interest in research such as mine, and I appreciated his detailed local knowledge.

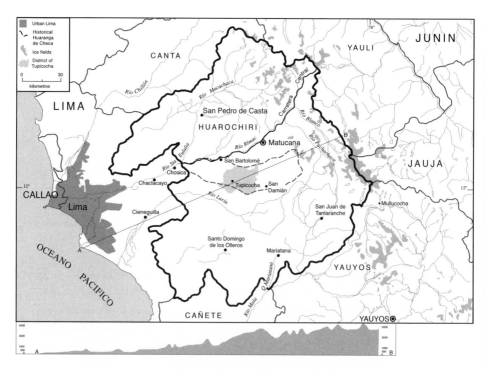

MAP 1   Map of Huarochirí Province, Departamento de Lima, Peru.

One evening, Milton said, "You know, Salomón, you should visit my home village, Tupicocha. I think you'd be interested in the equipos."

Equipo means a team, usually a soccer team. I said, "Well, I like soccer too, but I guess I can watch it at the field right here."

Milton half-smiled and said, "No, I really think you'd be interested in *my* village's equipos."

As the bus to San Damián snakes along the precipice it stops at Tupicocha, so I had seen it many times. Tupicocha was a smaller, poorer village than San Damián. The passengers who got off there seemed always to be talking about poverty and water worries: scanty rain, half-full reservoirs, withering or late crops, or disputes over land and irrigation. Every time we stopped there, I thought, "I'm glad I don't live here." I knew that the mythic path of one the most important heroes of the Huarochirí book passed through Tupicocha, but I had not given the place ethnographic priority. Yet eventually, needled by the feeling that Milton was setting me a half-satirical test by hinting at something important, I finally went there.

I arrived one morning just as the Tupicochans were making their daily vertical exodus, some up to the pastures and potato plots, others down to the orchards and cactus-fruit patches. My heart sank as distant couples with burros disappeared over the ridge. The tips of their steel tools glinted and were gone. But luck was on my side: I met a kinsman of Milton's, Sebastián Alberco. He was running an errand in connection with his duties as secretary of the Peasant Community, so he'd be in town for an hour or so. That gave him time to listen to my question, "Why are Tupicocha's equipos important?"

Sebastián shared the streak of dry wit for which his family is known. He guessed at Milton's sly way of educating me. "Ah, the equipos. Sure, stick around, I'll show you something."

While running the errand, he said, "We'll stop at my cousin's store. Our equipo is there, our *equipocamayo*." Suddenly I realized important information had arrived, in the humble form of a pun or folk etymology. *Equipo* had nothing to do with soccer. *Equipocamayo* would be the monolingually Spanish-speaking village's way of pronouncing the Inka word for a master of the knot-cord art, *khipukamayuq*. But could this rather ordinary-looking village retain a legacy that the classic places of Andean ethnography had lost?

Walking briskly, Sebastián explained that Tupicocha consists of ten parcialidades (sectors), informally known by the ancient term *ayllus*, and that all but the newest of them were symbolized in political ritual by quipocamayos. Now the rest of that punning folk-etymology fell into place: each *ayllu* really is a "team," not in the sports sense (though ayllus do in fact sponsor soccer teams) but in the sense of furnishing one team in the complex array of crews who, in friendly rivalry, do the village's basic infrastructural work.

When we got to Sebastián's cousin's store, the owner had not quite finished locking up to head for the fields. Sebastián rapped on the shutters and shouted

"Cousin! There's a foreigner who needs to talk to you!" Feet scuffed on a creaky stair, and the door opened. In the store it was deep twilight, the shutters open just a crack to discourage disruptive last-minute buyers. The brass of a balance scale showed through the murk with a Rembrandtesque burnished gleam. Sebastián's cousin pulled a plastic bag from a locked chest and upended it on the counter. Out flopped a multicolored tangle of heavy yarn. A few wine-red and yellow ornaments glowed amid a mound of tawny, dark, and mottled cordage.

Sebastián lifted the skein, demonstrating the first steps in handling a quipocamayo: one picks up the extremes of the main cord, shakes the pendants down to a hanging position, and calls on a peer to "comb" the tangled pendants out by separating them with the fingers. As the cords began to hang parallel, it became clear that this was nothing like the eccentric "ethnographic" khipus documented elsewhere. It was a khipu right in the mainstream of the canonical Inka design tradition. In fact it looked a lot like some of the grander museum specimens, except that, as my fingers soon told me, it was made of wool and not cotton.

Sebastián then demonstrated how one displays the object to the village in its annual ceremonial array. He held the main cord diagonally from his left shoulder to his right hip, while his friend caught the long "tail" up behind and tied it over his shoulder blade so that the whole object formed a "sash of office"—the metaphor he used in explaining this motion. We stepped out into the brightening morning and took a photo.

The survival of this complex put the matter of Huarochirí's lettered past into a different and more exciting light. The ayllus that owned the cords had, for the most part, the same names as the ones that made up the confederacy which the Inka regime called the "thousand" of Checa. And these were also the same ayllus which figured as protagonists of Huarochirí 400-year-old Quechua book of gods and heroes (Salomon and Urioste 1991:1–38). Could it be that the cords held content related to that legacy?

The chapters of this book describe how that day's initial and simplistic guesswork gave way to more informed hypotheses. Their overall concerns are the following:

1. At the level of theory, the goal is to adapt the "ethnography of writing" to a code which philological grammatology locates outside the domain of "writing proper." Writing proper is taken by many grammatologists to mean any "secondary" code which uses visual signs to represent a "primary" code consisting of audible speech signs. But we know many societies have produced inscriptive codes which do not work this way. And while there is no reason khipus *could* not stand for speech segments, we have no evidentially firm case that proves khipus *did* work in this way. We do know that they worked in other ways, and these other ways are worthy of ethnography. Putting khipus into a more omnidirectional model of inscription would contribute to interpreting a large and poorly understood portion of humanity's "technology of intellect."

2. From a historical perspective, the supposed death of political khipus is usually seen as an instance of alphabetic writing's triumph over "proto" or "partial" inscriptive systems. In the old Viceroyalty of Peru this is usually dated to the early colonial era and is attributed either to the alphabet's greater intrinsic capacity, or to the brute force with which it was wielded. Ethnohistoric inquiry into the Tupicochan context proves, on the contrary, that both systems coexisted for almost four centuries. This gives reason to think that the radical differences between them may have made them complementary rather than rival media from the local viewpoint.

3. On the plane of ethnographic synchrony—an "ethnographic recent past" devised for heuristic purposes, without imputation of real-world timelessness—I am concerned with reconstructing some macroscale features of the data-registry and documentary system in which quipocamayos worked at the end of their full-function life. The actual years to which this reconstruction applies correspond to about 1883–1919.

4. I will argue that khipus' double capability for simulating and documenting social action worked as the hinge of articulation between kinship organization and political organization. While we do not know whether ancient khipus worked the same way overall, the reconstruction offered here is compatible with the structure of many ancient specimens. The final chapters argue that Tupicochan practice demonstrates a root relationship between inscription and Andean social complexity.

The remainder of this introduction discusses why Huarochirí Province is a crucial locus for Andean studies. It then lays down contexts of khipu study, sketches the khipu research frontier, previews the argument, and summarizes research methods.

Huarochirí, Classical and Marginal

The phrase "canonical culture" is sometimes heard in anthropology about peoples whose ethnographic literature has durably influenced theoretical ideas or images of peoples.[3] Among Andean cultures, only the Inka empire would be recognized as "canonical" across the discipline—canonical because it is one of the clearest examples of "pristine" or "precapitalist states" and of divine kingship. But ideas of what makes "Inka culture" distinctive and important (in theories of state formation, political economy, ideology, etc.) are, on source-critical inspection, composites of scholarly experience from several regional polities and cultures. Among these, "Huarochirí" has rather a classical sound to Andeanists—so much so that one disadvantage of working there is to face a jaded attitude from sophisticated Peruvians, who have already heard plenty about it.

Indeed Huarochirí stands second only to the sacred Inka capital Cuzco, with its outliers around Lake Titicaca, as the place where Spain's, Peru's, and later the world's notion of what is "Andean" was constructed. This has everything to do with the fact that it lies astride what was until the twentieth century the main route from the Viceroyalty's City of the Kings—Lima—to the Inka capital Cuzco. It was along this route that in 1570, at the future provincial capital of Santa María Jesús de Huarochirí, Peru's first Jesuits set up an experimental prototype for their famous schools to teach the sons of native lords literacy, music, and Catholic doctrine (Mateos 1994:223–24; Wood 1986:66). One of the staff at that mission was the brilliant half-Inka novice Blas Valera. Later in life, Valera may have invented a way to emulate European "writing proper" and put Christian sacred discourse on cords (Hyland 2002:162–64). We do not know what young Blas had in mind circa 1570, but it may be that the notion he developed of a khipu art capable of carrying exalted meaning was influenced by Huarochirí experience as well as by his famous studies among the heirs of the pre-Hispanic god-king. Perhaps his presence in Huarochirí influenced the literate but simultaneously khipu-using semiotic pluralism which characterized the area through subsequent centuries.

The most famous thing about Huarochirí is the colonial book mentioned in the opening of this chapter—the only known South American text that bears comparison with Mesoamerica's native-language monuments such as the Maya *Popol Vuh*, namely the untitled, anonymous Huarochirí manuscript sometimes known by its initial phrase *Runa yn[di]o ñiscap*. Written in colonial Quechua and dated by Antonio Acosta Rodríguez to 1608, it alone of all known writings tells the myths of the pre-Christian deities and heroes in an Andean language, and it explains the duties of their priests (including the knotting of khipus). The immediate genesis of this anonymous treasure lies somewhere in an ugly colonial brouhaha. At the turn of the seventeenth century, Huarochirí was in the pastoral care of a brilliant clergyman, who, like Blas Valera, had enjoyed a Quechua-Spanish bilingual upbringing in the shadow of the Inka palaces, but who unlike Valera had a purely contemptuous attitude toward non-Christian worship. This man, Father Francisco de Avila, seems to have commissioned an unknown native ally to compile the text from oral testimonies. Faced with a lawsuit by his disgusted parishioners (Acosta Rodríguez 1987), Avila used the text to sleuth out incriminating particulars about Andean cults and stoke up the series of persecutions called "extirpation of idolatries" (Duviols 1972; Griffiths 1996; Mills 1997). Consequently, during the century and more when "extirpation" lashed the archbishopric, Huarochirí was one of the two most punished provinces. The resultant trial records (Duviols 1986; García Cabrera 1994) have enriched reconstructions of Andean religion (Doyle 1988; Gilmer 1952; Huertas Vallejos 1981). Huarochirí's great regional deity, embodied in the snowcap Paria Caca, was among those the indigenous chronicler Felipe Guaman Poma de Ayala (1980 [1615]:240) chose as a pictorial archetype of multiethnic "major idols."

Huarochirí studies (alongside those of Cajatambo, its counterpart to the north of Lima) have influenced dominant modern images of Andean culture far out of proportion to the province's size. It was here, early in the twentieth century, that the pioneer archaeologist Julio C. Tello and the Harvard physical anthropologist Aleš Hrdlička pioneered scientific mummy-hunting (1914). Tello's assistant Toribio Mejía Xesspe, a Quechua speaker from childhood, wrote a still-unpublished pioneer translation of the Huarochirí Quechua Manuscript and tirelessly roved the Huarochirí heights for his 1947 regional monograph. In the 1950s, a group from the country's flagship university under the leadership of José Matos Mar wrote a series of influential ethnographies which did much to place the country's "indigenous communities" into the paradigm of modernization theory (1958). Partly in response to the cultural thinness and overbearing modernism of such studies, Peru's Quechua-Spanish literary genius José María Arguedas translated the Huarochirí textual legacy so as to give Spanish-speaking Peruvians a more indigenous-based understanding of pre-Christian "gods and men" (Arguedas and Duviols 1966). By 1980 Huarochirí as conceived by Avila had so clearly become a locus classicus that when Ortiz Rescaniere set out to introduce "oral tradition" research as a resource for structuralist modeling of Peruvian archetypes, he could give his book a Spanish title meaning "Huarochirí Four Hundred Years After," without even having to say after what.

In the final quarter of the twentieth century, researchers countering the "modernization" paradigm with Marxian alternatives pioneered the argument that "Indian-ness" is a contextual attribute of social inequalities. Among these, Karen Spalding's 1974 *De indio a campesino* and her 1984 *Huarochirí: An Andean Society under Inca and Spanish Rule* provided an influential regional case study. Huarochirí was not at first a paramount theater for the "vertical archipelago model" which John V. Murra fashioned (portraying Andean political territories as assemblies of discontinuous "islands" stacked in different resource niches at different altitudes; 1975a). But as the geographic shape of ancient society emerges, we now see vertical organization as the substrate of that same organization which the Quechua stories explain in mythic terms (Feltham 1984). Among structuralist-influenced models of Andean society, María Rostworowski's pioneering interpretation of the Quechua mythology as the ideological self-image of a society formed by fusion between invasive highlander ayllus and locally rooted lowland peoples (1978a, 1978b) has stood alongside Pierre Duviols's 1973 *huari-llacuaz* analysis of the same fusion as a perennially fruitful insight into the "emic" side of vertical diversity.[4]

Because it is the nearest contact zone between the capital city and the "deep" Peru to which national ideology often appeals, Huarochirí has become influential in urban and schooled Peruvians' understanding of rural ways of life. Social science departments in Lima universities routinely dispatch students there for training fieldwork: in some towns on any festival day, one is likely to meet an academic outsider. A set of university term papers about Huarochirí became, for example, the special journal issue *Debates en Antropología* 5, 1980. Huarochirí figures disproportionately in social-scientific attempts to characterize modern peasantry (Echeandía Valladares 1981; Llanos and Osterling 1982).

Although foreigners seeking the "Andean" usually wing straight to Cuzco, Limeños of modest means enjoy weekend excursions to Huarochirí tourist zones such as San Pedro de Casta or the heights of Marcahuasi. School groups, families, and young couples toil up precipice roads by bus to seek vistas, both literal and conceptual, above Lima's smog. Bemused peasants see clubs of mountain bikers caked in the dust of archaeological byways pounding the locked doors of part-time rural stores in desperate search of soft drinks. Not infrequently, Huarochirí's stunning landscapes and "typical" central-highland ways of life (Olivas Weston 1983) appear in newspaper supplements (Noriega 1997; Ochoa Berreteaga 2000, 2001). During 2001, "adventure tourism" packagers put an ad for travel through Huarochirí "in the footsteps of the extirpators" onto the Internet.

At the turn of the twenty-first century, Tupicocha has caught the eye of journalists. This ordinary-seeming village is beginning to acquire a special mystique because its civic ritual appears emblematic of homegrown, responsible, democratic grassroots governance — a value for which Peruvians became hungry as they watched the Alberto Fujimori regime dissolve in a nauseating vortex of high-level scandal. *La República*, an opposition daily, greeted New Year 2001 with a color-photo spread (Ochoa and Herrera 2001) in which "the [Tupicochan civic meeting] Huayrona, basis of Andean democracy" figured as a pageant of rock-steady integrity. In 2002, Oxfam America and the Ford Foundation projected the same image toward a worldwide public through their multimedia synthesis "Indigenous Peoples of Latin America" (Smith 2002).

Limeños also notice many Huarochiranos among the in-migrating vendors and workers who recently swelled the city's numbers, especially while Shining Path warfare deepened the 1980s economic recession. One might expect the children of this province to disappear into the colossal maelstrom of Lima demography; 28.7 percent of the country's citizens by 1996 lived in Lima,[5] while as of 2000 the 59,238 Huarochiranos made up only about two-tenths of 1 percent of their country. But people from there are disproportionately visible because they fill roles that link urban and rural publics: market-stall vendors, operators of tent-restaurants in working-class neighborhoods, entrepreneurs in regional transport, and truck-farm wholesalers. Radio Inka, a pop station specializing in "chicha music" for a Huarochirí-born audience, blares in taxis and commercial galleries.[6]

Huarochirí is sometimes emblematic of what elite Limeños see as the racial masquerade of not-really-white immigrants. In his famous satirical novel *Un mundo para Julius*, Alfredo Bryce Echenique deflates an upper-crust Lima beauty's cosmopolitan pretensions by giving her hairdresser a resoundingly Huarochirano surname, Pier Paolo Cajahuaringa (1984:279). Despite suffering such racially tinged snobbism, Huarochirí villagers regard themselves as progressive campesi-nos (peasants) of Peruvian nationality, not as members of an indigenous "race."

Khipu Contexts

A khipu (or *chinu* in Aymara) is an Andean information storage device made of cord. The concept is not uniquely Andean, and indeed devices fitting this minimal definition are attested in many cultures. Herodotus mentions one in use during the Persian wars. Other cases come from peoples as far afield as the New Mexico Pueblos, the Ryukyu Islands, and Hawaii (Day 1967:2–3, 7–11, 13). In the He-brew Bible, Numbers 15:37–38 prescribes knotted "fringes" (*tsitsit*) as a vector of memory (Gandz 1931). Diffusionists have suggested that this far-flung distribu-tion reflects an ancient dispersion of an eminently portable medium (Birket-Smith 1966–67). There is no archaeological trail, though, and one could just as well posit independent inventions.

Only in the Andes were cord records central to the cultures they served, or abundantly produced. Khipu chronology is obscure because few if any specimens have been radiocarbon-dated. William Conklin (1982) has documented a highly developed khipu art from Middle Horizon times, about 600–1000 CE, that is, a half millennium prior to Inka expansion; one of its striking features, the lashing of bright-colored thread in bands around pendants (Radicati di Primeglio 1990b) also appears in an otherwise Inka-looking specimen (Pereyra Sánchez 1997), sug-gesting a continuous deep-rooted design evolution. As of 2004, pre-Inka khipu-related objects are appearing in even earlier contexts (Splitstoser et al. 2003).

Regarding Inka times (c. 1400–1532), Spanish chroniclers, including a few with close access to royal khipu masters, say that cords served virtually all the data needs one would expect an imperial state to have. The attested uses include censuses; cal-endars; inventories of all sorts including weapons, foodstuffs, and clothing; tribute records; royal chronicles and chansons de geste; records of sacred places or beings and their sacrifices; successions and perhaps genealogies; postal messages; crimi-nal trials; routes and stations; herd records; and game-keeping records. Respon-sible summaries of the complex and rewarding primary literature, which bristles with source-critical hazards, appear in Carmen Arellano (1999), Carol Mackey (1970:8–22, 209), Carlos Sempat Assadourian (2002), and Gary Urton (in press).

Pre-Hispanic ("archaeological") khipus are not rare. By 1988 Robert and Marcia Ascher (1978, 1988) had analyzed 215 museum khipus. As of 2001, specimens at-tested or published by scholars totaled 575,[7] or if one includes fragments, about 1,000 (Arellano 1999:231, 233). But they form a difficult research base because nearly all of them come from looting (mostly on the central and southern desert coast), which robs them of context.

A khipu is termed "colonial" if it was produced and used between 1532 and

1824. Many colonial khipus are mentioned or transcribed on paper—and some are important to this book—but no single museum specimen has been identified as definitely colonial. A relatively undamaged burial complex with khipus discovered at Laguna de los Cóndores (Von Hagen and Guillén 2000) may span the pre-Hispanic–colonial transition and seems to yield an early-colonial tribute register on cords (Urton 2001).

A khipu is termed "patrimonial" if it has been held as a historic legacy in its owner community but is not a productive medium at the time of documentation. Leaving out hybrid cases (Rivero y Ustáriz 1857, 2:84; Robles Mendoza 1990 [1982]; Tello and Miranda 1923), the only clear case besides those reported later in this book is one reported by Arturo Ruiz Estrada 1990. It too comes from the Lima highlands. Patrimonial khipus apparently date from the Republican or modern eras, as discussed below. All the known cases have much in common with Inka-era designs.

Khipus will be called "ethnographic" if they were studied in a context of productive use or were explained by people who retained productive competence. A few ethnographic khipus—those which herders made to keep track of flocks—have been interpreted, the best cases being Mackey's (1970:121–75, 267–99). Many deviate in basic design from Inka-era specimens. Other ethnographic cases were reported by Bandelier (1910:89), Adolph Bastian using Uhle's data (1895), Teresa Gisbert and José de Mesa (1966:497–506, plates 11–14), Olaf Holm (1968), Mackey (1990), Oscar Núñez del Prado (1990 [1950]:165–82), Rita Gertrud Prochaska (1983:103–5), Mariano Eduardo Rivero and Johann Jakob Tschudi ([1846] 1963:384–86), Froilán Soto Flores (1990 [1950–51]:183–190, Max Uhle (1990 [1897]:127–34), and Martha Villavicencio Ubillús et al. (1983:32–36). With the exception of Holm's Ecuadorian specimens and certain ones from La Libertad, Peru, reported by Mackey, modern khipus come from montane southern Peru through central Bolivia, and especially from the Cuzco area. Some authors do not give numbers of specimens seen, but the stated cases total under fifty.

The relevance of patrimonial and ethnographic khipus to pre-Hispanic ones is an open and difficult question. This book argues that for khipus of specifically political import, the patrimonial chain is continuous enough to shed light on archaeology.

Several good books on the khipu art are widely available. Marcia Ascher and Robert Ascher's *Code of the Quipu* (1981, republished 1997) presents a lively and accessible study of the mathematical makeup of cord records. Its complement is a microfiche compendium, the *Code of the Quipu Databook* and *Databook II*, of cord-by-cord descriptions documenting and mathematically analyzing 230 museum and privately owned specimens (1978, 1988). The most up-to-date compendium, Jeffrey Quilter's and Urton's *Narrative Threads* (2002), is rich on khipus in colonial context, and it contains findings by William Conklin that are seminal to Urton's *Signs of the Inka Khipu* (2003). *Quipu y yupana* (edited by Mackey, Pereyra et al. 1990) contains an equally important but earlier harvest of research, connecting the key findings of the 1920s with the current resurgence of khipu studies. The richest illustrations as well as strong documentation are in Carmen Arellano's "Quipu y tocapu: Sistemas de comunicación inca" (1999), which demonstrates (as do the Tupicochan specimens) that some khipus were made as craft treasures.

Khipu Research Frontiers

The next few paragraphs sketch the state of khipu research, especially for readers with interests in inscription, literacy, and decipherment formed outside the Andean area. It emphasizes the reasons why Andean scholars suspect the khipu problem of being uniquely difficult. As Quilter (2002:201–2) observes, we do not even know to what degree it is a single problem. Millennially old as it seems to be, and developed as it was among peoples who spoke a multitude of languages, the art of putting information on string may actually be a branching tree of inventions. In that case, studying the khipu as a single code would be as feckless as trying to study marks-on-paper as one code. Typological research to settle this doubt is only now beginning. We are also still in the dark about the diachronic dimension, since nobody has worked on khipu dating, much less developed an archaeologically grounded model of cord graphogenesis and evolution which might stand alongside impressive Old World research on origins of writing. And as already noted, it is still uncertain whether the idea of inscription as a secondary code for speech provides appropriate axioms for khipu decipherment. So at the start all bets are open. But that is not to say there are no existing landmark studies.

THE AGENDA OF KHIPU AND NUMBER
The first interpretative task broached in modern times was khipus' arithmetical structure. Leland Locke (1923, 1928) was able to establish base-10 positional notation as the numerical content of many knots. The plan is similar to Indo-Arabic numeracy except that zero is represented by an empty place rather than a sign. Ascher and Ascher explain the basic "Lockean" conventions as in figures 2–4.

Figure 4 could, for example, represent a small segment of an Inka census, encoding a village from which households have been sent to do *mitmaq*, or remote 'transplant' duty. Each pendant could stand for an ayllu, with its respective subsidiary signaling the number of its absent households, and the topcord with its subsidiary the whole population with a subsidiary expressing the number of absentees. The Aschers advanced past Locke by showing in principle that beyond this role, khipu numbers can function as "label numbers" (i.e., like a social security number, they register identity rather than quantity). They have documented mathematical regularities — many complex, some partial, and all enigmatic — in over 200 specimens. Mathematical analysis continues to be productive, dealing, for example, with the question of whether specimens express angles (Pereyra Sánchez 1996).

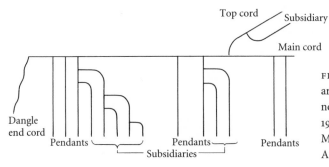

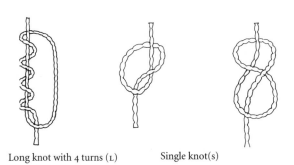

FIGURE 2 Basic khipu architecture and terminology (Ascher and Ascher 1997:17). By permission of Marcia Ascher and Robert Ascher.

Top cord
Subsidiary
Main cord
Dangle end cord
Pendants
Subsidiaries
Pendants
Pendants

FIGURE 3 Common Inka-style data knots. Left, Inka long (L) knot of value four, used in units place; center, single (s) knot; right, figure-eight (E) knot (Ascher and Ascher 1997:29). By permission of Marcia Ascher and Robert Ascher.

Long knot with 4 turns (L)   Single knot(s)

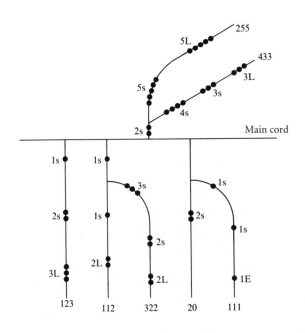

FIGURE 4 Khipu data deployed in "Lockean" Inka style. Note the regularized positioning of knots by their decimal "places." The topcord sums the values of pendants, and the topcord's subsidiary those of the pendants' subsidiaries. (Ascher and Ascher 1997:31). By permission of Marcia Ascher and Robert Ascher.

The Aschers write, "No amount of mathematical insight has budged the fundamental problem. This problem is that 'we are not party to the informational model that would permit us to associate a particular quipu with a particular cultural meaning'" (Ascher and Ascher 1997 [1981]:78). The research frontier is essentially the attempt to break through this difficulty.

THE AGENDA OF KHIPUS AS SIGN-BEARING MATERIAL CULTURE
One major approach is to interrogate the khipus for meaningful features outside Locke's and the Aschers' approaches. In a decade of research, Gary Urton has sought them by looking for features of cords which apparently mimic Andean logical structures (rather than taking Indo-Arabic arithmetic as the a priori frame). His point of departure is Andean "insistence"—the Aschers' term—on binarism as a pervasive organizing principle. Andean societies often rely on dualities as the first step in structuring human activity, such as village "halves" (moieties, *saya*) matched as rivals in work and ritual. It is because fiber working inherently requires binarisms—a series of decisions such as left/right, over/under, and so on— that it neatly mimetized logical operations that generate Andean cultural order. It thus became the favorite data-bearing medium not accidentally. In 1994 Urton demonstrated that the leftward- or rightward-tied directionality of knots, as well as the S- or Z-directional plying of cords, can be a data variable in its own right. (The direction of a knot depends on whether the first pass of the working end goes leftward or rightward past the body of the cord. S- or Z-plies result from twisting clockwise or counterclockwise as one unites primary threads.) For Urton, the sign which a cord contains is not "on" the cord, but rather is the aggregate of the binary decisions made in constructing all its features. Urton detects seven such decisions, starting with choosing wool or cotton, dying in one of two color spectra, spinning leftward or rightward, and so forth. Thus the finished cord is a "seven-bit" unit of information, with (so to speak) a zero or one value for each of the seven decisions. Urton emphasizes that such signs might be assigned to any cultural construct, much as an eight-bit segment of the data stream is coded to a letter when we are using ASCII alphanumeric computer character code but to a color or texture in a photo-editing computer program. Until assigned, any cord form is an empty vehicle. It is machine code, so to speak, as opposed to a human interface or surface code reflecting vernacular cultural entities. This theory is neutral as to whether the code consists of constructs that are parts of speech (words, syllables, etc.). It is therefore open to the possibility that cords are writing in the usual sense of the term, that is, visible signs corresponding to speech segments, and equally open to the possibility that the "surface code" or human interface registers other cultural entities.

Eventually, the methodological problems of such close reading will have to disturb a field heretofore marred by coarse reading. Can we ever find in the objects themselves "the place where 'subsemiotic' marks leave off and signs begin"

(Elkins 1996:186)? When I was exploring the Tupicochan khipus (at a time before Urton's seven-bit model was available), the villagers I consulted about the material makeup of specimens commented on five of the same variables as Urton's, but not exclusively on these. In the pages that follow, I have not attempted to count and total the number of meaningful variables, but rather have tried to follow all the locally perceived variation as far as possible "upward" toward the "surface" meaning. Given the fragmentary memories of the art, this does not lead to a consensual inventory of variables. I also seek to connect cord observations with surface meanings in the alphabetic writings and oral practices of villagers.

Villagers sometimes regard the fact that cords appear "used" or altered as meaningful, and I too argue that use marks are an important source of meaning. In my opinion khipu studies, with the lone exception of Radicati's, have erred by ignoring material traces of use as opposed to design. Overgeneralizing from Locke's reasonable statement that cords are not a convenient medium for calculating (because one cannot knot as fast as one reckons), scholars have assumed that khipus are textlike assemblies of finished arrays. I will argue, rather, that these local specimens were operable devices for simulating changing plans and performance.

THE AGENDA OF KHIPU SEMIOSIS[8]

Conventional grammatological books tend to parrot Bernabe Cobo's ([1653] 1964:143–44) uncorroborated statement that khipus were merely "mnemonic" in the sense that each was an aide-mémoire which only its maker could interpret. Urton (2003:17–26) has patiently argued against this implausible idea (implausible because such a system would have been useless to Inka administration). A visit to the main museum collections—the greatest by far being that of the Ethnologisches Museum in Berlin—quickly convinces anyone that despite regional tendencies in prehistory, certain far-flung conventions did prevail throughout huge and culturally heterogeneous spaces. Yet it is hard to avoid the impression that in the khipu art, standardization stands in dialectical relation to some other principle of anchoring in the particular. I suggest in chapters 6 and 7 that the incomplete standardization of Tupicocha's specimens may relate to high demand for "hooking" symbols into the performative particulars of the moments when the signs came into being. This ability to accommodate the particular may be related to localism and even the particularisms of ayllu and lineage. States demand of their record keepers conventional, maximally comparable accounts of different parts of society. But the local khipu is likely to have been actor centered, affected by a functional pull toward marking events (and other things) as unique. Resulting defects of comparability during the term of actual use may not have been a threat, since the context of use was a face-to-face community where any ambiguity could be immediately resolved.

This tendency may have to do with an insistent minor theme in khipu studies (mostly ethnographic ones): iconic and indexical significance. Khipus are sometimes characterized as "aniconic." Yet Prochaska found that recent Taquile Islanders saw herding khipus not as signs for the numbers of animals but as grouped tokens for individual animals, using a code of color resemblance. Older Taquileans saw the khipu as a likeness of the herd as a whole, rather than an abstraction of its numerical properties. Islanders inserted in knots sticks iconic of individual animals' attributes, for example, a half-diameter stick to signal a sick one (1983:103–5). Comparable insertions appear, without explanation, in a drawing of an unidentified khipu observed by Charles Wiener (1993 [1880]:826). The giant patrimonial khipu of Rapaz is thickly studded with "tufts of wool, human figures, and . . . a seashell" (Ruiz Estrada 1990:192).[9] Tupicocha also has tufts inserted. The presence of human hair (Pereyra 1997:194) in khipus even raises the likelihood that in some cases, the relation between sign and signified was motivated by indexical or consubstantial considerations. In the closing chapters I suggest that the khipu as a whole may have a dimension of iconicity, in the sense of a "data graphic."

THE AGENDA OF KHIPU AND LANGUAGE OR DISCOURSE

It is not unreasonable to suppose that if Inkas used khipus for multipurpose imperial records, these must have covered much of the functional range that "real writing" does. A small number of theories have been adduced about how they could have done so, two of which I describe here.

The first is that khipus embodied a conventional nonnumerical, signal-like code for a wide range of referents other than numbers: things, actions, and so on. Since the seventeenth century, scholars, most notably including Fray Antonio de Calancha ([1638] 1974:206–7), have entertained the notion that cord colors signify nonnumerical meanings. Calancha's specific suggestions, which obviously derive from common European color symbolism (red = war, black = death, etc.), have not proven verifiable. This remains a productive vein nonetheless. Martti Pärssinen (1992:31–43) suggests that colors combined with numbers to signal categorized nonnumerical referents. (For example, if black cords signify provinces, a black cord knotted "6" would mean the sixth in a standard list of provinces.) Transferred to Urton's seven-bit model, this would amount to reserving bits for attributes: bit 2, "color class," as inflected by hue, would be reserved for the attribute "class to which signified belongs," and bits 5–6 (knot direction, number parity inflected by digits) would be reserved for attributes identifying the member of the class. Such a system would either require use of a master key—and what medium would *that* be in?—or else a large memorizing task with apparently little redundancy to lean on. (Urton notes that his estimated 1,536 values for seven-bit cords fall within the range of characters a modern reader of Chinese memorizes; but are seven-bit sequences as easy to learn and scan as character gestalts?) This vein of theory does capture an important point usually neglected. To record a datum, it is not necessary to record it in any particular language. Recording in a way that is not language specific would have been very valuable in a multilingual empire, since it would mean people untrained in Quechua—and they were the majority in many areas—could take direct part in the imperial communication system.

The second vein of theorizing is that khipus did actually signify speech segments. Certainly there is nothing difficult about imagining ways in which cords might stand for speech segments. Urton notes that the inventory of 1,536 seven-bit signs is not out of scale for a relatively unphoneticized logographic or logosyllabic system of writing (i.e., one in which signs stood for relatively large segments, like words or syllables, a common early form in the development of writing systems). If verified, such usage would remove the Inkas from their anomalous perch as the only "civilization without real writing." In studying Tupicochan khipus, I sought traces and memories of categorical paradigms that might assign cord attributes to various referents, and I ranked the results as to believability. I also listened carefully for behaviors which might suggest that khipu inheritors actually treat cords as visible language (as opposed to merely asserting that they are), such as scanning for sentential syntactic relations among cords or hesitating between sound alternatives (as opposed to semantic ones) when interpreting. The results are compatible with a more-than-Lockean reading method and a far more than arithmetical content, but they do not confirm any systemically language-mimicking usage. The apparent survival of Tupicochan khipu competence through the transition from Quechua and the ethnic Jaqaru language to Spanish suggests that cords were not seen as being "in" any one language.

KHIPUS IN SEARCH OF CONTEXTS AND VICE VERSA

"[*Khipus*'] structures match the phenomena they recorded, whether they be tunes, plans for textiles or phases of the moon," wrote the Aschers (1997:122). This remains the indispensable axiom of most research to date, including this project, and yet it is a hard counsel to follow. The literature resembles a bridge half-built from two piers. On one side, we have khipus with elaborate formal structures and internal mathematical patterns. On the other, we see Andean domains of activity or thought said to have been encoded in cords. But finding promising matches has proven terribly difficult.

When seeking context for an opaque text, decipherers often get a break from the simple fact that texts are wrapped right onto the things they concern (as with Mayan or Indic temple dedication inscriptions, Roman makers' marks, or ancient Chinese turtle-shell oracles). Quilter suggests that the Andes deny us this break because khipus need no surface other than their own fibrous bodies to exist on (2002:198). But on the contrary, Tupicocha does present the "wrapping text" advantage in a most striking way: its khipus are wrapped onto the bodies of its officials at the moment when these men's bodies instantiate the "body politic." One could hardly ask for a more powerful suggestion about what the cords concern.

For other researchers, the most persistently attractive path toward context is calendrical systems. Erland von Nordenskiöld thought he saw prevalences of certain astronomical numbers (1925, 1979 [1925]). R. Tom Zuidema, using a more refined notion of the Inka calendar, adduced another (1989), and Urton used calendrical numbers as signposts to his persuasive interpretation of a Chachapoyas khipu as a biennial record of tributes (2001).

Another important known social structure is the Inka scheme of decimalization. Catherine Julien's account of "How Inka Decimal Administration Worked" (1988) persuasively explains the Inka method reconciling ideal (decimal) population numbers with de facto findings, a pattern worth remembering in view of the fact that Inkas may have classified Tupicocha's ayllus as "hundreds." The decimalization of Huarochirí society in "thousands" is among its best-documented properties (Dávila Brizeño 1965 [1583]; Espinoza Soriano 1992:124–27; Spalding 1984:28, 51–52, 54, 88).

Similarly, the rigid structures of Inka tribute-paying, age grades, and such, were expressed to Spanish bureaucrats through khipu readout (Brotherston 1979:75). Murra (1975b) pioneered the detection of the "ethno-categories" latent in what might be called "paper khipus." Indeed it is possible to construct retro-khipus, that is, hypothetical cord arrays which could have generated Inka artifacts (Lee 1996) or readouts on the Spanish page (Rostworowski 1990). But nobody has combed museums for specimens whose patterns resemble these analyses.

Andean space was also imagined as highly patterned (Gartner 1999:289–94). A number of observers have noticed that Cuzco's *ceque* system (schema of shrines on radial lines) is "beautifully adapted to . . . recording on knotted strings" (Rowe 1946:300). Thomas Abercrombie indeed argues that the Andean ideal of knowledge itself centered on the metaphor of pathway. The past was imagined as "chronotopography." Khipu cords are for him paths guiding the hand, eye, and mind to the transtemporal (genealogical, divine, etc.) sources of things, much as trails guide one to geographical sources such as shrines and water intakes (Abercrombie 1998:178–88, 259). For Abercrombie it is the spatial, not the verbal, faculty which organizes recall. Some Tupicochans also think of their cords as model spaces, and, as noted in chapter 8, some see a khipu as a holistic "chronotopograph" of a social domain.

Can one even hypothetically match cord structures with structures of narrative? As the Aschers (1997:75–76), Julien (2000:91–165), Lienhard (1991:16), and Marcin Mróz (1984) point out, many Inka-sourced accounts of the past seem to feature fairly regular episodic structures and "catalogs" — that is, for example, a report of a war campaign often appears "preformatted" with predictable "slots" open to contain data about the protagonists, the enemy force, the day of battle, the fate of the captives, and so on. A standardized cord device tipping off "readers" what genre format to apply would enable them to locate cord particulars (e.g., numbers, signs for provinces) within a coherent narrative. At the outset of this project, I harbored the idea that a retro-khipu mimicking major episodic structure of the 1608 Quechua source's narrative of Tupicocha's gods and ancestors might correspond to traits of the extant quipocamayos, but both chronology and functional indices point to less simple continuities.

In all cases—both narrative and nonnarrative—"reverse engineering" from non-khipu data has a severe limitation: it seems possible to design multiple khipus representing any one data set, and we have no way of knowing which simulation actually mimics ancient methods. The present book tries to build the arch from both ends. Given the structural characteristics of Tupicocha's khipus—and a notable lack of arithmetical regularity is one of them—we will consider what ethnographically observed classifications or entities they would have been useful to mimic. From the ethnographic side, we use observation and the village's rich self-documentation to narrow down the range of cultural entities after which cord signs were likely to have been modeled. While the arch is not complete, the range of possible "surface" code references does thus become manageable enough to frame a reconstruction of the macroscale articulation between cord media and community organization.

The Argument in Prospect

Chapter 1, "Universes of the Legible and Theories of Writing," concerns theoretical definitions of reading and writing. It argues that the major consensus about writing achieves clarity of definition at the expense of expelling from the field of study the exact systems ethnography must concentrate on, namely, those least similar to "writing proper." The chapter then probes less familiar theoretical openings to this unfamiliar graphic universe.

Chapter 2, "A Flowery Script: The Social and Documentary Order of Modern Tupicocha Village," provides a minimal ethnography of communitywide institutions, emphasizing that the "polycyclical" productive regimen puts a premium on record keeping as a key resource for rational adaptation. It also sketches the ritual control of labor, a probable link to the old khipu-producing system.

Chapter 3, "Living by the 'Book of the Thousand': Community, Ayllu, and Customary Governance," concerns the community's constituents: small kinship corporations that actually use quipocamayos. The past and present functions of these groups are reviewed as probable referents of khipu recording. It is argued that the cord system thus formed the exact hinge of articulation between kinship-structured and politically structured society. It is in this sense that campesinos call the patrimonial cords their "constitution" or "magna carta."

Chapter 4, "The Tupicochan Staff Code," concerns the simplest of the village's nonalphabetic codes, the signs inscribed on staffs of office (varas). Unlike quipocamayos, they are still being produced. These artifacts seem to be "writings without words" in a more radical sense than the one Elizabeth Boone and Walter Mignolo posited in their book of that title (1994). Although not closely related to khipus, they alert us to unfamiliar sign-using processes which may also occur among cords.

Chapter 5, "The Khipu Art after the Inkas," questions published estimates of khipu chronology and argues against the supposed political demise of the cord art in the early colony. Unpublished sources show that in Huarochirí khipu-making continued alongside what Angel Rama (1996 [1984]) called the colonial "lettered city" for centuries.

Chapter 6, "The Patrimonial Quipocamayos of Tupicocha," describes the Tupicochan cords themselves and explains their context of use, namely, the annual civic plenum. Technical scrutiny shows that despite probably late dates, they are much closer to the mainstream of Inka data technology than other post-Hispanic specimens. Physical scrutiny also suggests that operability was as important as fixity in quipocamayo functions.

Chapter 7, "Ayllu Cords and Ayllu Books," centers on written records which the quipocamayo-owning corporations wrote while the khipu art waned. Formal likenesses between the cord medium and the paper one are explored by study of vernacular "social auditing," which generated both.

Chapter 8, "The Half-Life and Afterlife of an Andean Medium: How Modern Villagers Interpret Quipocamayos," concerns popular exegeses of the quipocamayos. Two exegeses are explored. One is the reconstruction of the art as attempted by a youngster who was partially trained in it by his great-grandfather. The other is an esoteric mode of cord interpretation which seeks in the cords guidance from the superhuman.

Chapter 9, "Toward Synthetic Interpretation," combines the methodologies used in chapters 6–8 in order to suggest specific functional interpretations of the Tupicochan corpus. Quipocamayos come in two formats, color cycles and color bands. It is suggested that the formats relate to planning as against performance, forming in the ensemble a versatile interlocking set of simulation devices.

Methods and Coverage

The geographical scope of my Huarochirí ethnography is almost exactly that of the 1608 Quechua source, that is, from the south bank of the Rímac River, across the entire Lurín drainage, to the north bank of the Mala River (see map 1). It forms a single seaward-facing Andean rampart. The area extends downslope to the Pacific and upslope to the three rivers' respective headwaters in the icy crest of the Andean cordillera. Although I have been visiting since 1989, the first substantial fieldwork reported here took place in 1990–91. Additional periods of fieldwork took place in 1994–95, 1997, two visits in 2000, and one in 2001. The earlier phases concentrated on southern Huarochirí province including its eponymous capital, and San Damián (see map 2). Work from December 1994 on focalized Tupicocha and Tuna, in the middle of the province. The data set collected includes (1) early colonial records held in Peru, (2) observation of quipocamayos in Tupicocha, (3) internal documents of the community and ayllus of Tupicocha, (4) ethnographic observation and photographs in Huarochirí, San Damián, Sunicancha, Tupicocha, and Tuna, including consultation of fiber artisans, and (5) radiocarbon and fiber analysis.

I repeatedly availed myself of the fact that documentary and native-media operations become public during the wet-season ritual cycle—that is, the time which begins with New Year's Eve and ends with Carnival (loosely interpreted as most of February). Readers are reminded not to mistake this book for a general ethnography. I leave out much of Tupicochan reality, notably the "semiproletarian" or semi-migrant way of life which binds it in close relation to Lima and an international diaspora.

Each quipocamayo-owning ayllu kindly granted permission to photograph and study its patrimony. No cord records were removed from the village at any time.

In representing Huarochirí language, I treat etymologically non-Spanish words as Hispano-Quechuisms (etc.) within Spanish. Modern inhabitants do not know Quechua nor the Jaqaru (Aymara-related) ethnic language which formerly underlay it. I spell Hispano-Quechuisms using the same orthography villagers use for their own records (e.g., I use the spelling *quipocamayo* rather than using the reconstructed Quechua *khipukamayuq*).

The local way of talking about quipocamayos does not include unique names for each specimen, so I invented the binomials by which they are referred to from here on. The first term identifies the owning ayllu, and the second the order in which they were observed. For example, M-02 belongs to Mújica ayllu and was the second Mújica specimen observed.

Following local preference, I refer to people by their real names except if mentioning something confidential or harmful to legitimate interests.

This book explores a relationship between the nonalphabetic media and the alphabetic legacy, but it gives the former primacy. In this sense it is partial. At a later date, a work complementary to this one will put the no less remarkable heritage of unofficial rural alphabetic production center stage.

1

UNIVERSES OF THE LEGIBLE AND

THEORIES OF WRITING

ROM EARLY contact to recent times, South American indigenous groups learning the alphabet have often denied that writing is new to them. They say they "already" had it, because they could "already read" various things such as petroglyphs or spoors (Gow 1990; Hugh-Jones 1989:65–68; Perrin 1986; Platt 1992:143). Yet Andean mythology also abounds in motifs to the effect that letters were deeply puzzling when first imported. This polarization suggests that many Andean persons perceived European writing as a member of some larger familiar class of legible signs, but a strikingly deviant member. Certainly the few examples of South American inscription systems about which we have ethnographic evidence—*grafismo indígena*, as Lux Vidal (1992) classes them—do differ drastically from writing "proper" in their principles of legibility (Arnold 1997; Langdon 1992).

Where do South American models of legibility and legible objects fit in relation to grammatology as usually defined? Do nonphilological theories of inscribed meaning yield promising heuristic avenues for interrogating inscriptions where mimesis of speech is far from being an assured property?

"A Certain Kind of Writing": Grammatology and the
Problem of "Writing without Words"

By way of estimating the distance between indigenous South American notions of legibility and the extant corpus of theory and method about writing, we might give ear to an obscure man made famous by testimonial literature, a cargo porter in Cuzco named Gregorio Condori Mamani. In the early 1970s he tried to explain, via a legend, that Andean and European ways of recording information were *maximally* different:

> The Inkas didn't know anything about paper or writing, and when the good Lord wanted to give them paper, they refused it. That's because they didn't get their news by paper but by small, thick threads made of *vicuña* wool; they used black wool cords for bad news and for the good news, white cords. These cords were like books, but the Spaniards didn't want them around; so they gave the Inka a piece of paper.
> "This paper talks," they said.
> "Where is it talking? That's silly; you're trying to trick me."
> And he flung the paper to the ground. The Inka didn't know anything about writing. And how could the paper talk if he didn't know how to read? And so they had our Inka killed. (Valderrama Fernández and Escalante Gutiérrez 1977:50.[1] Translation from Valderrama Fernández, Escalante Gutiérrez, Gelles, and Martínez Escobar 1996:57)

This legend was not just Don Gregorio's. It has been collected and discussed over and over for 430 years. It seems among the most indelible of all Quechua-language traditions. Literally foundational to the Andean-European dialogue, it comments at the same time on its failures. It occurs in the oldest known book of Andean authorship, Titu Cusi's 1570 brief for the intransigent Inkas who had been defending a jungle redoubt since 1535 (Titu Cusi Yupanqui 1973:15–16) . Over 400 years later, it still occupied a central place in Andean folk history (Ortiz Rescaniere 1973:134–41, 146–49). In each version the rejection of writing (with or without provocation by the Spanish) triggers the first act of the colonial tragedy.

The story is no less a canonical theme in academic history (MacCormack 1988; Wachtel 1977:39). In some cases, it has become a charter myth for misguided treatments of Andean culture as being in an essential way "oral" or even antigraphic. One such article bears the title "Literacy as Anticulture" (Classen 1991). Another (Seed 1991) bears the astonishing subtitle "Atahualpa's Encounter with the Word," as if absence of alphabets meant absence of language! This misperception underwrites an attitude on the part of educators that Peru's rural literacy deficit results not from sociolinguistic difficulties, but from some fundamental dissonance between Andean culture and literacy.

And yet the myth has not been fully interpreted. European and Euro-American readers seem obsessed with Quechua insistence *that* Andeans found the alphabet radically strange. They are understandably fascinated by the world-historical importance tellers attach to this fact. But they rarely ask *why* the book, of all things, stands for insoluble cultural difference.

Condori was telling us precisely that Inka society *was* a graphic society. Since the Inka already possessed a system of visible "messages," a graphic artifact as such would not seem a fundamentally confusing artifact. By telling us first of all that Inkas used messages on cords—*q'aytu*, incidentally a word Tupicochans likewise apply to khipus—Don Gregorio tells us that the problem concerns *kinds* of graphic system, not the *presence or absence* of them. His story is about a comparison, not a singularity.

The reason for the Inka's confusion is mentioned, but unanalyzed: "paper *talks*" (papelmi *riman*). *Rimay* means speaking in words, specifically and exclusively (Lira 1982 [1941]:251). Although Condori says cords are like a book, he does not apply *rimay* to cords. He implies, then, that European paper used words, but in a way that did not involve sounds. In other words, the Inka was putatively puzzled not over the concept of legibility, but over the assertion that paper was legible by virtue of its being *rimay*.

To us, nothing could be more routine than the assertion that writing is a secondary code for a primary, oral-aural code, namely, speech. After all, thinkers from Aristotle to the modern heirs of Ferdinand de Saussure and Leonard Bloomfield have been insisting that this is its essence (Olson 1994:3). But the Aristotelian-through-Saussurean viewpoint is far from cross-culturally obvious.

Consider, then, what putatively stopped an Inka well versed in Peru's graphic code short of recognizing the alphabet as an alternate graphic code—and why this difference appeared as a fateful gulf between cultures. Writing "proper" operates not as a code whose signs correspond to objects in the world, but as a code whose signs refer to the sounds which a given spoken language uses as parts of speech in naming such objects. Whatever the fineness or coarseness of divisions at which written signs encode speech (real cases range from minute articulation features in Korean to whole words in Chinese, with alphabets occupying a middle ground), the mechanism is basically the same: visible signs stand for sound-segments of the speech flow, and the morphemes (e.g., words, suffixes) that make up the flow in turn stand for "things."

Perhaps the Inka was not unfamiliar with visual code, but unfamiliar with the notion that it stands for the *sounds* of "talk" as opposed to the *referents* of "talk." Commentators have emphasized the negative—what the Inka failed to understand—without asking the more interesting question of what his story did presume about legibility. This book sets out to consider the positive: what legibility did Andean culture posit? If not talk, what?

Let us restate the point in terms of theory. What the Inka was unfamiliar with was "writing with words," which Barry Powell (2002:64) terms *lexigraphy*.[2] (Lexigraphy is a broad term including all signaries that correspond to segments of speech, whether large ones, such as whole morphemes, or small ones, such as phonemes.) His expectations were apparently based on some other principle. Just to begin somewhere, we could consider the most broadly conceived alternative: what Geoffrey Sampson, following Gelb's 1952 neologism, calls "semasiography."

Semasiography is applied to the generally ill-theorized area of "mnemotechnologies," "pictography," "notations," and "tokens" (Sampson 1985:26–45).

Semasiographs purportedly do not stand for the sounds of the name of a referent, but rather for the referent itself. Taken abstractly, they are not "in" any particular spoken language. Productive competence consists of knowing or inventing signs that correspond to objects within the presumed common semantic grid. The reader's competence is to recognize the correspondence and, *optionally*, verbalize it in any appropriate tongue. The "No left turn" traffic sign, consisting of a leftward-bent arrow in a slashed red circle is a semasiograph of two sematograms, one iconic (the shape of the turn) and the other perhaps arbitrary (the slashed red circular cartouche). Whether a police officer verbalizes it as "no left turn," or "no doblar a la izquierda," depends only on local translation habits. This detour via verbiage is the operation which the Inka apparently failed to guess.

Because in any pure semasiography, elements of speech need not be retrieved in order to grasp a message, some authors call such systems "writing without words" (Boone 1994). Grammatologists disagree about whether this is an acceptable extension of the word *writing*. William Bright's and Peter T. Daniels's superb compendium *The World's Writing Systems* does cover dominantly semasiographic musical, dance, and numerical scripts. But in his theoretical keynote essay, Daniels enshrines only what the countergrammatologist Jacques Derrida calls "a certain kind of writing" as the real graphic McCoy (1979 [1967]:83; see Goody 2000:109–18). Daniels's definition demands "a system of more or less permanent marks used to represent an utterance in such a way that it can be recovered more or less exactly without the intervention of the utterer. . . . It is thus necessary for a writing system to represent the *sounds* of a language" (Daniels 1996b:3). In other words, for Daniels, "writing" must imply paper (etc.) that "talks." John DeFrancis, rebutting Sampson, argues for even more restrictive postures (1989:211–47). These, like most historians of scripts (for example, Coulmas 1989:18; Gaur 1984:22–23,77–79; Gelb 1952:4), regard khipus as irrelevant to writing.

Influenced by such theory, and by the unilineal evolutionism of its precursors (I. Taylor 1899 [1883]:1:18), encyclopedias and syntheses tend to treat semasiographies as "primitive" precursors of "true writing." Isaac Taylor's Victorian idea of a single continuum from signs for ideas, to signs for words or morphemes, to more analytical systems like the alphabet, has long outlasted other pre-Boasian unilinealist theories. Although practicing grammatologists no longer embrace it, the notion of "progress" from more aggregated to more analytical signaries still saturates virtually all Western popular literature. The *Encyclopedia Britannica* even retains (as of 2004) a special dungeon for nonlexigraphic systems under the heading of "subgraphemics." But before assuming that semasiography has something to do with simplicity, one should notice that music notations, chemical formulas, mathematical scripts, machine-readable waybills, and circuit diagrams are semasiographies.

Could khipus' reference system be a general-purpose semasiography, as opposed to functionally restricted modern semasiographs? Sampson imagines a limiting extreme: "There would appear in principle to be no reason why a society could not have expanded a semasiographic system by adding further graphic conventions, until it was fully as complex and rich in expressive potential as their spoken language. At that point they would possess two fully-fledged 'languages' having no relationship with one another—one of them a spoken language without a script, and the other a 'language' tied intrinsically to the visual medium" (Sampson 1985:30). In fact no such language has been found. Sampson suggests that such a system would be impossibly cumbersome because it would be unmanageably prolific of signs. The crux of the matter seems to be that semasiographs are superior where different users have a substantial domain of culture in common, but little spoken language in common (e.g., musicians), or where for other reasons the verbal detour is undesirable. (Such reasons include cases where the syntactic structure of speech obscures dissimilar logical structures, as when one obscures an algebraic equation by phrasing it as a sentence.) W. C. Brice, an expert on the ancient Cretan scripts, calls attention to the "self-sufficient function" such signs achieve:

> Most studies of the history of writing relegate non-phonetic systems, under various names, to a brief preliminary chapter, which stresses their limitations, before passing on to early varieties of so-called "real" or "true" writing in which, through the familiar device of the rebus, the symbols are used to designate sounds rather than ideas. But in fact the only truly independent writing is that which is non-phonetic, and can express a meaning without reference to sound. Phonetic script is writing deprived of its self-sufficient function and used not to express an idea but to freeze a spoken sound. Both systems have their separate advantages. But if non-phonetic writing had been so clearly inferior to phonetic . . . it would not have survived in use for special purposes. (1976:40)

Highly successful and persistent nonphonetic scripts such as math notation, music notation, chemical formulas, formalizations for linguistics, choreographic labanotation, and knitting and weaving codes, satisfy such purposes.

It would be pointless to deny that movement toward writing "with words" is a repetitive course of history. The association occurs in archaeological cases as diverse as Sumer, Egypt, the Maya lands, and ancient China. The system of glyphs associated with Aztec rule appears to have been acquiring some lexigraphic features when Spanish intervention diverted its history. It seems "real writing" in the Aristotelian-Saussurean sense did over and over again develop in sign systems that served complex institutions: states, priesthoods, and commerce. It has been suggested (see chapter 5) that Spanish invasion itself stimulated khipu development in that direction.

But the ethnographic evidence presented in chapters 6 through 8 does not confirm any systemic speech-mimicking function. It does suggest a khipu system elaborately keyed to mimicking other forms of action. What little we know ethnographically of modern and recent khipu competences depends on semasiographic composition with a "readout" method superficially resembling logography. Without prejudice against Urton's argument that khipus are theoretically capable of lexigraphic reference such as logosyllabography, I have found that actual cord lexigraphy remains conjectural. So it seems to me we should still give a high priority to asking how khipus could have served complex data registry independent of lexigraphy, with or without supplementation by it.

Could it be that Peruvian practice came closer than our own to that limiting case Sampson asks us to ponder theoretically—the extreme at which visible code and speech become "two fully-fledged 'languages'"? If one considers the phylogenesis of graphic practice in its pristine instances, thinking in a forward or historical direction rather than assuming a teleology toward "real writing," one quickly runs into considerations that bring real writing and its alternatives much closer together.

The first is that when people set about to inscribe, they do not a priori have the goal of recording speech acts. It would be silly to posit a pair of puzzled Neolithic ancestors asking, "How can we write down what we've said?" because the concept of representing evanescent, unself-conscious speech was itself unavailable. Indeed the psychologist David Olson (1994:105) persuasively argues that "writing introduced a new awareness of linguistic structures," only after it had arisen from nonlexigraphic processes. Even Florian Coulmas, a strong exclusivist, concedes that "the invention of writing . . . was not a clearly defined problem. . . . Rather there were a number of practical problems (such as record keeping [by priests, who would be held accountable by fellow priests], counting, conveying messages indirectly, etc.). . . . The establishment of convention is a kind of *social problem solving* and that is what the invention of writing amounts to" (1989:9). Coulmas may have been persuaded by Konrad Ehlich's (1983) formalization of such problem solving in semiotic terms.

The useful perception here is that the development of a writing system is *nothing other than* the practical case-by-case solution of social tasks, which produce *as an emergent* a new data registry system. An interesting research venture in the direction of studying legibility as problem solving is that of Axel Steensberg (1989), a Scandinavian archaeologist who associates complex signaries with problems of "labeling" in certain food technologies. Steensberg, like the Aschers, reminds us that the record-keeping art takes shape around the social problems it solves.

And this indeed is what the archaeological record seems to show. Denise Schmandt-Besserat's famous argument about how writing as visible speech evolved in Sumeria from a system of "tokens" that in themselves were mere chips for the solving of transactional accounts (i.e., a form of numeracy; 1980, 1988) has run into archaeological critiques (Michalowski 1993). But the critiques essentially question whether the graphic simulacrum of spoken language arose as a mutation in the labeling of tokens, not whether tokens had the function of problem solving by means of symbolic simulation. If one grants that they had that function, one can also grant that the elaboration of tokens and their labeled containers ("envelopes"), a code chronologically prior to "real writing," already constituted a path to inscriptive data registry.

Daniels himself is of the opinion that speech mimicry could just as well be epiphenomenal:

> It is often supposed that writing was devised for the purpose of communicating at a distance. . . . But this seems to be a case of overlooking the obvious: the sending of messages, and the writing of books for posterity, are happily accidental byproducts. *The earliest uses of writing seem to be to communicate things that really don't have oral equivalents.* In Mesopotamia, the earliest documents are business records: quantities of livestock, lists of workers and their rations and tasks. In China, the oldest writing is found in oracles. . . . In Mesoamerica, astronomical, life cycle, and other calendrical information is the primary topic of the many texts that can be interpreted." (1996b:5; emphasis added)

Lists of quantities or the trajectories of stars are awkward things to put into words. Utterances which do so are hardly typical speech acts. Jack Goody mentions the propensity to make lists as a specifically nonoral behavior, strong in the early phases of Egyptian and Near Eastern graphogenesis: "This 'non-textual' . . . use of writing embodied in lists of various kinds affected other areas of communication but it dominated administrative uses" (1986:54). So, if not speech mimesis, what do early legible artifacts achieve? Although much has been made of the "space-crossing" and "time-binding" potency of scripts (Innis 1950), that special functional "something" which early inscriptions had, and which speech lacked, may have been neither durability nor transmissibility, but manipulability. Tokens, for example, appear above all as aids to organization of data relationships.

Peter Damerow carries this line of discussion to forceful conclusions in his summation on proto-cuneiform script of the fourth millennium BCE. (Proto-cuneiform is a well-attested system ancestral to Sumerian cuneiform and thus crucial to the invention of writing proper.) Damerow protests against "the anachronistic projection of modern functions of writing into its early use" (1999:4; see also Larsen 1998).[3] He argues that the precursors of "real writing" were not deficient attempts to represent speech (e.g., through pictograms standing for nouns) but successful attempts to represent knowledge expressed in forms other than verbal sentences. Rather than matching the syntax of a language, they match the syntax of particular action sequences, such as taking inventory or calculating rations. "Phonetic coding" played little role if any in proto-cuneiform. Proto-cuneiform codes were standardized only within a particular community sharing such sequences. Inscriptions are highly structured, but the structures are nonlinguistic. Rather, they reflect administrative data hierarchies. Proto-cuneiform co-evolved with arithmetical notation. Its adaptation to "phonetic coding" was a subsequent evolution. And yet it was "proto" only in a phylogenetic sense; the survival of 6,000-odd texts attests that it must have proven stably satisfactory in its own setting.

If khipus were proto-writing in Damerow's sense, and thus far from "true writing," why did Spaniards perceive their use as a kind of reading? In chapters 6 through 9, I argue that a semasiographic method (taking the term with reservations discussed there) formed the basis of khipu production, but khipus might easily be verbalized, because many or most cord signs, like numerals, had verbal equivalents and could be taken as virtual logograms. Perhaps it was the spectacle of people doing this which caused Spaniards to compare khipus with their own writing. I suspect that the khipu art presents a genuine ambiguity between *semasiography of production* and *lexigraphy of recitation*—and that this ambiguity was a great hazard to Spanish attempts at understanding Andean code.

Father José de Acosta, a Quechua expert, explained that combinations of khipu knots and colors corresponded to "significaciones de cosas," or "meanings of things." He explicitly contrasted this with combinations of letters, which correspond to *vocablos*, "words" (1954 [1590]:189). Acosta was sophisticated in the philology of his day. If he had thought knots stood for words, he would have said so; instead he seems to be pointing at semasiography. Based on observed recording practices (chapters 4 and 7), I too approach Tupicocha's quipocamayos with a supposition that the local legibility theory of khipus centered on marks left by *significaciones*, acts of signing, that recognized things and deeds in their world—the small world of local political and productive relations. Such inscriptions would tend to calque action scenarios: the arithmetical sequences of an inventory, the rotation of a labor duty, or the sequential gestures of a ritual. Their insertion would obey the syntax of the respective domain of action, not of Quechua or Spanish speech. But since the referents do have verbal names, (e.g., a particular knot could be verbalized as "absent"), they could in practice be read out as if they were logograms. Whether this process led in the direction of logosyllabography, a common form of early "real writing," is not a question we can answer yet.

Some Nonphilological Accounts of the Graphic

Damerow thinks proto-writings encoded "simple patterns of semantic categories" (1999:6). But the organization of experience into inscribable categories does not seem so simple from the cultural anthropological viewpoint. Because philological grammatology has thrived on its dedication to "a certain kind of writing," it rarely defines an analytic common ground wide enough to cover the gamut of ethnographically known ways in which acts other than words are rendered writeable. Ventures in this direction come from elsewhere. I will highlight three: those of the semiologist Roy Harris, the philosopher Nelson Goodman, and the linguist Émile Benveniste. The objective is to explore their promise for an expanded ethnography of literacies, seeking points of applicability which will be taken up in later chapters.

Harris propounds a theory expressly designed to include *all* visual sign-systems, most explicitly in *Signs of Writing* (1995; see also Harris 1986). His project, globally intended as a critique of the Saussurean legacy, stands even further from the philological consensus than Sampson's revision. It has three main tenets:

The first is "integrationalism": "The view of human communication adopted here is integrational as opposed to telementational. That is to say, *communication is envisaged not as a process of transferring thoughts or messages from one individual to another, but as consisting in the contextualized integration of human activities by means of signs*" (Harris 1995:4; emphasis added). In a more exact restatement of this cardinal premise, "a sign is integrational in the sense that it typically involves the contextualized application of biomechanical skills within a certain macrosocial framework, thereby contributing to the integration of activities which would otherwise remain unintegrated" (Harris 1995:22–23).

The second tenet is an open-minded stance regarding the relation between the written signifier and the signified. Whereas Saussure and most grammatologists accept the Aristotelian judgment that the written sign is a metasign, that is, a sign for the whole or part of a primary speech sign, Harris asks us to consider the likelihood that writing may have other relations to the things it signifies. We know it can do so because there are nonspeech activities such as mathematical reasoning, music, dance, and (one could add) ritual, which are capable of integration through inscription. Like Sampson, then, he is open to the idea of the signary as primary code.

The third tenet is that the written sign is not a transparent medium merely *equivalent to* other cultural codes; rather, its own form inherently *contributes to* what the sign signifies (as, for example, the peculiar curl of a line contributes to a familiar signature the meaning that the bearer of the name is the very person who wrote it). Harris sees the attributes of the sign as both inherently and relationally meaningful.

It is important to notice that Harris is not proposing a return to the notion of ideograms (signs corresponding directly to "ideas") as the alternative to "lexigrams." He is renouncing "type-of-referent" altogether as a criterion for classifying signs. He is saying that a written sign, whose taxonomic status is an open-ended matter, comes into being whenever humans use a material symbol to place persons or activities into "integrated" semiotic relation. One knows something is a sign if people's activities come into a relationship by virtue of it. Whether the sign corresponds to a segment of speech sound, a culturally categorized ritual gesture, or any other set need not be stipulated. Harris also introduces the ethnographically useful notion of *emblematic frame* (1995:168–69; see also Parmentier's independent but comparable [1985] argument on "diagrammatic icons"). An emblematic frame is a cultural artifact within which a class of signs may be deployed, examples being games, calendars, uniforms, and rituals. "Emblematic framing" serves well to characterize the hypothesized planning role of khipus (see chapter 9).

The second attempt at an overarching analysis of sign systems is that which the philosopher Goodman set forth in *Languages of Art* (1976).[4] His focus is on reducing the seemingly endless differences in the ways meanings are organized in different media to a few principles. All media *refer* to things, but they do so under dissimilar rules. Goodman proposes that various codes carry meaning in different ways because they establish different kinds of reference depending on the relationship between the *formal* properties of the signary, and the *formal* properties of the cultural schema that forms the set of referents—that is, their respective properties simply as schemata (discreteness of terms, etc.; 1976:127–73).

Reference is a two-way relationship between a sign (*character*) and its *compliance class* (or *extension*), the set of "things" which satisfy its criteria of reference. The compliance class of the sign "b-flat major" on a staff is the set of actual sounds that musicians recognize as this note.

When the arrow of reference points from a character to a compliant, the character is said to *denote* its referent. This can happen in two ways: by *representing* it or by *describing* the compliant.

Simplifying a complex definition (Goodman 1976:233–41), *representation* may be understood as denoting a compliant by presenting selected features of it through an analogue character. (The curve in a pencil sketch of a pear is an analogue of a pear's outline, and *represents* it.)

The other kind of denotation, namely, *description*, occurs when we refer to a compliant by means of characters that are not analogues. The crucial point for the ethnographic application is that there are two ways to describe. One way is to apply the characters to an otherwise unlimited and unsorted array of referents. This is called *verbal description*. It is what we do when we use a character set (for example spoken words) as "natural language." We have presorted the set of words, logograms, and the like to be sure they have the necessary properties of distinctness from each other. But we have not tried to presort the universe of possible referents at all. This is what we mean when we call such usage "natural." Natural language yields a one-way definitional ordering. As long as we follow the arrow of reference from character to referent, each potential referent either does or does not comply. For example, the usage of the sign "Dr. Nelson Goodman, philosopher" is determinate in the character-to-referent direction; everything in the universe either is or is not what the sign refers to. But if we reverse the arrow of reference to point from referents back to characters, we are faced with choices that undo any determinacy: The particular entity I am thinking of is a compliant to the characters *mammal*, *professor*, *English-speaker*, and so ad infinitum.

The upshot is that there can be no one right way of verbally describing anything via "natural language." Sometimes a person, or some culture, or some métier finds this inconvenient. They will be interested in a system of denotation which provides a determinate route from the object in the world to the character that stands for it, as well as vice versa. For example, the music historian Leo Treitler (1981) notes that from the tenth century onward, European music masters demanded greater and greater control of music, not just in terms of controlling the performance from the page, but more and more ability to compose on the page (that is, put on paper a uniquely recognizable rendering of the sounds in the composer's mind). The actual sound of someone singing kyrie eleison in a certain key is an object that, like Dr. Goodman, could be a compliant to any number of characters, until one decides to classify it in a way that excludes all other ways, and assign unique characters (signs) to each chosen variable. The qualities of sound which Europe chose for this purpose were duration, pitch, and major or minor scale. Other cultures chose differently.

In other words, one achieves two-way determinacy between performance and text at the expense of the freedom of natural language. This is a pervasive choice in many contexts and cultures.

If one sacrifices the freedom of natural language for the accuracy of bidirectional determinacy, one is choosing what Goodman calls *notational description*. This is the point where Goodman's schema sheds fresh light on "writing without words."

To formalize the musical process in Goodman's terms, let us suppose that, in addition to making *rules about the set of characters that can denote referents*, we impose some *rules about the set of potential referents that can comply to characters* (pitch, duration, scale . . .). As Goodman puts it, notational systems demand three "semantic requirements":

1. Unambiguity: A sign system only works if the compliance relation (what x is referred to by symbol y) is invariant.

2. Compliance-class "disjointness": No two characters may have a compliant in common. "The requirement of semantic disjointness rules out most ordinary languages even if we suppose them freed of ambiguity . . . a notational system cannot contain any pair of semantically intersecting terms like 'doctor' and 'Englishman.' . . . The characters of a notational system are semantically segregated" (Goodman 1976:152).

3. Semantic finite differentiation: Any two potential referents must contrast with, not gradate into, each other. That is, it must be possible to determine without doubt which of two compliance classes an object belongs to. So if, for example, one is devising a notation for weight, it is not enough for the *signs* to be discrete. It is also necessary to pretend that *weight* is a discrete variable, even though, of course, it is not. One must divide it into nonoverlapping ranges such as the near-

est whole kilo. While scientists who need to take gradation seriously use devices such as calculus to avoid such fictions, the fiction (bizarre as it sounds when made explicit) is actually a common cultural practice.

Once one presorts objects culturally, placing them into categories that fit these imperatives, it becomes possible to *notate* them with equal control in both directions. This is, of course, common practice, from the social security number, to music notation or labanotation, to North American Indian clan insignia. Would it work well with khipus?

The usefulness of notational symbolism depends on what domains a population treats as "antecedently atomized." It also depends which ones it deems suitable to be consciously organized as "atomic." Extrapolating from Goodman's reasoning, one might suggest that in any given society the elaborateness of notations is limited only by the ability or disposition to presort domains of experience by imposing discretely cutting cognitive filters. Alexander Marshack's (1972) argument that markings on upper Paleolithic and Mesolithic objects are registries of lunations amounts to assertion of a notation based on days and months being taken as "antecedently atomic," millennia before scripts mimicking "natural language" arose. The archaeology of scripts seems to indicate that sky phenomena were likewise antecedently atomic in the eyes of ancient Maya, and agropastoral quanta (animals, storage units) in the eyes of ancient Mesopotamians.

Many if not most cultures seem to work up notations some of the time. The system's frequent appearances should not be surprising, because the conditions for calling things unitary, discrete, and multiple are very generous; they range from merely gathering perceptions preorchestrated by physics (e.g., days) to arbitrary cultural segmentations (e.g., measuring of space, weight, etc.) and rhythms created anew (ritual cycles, etc.). In the Andes broadly, the harmony between diurnal cycles and work tasks, climatic cycles and irrigation schedules, and, in Inka lore, the recondite correspondences of astronomy with agropastoral cycles, kindreds, and ritual spaces (Bauer and Dearborn 1995) set widely agreed-on imaginary templates to which people anchored discourse and practice. Rituals often served as "dotted lines" demarcating such domains.

But "natural" breaks are not enough. The Andean peoples seem to have perceived a very large range of their own practice as antecedently atomized. Otherwise they would not have been so inclined to naturalize such things as binary and four-part schemata on referents that look continuous to others (the horizon, the year, the geography of a valley, the color spectrum, the ages of man and woman, etc). It is as if they were interested in expanding the idea of the antecedently atomized outward to exceptionally far limits. Urton's emphasis on the succession of dual choices involved in spinning, plying, and weaving makes it plain how fiber work readily supplied a "sign" end to match the "referent end" in a bidirectional notation system. In chapters 6 through 9 I will propose that cords are related to varied kinds of social action like "notation" in Goodman's sense, and as its further derivatives "diagram" and "model."

The third opening to a freer ethnography of inscription is Benveniste's innovative "semiology of language," a synthesis of Saussurean approaches to sign systems with those of Charles Sanders Peirce (1985 [1969]). Benveniste is unusual among linguists in considering speech's coexistence with nonverbal "sign systems" a fundamental fact about its meaningfulness, and he, like khipu specialists, is urgently interested in understanding the terms of their coexistence. For Benveniste, coexisting sign systems justify their coexistence by being functionally different on four points. The first is their "modes of expression," that is, sensory channels; Andean speech was oral/aural, khipus visual/tactile. Second, coexisting systems have distinctive "domains of validity," that is, ranges of social efficacy. We have already mentioned some aspects of khipu efficacy, such as transtemporality and power across space, as well as a social domain in the ceremonial reproduction of power. Third, multiple sign systems have multiple sign inventories, differing in nature and number, adapted to their channel and rhythm of use; Inka khipus, like many "real writings," seem to have evolved in the direction of finite sign inventory, apparently across language communities. Fourth, coexisting systems differ in "the relationship that unites the signs and confers their distinguishing function," presumably meaning the specific physical points that embody Saussurean attributes of contrastive value and syntactical connection — attributes of fiber construction which relate systemically to each other in a different way than points of voice articulation, and so on, do. The point of having coexisting semiotic systems is that they are *nonredundant*. "We are not able to say 'the same thing' " in any two of them. "Man does not have several distinct systems at his disposal for the *same* signifying relationship" (1985:234–35; emphasis in original). Benveniste allows us to consider that instead of reinforcing orality by redundancy, as philological grammatologists hold, coexistent media engage speech in a game of related but indeterminately variable representations on shared experiential ground. This is obviously of immense pragmatic importance. It opens a way to a pragmatics-oriented attack on the problem of decipherment.

That khipus and speech were probably only partly equivalent is a caution against expectations of a Rosetta-stone approach. (How inviting it is to forget that the Rosetta stone collated script with script, not script with a dissimilar signing system!) Benveniste's theory suggests that speech and khipu were related in a less simple relation than one in which the latter secondarily encoded the former. William Hanks's exegesis of Benveniste's concept "partial equivalence" (1996:51) notes that two systems are partially equivalent "by homology" if they have corresponding shapes or values, as when a visual system (road map) works as homology to a verbal landscape description. Chapters 6–9 argue that khipu making was a conscious homologue to decision-making process and performance registry, rather than to words about these processes. If signs are assembled in homology to a process, regardless of whether they mimic its verbal form, the overall set — the khipu — will bear an iconic likeness to it, and this is an important part of the intelligibility modern villagers attribute to khipus.

Two sign systems can also be partially equivalent "by contiguity." They become so if they co-occur in space and time. "Words and gestures are contiguous systems insofar as they are joined in acts of utterance. Material symbols, speech forms, and gestures are contiguous in ritual events" (Hanks 1996:51). Tupicochan khipus were contiguous to ritual speech and labor, and even, from the local viewpoint, consubstantial with them. Accordingly, in some respects it makes sense to interpret some quipocamayos as indexical signs of work and ritual in concert with each other — a property which goes far toward explaining their sacred standing.

A Heuristic and a Methodology for Tupicocha

First of all we must be aware, as Powell says, that "speech is only one form of language." If, as we know now, the gestural languages of the deaf satisfy the "innate human faculty of symbolization" without secondarily re-encoding speech (Powell 2002:59), why should a visible signary not also be what is sometimes called a "parallel" (rather than secondary) language? In seeking exits from logocentrism, each of the above theorists heightens awareness of properties which a code might display. (Indeed, the word *parallel* itself implies too much similarity.)

From Harris we derive a greater ethnographic openness to "writing-ness" in speech-free cultural objects. "Integrationalism," the definition of signs as coming into being when a mark constitutes a social interaction, whether or not the signs obey a previously established code of correspondences, provides an axis of comparison among media which otherwise lack semiological common denominators (e.g., village record books and khipus). Harris's insistence that writing, in his extended sense, be taken as primary code for integrated action, rather than as secondary code for the spoken language it may entail, fits with Huarochirí views of all writing as primarily the concretion of a social act and only secondarily a reference to it. Likewise Harris's insistence that meaning inheres in the particular execution of a sign, and not just in a purportedly invariant underlying langue archetype of it, should help us accommodate villagers' wide interest in details of manufacture that exceed even Conklin's and Urton's maximalist views of significant traits. Finally, "emblematic frame" provides a more flexible paradigm for conceiving the structure and functional range of khipus than does the frequent but rather thoughtless equation between cords and texts.

From Goodman we derive a canon of formal coherence. Harris's understanding of the sign excels in comprehensiveness and flexibility but does not provide much guidance in understanding how a signing practice, as it emerges through interpersonal functioning, becomes infused with grammaticality. Unlike Harris, Goodman does not leave the organization of reference open. He classifies sign-object relations according to how both the objects of, and the means of, reference are sorted conventionally and logically. Different arrangements allow different sorts of correspondence: notational, diagrammatic, pictorial, narrative, and so on.

Goodman's typology of modes of reference opens the way to recognizing multiple kinds of grammaticality. While there is nothing wrong with searching khipus for formal properties that seem to reflect "natural-language" grammaticality (e.g., the subject-object-verb syntax of Quechua) or mathematical grammaticality (e.g., the base-ten syntax detected by Locke), the search becomes more worthwhile when informed by a wider and logically inclusive gamut of legible rules and not guided just by the habitual priorities of bookish or bookkeeping guilds. As we will see, the furthering of "notation" into the realms of "diagram" and "model" give some formal substance to the image of khipus which Abercrombie sums up with the word *chronotopograph*.

From Benveniste we learn to think of the distance between seemingly incommensurable sign-systems as a space of intelligible relationships. Their differences are eventually mappable in terms of pragmatics. Benveniste's comparisons imply that coexisting sign systems to some degree challenge and relativize each other — an implication he was hardly eager to follow, for his purpose was to revindicate speech as the sovereign semiosis, alone in its capacity to interpret all others and even itself. Nonetheless, to turn his work to Andean ends, it helps to ask whether interpretative potential and the unfolding of metalanguage really are the semiologist's passkey. In chapter 4 I will embrace his idea of the coexisting system but suggest that in Andean communicative practice, the game of multiple-system signing, including practices that pointed away from metalinguistic interpretation, acted as an important counterweight to hazards in the unequally tilted game of speech.

This Cook's tour of several partially discordant theories about the coexistence of symbolic systems may leave a feeling of disquiet about whether any single methodology can implement such disparate ideas. The answer lies in their shared property of opening paths toward the pragmatic, as opposed to grammatical, properties of plural semiosis.

Philological decipherment entails a relatively well-defined procedure (Gordon 1982) — one we are in a poor position to exercise, because we do not know when (if ever) the artifacts mimic speech, much less what spoken language or at what level of segmentation. I believe it likely that khipus functioned at a distance from language syntax, conforming rather to the nonverbal "syntax" of fixed social performances such as inventorying, accounting, attendance-taking, calendrical registry, quota-giving, sacrificing. In this they would resemble the "proto-writing" system Damerow has outlined for proto-cuneiform (1999). Khipus in my view were concretions of nonverbal action which, once made, were susceptible to verbalization by a method superficially like logography.

As for decipherment, what canon of method could correlate visible khipu traits to their action sources? Philological decipherment holds among its chief weapons the likelihood that a spoken language's rule-governed grammatical regularities will have surface counterparts in the artifact, and it treats these regularities as a heuristic for decipherment. (For this reason philology is of little use until one commits to a hypothesis about which spoken language is encoded.) But anthropological linguistics emphasizes the fact that grammar rules are not the only source of linguistic order. There is more pattern in parole than the rules of langue alone foretell because in speaking, humans employ fairly regularized schemata to achieve fairly repetitive ends. If grammar accounts for the rules of the game (langue), the anthropological linguist soon finds that characteristic ploys and moves in the game as actually played (parole) manifest schematic regularities as well as emergent novelties. Such cultural systems of verbal practice, the pragmatic dimension of speech considered as culture, comes to the fore in "communicative practice" theory (Hanks 1996). I believe our best avenue into the Tupicochan khipu problem is to model khipus as a trace of semiological pluralism shaped by practice. The khipus' surface regularities are likely to bear the stamp of schemata repeatedly employed to effect the social ends of gatherings where they were present. These ends and their schematic as programs of action are in part known, allowing one to link cord forms and the original contexts even when we do not know how closely the artifact was molded to the verbal discourse of that context. In all likelihood, too, they show a residue of "irregularity" not reducible to schemata; like speech in action, they record a dimension of agency in the form of emergent innovations.

It should be useful to view khipu patterns much as Hanks viewed Mayan speech practice. Hanks draws heavily upon Pierre Bourdieu's notion of habitus. "Habitus . . . locates the problem of what speakers share at the level of their actual embodied practices rather than in [grammatical] conceptual models. It incorporates the idea of habitual patterns of speech beyond the 'rule-governed' structures of grammar . . . [And] finally, habitus embraces linguistic facts along with nonlinguistic aspects of social knowledge, thereby helping to build a bridge between issues of verbal practice and social relations more globally" (1990:13). It might be a useful exercise in daydreaming about a khipu-using world, to try out Hanks's overview with a purposeful distortion: substituting the word *khipu*, and verbs suitable to it, for the speech-oriented lexicon Hanks actually used. If we try this, Hanks's transformed words would be:

> (1) Khipus and the world of human experience were everywhere interpenetrated, so that even the inner logic of a khipu system bore the trace of the routine practices to which it was adapted. (2) To make a khipu was to occupy the world, not only to represent it, and this occupancy entailed various modes of expression of which propositional meaning was but one. (3) Khipu makers and the objects about which they knotted were parts of the same world; a division between subjects and objects was one of the *products* of khipu practice,

something people create with knots, not the irremediable condition against which khipu arts had to work. (4) Andean people did many things through khipus, of which thinking and reasoning were a part—but not the only part. They also realized themselves; effected changes in their worlds; connected with other people; experienced beauty, rage, and tenderness; exercised authority; refused; and pursued their interests (altered from Hanks 1996:236).

Each of these four "doings" will have left visible traces in cord artifacts. Many of them took place in social scenarios that are at least in part ethnographically known. By the end of chapter 9, it should be possible to see khipu as codes representing such sequences in several ways: as signed registries in Damerow's sense; as marks of achieved social integration in Harris's; as nonredundant parallel language in Benveniste's; and as notations or diagrams in Goodman's.

2

A FLOWERY SCRIPT:

THE SOCIAL AND DOCUMENTARY ORDER

OF MODERN TUPICOCHA VILLAGE

W HEN THE members of Peasant Community San Andrés de Tupicocha assemble, they meet under a sign. It is the community's emblematic self-representation (figure 5). By unfolding its symbolism, this
chapter sketches the village's makeup. Because we are concerned only with inscription, much is left out — not least the village's fortunes in the era of the Shining
Path conflict and the 1990–2001 Fujimori dictatorship, which shaped its present
unstable and partly deterritorialized condition. We are only concerned with organizational properties formerly mediated by quipocamayos.

An Emblem of Village Polity

The mural commemorates the day the community undertook its most heroic
project, the thirty-kilometer-long Willcapampa Canal. Willcapampa is a stretch
of the western cordillera crest where mythic ancestors dwell. From the snows of
Willcapampa, these "grandparents" send melt-off water to irrigate Tupicocha's
parched fields and orchards. The Willcapampa Canal, built in the sweat of three
decades' collective labor days called *faenas*, or "tasks," is the crowning accomplish-
ment of an intricate complex of hierarchy, cooperation, planning, and political
self-discipline.

Asked about the mural, villagers explain it as an icon of society in production.
Flowering plants symbolize agriculture — both crops and the medicinal herbs and
flowers which are the village's market mainstay. Plants grow from artificially chan-
neled water. What makes the water flow is cooperation between the presidents of

FIGURE 5 The painting in the community meeting hall. Upper legend: "UNITED. Will-capampa [watercourse] staked out 12 to 22 July 1965." Lower legend: "Work begun XVI of VII of MXCLXV." Vertical legends: (on left) "Presidents of parcialidades"; (on right) "Community Directorate." This is the cartoon that Edelmiro Vilcayauri used (lower right) in painting the mural. From personal collection of author.

the ten parcialidades, or corporate kin groups, called ayllus in intimate speech (left), and the Junta Directiva Comunal, or board of elected officers of the Peasant Community (right).

At the center point of the design, these bases of social life cohere around a single all-important nexus: inscription (the pen). The actual letters of the book are visible but not legible. The visibility of "spirit" but not "letter" corresponds to an understanding that every transaction should be inscribed, but that the core social bonds that underlie all transactions should remain tacit. This image does reflect practice. Tupicochans rigorously record everything they do in groups, and they count *constancia*—"proof," in the form of permanent visibility—as indispensable to every action above the sphere of intrahousehold intimacy.

Land, "Nature," and Geographic Space

San Andrés de Tupicocha is one of a string of villages perched on small shelves of land about two-thirds of the way up the Pacific-facing rampart of the western Andes. The Spanish authorities who laid these villages out as "reductions," following commands of the 1569–81 viceroy Francisco Toledo, meant to concentrate Andean agropastoralists near the 3,000-meter level (pulling them somewhat down from pre-Hispanic habitations). Villages were built along roads where officials and priests on horseback could patrol. The village center of Tupicocha (11° 59′ 51″ south, 76° 28′ 23″ west at about 3,321 meters over sea level; see maps 1 and 2) fills a small ledge inside a westward-opening, horseshoe-shaped recess of the mountain wall. Its countryside reaches upward and eastward to snowcaps that glitter remotely in the thin air toward 5,000 meters. It reaches downward and westward into a vast chasm along whose bottom the Lurín, a bright thread of water, crawls its distant way to the Pacific. This landscape covers much of what was once the "vertical archipelago" (Murra 1975a) that Tutay Quiri and the heroes of the 1608 Quechua text conquered. The "vertical archipelago," an ideal-typical model of Andean organization, means a political assemblage of noncontiguous "island" territories at diverse altitudes, with diverse resources. Tupicocha's included icy heights; *puna*, or high-altitude pastureland; high tuber fields; herb and garden fields near the village; and hot valley lands below with orchards and maize. The mythology of this conquest is highly focalized in chapters 11, 12, and 24 of the Huarochirí Manuscript. Today Tupicocha's uppermost pastures are about 4,800 meters above sea level and its lowest fruit groves are near 2,500 meters. Holdings total 11,938.75 hectares (Martínez Chuquizana 1996:14, 21–24; Stiglich 1922:1084).

From the viewpoint of the nation-state, Tupicocha is first of all the capital of a district (a subdivision of Huarochirí Province, which is in turn a subdivision of the Department of Lima; see map 1). The nation-state exercises its basic authority through an office called the *Distrital Gobernación*, only tangentially involved in the khipu complex. Second, Tupicocha village has a *municipio*, or "urban" govern-

ment, theoretically responsible only for in-town functions such as street maintenance. It is a potent organization, but it postdates the era of khipu use and will not
be treated here except insofar as its precursor, the *agencia municipal*, was involved.
The important institution for khipus is the third, the state-recognized Peasant
Community (*comunidad campesina*). It is a self-governing corporation controlling
the rural orbit: community fields, pastures, and infrastructures including canals,
terrace walls, and reservoirs. It also leads the ritual part of in-town life, notably the
patron saint festivals. The Peasant Community, whose hall the mural in figure 5
decorates, is the traditional focus of loyalty and identity. Unlike the other authorities, which are legitimate but externally supervised, the community embodies "immemorial," autochthonous land and water rights, considered to be the legacy of
prehistory. The village also governs eight outlying "annex" settlements (*anexos*)
without khipus (see map 2, those towns labeled with a smaller typeface).

Of the village's 1,543 people (according to the 1993 census; Peru, Dirección Nacional de Estadística y Censos 1994:200), fewer than half live exclusively in the
community nucleus. The remainder live in the "annexes," have double domicile
in Tupicocha and Lima, or live full-time in Lima. In recent years, the households
registered as *comuneros* (community members) numbered 140–50.[1] The central
village is a tightly built adobe *agroville*, from which people commute on foot to

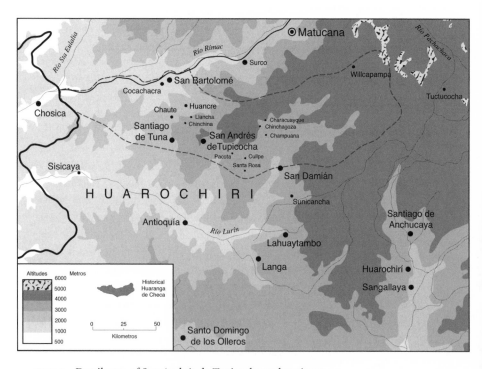

MAP 2   Detail map of San Andrés de Tupicocha and environs.

44

their fields, orchards, and pastures. The pioneering ethnographer Teresa Guillén de Boluarte strikingly called this pattern "an urban rural city" (1958:56).

Villagers say that in a not-too-distant past, Tupicocha owned much or most of its land communally. This village was spared the *latifundista* (estate-builder) landgrab that afflicted peasantries in many other provinces circa 1860–1910. It was correspondingly less sharply affected by the agrarian conflicts of the 1960s and the 1969 to 1973 agrarian reform of the Velasco Alvarado regime. These facts are important because the quipocamayos are likely to have served a labor-land nexus less interrupted by expropriation than in most parts of Peru.

Pressure for rigorous documentation arises from internal tensions, not just from state demands. Tensions arise among households that differently use the various "production zones" (in Mayer's terms)—in a word, tensions inherent in agro-pastoralism. The community still controls puna, or high tundra, in the form of common pastures. People heavily committed to pasturing there are distrusted by those heavily invested in planting, because herders sleep far away and often fail to show up for workdays. Villagers with many animals conversely resent those who dwell "below" because of pasturing fees and inconvenient labor demands. A village self-ethnographer mentions that high-dwelling herders tease lower cultivators with the term *cotucheros*, roughly "dumpsters," because they live close to their own refuse (Vilcayauri 1983–91:45A). Herders form a powerful bloc in community politics; before 1940, it was almost routine for the man with the biggest herd to be the community president. The need to document performance under these tense conditions—reminiscent of *huari-llacuaz* tensions in pre-Hispanic society (Duviols 1973)—has influenced the high demand for constancia that warranted khipu technology.

The association between herding and khipu-keeping has been amply documented by Mackey (1970) and others. Less known are the ways in which agriculture demands documentation. As will be discussed later in the chapter, labor deployment (in association with irrigation) is probably a key to the demand. In the days when the Checa commanded a "vertical archipelago" reaching into the bottom of the Rímac River chasm, the control of fields and waters at a distance likely demanded documentation. Its last pieces disappeared in the late nineteenth century. Privatization (*parcelación*) began a long time ago; in 1713 one José de la Cruz of Tuna already owned over 100 parcels, some in Tupicocha (Spalding 1984:197). "Parceling" lands compromises villagers' willingness to invest time in community infrastructure or in mutual aid, and this too reinforces concern for "proof." Since the Fujimori regime encouraged privatization, state representatives have handled the myriad folk-legal refinements of land use law casually and even disrespectfully. The community, fearing that a neoliberal attack on nonstandardized titles would create a forced sell-off, defends with dogged perfectionism its traditional claims, and tries to translate them into currently valid titles.

Migration to Lima (and beyond, to New York, Dallas, Rome, or Madrid) saps full-time population but creates an elastically deterritorialized version of village tradition. The loyalty of emigrants will decide the future of both the community and its quipocamayo legacy. Optimists bank on the fact that most emigrants love to attend ritual gatherings amid the unique horizons of their homes—not just out of nostalgia, but because the nexus of hallowed territory is also their subsistence "safety net" against urban unemployment (which is extremely high). As holders of the safety net and custodians of absentees' property, villagers are not without influence. They manage festivals which act as fund-raisers for the infrastructure, where emigrants supply capital and residents labor. In this emerging constellation, the quipocamayos enjoy renewed value as cultural capital.

Agriculture and the Basics of Labor Organization

In Tupicocha, as throughout the region, the uppermost croplands yield the Andean tubers (several kinds of potato, oca [*Oxalis tuberosa*], *mashua* [*Tropaeolum tuberosum*], and *olluco* [*Ullucus tuberosus*]), as well as barley. Middle-altitude lands yield alfalfa, beans, broad beans, maize, herbs popularly drunk as infusions,[2] flowers,[3] squash, and wheat. At both upper and middle altitudes there are irrigated and dry-farming plots, the latter being of marginal productivity. Irrigated warm lands below the village center are usually used for fruit groves (apple, cactus fruit, peach, plum) as well as herbs, flowers, and maize-bean-squash fields. A recent surge in the market for cochineal,[4] which grows parasitically on cactus, has raised the value of arid lower slopes.

Herds graze above the croplands, in two regimens: communal *moyas pastales*, or walled pastures, and *cerros mostrencos*, or unfenced, low-quality community grazing land. Moyas are walled off in fallowing sectors and made available to herd-owning families on a per-head basis, inspected as part of the communal regimen, and closely documented. Because grazing resources fall short of demand, the community also rents seasonal pastures from an adjacent community, and this too is part of a folk-legal documentary tradition.[5] It is an interesting clue to folk theory of writing that the bottle handed over in token of each year's rental is known by the term *escritura* (writ).

Given the variety of resources and infrastructures, each with its own cycle of labor demand, it is almost impossible to overstate the sheer busyness of campesino life—and the variety of ways families manage it. Everybody is always hurrying off to attend to one holding or another. This is one of the reasons compliance with collective duty becomes hard to enforce, and why enforcement relies so closely on record keeping. The working year requires intricate coordination among activities which are compatible only because they differ in their moments of peak labor demand. Scheduling is of the essence, for households as for the ayllu, and for the multi-ayllu community. Thus Andean agropastoral systems require not only what Murra identified as "vertical" diversification but also what Jürgen Golte (1980) labeled "polycyclical" synchronization. It is a matter of governance, not just domestic economy, for collective infrastructure work must be intercalated, and must defend its priority.

The scheduling process begins with the distinction between two kinds of labor: *trabajo*, or self-directed work among household members, and faena, or group work undertaken as an obligation of membership and as an act of reciprocity with peers (Gelles 1984:29). Faenas include much of the spectrum documented elsewhere as *minka* or with varying regional terminology. To manage the "suprahousehold" sphere—in effect, to levy labor in the collective interest even at moments when members' private interests clamor for it—challenges villagers' political resolve as well as technical skill. Traditionally, at two seasons of the year the "suprahousehold sphere" makes major inroads on work autonomy. One comes at the end of the rains, usually in late April or May, when the canal system must be cleaned and repaired (the *champería*) and the other in September, when the remaining collective infrastructures such as chapels and reservoirs must be fixed. But the old ayllu order discussed in chapter 3 made even more demands. Indeed, no month is free of faenas, some of them called at the last minute. Paul Gelles's study of faenas in a neighboring part of Huarochirí found that members of Casta Community were responsible for an annual average of thirty faenas, or about one every twelve days (1984:32–33).

Even this reckoning is an underestimate, because entities above community level—the municipality, the national state, and NGOs—also levy faenas. So do narrower groups, such as the Mothers' Clubs, private partnerships controlling small irrigation systems, or the religious sodalities. Most social scientists and villagers think the faena system is declining, and it is true that many communities have dissolved faenas into the cash nexus. But in the 1990s the system in Tupicocha, Concha, and Sunicancha appeared anything but relaxed. To sign on as comunero in these places still means committing oneself to thirty years' service in a regimen of almost military rigor.

Intricate scheduling and jealousy over precious working time help one understand the almost unlimited demand for exact planning and record keeping. Inherent uncertainty sharpens these concerns. Since most decisions depend on tenuous forecasts about water supply, there can be no rote or cookbook solution. Moreover, those who plan have little coercive power. Uncooperative people are publicly punished, and scofflaws lose water turns. But in practice, no sanction short of expulsion will stop a determined freeloader. Expulsion, however, is so destructive to the group interest (because it alienates kin of the expelled) that only flat-out insolence will bring it about.

Perhaps for this reason, faenas are heavily hedged about with rituals of sanctification as well as reinforced by documentation. The basics of faena etiquette are the following: Any faena must take place in the presence of the sponsoring corporation's "work cross," a small green cross planted at the work site and stored between

FIGURE 6 At the ceremony initiating 1997's faena to close communal grazing lands, members of Tupicocha Community take coca leaf as part of the morning armada, or ritual distribution. Their hats bear the herbal cockades, or enfloros, of the occasion. From personal collection of author.

times at the community hall or respective president's home. By bringing a work cross and standing his staff of office alongside it, an officer advertises which jurisdiction regulates the job. At the beginning of any faena, the authority assembles the crew ceremonially. Someone must write down attendance, usually the ayllus' respective elected secretaries. Two rituals sanctify work. The first is the *armada* (from *armar*, "to prepare, set up"): a distribution of cigarettes, coca leaf, and shots of liquor. It "sets up" an action group for the next task. The second is *enfloro* (enflowerment) or garlanding of the work cross, and the hats of all present, with rosettes of an appropriate plant (see fig. 6). Explaining this obligation, the sacristan of San Damián said, "When we begin any work we perform the enflowerment. It means that we ask the necessary permission from the [superhuman] owners of those canals or lands. We give them their drinks, cigarettes, coca leaf so they'll be happy and help us. Everything has its owners. We say, 'Grandparents, Owners, help us so our work will be easier, so no accident or bad luck will happen to us.' At the same time we ask [permission of] the Supreme One [i.e., the God of Christianity]." Rites must be repeated at the beginning of each period of work. Most work parties or meetings are divided into "custom times" (*horas de costumbre*), meaning periods punctuated by the ritual sequence.

At "custom times" the record is placed together with the cross, whip, coca, tobacco, liquor, and flowers, so one would not go far wrong by classifying it as part of the ritual gear—and, indeed, when ayllus began inventorying their khipus, they classed them with ritual gear.

Irrigation and Its Records

Production depends first and foremost on canals, reservoirs, and terraces begun in pre-Hispanic antiquity, and continued as a never-ending work in progress. Almost every ethnographer who has encountered the stirring drama of hydraulic mobilization and devotion has felt compelled to treat it at length: Arguedas (1956), César Fonseca (1983), Gelles (2000:75–117), Peter Gose (1994:95–102), Oliverio Llanos and Jorge Osterling (1982), Janet Sherbondy (1982:103–20), Ricardo Valderrama Fernández and Carmen Escalante Gutiérrez (1988), Humberto Vargas Salgado (1990) and the contributors to William Mitchell and David Guillet's (1994) *Irrigation at High Altitudes*, among others. Tupicochans celebrate the "owners" at the headwaters of Willcapampa Canal. There dancers costumed as the sacred personages called *huaris* ascend to a secret place where two ancient skulls are stored. These skulls are the persons of "our god and goddess, Pencollo and Mama María" (the latter also called Catiana), a divine couple who favor the village with water in the form of snow and ice on the mountaintops. With solemn and affectionate offerings, huaris thank them for the past year's water and ask permission to irrigate in the coming cycle. The deities reply with a "letter." Actually it is a rough jotting made by a huari at their telepathic dictation. Huaris "read" the letter to the massed public at their encampment. Speaking for the deities, they rebuke remiss members and praise and bless altruistic ones.

New Year's Day brings a ritual cycle inverse to the champería. During four days, 5–8 January, sacred clowns called *curcuches* take over the village center on behalf of the divinities of the heights. As children of the water "owners" and harbingers of rain, they put on skits featuring floods and dousing. Their arrival comes two days after the civic summit meetings, when the quipocamayos are displayed. What connected them was the idea that in return for the village's proof (constancia) of good productive conduct, the mountains sent messengers promising more water.

Water ceremonies are relevant to the inscriptive legacy because manuscript books containing the minutes of labor also contain descriptions of these celebrations, names of huari dancers, and the roster of sponsors and honored members. Canal cleaning is at once the crucial public work and the climactic cultural production, for in it the village both materially reproduces itself and symbolically defines itself. In former times such cardinal work-and-ritual days are all but sure to have figured among the denotata of khipus.

To maintain, improve, and govern these systems is the community's top responsibility. Villagers recall history largely in hydraulic terms. Historic factional splits often turned on disagreements about water projects. But canal work is also the core of solidarity. At any moment, a comunero will drop everything to defend the invested labor of millennia. One late afternoon when rain covered the hills with a slurry of slippery mud, I saw passengers climb off the bus from Lima, and slosh home from a harrowing, dangerous trip, only to be greeted with the news that soil washing into a drainage had dammed up water. A retaining wall over the village might burst. Within minutes they were back with shovels on shoulders, uncomplainingly ready to troop up into the dark, pelting rain and fog without stopping for so much as a warm herbal tea.

Were quipocamayos about water turns? Probably not, for reasons explained in chapter 3. Nonetheless, water administration is of interest. Actual assignment of irrigation turns lies in the hands of the Irrigators' Committee (Comité de Regantes), a board appointed by the community and responsible to it.[6] The Irrigators' Committee and the community board together set the schedule for canal faenas, a weighty and sensitive duty.

Every couple of weeks, the Irrigators' Committee holds open office hours. For the "old" or spring-fed systems (but not the newer Willcapampa system), the initial criterion of water access is seniority: along any given canal, the most senior member gets the desirable first turn,[7] on a different day the first turn of another canal, and so forth, provided he does not have any pending fines for unperformed faena work. This seniority principle, as we will see in chapter 7, is of khipu relevance. A given canal can supply two or more "turns" a day. Those with whom one shares turns are one's "water neighbors," and, of course, generation mates. The system is, however, more flexible and complicated than it sounds, because a water turn is alienable property. One may sell or exchange it.[8] Those who own a lot of land try to buy up turns from those who are fallowing, or from the land-poor or the absent or indebted. With members milling about to look for deals, a water meeting resembles a miniature commodity trading pit—and the results are far too complex to entrust to memory.

Catholicism without Clergy

San Andrés de Tupicocha's rich Catholic heritage, so complex and conservative that one might even speak of it as an instance of living baroque, links with the quipocamayo legacy at two points. The first of these is the community's responsibility for certain festivals. The community as a whole sponsors Holy Week. In connection with Holy Week, it conducts ceremonialized business meetings at which sponsors for other feasts are recruited. (Such meetings are called *fábrica de cera*, or "waxworks," an allusion to the extinct fund-raising custom of making church candles during the meeting and sending children out to peddle them.) The community also guarantees a Mass during the wet-season ritual cycle when the sacred clowns or curcuches dance. Most important, the community recruits sponsors for the patron festivals, the pride of the village and its fund-raising mainstays. These are Corpus Christi (a moveable feast, often falling in June), the patroness Virgin of the Assumption (15 August), and the patron Saint Andrew (30 November).

The link with the quipocamayos has nothing to do with clergy. It has to do with the fact that some burdens for these festivities fell on ayllus as corporations — notably providing parts of the food and drink to be redistributed. As will be shown in chapters 7 and 9, ayllus probably managed their portions internally via cord records.

A second possible khipu linkage occurs in fund-raising at ayllu level. Ayllus act as if they were something between a miniparish and a confraternity, each with its own cross and the responsibility to house it and parade it grandly. Like the larger, official parish, each is funded via a regimen of *limandas, cajuelas,* and *óbulos.* These terms are synonymous, all meaning "pledge token," except that they entail different material tokens and unequal rank. A limanda is a small statuette with religious connotations, such as a carved rooster, alluding to the cock which crowed in the gospel narrative of the crucifixion. It is the token of a modest gift. A cajuela is a portable glass-walled religious diorama. It is the token of a handsome gift. The person who temporarily adopts the greatest token of all, the large painted cross (*pasión*), will be lionized by the whole group during the post–New Year cycle and is expected to donate hundreds of dollars. An óbulo is a promise without a corresponding object. Courting donors is a nuanced diplomacy, involving visits and courtesies. Favorite prospects might be couples whose daughters have married into the parcialidad, migrants to Lima who have retired and returned with savings, or members of other ayllus with whom one's group has business dealings. One donates by choosing a token appropriate to the size of the pledge, then displays it at one's home, usually in a place where visitors can see it. One year later, the "devotee" will return it at a ceremony called "ricuchico." His "act of placement" will be canceled, amid warm candlelight; opulent displays of flowers; generous rounds of drinks, coca, and tobacco; and, above all, cordial words and handshakes or hugs. Donations may be large; in 1997 one man delivered on a promise of US$220.[9]

These practices generate no end of manuscript papers. Since the lower range of the ritual fund-raising system has been under ayllu control (in parallel with the religious brotherhoods and other corporations) as far back as records show, they are credible candidates as contributors of quipocamayo content. None of Huarochirí's churches have yielded the sort of ecclesiastical khipus which Gisbert and de Mesa (1966) inspected in Bolivia; nor does anyone remember any such. It has probably been a long time since clergymen handled local khipus.

Memory, the Political-Inscriptive Order, and Recent History

The 1982–92 decade of political warfare and economic free-fall sent many Tupicochans into urban migration, and some to overseas diaspora. This era had palpable effects on the complex of which khipus form an emblematic part. The community's ability to transmit traditional authority through its own patrimonial insignia implied uncompromised legitimacy, as contrasted with a state legitimacy damaged by nonperformance or worse. It contrasted even more sharply with the illegitimate institutions Shining Path tried to force upon groups under its sway. So as the old civic complex emerged from unheard-of travails, it acquired an aura of heroism. While many younger villagers are losing interest in the customary regimen, seeing it as needlessly complex, others acquire awareness of its unique connection to "Inka" symbolism, which is projected everywhere as a Peruvian essence. This shift has much to do with villagers' renewed interest in finding out what the cords "say," with their willingness to let me study them, and with a new willingness to exhibit them outside the village circle.

Another force altered consciousness about them. The Fujimori regime sought to buffer its exceptionally severe "structural adjustments" in various ways, of which the most striking was fostering ONG (nongovernmental organization, or NGO) interventions. Circa 2001, on almost any day, NGO "engineers" (as people call rural technocrats) could be seen bumping from village to village in trucks. Villagers view the NGO field as something like a free market in bilateral aid contracting, albeit one with lingering overtones of patron-client relationships. It could become a full-time job to handle all these contacts and negotiations, villagers complain, so many and so long are the meetings and faenas involved.

The community increasingly sees itself as entrepreneurial in its approach to the outside. Symbolic reproduction is no longer a matter of internal interest only. It is acquiring a marked "local/global" publicity dimension, as NGOs become interlocutors in the spectacle of legitimation. Nongovernmental-organization missions have promoted an ideology of cultural pluralism which values local idiosyncrasy. Such ideas partly erase the racial stain of "Indianness" which Lima's hegemony attached to the quipocamayos. One reason why the village receives students and researchers from Lima universities and elsewhere is to attract them as allies in the competitive development arena, and the quipocamayos help them do so.

Thus the quipocamayos, once a fetish of legitimacy treasured for inward-looking folk-historical reasons, now seem to have become banners of determination to perform strongly in the wider outside context. Since 1997 Tupicocha's officers have taken their quipocamayos out of the village twice, bringing them to the provincial capital of Matucana to parade for Peasant Day. Peasant Day 2001 added up to a neat pageant of the engagement between peasantry and state. It included a Native Potato Conservation prize, goose-stepping toddlers from rural schools, and brawny peasant women from the subtropical valleys on the march with avocados brandished like grenades. Dancing for Tupicocha, the ayllu presidents performed a five-minute medley of village ritual gestures. Draped in the ancient cords, they stomped and spun, whirling the cords about like Scottish kilts. It would all have looked sacrilegious at home, where quipocamayos go forth in solemn pomp. Yet by asserting to the eyes of state officials a writ of legitimacy older than writing, their strange show sketched out an emerging third-millennium chapter in the long tradition of record-keeping ritual. And finally, in 2004, Tupicocha sent delegates with two quipocamayos to a lecture at the National Museum of Anthropology and Archaeology in Lima.

3

LIVING BY THE "BOOK OF THE THOUSAND":

COMMUNITY, AYLLU, AND CUSTOMARY

GOVERNANCE

I N TUPICOCHA, as nowhere else, we know which institution made the khipus, and we have a chance to watch the institution at work. This institution is the "inner shell" of village organization, a kinship corporation called the ayllu or parcialidad.[1] (A kinship corporation is an imaginary family entity credited with a permanent virtual existence of its own, as, for example, an Iroquois clan or an Italian-American cousins' club.) This chapter asks which ayllu functions are likely to have left imprints in the cord records. To do that, one must first understand just how an ayllu works.

Tupicocha considers itself the union of ten ayllus. A quorum of the community board only exists when all ten ayllu heads sit together with the constitutional officers (president, secretary, etc.). Ayllus today are not legally incorporated, and not recognized by the state. Yet if one ayllu president is late, the officers kill time in the cold and dark until he arrives.

To Tupicochans, the community can be seen either as the federation emerging from the preexisting ayllus' banding together, so as to exert their shared rights through national law or, alternatively, as a legal corporation created afresh in 1935 (replacing earlier supra-ayllu entities) to subsume and govern the ayllus. Unwritten law ("custom"), not the local constitution written for the state, articulates relations between the totality as emergent and the totality as sovereign. We can see this from the fact that in 1897, before the modern recognized community existed, an older governing body, the *sindicatura*, made room for the claims of preexisting kin-based jurisdictions by doubling its leadership. Because the constitutional mayor (*alcalde*) was unable to attend all the "custumbres" [*sic*] or traditional functions, the Syndics appointed an *alcalde de costumbre*, or "customary law mayor" to carry out unwritten laws (ACCSAT/SAT_18 1891:10–11). Until the 1920s the community did not itself even count its own membership; it simply took the ayllu leaders' words for how many members each represented. Any given ayllu member could see the community as federative and the ayllu as autonomous. Since the state recognized the Peasant Community in 1935, the ten united ayllu heads embody the community as emergent, and the six constitutional officers the community as sovereign.

This Janus-faced folk constitution is ancient, even though its current legal vessel is recent. The quipocamayos, then, are products of two sorts of relations: peer relations within each ayllu, and each ayllu's corporate duties to the overarching multi-ayllu polity on which it depends for common infrastructure (see color plate 1).

The Community and the "Thousand"

Tupicocha's federated-ayllu organization was once part of something larger, and its khipus perhaps once formed parts of a larger khipu suite representing it. It is a basic dogma of folk legality that the federated ayllus as a village (*llahta*) formed part of the Huaranga[2] de Checa ('Thousand of Checa'; see maps 1–2). The extraordinary thing about this dogma is that the Huaranga de Checa has been a ghost jurisdiction for well over 200 years. The hierarchical series ayllu-llahta-huaranga is basically Inka. It formed part of the same system which transmitted political-administrative khipu-making from Inka to colonial times (see chapter 5).

The term *huaranga* is a Hispano-Quechua version of the Quechua word for 'thousand.' An Inka thousand (*waranka*) was a rounded-off total of tributary households (Julien 1988), which would in turn be subdivided by named "hundreds" (*pachaka*) often corresponding to then extant local corporate groups. The decimal structure of Huarochirí is remarkably well known, thanks to an early Spanish official with a good ethnographic eye (Dávila Brizeño 1965 [1583]). In Inka times, the Checa thousand was the fifth of five thousands that made up the Huarochirí cluster. This cluster, called "Lower Yauyos," in turn formed half of a ten-thousand tributary bloc (*hunu*; Spalding 1984:179). Perhaps khipus representing these bigger units lie among the many specimens looted at the vast shrine of Pacha Kamaq, where the huaranga and the hunu worshipped. In structure and in terminology, as we will see in chapter 6, the Tupicochan specimens bear traces of this decimal formation.

As mentioned in the introduction, Tupicocha is one scene of the only known book rehearsing the pre-Christian mythology of Peru in an Andean language. Some of the storytellers whose tales fill the Huarochirí Quechua Manuscript of 1608 seem to have been members of Tupicocha's ayllus. This gives us an extraordinary view of deep continuities, certain of which seem also to constitute precedents for quipocamayo structures (see chapter 9). These tellers did not see "Checa Thousand" with the cold eyes of Inka statisticians, but with the reverent and affectionate eyes of ethnic descendants. To them "Checa" was the name of a large quasi-kinship group, perhaps a phratry, comprising several smaller sets of people who all descended from one of the sacred snowcap Paria Caca's five primordial "sons." This common Checa ancestor (whose mummy, supposedly 600 years old, a Spanish priest found and destroyed in 1611) was Tutay Quiri. "In ancient times these peoples . . . since they were all brothers to each other, traveled into battle together as one. Because he was the oldest of them all, the one called Choc Payco traveled in high honor, on a litter. But Tutay Quiri was the strongest, excelling beyond the others. Because of his strength he was the one who first conquered the two river valleys [i.e., Lurín and Rímac]" (Salomon and Urioste 1991:166, 186; for Tutay Quiri's patronage of Checa, see 79, 184). The quipocamayos, then, are physical parts of the system whose higher levels included the Huaranga. This ghost-constitution retains vital importance insofar as it relativizes all the structures built up after it: cord records give archaic self-government a tangible presence against which everything else is measured.

Community Is the Sum, and Also More than the Sum, of Its Corporate Parts

Although the memory of the overarching "Thousand" is precious to them,[3] villagers consider ayllus the only organization that actually created extant quipocamayos. The ayllu or parcialidad is a nonlocalized, predominantly patrilineal corporate descent group (Castelli, Koth de Paredes, and Mould de Pease 1981; Cunow 1929 [1890–91]:50–78; W. Isbell 1997). The term *parcialidad* denotes the outer face of the corporation, especially its work as a segment of the community. *Ayllu* is a colloquialism, so markedly rural that villagers are a bit guarded about using it in earshot of outsiders. It is the inner term, used at closed meetings. It evokes brotherly and filial feelings. The double terminology reflects the institution's role as the hinge connecting kinship to political organization. Especially in chapters 6 and 7, I will argue that the quipocamayos were the material apparatus establishing this connection.

Today's ayllus articulate and negotiate the interests of kindreds sharing inheritances, with those of political entities that lay claims upon their interests and hold power over the "suprahousehold" infrastructure. The history that ayllus construct is a history of kinship-scale self-determination in articulation with this external constraint. Let us survey activities where this situation left material traces.

DESCENT MADE VISIBLE

Tupicocha's newest showpiece is its bullring, finished in 1998. It looks much like the cement arenas that have popped up all over Peru as villages hit on bullfight-

FIGURE 7　At the Tupicocha bullring, parcialidades commemorated their respective contributions to construction by using different masonry styles. In this portion, three are visible: at left margin, a few stones of a rounded fieldstone design; at left center, cement stucco scratched to evoke Inka masonry; at center and right, brighter yellowish stone with receding mortar; including at right, behind the wheelbarrow, flagstones patterned to make a sunrise. From personal collection of author.

ing as a fund-raising fad. But inside the ring, one notices an oddity: the walls are of heterogeneous masonry, differing in color and form. They resemble a World Cup soccer field, whose walls are plastered with corporate billboards. The designs are indeed advertisements but for a different kind of corporation, namely, kinship corporations. Each ayllu or parcialidad has marked the stretch of wall it built by choosing a distinctive masonry style (see fig. 7)

In 2001 some state-oriented leaders talked about cementing over this patchwork. This situation mirrors a structural dilemma probably as old as Inka rule. Because the state has bureaucratized the community level, it transforms the emergent whole into a reified structure with powers of its own. This makes the "parcialidad" view of segmentation more hegemonic and public than the "ayllu" view. Ayllus are stuck, having to rely on the larger political unit to back up their endogenous social reproduction, for example, in sanctioning noncompliant members tough enough to ignore kinfolk's moral pressure. It may even be that pooling the power of enforcement is itself one of the incentives historically driving federated-ayllu Andean governance. In any case, the annual display of quipocamayos is an array much like that "cast in cement" at the bullring: a visible demonstration that the totality which holds the suprahousehold means of production must defend the autonomy of corporate kindreds because it depends on them in their distinctive, modular, articulated capacity.

TUTAY QUIRI'S CHILDREN, OR THE MYTHIC ORIGIN
OF THE CHECA (TUPICOCHA) AYLLUS

It was mentioned earlier in this chapter that the Checa of colonial times saw themselves as the progeny of Tutay Quiri, the strongest of Paria Caca's "sons." Tutay Quiri, according to the tellings transcribed circa 1608, beat the other "children of Paria Caca" in the dash for the great river valleys of the Lurín and the Rímac. Tutay Quiri, like his progenitor Paria Caca Mountain, multiplied himself by having five sons. These were the putative founders of the Checa ayllus who joined with Yunca leaders to create a society segmented into a sixfold sib. This is worth a close look, because the modern ayllu constellation is a startling continuous descendant of their organization. Circa 1608, the founders and ayllus were named as

> Coña Sancha, founder of the Allauca,
> Yuri Naya, founder of the Sat Pasca,
> Chupa Yacu, founder of the Sulc Pahca,
> Paco Masa, founder of the Yasapa,
> Chauca Chimpita, founder of the Muxica
> and, as founders of Caca Sica, those yunca . . .
>> called Huar Cancha and Llichic Cancha.
> (Salomon and Urioste 1991:117–18, 216)

Tutay Quiri then imposed a hierarchy "ranking them from Allauca downward" and granting each hero certain heritable lands.[4] More important than the localities of these grants, some now lost to local memory, are the durable structural principles involved. (1) ayllus are sibling corporations to each other; that is, they owe each other fraternal solidarity. (2) They stand in fixed order. (3) The rank order is one of precedence, not of dominion. (4) Ayllus have separate endowments but coordinated duties.

AYLLUS BECOME PARCIALIDADES OVER TIME

The history of the ayllus in colonial and Republican times has yet to be written. But the gross outline of the ayllu array (see table 1) as glimpsed in administrative summaries affords some clues. First, it appears that although the Huarochirí Quechua Manuscript speaks of Llacsa Tampo, which is close to San Damián, as the main Checa ceremonial center, the actual center of gravity of Checa demography and organization shifted further north, to the Tupicocha-Tuna area, toward the middle colonial era, perhaps in the early seventeenth century. Second, by the later stages of the colony some ayllus had disappeared through demographic depletion (Spalding 1984:178) or fallen below bureaucratic notice. Third, it appears that as early as 1760, the Tupicocha organization had settled to the same six ayllus that existed circa 1900. The associations of ayllus traced in table 1 were called *llacta*, and in colonial papers *pueblos de indios* (Indian towns). They gradually acquired parish rank. During the interval between the delegitimation of ethnic lordships (1783 onward) and the implantation of Republican municipal forms in the nineteenth century, the ayllus were the main functioning governments.

AYLLU/PARCIALIDAD RANK AND IDENTITY

In every community that still has ayllu/parcialidad organization, the ayllus' precedence forms a sequence people know like the ABCs. At community meetings, the presidents of the parcialidades receive their drinks or coca in this order and speak in this order. At plenary assemblies, the whole population is seated in ayllu order.

Each parcialidad has regular business meetings of its own, at least once a month at the president's home, where the quipocamayo usually resides. The president has an old Hispano-Quechua title, *camachico*, which means, approximately, "one who imparts order and energy" or "one who sets things in order" (Taylor 1974–76; Guaman Poma 1980 [1615]:53, 121, 190, 286, 302, 312, 486, 556, 633, 696, 815, 824, 891, 909). The presidency had a uniquely local title of unknown meaning, *Hayllo-pach*, as late as 1939 (AP1G/SAT_01 1939b).

When a Tupicochano says, "I need to talk it over with my people," he means his ayllu/parcialidad. A whole gamut of totemic symbols reinforces this feeling of identity. When parading to visit their *devotos* (pledgers of donations), ayllus play characteristic signature tunes. Some use characteristic aromatic plants as garlands on their clothes, ceremonial tables, or vehicles. Each serves "typical" dishes. Each has a flag, displayed at the annual election meeting, known as the *báculo*. Each parcialidad has at least one nickname.[5] One might kiddingly greet a member of Segunda Allauca, "the Foxes," with a fox's bark, "huac!"[6] Seeing a friend who belongs to Segunda Satafasca, "The Mummies," a mother joshes her little girl, "Watch out, that guy might 'blow' on you!" — meaning, a "Mummy" person can blow "antimony," the poisonous exhalation of the dead.

In chapter 6 we will see that the quipocamayos have physical idiosyncrasies which neatly analogize such relationships: similar in overall structure as ayllus are in organization, they each have a syntactical slot — one extreme — into which a paradigmatically varying emblem, an elaborate knob, is fitted, as nicknames and insignia also form paradigmatic contrasts.

AYLLU/PARCIALIDAD AND SPACE

Each ayllu has a "chapel." The chapel is a large decorated cross (*pasión*) mounted on a *peaña*, or step-pyramid in a painted masonry shelter. The ten parcialidades each fete their chapel with a dawn ceremony on 3 May, the Festival of the Crosses, then bring them to the church for a common blessing and a meal of the early harvest. Space is always a dramatic medium for enacting social segmentation, as seen in seating and parading. Nonetheless, it is unlikely that ayllus governed separate territories in Tupicocha in any recent time.

TABLE 1   Ayllus in Villages of the Huaranga of Checa

UNDIVIDED CHECA 1608?[a]	SAN DAMIAN 1711–1751[c]	SAN DAMIAN 1760[d]	SAN DAMIAN 1839[e]	SAN DAMIAN 1877[f]	SAN DAMIAN[b] 1997
Allauca	Checa	Checa	Checa	Checa	Checa
Sat Pasca					
Pasa Quine		Concha	Mugica	Mugica	Concha
Muxica			Concha	Concha	
Caca Sica					
Sulc Pahca					
Yasapa					

	TUPICOCHA 1711–1751	TUPICOCHA 1760	TUPICOCHA 1839	TUPICOCHA 1877	TUPICOCHA 1997
	Tupicocha	Allauca	Allauca	Allanca [sic]	Primer Allauca[g]
	Allauca	Sadpasca	Sota-pasca	Sota-pasca	Primera Satafasca
		Guanri	Guangre	Guangre	Primer Huangre[h]
		Chauca Colque	Chaucacolque	Chaucacolque	Unión Chaucacolca
		Moxica	Mujica	Mugica	Mújica[i]
		Cacarima	Cacarima	Cacarima	Cacarima
					Segunda Allauca
					Segunda Satafasca
					Centro Huangre
					Huangre Boys

	TUNA 1711–1751		TUNA 1839	TUNA 1877	TUNA 1997
	Tuna		Satajacca	Satajacca	Satafasca Primera
	Satpasca		Mujica	Mugica	Satafasca Segunda
	Allauca		Cacasica	Cacasica	Mújica
	Moxica		Cacanina [sic]	Cacanina	Cacasica
	Huaracancha				Cacarima
	Cacasica				
	Sulpasca				
	Huangri				

[a] Salomon and Urioste (1991:119, 218). There is some variation between this, the fullest listing of ayllus, and the ones given on pages 117–18, 216, and 218.

[b] The Checa and Concha of San Damián form separate communities. Oral tradition recalls a moiety duality internal to Concha up to some date between 1920 and 1940.

[c] Astete Flores (1997:6), using AGN/L Derecho Indígena Cuaderno 677, 1711, and AGN/L Derecho Indígena 284, 1751.

[d] AAL/L Visitas Pastorales (1760:f.9).

[e] Córdova y Urrutia (1992 [1839]: 72–73).

[f] Odriozola (1877:210–11).

[g] Also written Primera Allauca.

[h] Also written Guangre.

[i] Also written Mójica.

Space is, however, keyed to parcialidades in at least two political ways. The first of these is the association of the kinship corporations with portions of public works. At every faena, each stretch of channel, wall, or excavation is assigned to a parcialidad. Segments align in precedence order. The path of a canal from headwater to distribution points can therefore be "read" as the rehearsal of social precedence, and it is indeed dramatized as such in the champería or major canal cleaning. The canal system as a whole, therefore, has a form like a giant khipu, on which parcialidades correspond to stretches of "main cord" (main canal) with the "pendants" being the minor branches that water fields. Chapter 8 will show that this iconic relation is a part of folk explanation about quipocamayos.

The second ayllu-space link is the demarcation of perimeter-security sectors by ayllu, which is discussed later in the chapter. For the moment it suffices to note that not only the village as an integral territory, but every culturally consensual space in it, has its edges marked by lines that can be regarded from without as unbroken contours, but from within as segmented lines whose sections represent the segmentation of society. When quipocamayos go on their annual display, they too are aligned as if forming a single long sequence, as the men wearing them stand shoulder to shoulder.

The Inner Makeup of the Kinship Corporation

In contrast to the outward-oriented definition of the ten corporations as segments — parcialidades or sectors — of an emergent whole, the inward-looking ayllu definition of the same body emphasizes its coherence irrespective of usefulness to a larger interest. This coherence is explained in terms of consanguinity and descent (and not the inheritances of property, etc., which run parallel to it).

"CHILDREN OF THE AYLLU"

A person is born as a "child of" his or her father's ayllu. Birth gives eligibility for membership, not membership itself. When a male reaches about eighteen, he is expected to decide whether he wants to become a member (*socio, ciudadano*) by assuming the expense called a *dentrada*, or "entrance." The dominant principle is patrilineality ratified by the paternal surname. One villager remarks, "In the old days, [our ancestors] used to be careful about surnames. We were pure Rojas. . . . The surname wasn't supposed to go to any other parcialidad. You had to join up where your surname was appropriate. And not out of liking [*simpatía*] but out of origin." Guillermo Astete Flores's survey of "predominant surnames" since 1760 shows that each parcialidad had one or two, rarely three (1997[?]:54–55).

The quipocamayo as a whole being the likeness of the ayllu, the stages of members' "entrance" and seniority seem to have influenced cord syntax (chapter 7). Novices pass a period as a *próximo*, or prospective, probationary member, with partial but far from trivial duties. On becoming a full member, one joins the community as an inscribed comunero, and commits to thirty years of demanding service.[7]

A daughter belongs to her natal ayllu and may stay in it if she marries a member. The chances, however, are that she will not, because it smacks of incest to marry a person with whom one shares a surname. By the time a young woman eliminates surname-mates and cousins of prohibited degree, few of her same-generation ayllu-mates remain eligible. The tendency is therefore toward ayllu exogamy (85.71 percent of marriages from 1988 through 1995, according to Astete 1997:59).

When a young woman marries out of her birth ayllu, "she gives herself body and soul to her husband's ayllu," as the local cliché has it. She will marry viri-locally, with a view to quickly forming a neolocal household near her husband's father's house. Parents usually confer advantages on male descendants, lest goods drift into the control of other ayllus. The resultant situation resembles that described by Denise Arnold in a Bolivian Aymara setting: houses or house clusters "formed around patri-, viri-local households are conjoined across space by a network of female ties" (1997:124). While Huarochirí has no named concept similar to Aymara *wila kasta*, or female bloodline, the small distances involved in the viri-local move (because the village center is so tightly built up) make it possible for married women to frequently restore connections with their female consanguines by socializing at cross-ayllu work gatherings.

The link between quipocamayos and population is head-of-household status. As long as the husband lives, membership in the ayllu and community is vested in his person. He may delegate his wife to stand in for him at meetings of either level. A woman can be a *comunera* or an ayllu member in her own right if she never marries but does inherit, or if she becomes a single mother, with or without inheritance, or if she is widowed. Rarely does a senior woman rise to become an ayllu officer.

ARE AYLLUS MINIMAL POLITICAL UNITS?

The fact that the surname is distinguished as a discrete inheritable feature separable from ayllu eligibility may cause the reader to wonder whether the ayllu is actually the minimum political institution. If it is not — that is, if smaller corporate entities exist within ayllus, above the "atomic" household — the actions of these smaller entities would be plausible matter for recording in ayllu quipocamayos, as considered in chapter 7.

The question has been debated with regard to the kinship system implicit in the Huarochirí Manuscript (Salomon 1997; B. J. Isbell 1997). The Quechua source there uses the term *yuriy* (birth) to mean a set of siblings, and *yumay* (sperm) to mean a patriline. It specifies that within a certain ayllu, there existed a "patrilineage that bears the name Chauincho,"[8] and that a certain goddess belonged to it. It also specifies that a water priesthood of Concha village had to pass not in an ayllu but in three named patrilines (Salomon and Urioste 1991:143, 243). As of 1608, then, we know that certain rights of public importance did move in patrilines more restricted than the whole ayllu.

Do modern ayllus similarly contain corporate patrilineages? In some respects, yes. We do not know when Huarochiranos adopted the Spanish custom of using the first surname as a token of patrilineal descent, but there are grounds for thinking of the modern ayllu as a set of politically bonded surname patrilineages. When ayllus wrote internal statutes, they sometimes specified that certain surnames were required for eligibility (cf. Vázquez and Holmberg 1966). Tupicochans refer to surname groups as *familias*. They do not highlight them in public kinship ideology. But familias are consequential, because they channel inheritance.

The familia, or patronymic patrilineage, then, seems to be the smallest corporate constituent of ayllu structure above the household, its "atomic" unit. Unlike the "sperm line" of old, modern patrilineages do not have differentiated privileges. They do, however, act as lobbies or blocs in controlling access to membership. The seniority order within each one creates a nonarbitrary ranking of "family" members. A tendency to hold members of a familia collectively responsible for each other's deeds (for example, absences at faenas) confirms that this level has corporate organizational status.

If the "family" was a minimal suprahousehold collectivity, one might ask whether it was ever mobilized as a group—the more so since group mobilizations are here held to be the content of quipocamayos. The answer is yes. When an ayllu as a whole had to perform a task (e.g., build a segment of reservoir wall) but did not need to finish it all at once, the ayllu was free to subdivide its "stretch" among itself as it saw fit. The usual way of doing so was to have separate "squads" (*cuadrillas*) do their respective portions on different days. These squads are occasionally referred to synonymously as "families" in ayllu books (AP1A/SAT_01 1955:18–20), and the same usage can be heard today. All these tendencies, as we will see in chapter 6, are likely to have structural reflections in the finer grain of quipocamayo syntax.

AYLLU SELF-GOVERNANCE, OR BROTHERLY BUREAUCRACY

Each year on 2–3 January, the village holds its town hall meeting, or huayrona—a plenum including the exit hearings of old authorities and installation of new ones. In the Huarochirí communities where Matos Mar's group studied circa 1955 (1958), the civic plenum was called the *huatancha*. This Hispano-Quechuism etymologically means "making its year" (i.e., the community's). As argued in chapters 7 through 9, year making is the core of quipocamayo tradition.

The first day of the huayrona is also called the "day of the ayllu," because on that day each ayllu holds its "family reunion." Nowhere can one witness more explicitly the ayllu's function as the hinge between kinship structures and processes, and political ones. The session is at once a formal parliamentary election, an audit of

FIGURE 8   "Signature" herbs—*yerbaluisa, chamana,* tobacco, and coca—accompany the special maize beer for Ayllu Segunda Satafasca's 2000 election meeting. From personal collection of author.

members' performance, and an intimate celebration of family feeling. The ayllu—including women, children, and elders—cram into a small space around a formal "table" (actually a mantle on the floor). It displays coca leaves, cigarette packs, bouquets of aromatic herbs, bottles of liquor, and, above all, at least one huge bowl of the special purplish-black, apple-seasoned maize beer which marks the occasion. The "winter cross," a medium-sized blue cross, stands nearby decorated with scarlet gladiolus. The quipocamayo, too, keeps company.

This meeting is worth a look because it is likely to have been the most important single past venue for reviewing (reading and/or inscribing) cord records, prior to their public display (see fig. 8). Together with faena workdays, it is as near as we can now come to ancient khipus' context of inscription.

First, everyone must be "enflowered" to create an auspicious context. As in all collective occasions, armadas of the triple gift—coca, tobacco, and alcohol—sanctify each phase of the meeting. Coca is especially important. It is scattered over the "table" as well as taken by mouth, because it is said to help one "find" (*adivinar*; more literally, 'guess') the next officers wisely. Although all present are close and even intimate kin, procedure is legalistic. Titles of office replace the affectionate nicknames (*quereres*) with which ayllu mates usually address each other. Max Weber might have seen the ayllu as a strange formation: an intimate bureaucracy. This combination of two ethoses makes "reunion" a demanding occasion. One may have to censure a beloved kinsman, or express as a dry motion some wrenching effort at reconciliation between estranged kin.

To ease such stress, the solemn cheek-sucking of coca leaf sets a calming pace. After each distribution, people must be given time to enjoy it and think. After perhaps five minutes, the presiding officer will say "Seems like it's time—"

"Not yet," say the others.

After about a minute, he asks, "Is it time?"

"Not yet." Another pause.

"Would this be the right time?"

"Yes, it's right." And discussion may begin.

Bureaucracy and brotherhood alternate as dominant notes. At intervals of an hour or so, the officers call for a dance break. Dancing in a circle, male and female members stomp behind each other, each clasping the shoulders of the person ahead, and loosing a unique falsetto whoop on the beat that ends the musical stanza.[9] The ayllu bond takes on a flavor of bodily warmth and of almost athletic excitement. Drinking intensifies it, creating a tightening circle of sentiment, and, when the meeting goes well, a glowing feeling of merged selfhood. It is important to reach or at least feign this state, because the appearance of credible solidarity is a reassuring sight to prospective "devotees" or donors, as to the community, which relies on the solidity of its components. An ayllu is among other things a caucus and a business corporation. It must look united.

Ayllus introjected more and more forms derived from the national state during the twentieth century. The formal order of business today is standard Latin American parliamentary procedure. The ayllus formulated written internal statutes starting around 1905, taking names such as Mutual Society of Parcialidad x (Sociedad Mutua de la Parcialidad x). Statutes were reformed repeatedly, especially in the 1919–30 *oncenio* (the presidency of Augusto Leguía), when modernization ideology became an obligatory platform for "native" legitimacy, and again after Tupicocha's 1935 recognition by the Indigenous Affairs Directorate.

To elect officers, parliamentary order requires a slate of three candidates, but it is usually obvious who must serve. The aging and shrinking demography of the village makes choices narrow, and tense. Since most mature men have already served, ever-younger men get pressed into candidacy. In the first and second rounds of voting, the young heir apparent may unhappily mumble, or even protest with understandable anger, that he needs a few years to build his household. But by the third round, the hesitant new leader—perhaps with tears in his eyes—gives in and accepts. Applause and warm cries of approval work a transformation; the downcast draftee becomes proud and eloquent. After that, remaining offices are rapidly filled. Maize beer and a heartfelt armada greet the resolution. After the swearing-in ritual, the ayllu congratulates itself on being ready to present its new leaders to the community the next day. Today, the minutes are drafted in ledger-size books, but of old this would be a moment for khipu manipulation.

Other rites of the same day include the round of dancing visits to the group's donors or "devotees"; the reception of visits from its *cajueleros*, or major devotees; and adornment of the major or chapel cross. These, too, may correspond to old quipocamayo content. Other meetings for self-governance include the annual and semiannual public audits (see chapter 7), as well as scheduled business meetings, ad-hoc special meetings, fund-raisers and receptions.

Ayllus' ways of ordering their members internally are historically multiple, and they are likely to have correlates in quipocamayo structure. One common principle is seniority. Ayllus have often internally used a system of age bracketing: (1) *activos* or *de obligación*, meaning those in prime of life, bearing full duty; (2) *mayores* or *pasivos*, meaning semiretired elders; (3) *enfermos*, or medically disadvantaged members; and (4) próximos, or youths aspiring to "entry" (e.g., AP1A/SAT_01 1948; AP2A/SAT_02 1932). Within category 1, members are called successively from the earliest "entry" down to the most recent. This sequence is called *número de orden* (order number). As time advances, each member's order number declines toward 1, until he fulfills his thirty years' service and applies for retirement.[10]

As noted earlier, another way of ordering members is by patronymic clustering, either longitudinally as "family" in the sense of patrilineage (i.e., all the members with one surname in their seniority order), or more horizontally in fraternal groups which also form de facto age brackets (i.e., clusters containing all the members of a certain generation bearing a surname, with name mates of a different generation appearing elsewhere). "The ayllu," one villager remarks, "is practically a symbol of the family. For that reason they used to set down the names of those present according to their families, or in other words, their surnames."

The ritualization of ayllu gatherings is an exacting discipline. Its effectiveness depends on a factor of production just as important as land, water, capital, and labor, namely, information. At every single occasion when an ayllu, a club, or even a delegated "squad" gathers as such, it must create a document of constancia, that is, an authoritative record. Constancias enjoy a ceremonial reverence. Books in use at meetings are garlanded with blossoms as well as aromatic and sacred plants. Any table that contains books will also glitter with bottles and shot glasses. Any room that contains them will also display crosses brightly enameled in blue or green, statuettes, and brilliantly colored vestments. It would be incomplete, then, to think of a book as being neutrally "about" the action done in its presence. It is felt to condense in itself the things done; it is the legible precipitate of goodwill and good conduct, summed up as *voluntad*. Records are felt to contain not just the data but the moral value of what they record. They are treasure. One reason why people comply with onerous obligations is that in records, their contribution will be treasured. For the same reason there is a tendency to start a new volume every time some collective commitment is made, even if it is not expected to generate much paperwork.

The conviction that the record is the concretion of achieved solidarity is felt to apply supremely to the now-illegible quipocamayos. Ayllu members feel sure that they embody a primordial bond above and beyond the contingent and minor acts lodged in writing.

The Functions of Ayllus as Such

Functions vary depending on whether one prioritizes the ayllu (kinship corporation) perspective, or the parcialidad (community segment) perspective. We will first consider the ayllu's value to its members, that is, the internal or kinship corporation view.

AYLLU AND LAND

Ayllus were formerly important landholding corporations. The ayllus of 1608 told myths whose "punch lines" were explanations of why each ayllu held certain shrines, and lands. One source (Anonymous [1613?] 1916:184) attests that a special type of shrine called *purun-huacas* (shrine [at the edge of] wild space) marked the edge of each ayllu's landed patrimony (*mayorazgo*). In early colonial *visitas*, or tribute inspections, such as the 1588 inspection of Sisicaya (AGN/BA 1588), which lies just down the Lurín valley from Tupicocha, households' land rights were classified by ayllu. In 1786, a man resident in a Rímac valley village mentioned in his will that he had "fields and lands. . . . of Mojica ayllo" by virtue of his grandfather's ayllu membership. This suggests that within ayllus, member households had hereditary usufruct rights to particular plots (AGN/L 1799:f. 5v–65v). As late as 1866, a lawsuit somewhat to the south was conducted strictly in terms of ayllu territories (AGN/L Tierras y Haciendas 1866).

Even in 1900, Mújica ayllu passed a resolution "so that they [officers] will know the territorial boundaries [*linderos*] of this parcialidad,"[11] apropos of holdings at Tampocaya which Mújica relied on for collective income (APM/SAT_01 1900). Segunda Satafasca had a collective property at Chamacha as its endowment (AP2SF_01 1921:15, 1928:48–49). Until the 1940s, most or all ayllus held communal walled pastures, and herds on them, as collective endowment. Mújica formerly held lands bordering Tuna. Its secretary in 1997 said he read a now-lost document explaining that they had an interesting use. Because this tract was rich in agave plants, the source of rope and sandal fiber, it was in demand. Mújica allowed each ayllu to extract fiber in one part of it, presumably for a fee. If correct, this tradition represents a late survival of the pre-Hispanic notion that ayllus had specific privileges affecting each other, and therefore cohered in organic rather than mechanical solidarity. (For example, in the 1608 Quechua tales, one ayllu is said to be the silversmiths; Salomon and Urioste 1991:119.) Cacarima had a patrimony in Mayani (APC/SAT_01 1923:85), now a forest. Before 1940 members of an ayllu sometimes donated the use of a private field to the ayllu, so the ayllu could produce something needed for its collective responsibility.

In Tupicocha the landholding functions of ayllus have shrunk to mere vestiges, with two exceptions that are significant because they represent attempts to reconstruct the ancient communal regimen. These are the large tuber-bearing tracts won in mid-twentieth-century intervillage "wars" and lawsuits, at Hueccho and at Masllaulli. Here the victorious community measured out tracts proportionate to the population of the ayllus, requiring each to wall its portion (to prevent inter-ayllu disputes, which happen anyway) and designating them as permanent collective endowments in usufruct (APM/SAT_03 1959:72–74). Each ayllu harvested its portion in a common faena, with each component household bagging its own share of potatoes. The ayllu then transported the whole harvest to the community storage, which was formerly in the Collca, or ritual center (hence its Quechua name, which translates as 'storehouse'). Now it is in the old municipal building.

Since this regimen furnished infrastructure for ayllu-level ritual reproduction, and since its administration was a core matter of equity among households as among ayllus, it is likely to have been an area of khipu content (see chapters 8–9).

AYLLU AND WATER

By contrast with the ayllu's role in land control, it had a slight role in water control in historical times. The crucial passage of the 1608 Quechua Manuscript, in which the victorious Checa parcel out the wealth of the aborigines by ayllu, apportions "fields, houses, ayllu designations [and] huacas" (shrines embodying superhuman beings) but not water sources, lakes, reservoirs, or canals (Salomon and Urioste 1991:119, 218). The detailed explanation of Concha water rights and ceremonies (chapter 31 of the manuscript; see chapter 8 in this book) treats water as the unitary property of the llacta, or community, with the administrative duty of water priests assigned to specific patrilineages (yumay, "sperm" lines) rather than ayllus.

Water control is par excellence the function of the supra-ayllu level and apparently has been for a long time. Indeed it may be that coordinating various ayllus' hydraulic development of a given watershed, or allying to defend existing water rights, was itself a spur to the prehistoric coalescence of multikindred polities (llacta). As far back as ayllu records reach, each ayllu made a collective contribution to the community water infrastructure proportionate to its demography, without claiming separate governance rights over it. In the early twentieth century, the community left the kinship corporations some leeway about deciding water consumption rights and details of labor levies. In 1933, the Cacarima parcialidad pledged itself to the communitywide Cosanche Reservoir project while reserving for itself decision on such matters as whether próximos (persons awaiting induction as members) would have full water rights (APC/SAT_01 1933:158–59). Today, the way water controllers refer to ayllus is to use them as rubrics for reckoning which persons owe labor debts (which disqualify one for water turns), and for apportioning construction and maintenance work. That is, the community executes water policy by deploying parcialidades, but parcialidades do not determine water policy. These facts make it likely that quipocamayos documented duties to the water system rather than benefits from it.

The most enduring and consequential function of ayllus both for their members, and for the larger whole, was control of members' work. Ayllu leaders began to write profusely about it as soon as they took up the pen (1870s onward). Collective labor remains the dominant theme of internal documentation. In chapters 7–9, we will argue that it is the single most important ingredient of quipocamayo content.

Up until the 1930s, labor reciprocity through the "round" of internal faenas made up the core of ayllu activity. Each time an ayllu wrote its internal regulations, it set down as members' first obligation the duty to "andar faenas entre los ciudadanos" (to walk workdays among the members). That is, the group as a crew would lend its collective labor to the needs of each member household by turn. Usually ayllus designated each Wednesday or Friday for such work. The householder of the week decided how to apply this labor: planting, harvesting, roofing, transport, and so on. He was said to be the "bearer of the faena." The bearer owed a small sum to the *fundo*, or service treasury, of his corporation. He had to feed the whole crew. He also owed a "fulfillment" (*cumplimiento*), that is, a ritual gesture of reciprocity—namely, coca, rum, and cigarettes sufficient for rounds at the rest breaks.

Since "polycyclical" agriculture depends on concentrated work power at successive waves of peak labor demand, this facility was the sine qua non of subsistence until the growth of a cash-wage economy. By enabling even poor peasants to rely on a substantial workforce, at a reliable date, without incurring major money debt, faenas among ayllu mates underwrote the very livelihood of Huarochirí villagers. For these reasons, any member's demand to use his faena eligibility overrode conflicting obligations (such as those of his ayllu to the community). Overall, the collective labor regimen owes its feasibility to liberal rules about scheduling. Such liberality and flexibility made the need for accurate record keeping more urgent, because it diminished automatic regularity.

The ayllu could also support its general fund by making itself available as a faena crew to outsiders, at an annually fixed day rate much higher than that for members (the rate being called *ganancia*, 'profit' or 'earning'). Any member short of land or water, or absent, could sell his faena entitlement, even to an outsider. Then the outsider would owe him the ganancia and also owe a higher fee to the fundo. The basic system is known under various names throughout the Andes. (Tupicochans of the 1930s sometimes used the general Peruvian term *tornapeón*, now forgotten, and still do say *tornamano*, or "turn of hand.") The ayllu could additionally levy labor days to support its own infrastructures.

Given such rules, the record would obviously be complex enough to demand a "technology of intellect" that would be central to the ayllu's efficacy.

Archaeologists often emphasize that Andean society reproduced itself symboli-cally through public acts of redistribution. Huarochirí ayllus did the same, in a surprisingly prosaic manner: they functioned as buying cooperatives. Plenary meetings occasionally authorize purchases of sets of equipment for member households. In 1912 and 1914 Cacarima bought shovels and pickaxes "for all who are linked as brothers . . . without leaving anyone out" (APC/SAT_01 1912:29, 1914:35). In 1951 Chaucacolca bought itself two dozen complete place settings (APUCH/SAT_03 1951:381–82), and in 1954 Cacarima did the same (APC/SAT_02 1954:170). The ayllu would name a buying committee, cover its travel expenses, and then name a "godparent" (usually an outsider) to subsidize and aggrandize the ceremony of redistribution. While archaeologists emphasize the show of lar-gesse and conspicuous consumption in Inka redistribution, these down-to-earth local transactions redistributed goods chiefly as capital equipment, putting osten-tatious consumption in the background. Dishes, for example, serve the need to host large numbers of people at feasts. Since dining with the ayllu morally obliges outsider guests to donate, the dishes are productive infrastructure. Today, dishes often form parts of recognizable purchase sets. In daily use, they are dispersed among households. They are pooled for festivals, then "loosed" back to the house-holds. Initials painted on the bottoms enable the cleanup crew to return dishes to each household. This pattern may be relevant to the archaeological distribution of some ceramic styles. In chapter 8, we will review folk memories to the effect that control of collectively owned equipment in its rhythm of dispersion and concen-tration was a quipocamayo function.

Ayllus provided "social assistance" (as their statutes sometimes called it) in other ways. At the turn of the twentieth century, the Mújica ayllu offered its mem-bers a seed bank (APM/SAT_01 1906a:27r). As Tupicocha became more and more enmeshed in a cash economy, the general fund of each ayllu functioned through the first half of the twentieth century as a low-interest credit union.

To be an ayllu member was to rely on the kinship corporation for various life-cycle transitions. In theory, the corporation helped the young as well as the old. In 1938 Primera Satafasca wrote into its regulations a commitment "to promote the study of artisanry" by "protecting" those who study it (AP1S/SAT_02 1938:100–101). ("Protecting" probably meant guaranteeing that the apprentice's fields and herds would be tended for his livelihood while he was absent.)[12] Similar relief was later proposed for those who went to the 1941 war against Ecuador or to schools out of town. For widows and elders, ayllus offered continued labor help with re-duced labor obligations. In the twentieth century, as welfare-state concepts be-came popular, ayllus started to use terms such as retirement and social security in formalizing these practices. A few explicitly took up relief for women's excess burdens. Ayllus also provided funeral benefits. Each member went to his grave in a burial habit supplied by his mates, under the glimmer of the two large candles (*sirios*) representing their solidarity. Any or all of these functions could be matters of quipocamayo content. The management of common-lot dishes and tools is among the uses still remembered.

The Functions of Ayllus as Sectors or Parcialidades

We turn now to this protean institution's parcialidad functioning: that is, what it contributed to its superior level of governance, the community. This too, as we will see in chapters 7–9, seems closely related to quipocamayo use.

RITUALS REALIZE THE TOTALITY

Ritual, inseparable from collective labor, is the hinge of articulation between the ayllu and the multi-ayllu totality. While some inconspicuous rites take place in the bosom of the kinship corporation, the great public shows take place as acts coordinated across parcialidades. It is impossible to decide whether these "really" belong to the community or the ayllu level; by dramatizing segmentary separateness they reproduce the former, and by dramatizing coordination they are constitutive of the latter. Some have already been mentioned: the massing of the crosses on 3 May and the joining of forces to enact the grand canal cleaning. In addition, some parcialidades' regulations oblige them to perform "social dances" in which their identities merge with the communal whole. Social dancing does not refer to ballroom dancing but to the robust theatrics of costumed rituals. Some social dances continue pre-Hispanic traditions: the huaris or priestly mediators with water deities; the *chunchos*, or "Amazonian savages" of patron saint festivities; and the divine clowns or curcuches who herald the mountains' gift of rain (AP1A/SAT_07 1948: 14). The rituals of fund-raising, and the financially vital patron-saint festivals for which fund-raisers "prime the pump," mobilize fixed scenarios at differing scales. The parcialidades, the two major dancing societies that crosscut them, and the extended community including its "children" in diaspora, all play parts.

On one level rituals simply dramatize ideal social structure and encrust it with symbols to which powerful sentiments attach. But there is a more interesting way to look at it. Tupicochans are born eligible for slots in an elaborate machine of ascriptive obligation. It was the resultant demanding regimen of reciprocity which caused early indigenists to picture such communities as communes or primitive socialist regimes, and this captures a partial truth (namely, their ability to command collectivist self-sacrifice, frequently unwilling). But the modern-era ayllu also behaved in some ways like an enterprise. It saved to capitalize itself, it commoditized its labor for outsiders, it charged interest, and, as it were, it advertised itself through feasting and parades. Indeed today's ayllu fund-raising complex might be seen as a sort of "stock market" in "reciprocity stocks." When an outsider to a given ayllu pledges on its limandas, he invests in it, and buys social status in it. Devotees pick and choose by considering several factors. Tokens (limandas, etc.), visible in one's house, exhibit one's friendships and alliances. These "stocks" do not pay off with cash dividends but with secure access to favors, political accommodation, and labor. Affection develops too, and it is no small reward. Playing such a field of options is not necessarily a modern game alone, since it does not depend on money. Traces of such politicking along the boundary of kinship and political organization proper are visible in the history of Cuzco's Inka ayllus and *panakas* (royal descent corporations). This may be a deep current in prehistory. Khipu traces of such affiliations are a likely possibility, because the system demands documentation of a dizzying variety of pending transactions.

PARCIALIDAD AS POLITICAL SEGMENT AND CAUCUS

In politics, the role of the ayllu is subdued but important. All the mechanisms of community-level administration are formally adjusted to achieve strict equity among segments so that, ideally, no particular decision (e.g., to engage an NGO, to hold a "water festival" on a particular day) will favor one parcialidad more than another. The parcialidades today are expected therefore to caucus on issues of general interest. Their respective presidents should come to community meetings ready to present crisply stated positions based on intrasegment discussion, so that a decision can be reached quickly. Parcialidades occasionally dig in their heels and resist unsatisfactory community policy. In 1933 the Primer Huangre parcialidad rebelled against the Community Directorate: "[Members protest] the grave situation this town is going through . . . in a very heated disagreement. . . . [It protests] immoral acts in the public meeting of the Guayrona. . . . [The Community officers] waste the income of this community like a bunch of tyrants. . . . We do not recognize anyone appointed by the directorate until they are audited"[13] (AP1G/SAT_01 1933:23).

Such open dissensus is rare. When the system works well, even Tupicochanos, who are their own severest critics, appreciate its efficiency at identifying issues or crystallizing consensus. Rarely is a vote taken. Rather, discussion proceeds until the president thinks he can formulate an *acta* (minute) expressing a consensus. Because there are so many crosscutting institutions, interests, and marriages, ayllus avoid mutual polarization in public. Actual negotiation takes place in drinking encounters, so that regrettable words can be retracted.

Thus the overt model is one of equivalence among segments. But this is not realistic. The ten presidents hardly represent similar portions of a unified common interest. Each parcialidad's interests depend on its size, degree of diaspora, dependence on public pasture or public irrigation, kinship with community officers, amount of private property, and a host of other contingencies. Despite the continuously high level of mobilization, which strikes outsiders as impressive, villagers feel pained by hidden undercurrents of conflict. Especially when drinking, many deliver searing judgments on their peers as 'selfish' (*egoísta*) or "crafty"

PARCIALIDAD	ACTIVE MEMBERS	RETIRED MEMBERS	TOTAL MEMBERS
Primer Allauca	9	12	21
Primera Satafasca	17	9	26
Primer Huangre	6	8	14
Unión Chaucacolca	27	30	57
Mújica	11	14	25
Cacarima	27	15	42
Segunda Allauca	14	12	26
Segunda Satafasca	13	6	19
Centro Huangre	28	27	55
Huangre Boys	12	11	23
Total	164	144	308

(*vivo*). Since the short-term costs of conflict are too high to allow flat-out confrontation, half-spoken resentments fester.

For these reasons, the display of articulation among parcialidades which marks the climax of civic ceremony, and which forms the context for displaying quipocamayos, is a test. At this moment, it is necessary to show that the segments are in a state of workable political relationship with each other, have successfully reproduced their internal hierarchies, and have satisfied their duties to the total community. By doing so they "make its year."

MANAGING THE WORK OF THE SUPRAHOUSEHOLD SECTOR

Executing decisions about infrastructural work and policy is by far the most vital role of the parcialidad system. In work as in ritual, the community puts levies on ayllus, just as ayllus lay levies on households. The ayllu then assesses its households for quotas of labor or (less often) of materials. Quotas of materials are called *porratas* (from pro rata). For example, when an ayllu schedules a workday to thatch a member's house, each household owes a day of able-bodied labor, plus as porrata a number of tied straw bunches. The same principle applies, by homology, to villagewide projects, for which the community levies quotas on its ayllus. In the Community Hall and the stadium, specific parts of the structure (beams, stretches of bleacher) are porratas of specific ayllus. This principle may be archaeologically relevant, because insignia or distinctive styles are inscribed.

As for equity in labor, the basic principle is the one Urton ably discusses under its Quechua name *chuta*, or "stretch, linear segment" (Urton 1984). In Huarochirí it is called *trecho* or *tramo* or *tupu* (Quechua: 'measure'). There must be ten measures of work for the ten parcialidades, but the parcialidades are of drastically uneven size (see table 2).

The smallest sector had only 3.7 percent of active members, and the largest, 17.0 percent. Equity demands unequal portions of work. Each ayllu receives a "stretch" proportionate to its size, adjusted for special difficulties, as for example a tupu of canal digging that entails drilling rock. The parcialidad is responsible for allocating its workers equitably to sections of its stretch, and for enforcing faenas, in cooperation with the community authorities. In maintenance jobs each parcialidad works the same stretch every year, adjusting for demographic change. The community assigns each parcialidad the annual task of checking the position of boundary markers along one stretch of perimeter, and repairing fences (APM/SAT_03 1960:92–93).

The timing of work on stretches is more negotiable than their spatial layout. Parcialidad records show a preference for having adjacent parcialidades work on the same day, because mutual vigilance will deter slacking and promote productive rivalry. Nonetheless, parcialidades do often let some members perform on alternative dates (usually to avoid conflict with irrigation turns). Such complexities contribute to the sky-high demand for accurate record keeping.

From the work-management viewpoint, parcialidades are indeed "teams" (equipos), as the folk etymology of the word quipocamayo implies. Almost everyone regards the rivalry among parcialidades as a harmonious stimulus: "Our groups work in counterpoint to see who wins." Tuna village's mayor recalls that when ritual reproduction was threatened, ayllus proved the strongest organizational tool: "Not even the least numerous group will let the children of another ayllu stand in for its own. In February 1997 there were problems organizing the [patronal] festival of Saint James the Apostle for July 1997. Five minutes were enough to solve the problem among sixty people who had been in disagreement. Cacarima [parcialidad] had only four active members, but with their feelings of being anybody's equal, they mobilized their well-off relatives in Lima and did as well as anyone."[14]

Huayrona, the Civic Plenum

As each new year begins, officials must face their public and be questioned. This gathering is the two-day huayrona, or open cabildo (roughly, "town meeting," in the New England sense). It seems to fuse a ritual of historically deep Andean origin with a Spanish colonial law requiring exit hearings for officeholders, and also with republican ideas of democratic process.

The huayrona is the moment at which the quipocamayos come into public play together with the other symbolic regalia of polity: the staffs, consecrated grass, and step-pyramids described in chapter 4; as well as "work crosses" and a panoply of flowers, coca leaves, liquor, tobacco, and banners. The fuller description of this display appears in chapter 6. Were we building a general study of political symbolism, it would make sense to group all these as an overarching syntagmatic line, a template for collective utterance in visible "language," within which the component sets (the staffs, the quipocamayos, the garlands, etc.) form paradigmatic columns. These symbols all partake of sacredness, and they have a special ontological status—a person who abuses any of them is subject to public whipping. The objects are not individually considered particularly beautiful. I never heard them praised aesthetically. But the perfection of their ensemble is held to be a beautiful as well as necessary thing, and any shortcoming in the display causes disappointment or even shame. In chapter 4, comparing quipocamayos with staffs, I will argue that distinctive rules of communication govern such regalia within, and perhaps across, paradigmatic sets. But for the moment, it is enough to emphasize that the cord records condense, as a single most potent symbol, the essence of the ayllu/parcialidad order this chapter has described.

In the course of the second huayrona day, when all the officers of the community board, the mayoralty, and the church stewardship have rendered their reports and been replaced, the outgoing presidents of parcialidades put the capstone onto the new political structure by draping the quipocamayos on their successors. At the moment when each new "camachico" has shaken hands with the constitutional officers, one year is consummated and the next inaugurated. As we will see, the common conviction that this ceremony contains the complete order of the ayllus may be well founded.

4

THE TUPICOCHAN STAFF CODE

ORD is not Huarochirí's only Andean medium. This chapter examines a different one, a far simpler one than khipus. It consists of inscriptions on staffs of office called varas. In some respects, these inscriptions seem relevant to the khipu enigma. Like khipus, staffs mimetize folk-legal and political processes. They figure in the same functions where quipocamayos appear, or did so in the past. And their pre-Hispanic precedents seem related to those of khipus.

These carved sticks demonstrate one kind of Andean semiosis. The path to understanding it is clearer than in khipu studies, because staffs are formally simple and because they are a living art. Whether they embody the same sort of semiosis as khipus remains open. The semiosis they illustrate is very different from that of "writing proper." It serves to alert us to just how wide a gamut of inscriptive practices we need to consider in looking at nonalphabetic media.

"From the Crooked Timber . . .": Staffs of Power in Andean Material Culture

Whether analogues to Tupicochan staffs existed before 1492 is unknown, but imagery of sign-bearing staffs abounds. The image of the Staff God, who holds what often looks like an engraved baton, is among the most far flung and long lasting in pre-Hispanic iconography. Michael Moseley (1992:53) sees it originating as early as Cerro Sechín of the Initial Period (c. 1000 BCE). The Staff God/Goddess, best known from the Raimondi stela at Chavín, was a core icon of the Early Horizon (c. 900–200 BCE) throughout its extent (Burger 1992:196–99). This deity much resembles the equally famous staff-bearing Gateway God at Tiwanaku (Bruhns 1994:245–49; W. Isbell 1988:180) and many other Middle Horizon artifacts (e.g., Castelli 1978). The Middle Horizon covers approximately 600–1000 CE. Throughout their amazingly long history, staffs in superhuman context usually show both iconic and geometric marks.

Three less obvious fragments of evidence bring pre-Hispanic staff insignia into closer context with the Tupicochan case. The first is the presence of wrapped staffs as accoutrements of many *mallki*, or mummy bundles from the area, especially in tombs thought to be of the Middle Horizon. One mummified ancestor lived in Chuquitanta, near Lima, perhaps in Middle Horizon times. She or he was mummified with nine stafflike objects that (1) are of about the same dimension as staffs, but (2) are at the same time corded objects, bearing (3) characteristic staff designs in (4) characteristic khipu colors (Herrmann and Meyer 1993:cover). So there may have been techniques carrying symbolic elements back and forth between staff and cord. In this example, it takes two sticks to make a staff, and the two sticks become a staff by being wound with thread that imparts a sign. A hank of half-spun fiber is left hanging, as if to emphasize the union of stick, yarn, and design process.

The second archaeologically suggestive fact is the presence on certain khipus of designs that resemble staffs. Conklin (1982:268–70) attributes to them a Middle Horizon origin (see also Arellano 1999:233). Specimen T-222 of the American Museum of Natural History and others of its class have information encoded in stripes and X's in vertical series like those on staffs.

A third fragment suggesting pre-Hispanic continuity is local. In the circa 1608 Quechua Manuscript, forebears of the Checa of Tupicocha told a specific tradition about their ancestral mummy Ñan Sapa, who "bore [a] staff named *quillcas caxo*" ("engraved rod"; Salomon and Urioste 1991:120). A late (1723) idolatry case against the Huarochirí native lord Francisco Julca Rirpo alleges that his adversary sponsored a ritual called "standing the staff" (*parar la vara*), suggesting some local *caxo* concept lasted centuries after Spanish conquest (Gushiken 1993:82).

For colonial and modern times, the role of staffs is well documented. Virtually all Andean communities formerly had, and some like Tupicocha still do have, hierarchies of political officers called *varayuq* ('staff-holders') in Quechua or *varayo* in Spanish (Ordóñez 1919). The staff makes its bearer an executor of folk law, as badges make the police executors of state law.

During the four centuries since the Toledan viceroyalty authorized a Spanish "high staff of Royal justice" for native use (Espinoza Soriano 1960; Salomon 1980), Huarochirí's local processes have worked it into many calendric and jurisdictional functions (Tello and Miranda 1923:539; Gelles quoting Echeandia 1984:68–69; Díaz Pinto 1935:24–26). Bernard Mishkin, who took a close interest in vara hierarchies of the 1930s and 1940s, judged that southern Andean staffs "parallel closely those of the Spanish village officialdom in the 16th and 17th centuries" (1946:443), yet he also took seriously Ordóñez's view that the system is of pre-Hispanic origin.

Unfortunately, ethnographers impressed with elegant silver-clad batons scorned the "roughly cut sticks" which could also embody authority (Mishkin 1946:445). They failed to notice that such sticks are "cut" with locally legible inscriptions. In some places, notably Ayacucho, the inscriptions are pictorial and/or alphabetic. In Tupicochan staffs, iconic allusion to divinity is present in the form of the *peaña* (described in more detail later in the chapter), but most signs are apparently aniconic.

A Tupicochan staff is a stick of *huarirumo* or *huarumo*, that is, an Alnus, or alder.[1] Huarirumo grows in curved stalks. If no straight piece is available, the staff-holder (or a contracted artisan) takes the green stick and alternately soaks it and heats it. While heating, he tightly lashes the saturated wood to a crowbar and holds it over fire so it will dry out straight, a low-tech analogue to the steam-bending process used in furniture factories. When asked why one does not simply use a straighter wood, a staff officer answered with a gesture of firm hands straightening something out. His suggestion was that "custom" patiently straightens out what Isaiah Berlin (quoting Kant) called "the crooked timber of humanity."[2]

Staff Investiture and the Bootstrapping of the Civic Year

In Tupicocha, unlike in Cuzco-area communities, staffs are not patrimonial objects; nor does the mystique of the heirloom stick to them. On the contrary, each staff is replaced each year, as part of the ritual reminding everyone that civic order is continually created anew. When a minor staff-holder (i.e., deputy of a major staff-holder) is halfway through his year, he must select wood and start preparing staffs for both his own successor and his superior's. Outgoing officers may keep their staffs, but they are not displayed in homes. They are often given to newly appointed friends for scraping and reinscription, though this is considered less than ideal practice. The actual act of incising the symbols of office on the staff is assumed to be a common competence. If verbal guidance is given at all, it must take place in private conversation between the staff-holder in charge and the carvers at this stage.

All this should be finished by 24 December, when the community board meets to choose slates of eligible candidates for the coming year's staff offices. By that date, the new staffs should be ready and inspected. They are not, however, collected at that time and therefore cannot be collated as a set. As we will see immediately below, this matters for the overall functioning of their signs. The investiture takes all of New Year's Eve, continuing until dawn, and reveals a lot about how staff legibility works.[3]

At the start, two governments, which each employ staff-holding officers, assemble in their seats: the Gobernación, which is the local office of the national state, in the building of the same name, and the comunidad campesina in its meeting hall.

Staff offices are the lowest part of the village's intricate political hierarchy. Their investiture is the first order of business because they constitute the mechanism for "bootstrapping" all the rest. It is they who will, on New Year's Day, clean and mark out the sacred civic space for the two-day civic summit meeting that starts the year's public business. If there were no staff officers in place on 1 January, there would be no way to get started.

Where inscription is concerned, carvers propose and the community disposes. The vara holder in charge is called the *regidor* (regulator). He judges staffs. The secretary of the community also has, or anyway uses, authority to correct those judged wrong before investing new staff-holders. No staff may be used until the Community Directorate has approved it.

The authority to ratify staffs changes hands with every community election. As a result, authority responds sensitively to changing political and folk-legal currents. Via them, the creation of signs is politically mediated.

A little before midnight, the presidents of the ten ayllus or parcialidades assemble with the community board. Meanwhile, the state-salaried district governor — for many years, a curly-haired coastal creole of conspicuously nonlocal manners and habits — waits in his office to receive the outgoing staff-holders. One by one, the outgoing staff officers arrive carrying the staffs for their replacements (see fig. 9). Each places the new staff on the governor's desk on an embroidered mantle (visible in fig. 10).[4] As the staffs accumulate, the regulator anxiously inspects them by candle or lantern light. The governor ostentatiously ignores them, toying with his whip of office. At this inchoate stage, that of accumulation, the staffs are not arrayed in determinate order. They may be moved around.

The second stage begins around 12:45 AM, when the outgoing staff-holders walk in procession to the Community Hall and are greeted with drinks by the board. The board authorizes them to close out their year of office.

In the third stage, around 1:15 AM, the outgoing staff-holders troop back to the Gobernación to "verify" the staffs. The regulator places them in array on the board's desk. (Orders of array are discussed in the later section "Variable Array.") He inspects them carefully, since this is the last chance to detect errors. It is done in virtual silence. Other staff-holders also anxiously study the array, and occasionally they pick up or point to a staff, but — and this becomes important in the next section — this is not an occasion for discussion. It is all but silent, with at most a taciturn comment such as "It's OK" (Está bien) or "Check this one" (Mire ésta). Staff-holders look closely at each others' submitted staffs. They count insignia elements while moving their lips but not speaking, or they run a thumbnail down the incisions to be sure of the count. In 2000, for the first time, the new staffs were submitted with paper labels around them. Meanwhile, the *gobernador* (salaried officer of the Gobernación) stands various rounds of drinks. If the regulator decides that any staff has an error, he wordlessly reserves it for later correction before reassignment.

In stage four, about 2:20 AM, the outgoing staff-holders troop back to the com-

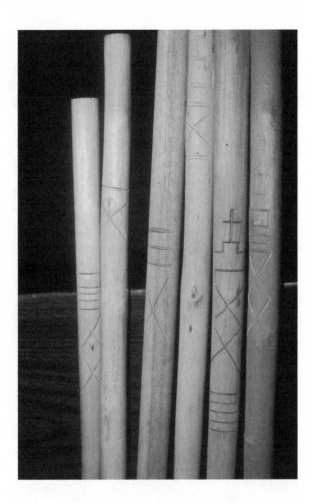

FIGURE 9 After midnight of 1 January 1997, staffs (not in rank order) await distribution on a table at the Gobernación. From personal collection of author.

munity hall, this time in formal parade, with all the staffs wrapped together in their mantle, or, in other years, carried by outgoing holders. The regulator formally surrenders them to the community president.

They are then laid in array. Speaking for all the outgoing staff-holders, the regulator tenders resignation, and the community president replies with a speech of thanks. (Meanwhile the governor locks up his office and goes home.) The president carefully studies the new staffs (see fig. 10). Now is the time for any residual business, such as judging an outgoing staff-holder who failed in his duties. Sometimes this part becomes long and contentious. Then, at last, each outgoing staff-holder is asked to go call on the three men nominated as his potential successors and bring them back.

This is the crunch. It breeds tension because all but a few try to evade staff office. Into the wee hours, the board receives disheveled men torn from much-needed rest, each determined to keep the burden off his shoulders. Some recite hard-luck

FIGURE 10   In the wee hours of New Year 2000, President Miguel Chumbipoma inspects staffs about to be assigned to new officers. From personal collection of author.

stories or protest that particular peers have owed staff service longer. Others get enraged about intrusion on their careers (understandably, since staff service sabotages the combined urban-rural strategies on which a young man's prosperity depends). An otherwise able man says he needs a year's delay because he has just returned from refugee life in Lima and "doesn't know customary law properly." The board scoffs, "Your wife knows everything." Still others mumble weak protests, too sleepy to fight back. A few rise to the occasion, or at least know when they are beaten. These accept office gracefully, and get a warm round of applause.

Each man is invested with his staff. New staff-holders curtsy to the shrine of authority, and they shuffle away staff in hand. By the gray dawn all of the offices should be filled, but usually some remain vacant. By 6:00 AM the board runs out of nominees, so it takes note of these failures in the closing minute. These cases must be taken to the civic summit, where they cause embarrassing acrimony.

The Ambiguous Hierarchy of Staff-holders

Borrowing a metaphor from Ayacucho villagers, the ethnographer Hilda Araujo aptly spoke of the community board, and its staff-holders, as respectively the "head" and the "hands" of traditional legality.[5] The job of staff-holders is to carry out decisions of the head. They notify and remind people about policies, they detect infractions, and they bring noncooperators to justice (see fig. 11).[6]

The system employs three major contrasts.

CONTRAST BETWEEN GOVERNMENTS
The staff offices belong originally to the folk-legal internal work of the community. But the community, when it became state recognized in 1935, conferred legitimacy on the state's agency in Tupicocha by "lending" it four "hands" (see fig. 12).

The state's Gobernación and the community's board have two quite different styles and associations. The community is the plenum of ayllus, with deep pre-Hispanic antecedents. The district government, on the contrary, is a creature of national law, that is, of Lima's hegemony. This contrast makes the staff system complex, problematic, and inorganic. "Hands" loaned to the Gobernación uncomfortably serve two masters — those who appoint them, and those who command them. As the Fujimori presidency of the 1990s evolved into a meddlesome dictatorship, this discomfort became almost intolerable.

CONTRAST BETWEEN THE MAJOR STAFF OFFICER
AND HIS DEPUTY (ALGUACIL)
These form higher and lower members of a pair, likewise being "head" and "hands" respectively. Each male member of the community is expected to carry out at least one deputy office and one major one, in that order, ideally in his youth.

FIGURE 11 Entering the huayrona or civic summit meeting of 2000, a staff-holder makes obeisance to the shrine (peaña) of the meeting space. From personal collection of author.

CONTRAST OF SPATIAL JURISDICTIONS (ORBITS)

Community authority employs a threefold division of concentric spaces, whose relative standing depends on the point-of-view issues discussed in the "Variable Array" section. These three parts of the system are here termed its "orbits": central, peripheral, and national.

> First, the community rules its *center*, the grid of streets. The regulator or staff officer-in-charge is also titled *jefe de plaza* ('plaza boss') because he maintains in-town law and order, partly through his deputy.

> Second, the community rules the *periphery*, the countryside. Two *alcaldes campos*, or rural constables, enforce folk-legal use of water, pasture, and fields, each with his own deputy.

> Third—and here is where the ambiguities begin—the community rules in partnership with the *national whole* beyond its own space. To this end, the community and the district government link up via the first and second *tenientes gobernadores* ('lieutenant governors'). The governor is unambiguously a national official. But his staff-bearing lieutenants and their deputies are hybrid officers: community "hands" on loan to national policy. They round up conscripts or call witnesses to the justice of the peace.

The ten staff-holders as an ensemble, then, represent both totality and discontinuity. From one viewpoint, that of community, they express the supremacy of the village center, radiating outward. From another, they represent the supremacy

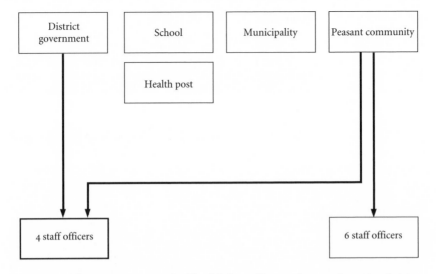

FIGURE 12   The peasant community "lends" four of its members to the national state as staff-bearers, so as to endorse "constitutional" legality with the authority of custom. From personal collection of author.

of Peru, radiating inward. These two perspectives imply discrepant rules of hierarchy. To understand this helps interpret not only what is written on the ten staffs, but why it is written through staffs and no other way.

What Was Inscribed on the 1995 Staffs?

Figure 13 is a summary of one year's staff inscriptions.

To attack the script, one must know the graphemes that make up the signary or notation and their basic syntax.

THE SIGNARY

The notation uses three graphemes (fig. 14), sometimes called the "initials" of the office.

The first is the *raya* (stripe), a bar cut transverse to the axis of the staff. In the annotations that follow it is signaled "R." It is sometimes also called *tallarín* ('noodle').

The second is an X (*aspa*) It will be annotated as "A." In common usage, "to make an aspa" means to mark with an X or a check mark, or even a thumbprint. An aspa is specifically not a letter of the alphabet but simply material proof of personal attention to the text (even by one who cannot read). This last detail sounds small, but it is actually a first clue to the way staff code works. An aspa in the colloquial sense is neither a specific design, nor a sign for any referent, but an index of a social act.[7] This is our first good lead: staffs work with signs that do not sig-

DISTRICT GOVERNMENT *(Gobernacion)*

First lieutenant governor *(primer teniente de gobernador)*	OP , 6R, 4A	
First lieutenant governor's deputy *(alguacil del primer teniente de gobernador)*	OP, 1R, 1A	
Second lieutenant governor *(segundo teniente de gobernador)*	OP, 5R, 4A	
Second lieutenant governor's deputy *(alguacil del segundo teniente de gobernador)*	OP, 1A, 1R	

PEASANT COMMUNITY

Regulator or plaza boss *(regidor* or *jefe de plaza)*	OP, 5R, 3A	
Regulator's deputy or chief deputy *(alguacil del regidor* or *alguacil mayor)*	OP, 2R, 1A	
First rural constable *(primer alcalde de campo)*	1P, 2A, 5R	
First rural constable's deputy *(alguacil del primer alcalde de campo)*	[P-space], 1A, 1R	
Second rural constable *(segundo alcalde de campo)*	1P, 5R, 2A	
Second rural constable's deputy *(alguacil del segundo alcalde de campo)*	[P-space], 1R, 1A	

FIGURE 13   The staffs of 1995. From personal collection of author.

FIGURE 14   The staff signary. From personal collection of author.

raya (R)   aspa (A)   peaña (P)

nify referents, but rather are contextually determined, performative concretions of achieved relationships.

The third is called *peaña*, a pervasive symbol in regional culture. Iconically, it represents a two-step pyramid surmounted by a cross.[8] Peañas mark sacralized boundaries. A three-dimensional peaña is found in every ayllu chapel. Similar structures mark divisions between central and peripheral space, or between communities. Even if no physical pyramid is present, or if (indoors) there is only a token pyramid made of a few cement blocks, any spot where a "work cross" is planted to establish ceremonial space is spoken of as the peaña (see fig.17). A drawing of a peaña is posted over the door of a house in mourning. The peaña is the only icon used on staffs, and it is also the only sign making reference to divinity.

THE BASIC SYNTAX

A complete inscription, that is, each whole staff of the sets documented in 1995 and 1997, consists of a P or nothing in first position, and varying numbers of R or A in second and third. The notation was devised by my consultant and me. The annotation P 2R 3A would mean a staff with, in descending vertical order, a peaña, two rayas or bars, and three aspas or X's. If a staff has at its top a blank area big enough to hold a peaña, it is described as having a P-space. Otherwise, inscriptions of 1995 start at the top of the staff.

THE POLITICS OF INSCRIPTION

We already noted that the ten staffs serve two governments, which stand in an inorganic, incommensurable relationship. Evidence for slippage and unease between them includes a tendency for villagers to forget the Gobernación staffs when asked to list staffs, unwillingness to accept this office, uncertainty about where the Gobernación's staff-holders should stand when all staff-holders stand together, and friction about their responsibilities. Despite much questioning on my part, no clear or consistent explanation of how the two subsets of staffs relate to each other was forthcoming.

The dawning realization that in asking for a context-free exegesis of how staffs are ranked I was asking for the impossible gave a second clue to the way staff signs work. By 1997 it was becoming clear that marks on the staffs encode the overall relationship among staff offices and that this relationship, though structurally important, is not expressed any other way.

It is not that staff signs record information which could be expressed in words but is not. It is, rather, that they encode information which Tupicochanos organize through means other than speech. The graphic act involved is not a translation from spoken language, but an act of wordless inscription.

Nobody can decompose and read the staff signs as words, though Tupicochans readily read and analyze many kinds of verbal artifacts. Nobody spontaneously or under questioning can give a gloss such as "one aspa means second-ranking

TABLE 3   Distribution of Aspas in 1995 Staffs

NUMBER OF ASPAS	OFFICE	GOVERNMENT TYPE AND LEVEL
4A	First and second lieutenant governors	District government
3A	Regulator	Community (Center)
2A	First and second rural constables	Community (Periphery)
1A	The five deputies of all the above	District government and community

deputy." Why? First, no such gloss is correct. The system does not work with unitary equivalences, but with context-sensitive sortings, as will be proven in this chapter. Second, there is no social context appropriate for verbalizing staff marks.

When the outgoing community officers of 1994 met in session from the wee hours to dawn to prepare for the rites of succession, they displayed the staffs to be held in 1995. Figure 13 lists them in their functional groupings.

What is communicated in the 1995 display of staffs? The most obvious feature is the *binary distinction between peaña-bearing staffs and those that lack them.* All but four lack not only sign P , but a space in which P would fit. The P was evidently irrelevant to these offices. The staffs that bore P were those of two rural constables. Their respective deputies' staffs bore blank spaces in places where P would fit, as if to allude to their superiors' insignia. This is referred to below as "P-space," an allomorph of P. We conclude (1) that in the distinction P/OP, P means "rural" or "peripheral" and OP means village or central. (2) Of these, P is the marked (more special, less frequent, less dominant) case. (3) The symbol P is iconic of the important ritual division between village and rural space, meaning that these officers' authority begins at the peaña marking the village-countryside divide.

The *distribution of aspas* appears in table 3. In the 1995 set, it registers *stratification among agencies of government.* The national state commands high positions, the community two middling but unequal levels (village center and community periphery), and both jurisdictions low ones. It recognizes, in other words, the supremacy of the national agency and more broadly the pervasive centralism of Peruvian government: while both central and local governments are entitled to have low-level deputies and enforcers, the former stands supreme and the second subordinate.

The *distribution of rayas* (table 4) registers a quite different hierarchy, namely, one among officers (as opposed to the jurisdictions that control the officers). It comes much closer to representing public sentiment about the actual importance of each office. It does so by placing the community staff-holders, who really do the work of maintaining order and protecting communal interests, in both town and country, as high as the nominally prestigious but usually otiose staffs which the national state commands. It puts a wide space between the higher staffs and the deputies who are to expend shoe leather on their behalf, thus building up the former. And it registers uneven levels of prestige among deputies, reflecting the community view that the regulator's deputy is "greater" (*mayor*) rather than lumping him, as does the jurisdictional bracketing, with mere messengers.

Finally, one must ask about syntactic practice and its implications (see table 5). The formula for a staff is simple: Emblem P (values "present" or "latent" versus "absent"), followed by two "token-iterative" (T-I) signs: x number of R's, and y number of A's. But it has an interesting wrinkle. Look at the way the token-iterative elements are lined up in those brackets which have paired (*Primer*, "first," and *Segundo*, "second") offices.

The schema shows the following regularities:

1. For community offices that govern the village center, R-before-A signifies first status with a pair and A-before-R the reverse. This applies to both the community's in-town functions, and the national government office. Both of the nonpaired offices, which are those of the regulator and his chief deputy, regulate the center and are marked with R before A.
2. Conversely, for all community offices that govern the periphery or countryside,

TABLE 4   Distribution of Rayas in 1995 Staffs

NUMBER OF RAYAS	OFFICE
6R	First lieutenant governor
5R	Second lieutenant governor, regulator, first rural constable, second rural constable
2R	Chief deputy (i.e., regulator's deputy)
1R	Deputies of first and second lieutenant governors, deputies of first and second rural constables

TABLE 5   Syntactic Summary of 1995 Staffs

OFFICE	FIRST T-I SIGN	SECOND T-I SIGN
First lieutenant governor	R	A
Second lieutenant governor	R	A
First rural constable	A	R
Second rural constable	R	A
First lieutenant governor's deputy	R	A
Second lieutenant governor's deputy	A	R
First rural constable's deputy	A	R
Second rural constable's deputy	R	A

(i.e., the rural constables and their deputies), A-before-R signals first status and R-before-A the reverse.

3. However, the distinction is different in the noncommunity offices, the Gobernación. These paired offices do show, as one would expect of an in-town authority, R-before-A in the first-status position, but rather than reversing to show second status, they retain R-before-A and diminish the quantitative value of R.

The inorganic members of the set, the staffs attached to a noncommunal authority, are marked by an irregular syntax. It is as if to say, "the A/R ordering rule does not affect us because our jurisdiction is not divided by center/periphery."

The suspicion that the irregular marking of staffs corresponds to a political irregularity is confirmed when one looks at the book where the directorate records the staff and other appointments. It also occurs in elicitation.

In other words, staff insignia coexist with a verbally labeled hierarchy of titles, but verbal titles are not what they encode. This set has been seen on close reading to embody three separate "takes" on the relations among the staff authorities, and to register dissonance among them.

For the purposes at hand, the interesting point is that none of these analyses is expressed in words or in any other code. The characters form an orderly notation of social relations, but the variables and some of the relationships which they notate do not have verbal names. When I explained them to a highly intelligent consultant who has himself directed staff work, he agreed in the end with my analysis, but only after a ponderous discussion in which he found himself inventing circumlocutions as far from normal speech as my own. Neither of us, for example, knew words for the contrast between jurisdictional prestige as against prestige of office.

Does Staff Code Possess Its Own Metalanguage?

In observing the New Year's Night political cycle, it was noted that there is next to no scope for discussion. What talk does take place is sociable chitchat, ostentatiously off the point. This marks a striking exception to the usual meetinghouse loquacity. Taciturnity is even more surprising when one takes note that this is the first occasion in which the new collection of staffs comes together as a total set. Since they have been produced in five separate pairs, preinspected and precorrected only as pairs, the risk of error is far from negligible. This is a source of tension that chitchat must cover over. Any suspected anomaly will be pointed out with a barely audible murmur, or only with a gesture. It then devolves on the regulator and the community secretary to decide whether to set the stick aside.

This is an eloquent silence if there ever was one. It begs the question of whether there is a metalanguage for discussing staff code as there is for discussing alphabetic writing. There appears to be strong variation among cultures in metalinguistic disposition even apart from literacies and genres (Mannheim 1986).

In order to learn more about any possible verbal "metalanguage" concerning the staff code and about properties of staffs as a medium over time, detailed 1997 interviews were undertaken with three men who had been active in the hierarchy over past years, all esteemed as *costumbreros*, that is, experts and loyalists of customary law. In two cases they also served as artisans who carved staffs for their peers. The findings highlight two striking functional differences from the written word.

The first is that the verbal "muteness" of the staffs extends also to metalanguage. As noted above, there are only two intervals when authority—chiefly the regulator and community secretary—can impose "correct" signs on a submitted stick: during preinspection between 24 December and New Year's, and as a last resort, during the interval from New Year's morning to the 2–3 January civic summit. On none of these occasions as observed did the regulator or secretary say anything like "It has one aspa too few." Rather, if they saw fault, they simply confiscated the stick and made the correction later. It is in these intervals of reserved action, not particularly secret but not public either, that they correct the inscriptions to match the model of harmony which constitutes their envisioned suite of power for the incoming year.

By exploiting the privilege of the "expert" and "outsider," I was able to elicit remarks about inscriptions. But no other ethnographic moment gave me such a clear feeling of "pulling teeth." The community officers felt uncomfortable. Their replies were atypically curt. I was apparently embarrassing them, even in private, by asking them to do something inappropriate, and yet I had too high a rank to be flatly refused. At first I thought they were mistakenly hearing my question as a challenge to their expertise in "custom" (this being a common source of anxiety). But it later turned out the difficulty was more intellectual and more fundamental than that.

I had naively assumed that to verbalize the ordering of incisions on a staff was analogous to the spelling out of a word; that is, a neutral, technical metacommunication, in which the contrast between audible signs and visible signs is not in and of itself significant. However, this proved a faux pas. The staff set is not an analogue for words as the alphabet is. Instead, it registers social knowledge that one does not put into words in the first place. It is an alternative to words. The metacommunication of words is words about words (e.g., spelling out, whether in sound or on paper). The metacommunication of staffs is handover, alteration, and acceptance or rejection of "initials." It is carving about carving.

The proof that verbal metalanguage is not the crucial mechanism is that there is no standard way of verbalizing staff incisions, and yet this does not compromise the viability of the staff as collective product. Having flopped at a discursive method, I interviewed by asking men to sketch staffs (on paper, in dirt, or with chalk on a shovel handle), without simultaneous questioning. This worked much better. But no amount of ex post facto dialogue yielded a uniform metalanguage.

When Justo Rueda, a senior villager experienced in several artisan crafts, drew staff inscriptions, he registered figure 15 as the sign for first lieutenant governor.

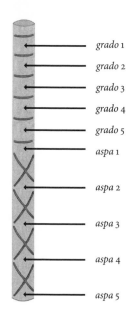

grado 1
grado 2
grado 3
grado 4
grado 5
aspa 1

aspa 2

aspa 3

aspa 4

aspa 5

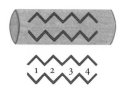

FIGURE 15   Justo Rueda's method of "reading" staffs. From personal collection of author.

FIGURE 16   Marcelo Alberco Espíritu's method of "reading" aspas as "puntos" on staffs. From personal collection of author.

In other words, he drew what my notation calls OP6R 4A, which agrees with figure 13. Asked what design he had just drawn, he replied, "Five degrees and five aspas" (Cinco grados y cinco aspas). Disconcerted, I asked him to point them out. The result was the labeling on the right side of figure 15.

Justo Rueda had reversed my consultant León Modesto Rojas Alberco's notion of the relation between character and delimiter, or figure and ground. In other words, he read spaces as characters and incisions as delimiters. To him a "degree," or *grado*, is a space separated by lines, and an aspa is a space adjacent to an X. The two agreed on the "utterance," but since they had no occasion to jointly analyze it in terms of a code exterior to itself, they did not have any shared terminology for doing so.

The third consultant was Marcelo Alberco Espíritu. He also agreed that the first lieutenant governor should have four signs that are neither rayas nor peañas. He calls these signs *puntos*, or "points," rather than aspas. For staffs that have only one "point," he drew the same X that others call aspa. But for staffs with multiple points, he used another convention. In order to indicate the four points of the first lieutenant governor, he drew the upper part of figure 16.

There was a clear space between the two horizontally deployed lines of zigzags. This seemed puzzling because no aspas were evident. "Points" appeared to me to number seven or fourteen (if one takes puntos to mean "peaks, vertices") or else eighteen (if puntos means "loci"). In response to my question about where the four "points" are, Marcelo drew the lower part of figure 16.

The interesting inferences here are (1) the absence of consensual analyses of the sign, (2) the absence of consensual verbal metalanguage for analyzing the sign, and (3) the fact that these absences do not impede the functioning of the sign as a vehicle to integrate social action. Indeed, as we have just seen, to verbalize norms about insignia is only to foment confusion.

This schema recalls Sampson's assertion that to the degree a society develops semasiography, it moves toward a situation of "two fully-fledged 'languages' having no relationship with one another—one of them a spoken language without a script, and the other a 'language' tied intrinsically to the visual medium" (1985:30). Sampson holds that to think of the latter as a general-purpose language is to dream of an unrealizable extreme. But within the confines of a special-purpose code, the staff incisions realize his theory in the strongest form. Unlike well-known insignia, which have precise verbal equivalents and are easily transferred to the verbal medium, these occupy a functional space all their own.

In other words staffs are more radically distanced from speech than Old World insignia. A familiar insignia code is, for example, heraldry. The visual code of armory has as counterpart a verbal code called blazonry, which consists of a set of syntactic and lexical conventions sufficient to verbalize any coat of arms. For example, the coat of arms of France is blazoned as "ancient, azure, semé of fleurs-de-lis." Tupicochans cannot blazon staffs because they lack a common language for it. Heraldry is a limited "language" convertible to words, while the staff code is a limited language insulated from words.

Variable Array: Contextual Meaning and the Productivity of Staff Code

In early stages of this research, interviewees were asked to set, or sketch, the staffs, "in rank order" (según sus rangos respectivos). Each pondered at length, treating the question (to my surprise) as a hard one, and then provided an array. But their arrays did not match. Moreover, elicited arrays deviated conspicuously from the "natural" arrays visible in actual staff use. And this natural class seemed to vary wildly within itself.

My premise that staffs stand in fixed rank order to each other was false. But the absence of verbal metalanguage for discussing what staffs "say" prevented staff experts from telling me so. Still less could they state what turned out to be the key to arrays: the "correct" array depends on the folk-legal context, inflected by the political contingencies of the moment.

For example, on New Year's Eve 2000, when the incoming staffs had been accumulated on the desk of the governor, the regulator, with the intense concentration of somebody doing a puzzle, arranged them in the following order:

    first lieutenant governor
    second lieutenant governor
    first lieutenant governor's deputy
    second lieutenant governor's deputy

first rural constable
second rural constable
first rural constable's deputy
second rural constable's deputy
regulator's deputy or chief deputy
regulator or plaza boss

(Note that the use of "first" and "second" removes doubt about the proper direction of reading.)

This array looks completely "wrong" in comparison to the array used at the Community Hall. But it snaps into clarity once one notices that it embodies the system as seen by the governor. His own two staff-bearing lieutenants top the list, and their respective deputies follow. The two rural constables in charge of land and water use form the middle of the list, trailing their deputies. The end of the list is the most interesting part, because in it, a master structural polarity trumps the common ordering of major officer above deputy. The last two positions show the deputy for village-center affairs, followed and not led by his boss, the regulator. The sense is that the regulator and the governor are, in the context of this event, polar opposites. So they needed to be maximally distanced. As we saw above, the ritual of the night shuttles back and forth between their respective seats. The regulator "rules" (as his title proclaims) the innermost or in-town domain of the political system, with his seat of office being the chamber of the Community Hall. It is he who regulates the inner affairs of the staff-holder corps, for example, by approving inscriptions. The governor rules the outermost or national orbit, and his seat of office is a "mini-Lima" lodged in the Gobernación. He sits so far from the inner ethos that it is his custom to studiously pretend ignorance of it. (Although this looked at first glance like racially tinged disrespect, it turned out to be a part of the modus vivendi that makes an awkward relationship livable.) To manifest this polarity is the overriding logic of this array. To reconcile two contextually appropriate rules of ranking that yielded contradictory arrays was the "puzzle" involved.

By contrast, when staffs are arrayed inside the Community Hall, which is the regulator's own seat, the regulator leads the list. Order in the Community Hall places officers of the central orbit first, and of the peripheral orbit last. Since those of the national orbit do not report to the community, they are not in play. But the totalizing view as seen from the community becomes more visible on one occasion when the community is forced to deal with it, namely, in nominations. It is revealed in the nomination slate of eligibles prepared on 24 December 1999. On that occasion, the regulator and the board dealt with nominations in the same order that was eventually manifested in the distribution of A's and R's on staffs as in table 6.

(The anomalously high A and R count of the last office is commented on in the

OFFICE	ASPAS	RAYAS
Regulator	A3	R5
First rural constable	A2	R5
Second rural constable	A2	R4
Chief deputy	A1	R3
First lieutenant governor's deputy	A1	R2
Second lieutenant governor's deputy	A1	R2
First rural constable's deputy	A1	R2
Second rural constable's deputy	A2	R3

next section.) The two missing offices, the lieutenant governors, were nominated from the Gobernación. The interesting point here is that the officers set the order of nomination not by the above polarity, but by the consideration that was probably uppermost in their minds—the degree of political responsibility involved, and the relative weight of these offices as assertions of the community's interest.

A third logical rule of ranking arises where the peripheral or *campo* (rural) orbit becomes paramount. This in fact occurs on the many occasions when the community assembles in its fields, pastures, or high canal routes, or when it gathers to conduct the annual inspection of boundary markers. At such outdoor meetings, it is the planting of "work crosses" and staffs which establishes the ritual space and social context. In these arrays, as one would expect, the staffs of the rural constables precede the rest, and their respective deputies precede other deputies.

No public function can be convened without at least one appropriate cross and staff. The many occasions at which only one or two are present may be taken as elliptical statements which "zero out" reference to authorities without immediate relevance.

It should at this point be clear that no single hierarchy ranks offices. That is why asking consultants to place the staffs "in rank order" only created confusion. The hierarchy of staffs is contextually determined. The actual determination is complex. It is grossly framed by the relation among jurisdictions in a given task. But, as with the initially puzzled regulator at the beginning of this section, the person who places staffs (the highest member of the hosting orbit) must also take into account all the factors which are actually on the minds of those present.

At this point, wordless inscription—the public concretization of a reckoning of the roles and problems at issue—emerges as a subtle art. The person who executes it sometimes fidgets with uncertainty or tries out multiple arrangements before settling on one. Onlookers, if they feel uncomfortable with a solution, sometimes express themselves audibly, but not verbally, with scoffing grunts or mumbles of discontent. They mean that the person in charge should think about rearranging. Once in a while, somebody will go as far as indicating a staff he considers misplaced and saying "over there a bit" (*allacito*, pointing with the chin). On the whole, however, participants stubbornly, consistently, and (I think) unconsciously keep the whole process nonverbal.

And yet it is at this point, in the midst of verbal inhibition, that one can begin to use the term *writing* in a weightier way than merely alluding to inscription. The crucial fact is that staff process is productive. The array of a given set of staffs in different situations yields wordless but unpredictable, nonpredetermined statements about those situations. They approach, therefore, the properties of utterance. And since they do this wordlessly, they also approach, as Sampson suggested, the productivity of a parallel system of utterances—a language—disconnected from speech.

Indeed, in the abstract, one could say that the year-long, politically choreographed movement of the staffs through space, time, and society "inscribes" upon Tupicocha's space the unpredictable "event history" of 365 days. The ensemble considered in synchrony, simply as a suite of signs, might be taken to deliver a constant message such as "there are ten minor offices patterned in principal/deputy pairs (etc)." But the ensemble taken in diachrony might be considered as delivering a series of messages about successive deployments in practice. It would not be sensible to call the "utterances" of staffs in action a historiography, because the comings and goings of staffs and their bearers are never discussed in retrospect. In the absence of metalanguage, there simply is no way to recall a given "utterance" once it is dissolved by the removal of the staffs—and that, as we will see below, might be part of the genius of the system.

The Staff Code Is Its Own Reinvention in Practice

So much for the synchronic langue and the everyday parole of incised sticks. What about staff code over longer periods of time? How does staff diachrony compare with that of "writing proper"? The answer is that staff code proceeds through time in a manner radically different from writing proper.

Table 7 compares six versions of the staff hierarchy: the ones recalled by men who directed the system in the 1950s, 1960s, and 1970s to early 1980s, plus the observed ones of 1995, 1997, and 2000.

What diachronic comparison reveals is, alongside their nonverbal quality, a second big functional difference from writing proper. As a code, staff inscription is strikingly inconsistent over time. Writing as we know it goes through time by producing varied messages in a constant code. The staff corpus does the obverse: it produces putatively constant messages in a varying code.

Every staff must be made afresh yearly. The code itself is therefore an emergent of each year's reproduction. It is an integrative product of the relations in process. There is no guarantee, and apparently no need or expectation, that integration will take place the same way every year. Participants create its symbolism as they go. So successive iterations yield not varied messages in a constant code but varying code which expresses the ten-office constitution as inflected by the emerging political constellation of the new year. Since the referent of the staff inscriptions as a set is a group of simultaneous relationships, their mutual synchronic fit and not their longitudinal consistency over time is the prime concern. Their historicity takes the form of code variation and not message variation.

Staff Code Changes Faster and More Fundamentally than Alphabetic Code

This variation is not drift but the silent registry of social reasoning. Let us first consider differences among the three systems the veteran staff-holder directors recall.

A "HYPERDIFFERENTIATING" STAFF CODE (C. 1970S–EARLY 1980S)

In the staff lexicon over which León Modesto Rojas Alberco presided, two characteristics stand out. First, with regard to distribution of A's (aspas), he differentiates two discrete classes of officers. Those who give commands to a subordinate have A's, and those who do not, lack them. At the same time, this bipolarizing tendency goes with a countervailing tendency toward continuum in the second characteristic.

This second characteristic is distribution of R (rayas). Here, Rojas's schema takes the idea of smooth gradient to its final extreme. The staff officers display an uninterrupted continuum of importance, from 1LG (7R) down to 2RCD (1R).

In sum, Rojas's array does two things: it maximizes the distinctness of each office from all others, and it makes a sharp break between two sorts of rank that somewhat resembles the break between commissioned officers and noncoms in the military. It may be relevant that Rojas, while a major promoter of community self-government, also belongs to the generation whose politically formative years coincided with the Velasco Alvarado military regime.

A "BRACKETING" STAFF CODE (C. 1950S–EARLY 1960S?)

A man sixteen years older than Rojas, Marcelo Alberco Espíritu, remembered a different set of norms, presumably an idealized version of the system he helped carry out in the 1950s–1960s.

Table 7, column 9 contains his scheme as "translated" from his distinctive "points" verbalization.

Unlike Rojas's scheme, which goes to an extreme of splitting (there are no overall equations, i.e., no two identical staffs, in his system) Alberco inclines toward bracketing or lumping. (There are two "point" staffs that look the same, with 3 puntos, and four deputy staffs that look the same, with 1A 2R.) In other words,

TABLE 7   Staff Code Inscriptions as Recalled (1950s–1980s) and Observed (1990s–2000)

A.

ABBREVIATION	OFFICE
1LG	First lieutenant governor
2LG	Second lieutenant governor
1LGD	First lieutenant governor's deputy
2LGD	Second lieutenant governor's deputy
R = PB	Regulator or plaza boss
RD = CD	Regulator's deputy or chief deputy
1RC	First rural constable
2RC	Second rural constable
1RCD	First rural constable's deputy
2RCD	Second rural constable's deputy

ABBREVIATION	SIGN
A	Aspa or x
R	Raya or bar
P	Peaña or step-pyramid with cross
P-space	Blank space at top of staff equivalent to a peaña's size
Punto	Conjoined aspas in the reckoning of Marcelo Alberco Espíritu (see figure 16)

ABBREVIATION	CONSULTANT
LMRA	León Modesto Rojas Alberco
MAE	Marcelo Alberco Espíritu
JR	Justo Rueda

TABLE 7 Continued

B.

STAFF	RECALLED, JR c.1940s–1950s	RECALLED, MAE c.1950s–1960s	RECALLED, LMRA c.1970s–1980s	OBSERVED 1-1-95
1LG	6R, 4A	4 *puntos*	OP, 6A, 7R	OP, 6R, 4A
1LGD	1R, 1A	1A, 2R	OP, 4R	OP, 1R, 1A
2LG	5R, 3A	3 *puntos*?	OP, 5A, 6R	OP, 5R, 4A
2LGD	1R, 1A	1A, 2R	OP, 3R	OP, 1A, 1R
R=PB	5R, 3A	3 *puntos*	OP, 4A, 5R	OP, 5R, 3A
RD=CD	2R, 1A	1A, 2 *puntos*	OP, 1A, 2R	OP, 2R, 1A
1RC	1P, 4R, 3A	1P, 1R	1P, 3A, 4R	1P, 2A, 5R
1RCD	1R, 1A	1A, 2R	1P, 2R	P-space, 1A, 1R
2RC	1P, 4R, 2A	1P, 2R	1P, 2A, 3R	1P, 5R, 2A
2RCD	1R, 1A	1A, 2R	1P, 1R	P-space, 1R, 1A

STAFF	OBSERVED 1-1-97	OBSERVED 1-2-97	OBSERVED 2-26-97	OBSERVED 3-29-97	OBSERVED 1-1-00
1LG				OP, 6R, 4A	6R, 4A
1LGD	OP, 1R, 1A			blank	2R, 1A
2LG		P-space, 5R, 2A		P-space, 5R, 4A	5R, 4A
2LGD		OP, 1R, 1A		P-space, 5R, 2A	2R, 1A
R=PB	P-space, 5R, 2A		OP, 5R, 3A	OP, 5R, 2A	5R, 3A
RD=CD	P-space, 3R, 1A	P-space, 3R, 1A	P-space, 3R, 1A	P-space, 3R, 1A	3R, 1A
1RC	1P, 2A, 5R	1P, 2A, 5R		1P, 2A, 5R	1P, 2A, 5R
1RCD		1P, 1R, 1A, 1R	1P, 1R, 1A, 1R 1R	1P, 1R, 1A, 1P, 1R, 1A, 1R	
2RC	1P, 1R, 1A, 1R			1P, 3R, 2A	1P, 2R, 1A, 1R, 1A, 1R
2RCD	1P, 3R, 2A			1P, 1R, 2A	1P, 3R, 2A

when he and his peers integrated this system, they had interlocked themselves with each other much less by acting out incommensurability, or by gradating each other within commensurables, and much more by establishing correspondences that clarified who was an exact equal of whom else.

A "COMMON DENOMINATOR" CODE (C. 1940S–1950S?)

Justo Rueda is another decade or so older than the previous consultant. His scheme makes R (delimiter of grado) and aspa, in that order, necessary constituents of all valid signs. Aside from his radically different verbal treatment, the most striking thing about Rueda's scheme is that it maximizes syntactical simplicity and regularity by focalizing an instantly noticeable gestalt-level "vareme" formed by the union of signs. This shape, a bar-topped X, is the common denominator among all office symbols. In substance, that is, the organization of inequality, Rueda's system does not differ much from Alberco's or the 1995 array. Yet it differs in the rhetoric (so to speak) of presenting that hierarchy.

Whereas one may say that Rojas's scheme emphasizes gradation and Alberco's emphasizes bracketing, Rueda's emphasizes harmonization. His set of staffs comes closest to being a uniform. It might correspond to a round of integrative practice in which the staff-holders were supposed to cohere as a corps more than they do now.

The Staff Code in Ongoing Transformation, 1995–2000

The recalled sets given by older experts may be distorted by idealization (chiefly in the direction of enhanced regularity according to the individual's notion of the rules). But this idealization itself served as a heuristic guide to understanding the not-so-ideal practice of staff use, since it has shown us how a synchronic set coheres when it coheres perfectly — as perhaps occurs mostly in imagination.

This helps to interpret how the sets actually did vary over time. In other words, the varied ways in which the "same" message was inscribed over three observed iterations, namely, 1995, 1997, and 2000, reveal through their sign-logic a pattern which actually does match identifiable changes in social practice.

This interpretation may be taken as a decipherment in a special sense — a sense appropriate to the idiosyncrasy of wordless inscription. Deciphering wordless inscription is a matter of recapturing past operations of social integration-through-signs. The "messages" recaptured here are differing instances of the simultaneous and mutual coming-into-being of social constellations and their signs. Comparing the 1995, 1997, and 2000 observed data sets, one can trace the following tendencies:

First, one sees an intelligible trend in the relation between major staffs as a set, and their deputies as a set. Irrespective of the specific number of A's awarded the staffs, in successive years, the number of R's attributed to deputies of any given major staff-holder rose. In 2000 the rise was universal and striking. It will be remembered that in the "importance-of-office" view, R's correspond to the esteem in which his individual office is held as a functioning part of the community. In recent years, migration to Lima and declining enrollment in the community have shrunk the pool of eligibles, so it becomes necessary to call on younger and younger men. Young men in their teens perceive deputyships as almost servile. The "upgrading" of their dignity of office responds to pressure from below. It will be borne in mind that deputies are the ones who actually manufacture staffs. There is a certain democratic logic in underdogs' being well placed to bid for political relief through the staffs they submit. Faced with the demographic facts, the community board of 1997 and again 2000 allowed these offices more dignified R- ratings vis-à-vis the rest of the set. The change is particularly noticeable in the staff 2RCD, which is often the point of entry for youngsters doing their first service.

Second, in the national or Gobernación orbit, a shift in syntactical usage has occurred. It was noted above that in 1995 (see table 5), the two orbits that fully belong to the community used a reversal of syntax (A before R, R before A) to signal, respectively, first and second of a pair. This applied in 1995 to the deputies whom the community loaned to the national orbit, 1LGD and 2LGD. Extracommunal 1LG and 2LG set themselves a bit apart from intracommunity hierarchy by not using this distinction. It will also be recalled that the deputyships of 1LG and 2LG are unpopular offices. In 1997 the insignia for deputyships 1LGD and 2LGD were in disarray. ("Erroneous" cases may not be disallowed under the present methodology, since disarray no less than array is the imprint of "integration"—or its failure.) By 2000, 1LGD and 2LGD had acquired a new array: they followed the same rule as their masters, 1LG and 2LG. Put into words (as no one ever would), the gesture signals that the villagers cede a trace of the community's authority in order to ease the incumbents' "two masters" dilemma and let them simply mimic Gobernación agenda.

The third, fourth, and fifth tendencies mark a single political direction, via semiologically different means. That direction is to distinguish ever more sharply between the peripheral or campo orbit and the other two orbits.

The third tendency is, like the second, a syntactical change, but a more fundamental and puzzling one. Through 1995, a universal rule, never contravened in sets as remembered by older men, required that aspas and rayas form separate sets. On New Year's Day 1997—the last possible moment for "corrections"—the community secretary noticed that someone had marked an incoming second rural constable (2RC) staff with P 1R 1A 1R. This interspersed pattern, which looks like "|X|," was silently set aside and scraped off. Nonetheless, the same "|X|" appeared again in February and March 1997 on the staff of the first rural constable's deputy's staff (1RCD), and it stayed there. All this recurred in 2000, and this time too it stayed there. "|X|" has great naked-eye salience. Its increasing popularity in the campo orbit seems to mark an emerging sentiment that the rural constable post, although of the same substance as other staff authority, partakes of a different order (much as the Gobernación orbit implicitly claims a unique order). The 2000 community board let this incompletely accepted notion "show" in public by not correcting the staffs.

One may take this as a subtle move in a political conflict which has troubled the community of late: the increasing assertiveness of the municipality in affairs outside its spatial jurisdiction, notably in rural canal construction. (The municipality does not itself command any staff-holders.) Because the mayor is an enterprising, able, and factionally strong man, one rarely hears the community assert flat opposition. But this silent split is actually the main political event since 1995. Deviation in the 1997–2000 staffs works almost as if to say, "the rural sector speaks a different language"—a claim to authoritative utterance in its own medium, parallel to the national orbit's syntactically encoded uniqueness. However, the new device "|X|" has a conservative dimension too: if one tallies numbers of A's and R's without regard to this novel syntax, their respective numbers come out as rankings similar to previous years.

The fourth tendency is the disappearance of the allomorph P-space (i.e., the leaving of an unincised area at the tops of some staffs in the location that P would fill were it present). P-space was used consistently in 1995 on staffs of deputies serving rural constables. P-space was then a sort of "implied" peaña. (Unfortunately, the notational system used in interviewing elders does not reveal whether they remembered P-space as an older norm, because as of those interviews I had not yet perceived the issue—and as usual, no verbal help was available.) P-space has a structural vulnerability: since staffs are carved in separate times and places, each carver must guess how much blank space to leave at the top. In 1997, a number of staffs outside the rural orbit appeared to have spaces big enough to be P-spaces, and I recorded them as such. The community board seemed puzzled about these spaces at the New Year's Eve inspection. They slid the staffs along each other as if measuring (but neither actually measured nor discussed). In the event, they did not recall any of these for correction. The result was that when the staffs were arrayed, P-space could no longer be visually associated with the campo orbit. In 2000, nobody made P-spaces. Many staffs had more than a P-space of blank wood, others less. None were corrected on this score.

The fifth tendency is probably a compensation for the fourth: The staffs that would have had P-spaces in 1995 now had P's, i.e., explicit peañas. P is the most naked-eye salient of all signs, so this change more than restored the visual distinctiveness of the periphery or rural orbit when staffs are arrayed. When a single staff is planted at a work site to show under which orbit the work falls, the claim is emphatic.

One might argue that this is simply a determined allomorphic shift, not an instance of the "new code for a new year" argument. But the gain in explicitness and conspicuousness is so emphatic that it makes sense to attribute greater importance. At the time of writing, there is no longer any "shading" of the peaña usage to make the peripheral orbit quartet of staffs "same and different" vis-à-vis the rest. That is, no longer can one say that the deputies of the peripheral orbit resemble those of other orbits by lacking overt peañas. Visually, center and periphery no longer overlap. Today, as a set, the peripheral orbit looks just plain different. The growing exaltation of peaña became notable in 2000 when the board carried along a portable stone peaña wherever its delegation represented villagers specifically as peasants, literally a weighty declaration.

I think this was a statement, in wordless inscription, of public resistance to the anticommunal policies of the 1990s Fujimori regime. For the rural orbit enjoys great public legitimacy as the quintessentially campesino orbit. It contrasts with the two orbits which, respectively, express functions common to all townsfolk and to all Peruvian citizens. For example, it is the peaña-carrying officers who take the lead when the village approaches the "grandparents" or pre-Christian deities as "owners" of their irrigation water. This is the most sacred of all identity-marking ceremonies, and the least similar to "national" or urban norms.

To make its champions more distinctive is to underline a feeling of "we, the campesinos." The staff change is a bit like orally overstressing the first word of the phrase "peasant community." This was, in my opinion, a sign of resistance to the Fujimori-era policy, which neglected recognized peasant communities in favor of agroindustry. (The community was at best eligible for fixed-term project loans, while all the other entities shown in fig. 12 got budget lines.) Staffs express determination to keep the campesino dimension before everyone's eyes.

Let us synthesize, reviewing these tacit shifts with the eye of an exterior historian. Integrative acts were the actual practice of agency in time, that is, the making of history. The carving of staffs was indexical of proposals for action, and their ratification indexical of integration as implemented. Innovation happened, but without verbal process to label it as such. The retirement of past staffs each year rendered innovation documentarily irretrievable, except in the private sphere and with difficulty. So the explicit argument is one of continuity. Tacit adjustments in implementing a nominally constant scheme are what make practical continuity possible.

The five changes reviewed above are, in a sense, only one change. They mark a broad effort to improve the always-difficult integration of roles in a partly inorganic system, in the face of additional political stresses, by marking its parts as more functionally specialized, more different from each other, and more dignified.

Why "Write" Wordlessly?

The work of this wordless code is (in Roy Harris's terms) integrational and not telementational. That is, it does not serve to make ideas explicit and shareable, but to coordinate actions.

One may well ask why Tupicocha chooses to arrange some parts of its polity using a set of signs even more isolated from language than chess pieces are. After all, a staff bearing verbal initials such as 1AC (*primer alcalde campo*) for the post "first rural constable" would seem to do the job. Indeed, in Ayacucho Department, where staff customs otherwise resemble Tupicocha's, staffs are incised with both alphabetical labels and icons.

Moreover, to explain Tupicochan usage, it is not enough to speak of carryover from an age when literacy was less common, because on the whole the village has enthusiastically alphabetized its internal process. By 1997, its literacy rate surpassed the national average. One must look for a positive reason why it is better to use a set of sui generis nonverbal signs.

The set of staff signs visibly does something that the open-ended stream of letters does not: it forms a closed ensemble. Staffs form, in a sense, a single meta-utterance on the collectivity's part. This helps us understand why staff signs do not overlap any other signary.

But why not do so via icons? It is worth noticing that the discussion up to this point has been thoroughly political. The actual task of integrating a staff corps has been expounded in some of its fractious disharmony. The "two masters" dilemma is only one of the many dilemmas that can make "a little town, a big hell" (as a Spanish cliché has it). It is useful, therefore, that when a new rural constable, for example, sets about cooperating with a new lieutenant governor, they take as common badges highly abstract signs relevant to their joint task and nothing else.

These signs are insulated from political electricity by being untranslatable, and empty of propositions, even of connotations. In all states, functionaries use colorless, noniconic, repetitive, connotation-poor signs—boring signs—to articulate bureaucracy. The staff system carries this logic to its extreme. The "hands" which must get together for touchy work—coercion—are, in other contexts, each other's friends or enemies, kin or creditors. The same applies to people they must coerce. Drily schematic signs keep attention on the ideal structure.

The fact that noniconic, nonverbal signs grow in the very guts of community politics also helps one understand the surprising finding that it is at the same time highly integrated (synchronically) and unstable (diachronically). The pattern that gets inscribed on each new staff set is the direct reflection of a current political interaction, influenced by speculations about the kind of integration among government organs which might be useful in the coming year (bracketed, hyperdifferentiated, solidary . . . ?).

By this route, a purportedly unvarying message ("there are ten offices, arranged in pairs, in three jurisdictional orbits" and so forth) gets expressed in a code that does vary. To the surprise of any researcher beguiled by the notion of tradition, it varies much faster than the institution it represents. It varies much faster than alphabetic norms. And it even varies much faster than oral language. Indeed, it is the ability to vary on the formal level which has made it possible for the bare-bones institutional message to remain "the same." The reason the code varies over time is that it bears the traces of an adapting process of integration. Had the staff hierarchy's symbolic infrastructure not been flexible, political friction might have demolished the staff system here, as it already has done in most Andean villages (B. J. Isbell 1972).

Andean villages create intricate political hierarchies among peasants jealous of their status as equals. According to ideology, differences in authority are steep, but they change hands quickly and equitably. Like every ideology, this one is a mixture of self-insight and self-deception. In fact, differences of wealth do affect political process, including staff recruitment. What staff code "propagandizes" for is not the political ambitions of a person, lineage, or polity, as in Mesoamerica (Marcus 1992:11), but the ideological proposition of an order that claims to be hierarchical in synchrony, and yet egalitarian in diachrony. The creation of a limited "parallel language" segregated from ordinary discussion helps to reproduce this order and guides people in using it.

In the end, is it helpful to call this system "writing without words"?

In critiquing a version of this chapter (Salomon 2001:23), Urton argued that staff signs resemble algebraic "ligatured expressions" (e.g., $3x$), which belong to the history of calculus, rather than signs of writing. Staffs then represent the social forces in play in terms of "relationships among magnitudes and sets." Once conceived in terms of abstractions such as magnitude, political entities become referents dissimilar from those of "normal types of discourse units." The reason why Tupicochans resist translating staffs into normal language, he says, is the same reason why mathematicians use a symbol set (equations, etc.) that resists rephrasing in sentences. Mathematicians could put their meanings into ordinary language, but ordinary language is poorly suited to the task. As Brice commented about related properties of Old World "proto" writings, including Linear A, "Ligatured combinations and differences of relative size and position" among signs make possible "a wide range of subtle distinctions of meaning," more economically than in *scriptio plena*" (1976:43). The staffs clearly do show traces of thinking about social relations represented as quantities in formulas. Urton's suggestion yields an acceptable characterization of staff signs' formal properties in synchrony, and it poses no obstacle to explaining why they vary in diachrony.

But detecting mathlike rather than "natural-language"-like structure in these artifacts does not make them irrelevant to khipus' general inscriptive functioning. Rather, it suggests that inscriptions formulated thus might belong to a semiosis that has calculuslike forms, yet operates in areas which local people do not think about mathematically.

Tupicochans have apparently devised a formal notation for certain social relations. Its annual deployment seems a sort of tacit social science. It offers a versatile system for schematizing relationships, with a compact notation of its own. But the work of expressing power in terms of sets, magnitudes, and hierarchies is blocked off from the arena of ordinary discourse, where we normally expect to find societies analyzing themselves. This may have to do with mathematical reserve with regard to ordinary language, as Urton holds. But one could also turn this around and say that a nonordinary language with number as a component has evolved as a way to denote nonmathematical entities. Certainly the mathematical viewpoint Urton mentions is not in any evident way the operant viewpoint. Not a single math-like expression arose, even by elicitation. Rather, code users seem to think of numbers (of aspas, etc.) as submeaningful features that contribute in the aggregate, through contrasts, to meaningful signs. The process of creating formulaic simulacra for social action is locally understood as performative process, not as the use of referential signs "about" political action. Staffs are taken as the visible impression of a new set of power relations emerging as a result of members' having exchanged tokens for the coming year. In short, the staff code example seems to remind us that Lockean numbers are only one of the kinds of numbers cords may contain. Formulaic and relational expressions of activity that the actors saw as nonquantitative may be just as important to khipus' "numerical" aspect as the accountancy which so impressed chroniclers.

What, finally, could be the relation between staff code and the quipocamayos? In the narrow sense of whether khipus might register staff contents, there is no obstacle. The reader can easily imagine a set of staff-to-khipu sign equivalences. If we were to find a khipu with knots forming an appropriate suite of ligatured expressions, we could suspect a roster of officers to be the content. That khipu would hardly be a "numerical" one in the sense that claims to bifurcate accountancy cords from the other, allegedly single kind associated with "nonnumerical" uses.

But more searchingly, one might ask whether the functional differences between them allow seeing them as parts of a unitary signifying system. This question breaks into two. First, it is argued that staffs have "emergent" meaning, insofar as they do not rely on a complete code existing prior to any given realization but rather contrive a code of composite signs anew each time they concretize ongoing process. Did khipus ever work the same way? The possibility may be held open, at least for small local systems where people can adapt quickly to tacit agreements, but it is unlikely for higher-level imperial records. It seems plausible that staffs and khipus share a small store of all-purpose visible "emes" which come into play whenever people visualize interaction, with "surface" relevance varying according to context. For example, aspa appears in consecrated grass, in manuscript, and in gesture — holding drinks with crossed arms when serving authorities — expressing different contrasts in each case. (This is also the case in Urton's binary-code model.) Second, staffs have "compositional" meaning, insofar as their meaning is only revealed vis-à-vis each other. Do cords? Archaeology yields many khipus whose strings form suites (one example is discussed in the Conclusions chapter) perhaps comparable with the suite of staffs. A string fallen from such a suite might well have been unintelligible, and indeed not a single chronicle source mentions any possibility of reading *one* khipu cord. It seems realistic to think that some cords had "compositional" meanings. If "atomic" signs such as aspa and raya were restricted to no one medium or context, but rather figured as recyclable multi-purpose tokens across media, we might think of staff and cord as two differently evolved templates or applications for an underlyingly common set of signifying habits.

THE KHIPU ART AFTER THE INKAS

TUPICOCHA IS exceptional in entering the third millennium with a set of khipus as its civic insignia. Their endurance is a historical enigma. Are they a direct continuation of a pre-Hispanic technology? A colonially modified descendant? A more recent reinvention or readaptation?

The present chapter is a probe into khipu history, proposing a long chronology. Several studies (Loza 1998; Sempat Assadourian 2002; Urton in press) synthesize what is known about general contours of the colonial encounter with khipus. These are briefly summed up in the next section, and a fuller Huarochirí regional case study follows. Huarochirí's abundant unpublished documents prove that the khipu art did not disappear from political life early in the Spanish era as khipu studies usually affirm. Rather, cord media persisted in the interstices of colonial rule as a parallel information system providing data independence from colonial scribes. Confidentiality and ethnic legitimacy also underwrote the cord system.

The Khipu Problem and Colonial Context

Hardly had the Spanish invaded Peru in 1532 when they found themselves startled by the Inkas' ability to keep accurate accounts on strings. The first khipu eyewitnesses, none other than the original Pizarran invaders, observed them during the invasion, when, in 1533, an Inka storehouse-keeper knotted down goods the invaders were taking from a state storehouse. Untying some knots and tying knots on other cords, the Inka official may have been using a double-entry method, which was at that time Europe's newly invented state-of-the-art accountancy (Pizarro 1920 [1533]:175). As early as 1542 a high Spanish governor took the khipu-based deposition of four cord masters in order to clarify dynastic claims (Collapiña, Supno, et al., 1974 [1542, 1608]). Although early Spanish warlords and missionaries usually were anything but credulous about native intellect, personal familiarity with cord-medium experts convinced many. By 1555 Agustín de Zárate's apparently accurate Lockean understanding of cord accountancy was in print (1995:28).

At a time when Indo-Arabic numeracy was only just becoming common among Europeans, many early chroniclers seem to have admired the cord art's efficiency while understanding it only slightly. Among the best informed were Pedro Cieza de León (1985 [1553]:57–60), who worked largely by interviewing local native notables; Juan de Betanzos, husband of an Inka princess and beneficiary of her access to Inka court information (1987 [1551]:96–97); and Juan Polo de Ondegardo (Fossa 2000, Julien 2000:55), who by 1559 was convinced that khipu masters really could "configure" laws, royal successions, and dynastic marriage records on cord (Sempat Assadourian 2002:126). Polo put khipu lore to the test by using it to sniff out politically dangerous foci of an Inka royal cult. These and a few others had already begun looking into khipus substantially before Spanish officials began to influence production of cords for trials and tribute records. Their assertions may therefore be taken as referring to a primarily pre-Hispanic technological legacy and not to khipu technology as reshaped along the colonial interface.

A Bolivian khipu specialist, Carmen Beatriz Loza, has parsed out three periods in early-colonial interaction between cord media and the alphabetic world of Spanish legality (1998). Her scheme sets an initial context for understanding the Huarochirí region's intra-indigenous media history, which is the main theme of this chapter.

Loza's first period corresponds to the 1550s. By this time cord masters had integrated colonial facts into their art. Garcilaso Inca de la Vega wrote that in his youth, which corresponded to that era, local ethnic lords used to ask him to read them the Spanish ledgers as a check against falsification of knotted tribute data (1991 [1609]:348). In this period, cords first attained cross-cultural recognition as testimony of transactions in Spanish legal forums. In 1554, Huanca ethnic lords whose homeland lay just over the cordillera from Huarochirí adduced their khipus as accounts of the many goods seized by Spanish armies during the early days of the Spanish invasion. For these they asked compensation payable by the Council of the Indies. At first the jurists could hardly believe that *indios* equipped only with strings could account for every bag of corn or pair of sandals seized in the hurly-burly of war decades before. Indeed their first claim went unanswered. In 1561 Francisco Cusichaca, as spokesman for the cacique of Hatun Xauxa, had khipu contents reformulated into a lawyer's memorandum. The conjoint cord-paper technique proved persuasive, and the court did recognize the double presentation as "accounts" (*cuentas*; Murra 1975b). This practice was soon taken as acceptable accounting in much of Peru, even though the Council of the Indies sent no mandate licensing it. In the same era (1559 and 1569) royal descent groups are claimed to have drawn on cords to explain the conquests of long-dead Inka kings (Rowe 1985; Julien 2000:134).

Loza's second period begins in 1570. It reflects the policies of Francisco de Toledo, the viceroy (1569–81) whom Philip II sent to hammer down nonstandard practices that had grown during thirty-seven years of invasion, warlordism, haphazard royal administration, and indigenous-Spanish deal-making. In the early Toledan years, colonial policy passed beyond merely receiving khipus. The colonial regime began to regulate their usage and even to require indigenous lords to maintain specific kinds of cords. This policy owed much to Juan de Matienzo, theorist of the Toledan regime. Matienzo prescribed that "every six months the *tucuirico* [supervisor] is to send a memorandum by writing or by khipu of the Indians who have died, or increased, or reached the age of eighteen, or fled" (1967 [1567]:67).[1] Francisco de Toledo in 1572 ordered that khipu masters were to aid judges in receiving native cases (Toledo 1986–89:237–38) and ranked them as equal in standing to assistant scribes (Loza 1998:155). In this way the colonial khipu proper, the one shaped around the colonial legal interface and molded to Spanish power, came into being. In Tapacarí (Bolivia) in 1571, the executor of a local lord's will adduced a long khipu inventory of his properties, apparently sorted by ethnocategories, and explained that the part about livestock was based on a specialized khipu made by the decedent's herdsman (Del Río 1990:107–8). Indeed, in Toledo's time many pre-Hispanically trained khipu masters still lived. Toledo had a panel of them interviewed by his official historian, Pedro Sarmiento de Gamboa, in 1571–72, so as to establish the "true" history of the Inka state (Sarmiento de Gamboa 1942 [1572]).

It was in the 1570s that cord media reached their most officialized colonial status. Cristóbal de Molina, a cleric who reached Cuzco before Toledo and stayed on to serve him, knew Quechua well, and was connected with colonial Inka elites. His high estimate of khipu capability expressed an opinion widely held in the period: "[The Inkas] had a very cunning method of counting by strings of wool and knots, the wool being of different colours. They call them quipus, they are able to understand so much by this means, that they can give an account of all the events that have happened in their land for more than five hundred years. They had expert Indians who were masters in the art of reading *quipus*; and the knowledge was handed down from generation to generation, so that the smallest thing was not forgotten" (Locke's translation in Urton, 2003:30; Molina 1959 [1573]:35–36).[2] Father José de Acosta, a Jesuit with a notable appreciation of khipus, observed in this period that women used "threads" to record their sins for confession and elders to itemize points of catechism. He explicitly contrasted alphabetic characters, which he understood as referring to submeaningful sound segments, with khipu codes, which referred to a class which Acosta called "significations of things" (significaciones de cosas) (Acosta 1954 [1590]:190, 275, 280, 287).

Huarochirí was one of many provinces where cord masters still understood historical khipus in the later 1570s, according to Sempat Assadourian (2002:134–35). The anonymous author of the Report on Ancient Customs of the Natives of Peru (*Relación de las costumbres antiguas de los naturales del Pirú*; 1968 [1594]), who seems to have been Blas Valera, at that time consulted Don Sebastián Ninavilca, Huarochirí's paramount native lord, as an authority on the khipu record of Inka times. Ninavilca numbered among the most biculturally sophisticated pioneers of the colonial indigenous order. Such intervention may exemplify the contacts which carried the ancient technology into a new kind of local administration.

Indeed, some Spaniards thought the Toledan regime went too far in legitimating cord accountancy. This was the opinion of a certain Doctor Murillo de la Cerda, who wrote a short memo with interesting detail on colonial accounting by khipu as the Toledan age practiced it. It is labeled as copied from a source in the "Biblioteca del Escorial que fue de Ambrosio de Morales," which suggests that it was originally tendered to Philip II. It is preserved in Spain's National Library (BN/M Manuscript 1589a), and its alleged date is 1589. In part Murillo says:[3]

Today [1589?] there continues the use of some quypos, which we call books of account [although] the Indians had no such [thing as account books] except those quipos, which are some woollen cords of various colors and on them many knots as is here shown [an illustration may be missing]. Some [are] different from others, such that by the difference they recognize and know the amounts that entered and left the account, and the gold and silver pesos which have been given and paid and received. The Spanish did not catch on to [*no . . . alcanzaron*] this kind of account when they won that kingdom, nor have they been able to learn it up to today. [This accounting] has good faith and credit only through some trustworthy Indians in those towns, whom they call quypo camayos, as majordomos of those accounts and as senior accountants [*contadores mayores*]. The accounting of all the livestock, and fruits and fields of the communities is in their charge . . . and these quipo camayos do the accounting before the judicial authorities, and verbally give account of everything. Up until today they have saved a great infinity of these knotted cords. Although the cunning and aptitude of some leading Indians [*principales*] has already extended in that kingdom as far as learning Romance [i.e., Spanish] and Latin and to singing and playing various instruments, and counting with Arabic numerals, in reality they do not use them [Arabic numerals], nor do the crown district governors [*corregidores*] allow them to take anything or give anything according to our counting and numerals, but rather through these quipos. And the quipocamayos themselves choose these same instruments, before the crown district governor, in their town council [*ayuntamiento*]. This order is maintained today. The other order, our own [i.e., accounting by numerals], serves as a curiosity and refinement [*policia*] of the leading Indian who chose to learn it.

This testimony may have been meant to alarm the king about the nonauditability of revenues in Indian hands. Spain's crushing military expenses had made revenue a hot-button issue of the 1580s, and careerists promoting "revenue enhancement" nostrums were hardly rare. But Murillo's details ring true, and they are fascinating.

Murillo tells us, then, that a half century after the conquest, Andean notables had learned Spanish numeracy but did not consider it important. It seemed to them a mere affectation of biculturalism, by comparison to the real working technology of cords.[4] (We can sympathize today, because the Spanish numeracy of the early colonial era, dominated by Roman numerals and verbally spelled-out numbers, seems awkward to us too.) Moreover those Spanish officials charged with extracting tribute through the notables' good offices preferred to keep things so, relying on cord masters even though they themselves did not control them, and apparently did not even understand them. Did the Crown officers prefer cord records because that would prevent higher officials from noticing finagling? Or did cords really provide superior administration? We cannot tell, but in either case khipu technology had evidently worked its way deep into the Toledan order. The regime not only allowed pluralism in data systems; it positively gave Andean people a mandate to create records Spaniards could not read. This helps one understand why, in later times, when Spaniards lost interest in cords, natives felt entitled to maintain them.

By the time Murillo de la Cerda wrote these words, the whole hybrid regimen was already coming under attack. In 1583, the beginning of Loza's third period, the Third Council of Lima (a summit meeting of churchmen at the all-viceroyalty level) ordered the universal destruction of khipus. The churchmen had learned that cords were the usual way to keep track of offerings to the pre-Christian deities. They jumped to the conclusion that any persisting khipu competence would undermine conversion. From this point onward, Loza holds, khipu masters worked secretly, for fear of being discovered in a practice that Spaniards associated with punishable "idolatry." Clandestinity in this era may cover up important processes in the readaptation of the ancient art. Sabine Hyland suggests that the half-Inka Jesuit Blas Valera, author of a lost chronicle which influenced Garcilaso Inca, may have "invented . . . on his own" a system for representing syllables or words on khipus, somewhat as Sequoyah later became inspired to invent the Cherokee syllabary (Hyland 2002:164–65).[5] Despite the official downgrading, mid-seventeenth-century references describe an interface between the khipu art and the *libros de rayas* (tally books) which regulated wages in colonial workshops (Cobo 1964 [1653]:2:143; Costales 1983:276–77; Meisch 1998).

Inkas and the Khipu Art in Huarochirí

For most places, that is about all we know. But Huarochirí offers more. First of all, it yields clues about how cord technology fit into provincial society just before the Spanish invasion. Khipus are mentioned twice in the 1608 Quechua Manuscript, both times in context of testimonies about ritual life. The first reference concerns the role of cord records in Inka subsidies to local religious cults. The Inkas kept a cord account of his subsidies to the superhuman powers, or huacas: "And likewise the Inca would have offerings of his gold and silver given according to his quipo account, to all the huacas, to the well-known huacas, to all the huacas. He used to have them give gold and silver *auquis* . . . and also gold and silver *urpus*, and gold and silver *tipsis*; all this exactly according to quipo counts. Of these major huacas, not a single one went unattended" (Salomon and Urioste 1991:112, 211).[6] This remark occurs in a chapter which deals with Tupicocha's own territory and ritual regimen.

The second reference concerns an intravillage rite in which Inkas played no part. In a chapter about the ritual reproduction of water rights, we learn that when the people of Concha village went to visit the lake deities which owned their water, they "took a quipu account of all the people who were absent and began to worship"[7] (Salomon and Urioste 1991:142, 242).

Comparing these two passages, one may note that in the Inka era, as the authors remembered it, the khipu art was not exclusively the domain of Inka specialists. Rather, it was an informational common ground. Local ayllus such as Concha, and imperial authorities, each made cord records for their own interests.

The great shrine-citadel of Pacha Kamaq, which had attracted pilgrimages and offerings from up and down the Andes since the Middle Horizon or earlier, continued to command religious awe in the days when it belonged to the Inka province of Lurin Yauyos (i.e., Huarochirí). The makers of the Huarochirí Manuscript regarded the deity Pacha Kamaq Pacha Kuyuchiq ("World Maker and World Shaker," an allusion to earthquakes) as the parent of one of their local deities. The temple grounds and environs of Pacha Kamaq have been one of the main sources of archaeological khipus (Bueno 1990). It is likely that at least some of them record offerings made in the same way the Checa witnesses were talking about. Some physical resemblances connect Pacha Kamaq khipus and Tupicochan quipocamayos, notably camelid wool fiber (unusual for the coast) and the ample use of mottled bicolor cordage.

A Huarochirí Cord Master in the Days of Spanish Invasion

How did cord technology fare in the transition to colonial rule? Huarochirí offers a rare glimpse of the process in terms of actual historical agency. The data concern the career of a khipu master living through the first confused days when seaborne barbarians, who turned out to be the Spanish, were debarking on the northern beaches and then beginning to desecrate Pacha Kamaq in the course of their assault on Inka rule. This man's story helps one envision in greater detail the tendencies leading up to the first of the three colonial stages that Loza sketches. It gives an idea of how khipus came to be seen as a resource for defending specifically indigenous interests.

In 1585 a lawsuit about the colonial lordship of Mama, an important yunka or coastal lowland polity in Huarochirí, came under the jurisdiction of an ethnographically intelligent Crown official named Diego Dávila Brizeño (1965 [1583]). Dávila had the wit to assemble relatively neutral senior natives from around the region, as well as the parties' own chosen witnesses. He even thought of asking them to use a Quechua expository technique of diagramming genealogy with stones (AGN/BA 1588–90:f. 83r).[8] The witnesses include at least one of the individuals mentioned in the Quechua Manuscript of Huarochirí.[9] In their version of the invasion crisis, khipu knowledge appears crucial.

At that dawning moment of the colonial era, when Spaniards had just seized the Inka sovereign and were starting to loot the great shrine-citadel, the non-Inka ethnic lords of Huarochirí scrambled to reposition themselves politically. One of the quickest was a certain Pomachahua or Pomachagua, a native lord of Huánchor in the middle Rímac valley. (His lands would have adjoined Tupicocha's valley outliers.) The Inka state had classified his ethnic lordship as a waranka, or "thousand," analogous to the "Thousand of Checa" (chapter 3).

Pomachahua held a Janus-faced power. He inherited a locally important pre-Inka ethnic privilege, but he was also known first and foremost as a manager of Inka royal property. The most potent title he held was "khipu master and majordomo of all the estates of Ynga Topa,"[10] a post his father had also held (AGN/BA 1588–90:f. 146r). In this capacity Pomachahua "was camachico [administrator] of the Indians who used to guard the Inka's livestock and likewise he was in charge of caring for the luxury textiles and maize and potatoes and the other belongings of the Inka" (f. 121v).[11] He may be the same "domain administrator lord Pomachaua"[12] pictured by Guaman Poma (1980 [1615]:309; see also fig. 18). The "Ynga Topa,"[13] who owned all this, and who is also present in Guaman Poma's drawing, was by then a mummy, an eternal person enshrined many years before the Spanish invasion. In practical terms Pomachahua must have been employed by "Ynga Topa"'s panaka, the rich commemorative corporation formed by the enshrined sovereign's descendants. Panakas had a sort of residual sovereignty over their hereditary endowments. Pomachahua was therefore hardly a well-controlled tool of the reigning Inka sovereign (in any case weakened by dynastic warfare even before Pizarro kidnapped him). He was, rather, a potentially disruptive factional contender, whose room for maneuver grew as the captive Inka lost his grip and his reign fell apart.

"Warlike and intelligent"[14] in his contemporaries' eyes, Pomachahua immediately "went to Caxamarca to give his allegiance to the Marqués Francisco Pizarro, just as many ethnic lords and Indians went, and they took gold and silver and Indian servant men and women" (AGN/BA 1588–90:f. 1r, f. 66v). While he was away forging what he thought would be a liberating anti-Cuzco alliance, his brother took over as lord of Huánchor (a major town of the "thousand" in the middle reaches of the Rímac River canyon). This brother, named Condorchagua, was also an "accountant" under the Inka regime (f. 68v). He may be the same "chief accountant and treasurer, khipu chief of Tawantinsuyu Condorchava"[15] drawn by Guaman Poma (1980 [1615]:332). Pomachahua's ploy was a short-term triumph. He came back instantly transmuted into the first colonial chief the Huarochiranos had ever seen, complete with a baptismal name and a new red suit: "The said Gerónimo Pomachagua gave [the Huánchor natives] orders by virtue of the grant of power that the Marqués Pizarro gave him, and because [Pizarro] had given him a lot of things, [including] a red suit and a sword and a dagger, and when the Indians saw him with those weapons and learned that he was carrying them with the Marqués' permission, they began to fear him and serve him" (AGN/BA 1588–90:f. 110v).[16]

To understand Pomachagua's coup de théâtre, one must remember that the people had never before seen steel weapons. The former khipu master with his Spanish arms "came on assertively and began to lord it over the chiefdom, but not because he really was the chief" (AGN/BA 1588–90:156r).[17] Rather, he was gaining ascendancy because people were beginning to believe his claim that the seemingly unstoppable Spaniards "had given him a grant of power as colonial chief of the three Thousands belonging to the *repartimiento* (tribute overlordship) of Mama" (f. 146r).[18] If true, this would have made him the paramount power in the Rímac valley.

One point that stands out is the startling ease with which Pomachahua and his brother could parlay Inka "accountancy" into a colonial power base. Of course many other upstarts gained ground in the confusion of 1532–48, and there is no reason to think that cord masters as such formed a distinctive colonial elite among them. But one can imagine that the "majordomo" Pomachahua was the first in his area to land a political punch because he had exact information on disposable political resources, as well as authority to move them. He was both in charge of a large fund of Inka wealth, and firmly socketed in the local ethnic power structure.

Certainly, khipu accountancy was among the firmest of Andean institutions during those chaotic times. We know from many lawsuits that while virtually all other Inka institutions crumbled, accountancy held amazingly firm. When actual warfare subsided after 1548, native accountancy was to become the strong right arm of attempts to regain lost wealth by litigation. These facts could hardly have failed to impress both Andeans and Spaniards. These events shored up colonial lords' as well as ayllu commoners' convictions that cord-keeping—an accountancy no Spanish functionary could distort—was indispensable.

Father Avila's Trial, Khipus, and the Sources
of the Huarochirí Quechua Manuscript

Hopes of Inka resurgence were crushed during the second of Loza's periods, when Viceroy Toledo destroyed the remaining Inka redoubt east of Cuzco. Spanish bureaucracy intervened more and more in village institutions, including their data regimen.

In Huarochirí, Spanish authorities not only received khipu evidence but demanded that natives compile it. When the Toledan administration set out to improve road services over the freezing heights of Paria Caca, an important step for restoring war-disrupted traffic between the new Spanish capital and the old Inka one, Lima sent an order requiring local lords to document their help "providing by quipo and in writing the names of those Indians who serve in this [i.e., highway service] and of what aillos they are and how many trips up they made and how many down . . . so as to make payment for their service."[19] Tupicocha served the way station, or *tambo*, at Sisicaya.

Likewise, in 1589, when a Spanish official named Francisco López prepared for the Viceroy a detailed report about the Crown's gunpowder factor at Santa Inés de Chíchima, he explained that its whole labor system depended on quipos. Santa Inés lies in the lower Rímac valley, a part of Huarochirí at the edge of Checa territory. Its labor force arrived in rotating contingents from all over the province. Each contingent brought along at least one of the "leading Indians they call quipocamayos who takes charge of putting onto quipo and memorandum[20] the Indians who were working, and of giving them labor chits [*recaudos*]."[21] The time-keeping quipocamayos drew salaries for this service (BN/M 1589b).

Throughout the first colonial lifetime, cord work articulated colonial Spanish and Andean societies in the realms of tribute; forced labor service, or *mita*; catechization; and commerce. In colonial papers of the late sixteenth century, phrases such as "let them bring their khipus" or "by the reckoning of khipu master accountants" were quite routine. They especially formed part of the structured expectations of those who conducted visitas, or tribute-quota inspections. Khipus are mentioned as sources of the 1588 *revisita* of Sisicaya (AGN/BA 1588:f. 8r).

It seems that late in the sixteenth century, as the Spanish Viceroyalty's horde of scribes and notaries solidified their grip on authoritative discourse, khipu experts functioned less and less frequently as authorities in their own right. Even though the Third Council of Lima allowed the keeping of personal cord records for purposes of confession, from 1583 onward the Archbishopric's general policy of burning cord records tended to force the cord medium off the margins of the legal record. We may guess that khipu-derived data continued to be common, but that it reached official attention only when mediated or eclipsed by the authority of scribes and accountants.

Most scholars of colonial media say the khipu art was pretty well silenced by

1600 (Urton 1998:410, 431; Pease 1990). Loza (1998:156) suggests that khipu masters practiced in a poorly documented "space of informality" or even clandestinity. A close look at the regional record, however, shows that this deofficialized continuity was more than a marginal contraband. After all, it hardly seems likely that the elaborate khipu-paper colonial interface, which Spaniards had themselves helped to build, evaporated without a trace while the institutions and relationships that mandated it stayed in place. It would be puzzling if "yndios" willingly sacrificed their independent database vis-à-vis possibly distorted Spanish data (or, for that matter, missed the chance to "cook" data before presenting it to Spaniards). In 1653 a report on a textile plant (*obraje*) in the jurisdiction of Quito said: "A khipu master is needed in the obrajes so that he too can keep account of the days that the factory hands have worked. He should make a large khipu with different strings according to the Indians who work at different tasks. By this means the workers will be able to check what is shown [*señalado*] by the khipu master and what his administrator has noted down, and in this way they may reach agreement (Costales 1983:276–77; see also Meisch 1998)."[22]

As Spaniards relinquished their tenuous connection with the cord-making orbit, and became consumers of paper only, the khipu art apparently lodged in folk-legal proceedings off the colonial ledger. These records, though not procedurally visible within the legalistic orbit, were vital in establishing the positions "yndios" held toward legality.

In the region of this study, it seems that khipus, even while they were forced from the official register, became the database which natives used in formulating responses to officialdom or protesting abuses by it. One fateful case occurred right in and around Tupicocha. This was the 1607 ecclesiastical trial in which members of several central Huarochirí villages turned against their brilliant but exploitative curate, Francisco de Avila (AA/L Capítulos 1607–9). While the importance of this trial has been amply recognized through researches of Antonio Acosta Rodríguez (1979, 1987), its khipu-based evidentiary structure has not been studied.

In the trial's early phases, several officials of central Huarochirí villages adduced khipus as records of the goods and services Avila had stolen from them. Don Martín Puyporocsi, who promoted the case (but was later dissuaded from it by Avila's ally Cristóbal Choque Casa; Taylor 1985, 1986), was an ethnic lord of Tuna village, adjacent to Tupicocha. He promised to have the "Indian accountant of these villages" prove by "quipo" the seizures, and did so. His part of the case demonstrates three important properties about the art of cord-based record keeping after its demise as a matter of state legality:

First, Puyporocsi and his peers felt that cord record work enjoyed a priority and a dignity that privileged Spaniards had no right to override. One of his complaints was that "having come to this area on his business he [Avila] busied four khipu-master subchiefs [*mandones quipocamayos*] making them do an all-day turn of guarding a mule. . . . [Avila] owes these day-wages and service" (AA/L Capítulos 1607–9:f. 3v).[23]

Second, the testimonies suggest not merely the persistence of khipus but their persistence as a multilevel data collection system, even though more than seventy years had passed since the Inka state ceased to coordinate khipu registry. To see this, one may start by asking, what are we to make of the "four" cord masters just mentioned? Tuna was at that time a tiny village. It would hardly have needed four cord-record accountants for its internal business unless that business was segmented. The four may have been representatives of its component ayllus, which numbered four into the nineteenth century. This might explain why they have the less-than-chiefly *mandón* title. When people from Guamansica village complained that Avila helped himself to their horses, their ethnic lord brought along a specifically designated "khipu master and accountant of the said ayllu." Yet the trial also repeatedly mentions a higher-level "Indian accountant of these towns,"[24] speaking unambiguously of a singular official for multiple towns—that is, speaking of an administrative position at least one level, and seemingly two levels, up from the ayllu.[25] We do not know whether the term refers to cord masters at the level of the "thousand," or to one attached to the *kurakas* ('ethnic lords') of multi-ayllu polities. Perhaps the reference connects with, but forbears to involve, the paramount Ninavilca *curacazgo* ('colonial chieftaincy') seated at Santa María Jesús de Huarochirí.

Third and finally, the testimonies give an intriguing idea of the scope and format of cord record keeping circa 1607. The most prominent subject matter is work performed, which was apparently recorded in a basic schema concerning the number of persons affected, type of work, quantity of tasks or products, number of days, and monetary outcome, with room for optional details (AA/L Capítulos 1607-9:f. 3r-v, 10r, 108r). Although only a few witness utterances are earmarked as khipu-based statements, many other statements about labor have similar format properties without mention of khipus.

Additional, explicitly khipu-based accusations concern goods tendered to Avila. One concerns Avila's demanding fifteen loads of fodder daily for his horses, another his having sold eighty sheep belonging to the community at state-set prices (AA/L Capítulos 1607-9:f. 3r, 70r). Some of the statistics involve huge numbers, presumably aggregates over substantial periods, such as the 1,001,630 fish which Guamansica ayllu supplied (f. 109r). If this is a khipu datum, it corresponds to a very high-capacity khipu. Some sections strongly resemble the khipu readouts which form the basis of Murra's (1975b) article on "ethnocategories" of economy. One of these (f. 110r-111r)[26] is signed by Andrés Macacaxa as "accountant" of Sunicancha; perhaps he was a cord keeper also familiar with alphabetic writing. Numerous testimonies (e.g., f. 66r, about how an "Indian" called the name of each person in order to take down an account of offerings for the dead on All Saints' Day) leave room for doubt about which medium was used.

Overall, the trial makes it abundantly clear that (1) khipus were in general use for village accounting, (2) accounting was a political office, and (3) accounting covered at least the following matters: community/ayllu herds including sale of animals, work levied on community/ayllu members, and disposition of products made with community/ayllu resources. It amply confirms, as the chronicler Martín de Murúa had affirmed in 1590 (1946 [1590]:124), that local ethnic groups had their own khipu resources apart from Inka bureaucracy.

In 1609, when Avila had emerged victorious from imprisonment and was spearheading the assault on Andean worship, a Jesuit Annual Letter signed by P. Juan Sebastián de la Parra reported that amid the uproar of Avila's attack on the gods and ancestors of the San Damián–Tupicocha area, converts eager to get on the right side of Christianity engaged in a furor of khipu activity. "Everywhere people were making quipos to confess, to learn what they didn't know about the doctrine in order to confess, to fast, and discipline themselves, and . . . generally attend, each one, to the salvation of his soul" (Polia Meconi 1999:273).[27] Strikingly, the Jesuit observer saw this as general activity and not as the charge of cord specialists.

A Late-Colonial Episode of Rebellion, Ethnicity, and Media Pluralism

From the mid-seventeenth century onward, an ever-widening lacuna in documentation separates the colonial cord record from the written one. Rarely, mentions of khipus surface, such as a 1623 lawsuit in which leaders of two Huarochirí communities claimed that a priest forced them to make unwilling contributions for Corpus Christi and the Day of the Dead "by the tribute quota lists, quipos and registries" which each ayllu maintained.[28] From 1705 to 1719 a coalition of villages in Huarochirí and its environs brought a series of protests against curates for dubious dealings in community livestock. One of the accused padres defended himself by showing a set of receipts among which are notes attesting khipus about herds. One of the cord records denotes 9,011 ewes. Others are described as "straw khipus" (*quipos de paja*), which apparently served as jottings of single-animal transactions (AAL/L Capítulos 1705–19). Casual techniques such as straw knotting, rather than suggesting degradation of the art, suggests that it was available as a commonly known vernacular. In 1725 a priest averred that an accused idolater "used to walk around always loaded with a cord quipo, through which he recognized everyone of his panaca and knew by the quipo the persons who owed labor turns, their names, condition, and what livestock and property each one had" (Radicati 1979[?]:55).[29] These examples attest specific ayllu-level khipu functions from a time within the possible radiocarbon intervals of the Tupicochan specimens.

By the middle of the eighteenth century, many of the old markers of ethnic difference between Spaniards and "yndios" had become blurred or obsolete in Huarochirí. Alphabetic literacy, like some formerly distinctive habits in dress and ornament, was one of them. But interethnic literacy did not cause a merger of Spanish and native political societies. This became explosively evident during the age of the great neo-Inka rebellions. While the better-known rebel messiah Juan Santos Atahualpa and his army of tropical forest guerrillas were rousting Spanish forces out of western Amazonia and extending a rebel network into the Tarma highlands, a Lima-dwelling Huarochirano named Francisco Ximénez Inga took part in a short-lived attempt at a parallel urban insurrection. Spanish forces, tipped off, quickly snuffed it out with executions. Ximénez Inga was among the few who escaped. Fleeing to his homeland, he succeeded in touching off a fierce regional revolt throughout most of Huarochirí. Karen Spalding (1984:272–90; see also Sotelo 1942) has detailed its history. The anticolonial surge began with a swift buildup of rebel alliances among native lords contacted by Inga's faction, each concerned lest commoners' fury over forced labor and frustrated petitions for tribute justice turn into rage against colonial chieftaincy itself. During a climactic explosion of anger, on 25 July 1750, villagers in the provincial seat of Huarochirí killed, injured, or drove away all but one of the party defending the *corregidor* ('Crown governor'), José Antonio de Salazar. For a matter of days, the rebels actually expelled Spanish power from the agropastoral heart of Huarochirí.

But an astute Spanish mine operator from Yauli, Sebastián Franco de Melo, saw a way to pry rebel alliances apart almost as fast as they formed. Even before the official Spanish militia was able to mobilize—in a total of only two weeks—Franco de Melo used his many ties of co-godparenthood to sow Machiavellian misinformation among the rebel communities. By playing on each one's hardened rivalry with its neighbors, he cracked the fragile solidarity of the anti-Spanish front. Francisco Ximénez Inga was one of two leaders betrayed and captured early in the game. Before long, in the Huaranga de Checa and the other regional native polities, village leaders one after another hurried to build safe positions by betraying rival villages' rebel chiefs while themselves posing for internal consumption as steadfast revolutionaries. Before long Franco de Melo was able to snuff out village resistance at his chosen pace. A few days later he corralled two thousand highlanders under the gun, and forced them to watch in silence as seven rebel leaders were shot and mutilated. Each was butchered into five pieces—maybe Franco knew the significance of five-in-one symbolism since ancient times—and the trophies were exhibited in "pacified" villages.

The interesting point for the present study is just how Franco de Melo stimulated this cascade of factional collapses: with letters and khipus. His remarkable diary (MM/BA 1761),[30] which Karen Spalding is preparing for publication, clearly shows that at every stage, sending political and military intelligence by letter, and intercepting the enemy's correspondence, was the key to tactical success. Throughout the campaign, both sides relied on Quechua for face-to-face business, but also operated on the assumption that every village potentate could handle Spanish-language letters, or at least had native scribes who could. Franco's stratagem was to send confidential letters whose untrue contents would provoke native lords to self-destructive action. In fact, crowing over his victory, Franco de Melo wrote that when Crown troops arrived, "I had already pacified the province with my . . . letters to the villages" (f. 43r).

The crucial moment in his epistolary war came when Franco de Melo climbed up to a high pasture where he plotted with a woman herder who owed him the fealty of ritual kinship, but who (as pasture renters often did and still do) held a grudge against local villages. This woman's name was María Micaela Chinchano. She was an "outsider," but one with fifteen years' residence and sons whom the rebels were holding captive. Franco de Melo's remembrance brings to life the sinister meeting:

> I grabbed paper and an inkwell, and went all alone to María Micaela's house, and after chatting with her about various things, . . . I offered to . . . give her fifty pesos if she would spread around in the villages some papers which I would give her. She agreed she would do that, trusting that I would protect her and that she could carry the papers under cover of looking for her sons, and that if she didn't come through with what she offered I would punish her.[31]

Melo dispatched María Micaela Chinchano with messages to convince each rebel village leader he had best beat his treacherous neighbors to the punch by switching sides.

> So I wrote twenty-two papers for as many villages in this repartimiento. I will set down their content, because they were all the same.
> *Children, alcaldes ['vara officers'] and principales ['ayllu heads'?] of the Town of Langa: I received your letter in which you say that you are loyal vassals of His Majesty, and that it was only out of fear of the Lahuaitambo rebels that you joined in the insurrection, but that if I pardon you of this crime in His Majesty's name, you will hand over to me the dead or captive bodies of Francisco Ximenez Ynga* [and five other named rebel leaders]; *for which I thank you, and in the name of Our Lord the King I accept, and you will be rewarded, and I will hand over your lands* [. . .][32]
> I had her [María Micaela] drop this paper written to Langa, in Lahuaitambo;[33] and as for the one written to Lahuaitambo, I had her drop it in Langa; and so forth in the other villages, always switching them around, because I calculated that being so close together, they would begin to distrust each other. . . .[34]
> My Indian woman set out about three in the afternoon, giving me her word that all day and night she would walk through the villages of Tuna, Tupicocha, San Damián, Sunicancha, Lahuaitambo, Langa, and Chorrillos, and the next day she would walk through the native parish of Olleros. And if she were to find her sons free, she was sure they would go around through other villages to help her.
> For this reason she carried the papers tied up with threads of different

colors made into quipo[s], which is the means by which they understand each other.

That is what she promised, but she carried it out even better. . . .[35]

A few days later, María returned:

Maria Micaela came back from carrying her papers, assuring me that she and her sons had dropped them off, and had carried out my orders in all the villages, and that my letters had had such an effect that all the rebels who were under the traitor [Ximénez Ynga's] command, had cut themselves off from him, and raised [battle] flags one village against another, hurling themselves murderously at each other, each accusing the other, [saying] "It was you who wrote to the mine-owning Spaniard!"[36]

In the outcome, de Melo's reliance on local cultural savvy paid off. He called in his thirty co-godparents and his clients, fed and feted them in traditional highland style, and made good on his promises, both paying the combatants and compensating everyone for supplies and services. Brutal to the rebels he captured and interrogated, he listened attentively to his Indian allies and frankly blamed his fellow Europeans for the danger they had brought on themselves. In triumph he displayed the mutilated bodies of rebel leaders while making a show of forgiving lesser fighters. In short, de Melo set himself up as the exemplar of an acceptable Spaniard: one who was better tolerated than resisted, because he could be counted on to keep promises and protect friends.

The Implications of a Campaign of Corded Letters

María Micaela Chinchano's daredevil part in this fakery has several implications for the history of alphabetic and khipu media. What we take her part to mean depends upon what we suppose the function of her cords to have been. There is room for three hypotheses.

First, at the most conservative end of the interpretative spectrum, one might hypothesize they were merely address labels. Since Chinchano had twenty-two similar-looking letters in hand, and was presumably unlettered, she might have needed cords just to be sure each would reach the intended destination. Misdelivery would obviously have been a disaster.

A second hypothesis is that they served as accrediting information, warranting on (false) native authority that the message was what it appeared to be.

A third hypothesis is that they offered a paraphrase of the letters' content, so that unlettered rebels would not have to rely on readings by village lords of suspect credibility.

Under any hypothesis, even the most conservative, the case warrants questioning some common assumptions about cords and letters in the late colony. First, as to chronology: Chinchano's messages show that khipu use was apparently normal circa 1750. This contradicts Spanish books of that period, which treated cord records as a matter of antiquity if they treated them at all. Local chronology could bear either of two interpretations. On the one hand, Chinchano might have been relying upon a conservative and routinized regional tradition. On the other, given enthusiasm for Inka memories among Andeans of many ethnic groups during the mid-eighteenth century (Burga 1988; Flores Galindo 1987; Stavig 1988), one may entertain the notion that khipu competence was in some way a resuscitated medium, significant in itself for its connotations of Andean nobility and sovereignty. The former seems likelier, given the factors noted later in this chapter.

Second, on gender: It is interesting that de Melo, who knew the district intimately, showed no surprise that a woman could readily create khipus. This suggests that circa 1750 khipu competence was not limited to men. Whether it was in any way a female specialty remains unclear. Alphabetical political messages by eighteenth-century Andean women are rare even among notables. The fact that a woman could easily make cord documents suggests that cords were less gender-exclusive than paper.

Third, on standardization: Purportedly unstandardized "mnemonic" usages could not have been the norm in Huarochirí if hypothesis 2 or 3 is correct. For in that case, María's code was meant for the eyes of people in twenty-two different villages. It is easier to believe that these villages had code norms in common than to believe Maria falsified multiple cord dialects.

Fourth, on specialization and manufacture: Melo was unsurprised that preparing khipus was not difficult for a herdswoman, apparently a person of no particular eminence, and not even a native of the region. Nor need we be surprised. A herder might well have enough fiber on hand to produce cords quickly. Modern artisans only modestly trained in textiles can produce a pendant-length one-color woollen cord in a matter of minutes. We have no way to estimate how many cords would be needed to complement de Melo's letters. But if we assume the khipu tied around each letter was short and simple, Chinchano could easily have made twenty-two small khipus while de Melo was busy with his inkwell. All told, the case suggests that cords could be used by ordinary people, quickly and ad hoc — an interesting deviation from Inka-oriented sources' image of the khipu as a treasure-object and its master as a ponderous specialist.

Fifth, on social function: The khipu, Melo explains, "is the way they communicate" (es el modo conque ellos se entienden). The emphatic third-person phrasing with the explicitly distancing *ellos* implies a disclaimer of khipu knowledge on Melo's own part, and a reminder that cord messages were for him firmly on the other side of a cultural divide. Proud of his bicultural accomplishments, such as conducting politics in an Andean tongue, Melo would almost surely have mentioned khipu competence had he possessed it. The pronoun also implies that he meant indios in general, not some special subset. Moreover, Melo's comment that the "quipo" was how indios "understand each other," that is, exchanged information, as opposed to merely reminding themselves, tends to support hypothesis 2 or 3. Mere address tags made by Chinchano as aide-mémoires would have called for explanation in terms of mnemonics, not of communication. So Chinchano's cords may indeed have functioned to certify the authenticity of the letter as really emanating from Melo, and thus to warrant, by the code itself, that he had made his plan known to an indigenous ally. As noted in relation to Cerda's testimony, the loss of jural standing for khipus might have infused them with a different value: that of immunity from Spanish tampering.

Sixth, of syntax: Since we do not know the cords' content, the testimony sheds little light on how the code worked. If we stick to the most conservative hypothesis—that the cords were only address labels—it would have been possible to do the job by single cords containing ordinal numbers: a cord knotted with numeral "2" could signify Tupicocha, the second point on the above-quoted itinerary. The itinerary itself is self-evident, being the sequence of villages along a southward route at about the 3,200-meter elevation. But that fails to explain the one physical fact about the cords which caught de Melo's eye: they were of varied colors. So even if they were only address labels, they expressed something nonnumerically. Perhaps colors corresponded to villages, and knots on them, if any, their ordinal standing or other data.

If we entertain the second or third hypotheses, we are speculating about these cords' membership in that elusive class of "narrative" khipus about which Urton (1998) offers suggestions. Hypothesis 2 suggests the cords were "meta"-messages telling how to take the contents of the paper messages. Perhaps the sense was something like "This letter really is from Melo, warranted by the cord maker at so-and-so place and date." Since the false-address trick was the core of Melo's ploy, a sign corresponding to the purported addressee village would also be a likely content.

Under the third, or maximalist, hypothesis, the cords were redundant to the alphabetic message given above. In that case they must additionally have contained, either lexigraphically or semasiographically, signs for many features.

In terms of message structure, a cord equivalent for the full letter would have needed a sign for contingency, of the form "if . . . then . . ." to express the sentence "if I pardon you of this crime in His Majesty's name, [then] you will hand over to me the dead or captive bodies" (si os perdono en nombre de Su Magestad este dicho delito, me entregareis muertas o presas las personas). Quechua expresses such patterns with distinctive constructions, one for cases when the subjects of the two clauses are the same, and the other (using suffix -pti or variant) when they are different. The overall structure of Chinchano's message would include (1) cords expressing a vocative or addressee identifier with three items corresponding to the salutation terms; (2) cords expressing the receipt of the putative earlier message; (3) a device signaling quotation of the contents of that message; (4) a structure stating the "if" clause that it putatively contained; (5) a sign equivalent to the morpheme *-pti* (switch-subject subordinator introducing the "then" clause); (6) a structure conveying content of the "then" clause, having within it a series of six paradigmatically similar signs corresponding to the names of the accused; (7) a sign indicating the end of the quotation and the beginning of Melo's response; (8) a structure, perhaps threefold, expressing the three actions Melo promises to compliant villages. A signaturelike sign could also be expected. The invocations of the "King's Majesty" which delimit the major periods of the letter might be signed in some way, perhaps forming major demarcators.

Among these three hypotheses—that of a minimal addressing function, a "meta" comment on the Melo letter, or a substantially redundant counterpart to it—the first two seem more probable, since the hypothetical full equivalent seems too bulky for one person to inscribe twenty-two times in one night. The minimalist, or first, hypothesis suffices to fit Melo's tactical aim. In defense of this hypothesis, one must note that the document says nothing about the reception of khipus after delivery of the letters. If the strings were only address labels, they were incriminating, and presumably María Micaela would have destroyed them after use—the last thing the counterinsurgency needed would be to have the letters found with address tags contradicting their explicit salutations! However, the minimalist hypothesis only weakly suggests a reason why María Micaela would have used multiple colors.

Even if the cord message itself was minimal, the incident remains significant and intriguing. It shows that cords did function as a vehicle of inner process within peasants' own polities, and outside the reach of the scribal ascendancy. It shows that circa 1750, the khipu art not only persisted, but was known in a wide communicative universe that included humble social strata and both sexes. "The people called Indians" had by that date built factional and local alliances across ethnic boundaries, and against enemies on their own side of the ethnic fence. "Indian rebellion" did preach pro-"Indian" ideology as an alternative to interethnic dependency. Yet both sorts of political practice—anti-Spanish nativistic practice, and interethnic alliance practice—depended on intimately Indian cultural competence. A cultural divide was indeed in play, but it inhered in techniques of political behavior rather than in the resulting strategic blocs. An indigenous channel, maintaining a margin of intellectual autonomy from the interethnically transparent medium of writing, apparently survived the failure of all the insurgencies.

The defeat of Francisco Ximénez Ynga, of Juan Santos Atahualpa, and, three decades later, of the vastly more powerful southern neo-Inka leaders, brought an end to the age when hereditary native nobles were the key political actors. We are only now beginning to glimpse the emergence of successor organizations. As for the place of khipus and letters in these successors, lack of research still forbids any generalization. Urton sums up a consensus in saying that "during the eighteenth and nineteenth centuries . . . the arts of *quipu*-making and reading had clearly become 'disestablished'—i.e., eliminated from the practices of record-keeping among native officials" (in press).

From the late eighteenth through early twentieth centuries, Peru has yielded only faint evidence on cord-record practices at the village level, and few if any from Huarochirí. In the mid-nineteenth century, Mariano Rivero observed that herders in the south highlands were recording flocks on cords. Parishes used "khipus . . . attached to a panel with a register of the inhabitants," the cords being used to signal their absences from religious lessons (Sempat Assadourian 2002:136). Such hybrid tablet-khipus apparently enjoyed wide usage. They are documented from the Huarochirí area by Julio Tello and Próspero Miranda (1923:508, 534); from Mangas, Cajatambo, by Román Robles Mendoza (1990 [1982]); and earlier, less clearly, from the north coast by Baltasar Martínez Compañón y Bujalda (1985 [c. 1779–89]:5.2:53–54). "Ethnographic khipus" registered in the southern Andes from the early twentieth century onward have already been discussed.

Of the ethnographic examples, the most relevant to the Tupicochan data is Ruiz Estrada's unfortunately short report (1990) on a huge khipu which the central-Peruvian village of Rapaz holds as a holy civic patrimony. Its date is unknown. When observed, its function and origin had seemingly passed from memory, as in Tupicocha. The Tupicocha quipocamayos seem to fit somewhere in the same late and obscure transition from attested colonial khipus to ethnographically observed modern ones. But the gigantic size of the Rapaz specimen suggests that it aggregated a far greater data set. Perhaps it was an all-ayllu, village-totaling document at a level which Tupicocha lost.

The Chronological Problem of Tupicocha's Quipocamayos

No local person seems to have a definite opinion about how old the cord records are. If asked why their village has kept what other villages lost, Tupicochans say that when Chileans attacked neighboring Tuna and set it afire (a documented incident in the War of the Pacific; Sotelo 1942:69–77), Tupicocha cached its regalia in a cave. Beyond that, the quipocamayos seem to them simply immemorial. Nothing in the village's impressive stores of historic documentation (see chapters 6–8) reveals when the present quipocamayos were made, though many documents from 1876 on mention their existence.

Because quipocamayos shed some shreds in storage (they are held loose in plastic bags), and because the ayllus gave permission to take the few hairs needed for radiocarbon dating,[37] it has been possible to date shreds which are apparently parts of three quipocamayos (UCh-02, M-01, and C-01).[38] The results, however, are not as easy to interpret as pre-Hispanic archaeological dates. The reason is that ten of thirteen fall within the three centuries starting in 1650, a period for which radiocarbon dates tend to be inherently ambiguous. In this interval, fluctuations in solar activity, in the earth's magnetic field, and in deep-space cosmic ray emissions caused the proportions of C_{12} and C_{14} in the atmosphere to "wiggle" erratically. As a result, any given proportion of isotopes within the range associated with that era corresponds to benchmark readings for more than one date. Ten individual quipocamayo samples are each made of fiber that might date to any of two or more intervals within the 1650–1950 period.

With all its ambiguity, this is an important clue. It proves that at least some of the cords composing these three artifacts definitely postdate the period when Spanish colonial officialdom left khipus behind. So we must greatly extend our estimate of the period when conspicuously "Inka"-looking khipu work was done. At a minimum we must extend it far into the middle colonial era, a time when cord reckoning has previously been thought to subside into simplified herd-keeping form.

But can we get any closer to the actual date when villagers made these specimens? The radiocarbon chemist David McJunkin and his associate Melanie Edwards have devised a probabilistic method of working with sets of samples which individually yield multiple dates of approximately equal probability. They work with the assumption that if the samples as an ensemble in reality date to a single unknown interval, but each yield multiple possible dates in radiocarbon profile, then the date range which they as a group yield most frequently is more likely to be their collective or average period of origin than the various date ranges which they as a group yield more sporadically. This is a novel inference, not a part of the radiocarbon canon, and is not offered as any more than a suggestion for how to prioritize interpretations among results that remain ambiguous. Using this inference, McJunkin and Edwards suggest that the ten samples not containing "bomb carbon" are more likely to have originated in the nineteenth century than in other centuries.[39] The collective tendency of their possible date ranges suggest years near 1870 as the likeliest overall time of production. That is, the period shortly before Peru's War of the Pacific shows up as a suspected interval of origin significantly more often than do the other possible intervals, which include both earlier and later dates. This does not define when the quipocamayo-making complex as a whole began or ended. It only implies that enough quipocamayo activity took place during the late nineteenth century to show up heavily in shred samples. (NB, on the assumption that new cords are less likely to shred than old ones, the shred sample seems biased against showing late activity. We will use other methods to explore the dates of the end of activity.)

The startlingly late date raises questions about articulation with alphabetic writing. By 1870 written Spanish was long since omnipresent in the Huarochirí countryside. In fact, as chapter 7 will show, it was not only present as the imprint of outside authority, but lay well within the competence of many peasants. Are there, then, any points of articulation between the cord and paper records? Mújica ayllu in Tupicocha started to write books of records just before the War of the Pacific, and ayllus in general began to keep written inventories of corporately owned goods starting around the turn of the twentieth century. Mújica's oldest book (APM/SAT s/n f. 3r) in 1897 already inventories the quipocamayos as artifacts "de anterior" (of former [times]). It is hard to guess how far back "former" meant to the writers. But the short interval between a likely date of active khipu use and the rise of intra-ayllu writing makes it likely that ayllus began writing books at a time when cord-media competence had not disappeared. Since the 1870 estimate only suggests a year within a radiocarbon interval that extends well past the onset of intra-ayllu writing, the two eras may have overlapped.

As for three radiocarbon dates which lie outside the 1650–1950 era, they are very late. One (WG454) comes from unidentified fallen fibers of the Unión Chaucacolca ayllu's UCH-02, a deteriorated specimen kept out of ceremonial service. It measures 1959 plus or minus two years at one standard deviation. The others (WG521, WG522) come from pendants 48 and 66 of Mújica ayllu's M-01, the "freshest"-looking quipocamayo. They measure respectively 1990 and 1979, both with the same two-year margins.

These late dates are unlikely to be erroneous, because they fall within the era of "bomb carbon," which yields secure chronology. They suggest that quipocamayo activity continued very recently. But what kind of activity? Should we suppose a quipocamayo art exists today in clandestinity?

Modern fiber on a quipocamayo does not necessarily come from acts of competent quipocamayo inscription, for two reasons. The first is that modern villagers routinely tie modern cords onto the artifact to facilitate draping at the investiture ceremony. These may be cotton shoestrings or other industrial cord (including synthetics), or homemade yarn. The other reason is curatorial behavior. A recent secretary of one ayllu admitted, with the air of vouchsafing an uncomfortable confidence, that his peers have in recent decades made repairs on the sacred artifacts. (This is detailed in chapter 9.) Indeed it would be surprising had they not, for quipocamayos show substantial wear and tear from year to year. Officers would hesitate to hand on a noticeably worsened quipocamayo.

One way to check on the repair hypothesis is by referring to fiber content. The samples from the quipocamayos, according the Richard Bisbing, a fiber identification specialist, are mostly of camelid wool. Tupicochans today do not have any llamas or alpacas. Given the village's intense cultural focus on agropastoral know-how, it is highly unlikely that such an important fact as camelid herding would be quickly forgotten. Elders consistently say their grandparents wore alpaca clothes but did not produce the fiber. They do not remember a time when the Tupicochans herded camelids; nor do they say their own elders spoke of owning any. Oral tradition seems to preserve identifiable events for about a century, and documents about pasture usage match this testimony. An oral tradition says that circa 1860–80, Tupicochanos hunted and killed the last feral remnants of old herds. They do own a substantial number of sheep. So it makes sense that new local materials added to quipocamayos in the last century or so would be of noncamelid fiber. The fiber content of WG454 is unknown, but WG521 and WG522 do come from cords which appear to be of sheep's wool. So curatorial behavior is a plausible explanation for the presence of modern fiber.

Many quipocamayos contain obvious repairs, and indeed their obviousness (e.g., tying a pendant onto a main cord with an overhand knot instead of the normal half-hitch) may reflect a preference for repairs that cannot be mistaken for falsifications. Most are matters of mending or reattaching fallen camelid-fiber cords. Sometimes cords missing their proper attachments seem to have been tied onto the end of the main cord as a means of conservation. (M-02 may have several such.) Chapter 9 discusses the possibility that M-01, with late dates and sheep-wool components, is a replica or heavily reworked restoration.

When, then, did the quipocamayo art die out in Tupicocha? The beginning of the quipocamayo-making era presumably belongs to Inka or pre-Inka times, but its end seems to have been recent. As is discussed in chapter 8, the grandfather of several men now living in Primera Satafasca ayllu is widely said to have been the last to understand the art, but the descriptions of his "readings" are vague. Silvano Rojas, aged seventy-six in 1994, said his grandparent's generation was the last to understand the cords. He would be speaking of the generation which was born about 1875 and which would have reached its sixties in the 1930s. This accords with most local opinion of elder men. Such elders would have grown up in contact with khipu-competent holders of cords made late in the nineteenth century, and carried that competence onward with declining productivity into the twentieth century.

In one case, a Tupicochan was able to associate the making of a khipu with a specific date, namely, 1914. That man, an elder of Chaucacolca, says his mother recalled working at top speed on a new quipocamayo, in haste because she felt labor coming close. She finished it just three days before the teller's birth, which the teller recalls as 1914. While unverifiable, this memory does have the ring of truth. It is not a genre stereotype. Does the testimony mean women were authors of cord records? Women today are the main spinners of yarn, but elder women, when asked about whether they had seen their mothers work quipocamayos, deny it. Perhaps women in the age of quipocamayo use provided cords — which were not "raw material" but material with much data value already encoded — while men knotted cords and mounted them.

An additional clue to the erosion of quipocamayo competence comes from the phenomenon of ayllu fission. Before fission, ayllus always inventoried their respective quipocamayos in pairs. (The function of pairing is discussed in chapters 6 and 7.) The wave of fissions which gave birth to Tupicocha's four junior ayllus (Segunda Allauca, Segunda Satafasca, Centro Huangre, and Huangre Boys) began in the 1920s. At that time quipocamayos were thought necessary to the legitimacy of an ayllu, so the junior divisions of Allauca and Satafasca took along one of the parent ayllu's pair. (The junior Huangre segments do not have quipocamayos, but at the 2000 huayrona, Centro Huangre went public with a demand that its parent ayllu hand over an allegedly hidden mate to its public specimen G-01.) It is quite significant that the breakaway groups thought it suitable to own just one quipo-camayo. Neither the junior nor the parental segments felt the need (or ability?) to restore the pairedness of quipocamayos. So by this time cords are likely to have been functioning as regalia, rather than as current records. Of course it is possible that fission itself is what put an end to their recording functions. If so, the ayllus which did not split—Chaucacolca, Mújica, and Cacarima—could have kept the dual-quipocamayo regimen alive longer. But this does not seem to be the case; none of these dispute the fact that the divided ayllus Allauca and Satafasca retained cord expertise longer than others.

On quipocamayo 1SF-01, pendants 23–24 bear smudges of what looks like blue-black water-based ink, which suggests that someone handled them while also writing on paper at a date before the introduction of ballpoint pens (c. 1960). Satafasca members agree that it is the kind of ink formerly used to write their ayllu books. Satafasca began writing books in the 1910s and inventoried no papers older than its books. Perhaps, then, around 1910–60 the cords were still handled together with books on the same table, that is, the table for writing acts, which forms part of every meeting and ceremony. However, the latter part of this range is unlikely, because by the 1920s members inventoried quipocamayos together with the "cloth-ing of the cross" and other liturgical "ornaments," rather than with books. Today liturgical ornaments are not put on the recording table. From 1913 through 1921, undivided Satafasca wrote inventory entries for its "pair of quipocamayo with its markers [motas]" (e.g., AP1SF_01 1918a:17), but from 1922 on, the markers fell be-neath notice (AP1SF_01 1922:35), suggesting that only the object as a whole was perceived as significant. These facts reinforce the idea that quipocamayos were regalia rather than records during the 1920s.

Given these findings, the period that seems likely to have witnessed the waning of the general quipocamayo regimen—the communitywide standard which re-quired all parcialidades to maintain cord records and share them at the huay-rona—seems to be roughly the one extending from the War of the Pacific (which began in 1879) to the beginning of President Augusto Leguía's eleven-year near-dictatorship (1919). The generation which came of age around the wartime appar-ently used quipocamayos in full competence. The generation that matured after it was perhaps the last to have competence and the first to begin relinquishing it. Those born about 1890–1900 would have made their civic-political careers in the Leguía years, a time when ayllus strove to adopt modern forms and abandon old ones. As they replaced the term camachico with presidente, so they may have been pleased to leave cord use behind. However, fragmented or unofficial knowledge of the art would have lingered quite a while longer, for the generation born before 1890 had living members as late as the 1960s. In chapter 8 we examine a family in which this generation's lore was fragmentarily passed on. Even assuming that no younger people learned the method for official purposes, it is credible that the last people with some inherited knowledge of quipocamayo were still alive in the early 1980s, as villagers assert.

It may be significant that despite fission, the ayllus of highest ritual rank were the most conservative of khipu lore. Primera Allauca is the first of the kinship groups in ritual rank. In the normal Andean scheme, it would have held the extinct hereditary chiefdom (kuraka lordship). If one had to guess which corporation might be more tenacious about Andean protocol, Primera Allauca would be the first guess. And indeed, it was not only the last ayllu to commit its internal deliberations to books but also the only one which saw the details of its cords as worth recording. From 1958 to 1974, Primera Allauca described, as opposed to merely inventorying, its "quipo Camayo emblem of this parcialidad." In 1958 it mentioned that the object "with its *frontales*" had "a hundred and eleven points" (AP1A/SAT_01 1958:23). The term *frontal* today refers to cloth draped so as to hang over the front of something, for example, an altar. It may mean "pendants" as draped on the body. In 1959, Primera Allauca specified 123 "points" (puntos) and also "its 5 balls" (*bolas*, perhaps meaning "markers"?; AP1A/SAT_01 1959a:29). From 1960 through 1966, the number of points was reported as varying slightly. From 1967 through 1969 the number was unrecorded, and from 1970 to 1974 it stayed constant at 118. The word *punto* is not now in quipocamayo use, and these numbers do not match the 1995 number of pendants (106). The term *punto* now commonly means "stitch." In the 1970s and earlier mentions, it apparently means "attachment," that is, attachment loop. It makes sense that this would be taken as the initial counting variable because counting bottom ends of cords confuses pendants with subsidiaries. Quipocamayo 1A-01 has stretches of bare main cord long enough to have accommodated the maximum number recorded, 125 in 1962, with a close fit.

The important point is that Primera Allauca still thought it important to report the data state of their knot record as long as their last experts lived. What is more, from 1958 through 1966 they perceived change in that state. Whether the change is due to inaccurate counting, or to real alterations, is a point on which no one claims knowledge. But it is credible, just barely, that until 1966 someone was still updating something on a quipocamayo. Assuming this person had been born circa 1900–10, and thus a "last chance" learner of cord lore, he would have become a pasivo, or semiretired member, toward 1966. Retirees do not write records, so the date of cessation in punto change is understandable. In 1970 someone continued the custom of recording points, but by this time updating had ceased. Indeed, since 1968 entries specify that the quipocamayo was kept *de recuerdo tradicional* ('as a traditional memento') or *de recuerdo de años anteriores* ('as a memento of former years'). From 1973 on, it is described as *de los antipasados* [*sic*] ('of the ancestors').

Could Tupicocha's Quipocamayos Be "Reinventions"?

The span of possible radiocarbon dates for Tupicochan specimens covers not one but two periods during which Peruvians "reinvented" the pre-Hispanic past. The first was the peak era of neo-Inka rebellions, around 1742–83 (Sala i Villa 1996).[40]

The second was the heyday of modern indigenism, around 1909–46.[41] It seems only prudent, then, to consider the likelihood that at some point the cord art was reintroduced as part of a conscious harking back to prehistory.

As we saw in the section "A Late-Colonial Episode of Rebellion, Ethnicity, and Media Pluralism," in 1750 Tupicocha was close to the heart of a short-lived but intense anti-Spanish uprising in which Inka motifs played some part and khipus a clear-cut role. The period leading up to the neo-Inka revolts of the 1750s–1780s was also a period of "reinvention," when rural and urban elites enthusiastically displayed images of Peru's golden Inka age in artifacts from rugs to parade floats (Fane 1996). It is not impossible that the 1750 movement electrified old forms of native knowledge with new political meaning. But if so, María Chinchano's making of khipus as described above could hardly have been the innovative work of the political moment alone, because the whole narrative presumes a preexisting general pool of cord competence. As in other rebellions, neo-Inkaism was the characteristic position of urbanized native elites in search of rural clienteles. It is most unlikely that an urbanite such as Francisco Ximénez Ynga could have conjured Inka data technology back into being during his brief, tragic campaign.

The other great wave of "reinvented" Inka lore corresponds to Peruvian indigenism. For the most part, Peruvian indigenism was a matter of "indigenism without Indians." It attracted provincial urban elites interested in attaching the mystique of the Inkas to their cities, artistic cliques, or factions, and also attracted politicans interested in packaging state social control as betterment of the race. For still others, indigenism meant meliorist outreach to pariah sectors, or an attempt to reinvent socialist revolution as a rebirth of aboriginal communalism, or a semiracialist nationalism imitative of Mexico. For some time, particularly during the 1920s ascendancy of the "Tawantinsuyu Committee for Indigenous Rights," radical peasant activists themselves also took on an ethnically conscious agenda (De la Cadena 2000:89–118). Indigenism stimulated a regional ferment of Inka nostalgia in Cuzco and Puno, starting in the 1900s, and fomented a would-be-scientific archaeology by 1920. The regionalist indigenisms of highland regions, and the assimilationist indigenism of metropolitan Lima elites, both influenced the countryside via public schooling from the 1920s through the 1950s, and to a lesser extent still do so.

Is it possible that rather than prolonging a deep-rooted local tradition, Tupicocha imitated ancient khipus as part of a campaign to have itself included as part of an "authentic" Peru? After all, the archaeologist Tello and his assistants, who passed through Tupicocha at least once during this period, had the opportunity to stimulate interest in prehistory. This might have come in handy for political purposes during the age when "Inka" pageantry returned to national fashion.

This strong version of a "reinvention" thesis does not hold water. First, as we have seen, the oldest written references to khipus as patrimony (in ayllu Mújica, 1897, cited in APM/SAT_01 1897:f. non num. 3v) predate Tello's visits. Tello was seventeen at the time of this reference, and was living in Lima. Even if he had shown up in some undocumented trip as a young traveler, he would hardly have been in a position to revolutionize the workings of six proud and deep-rooted ayllus. His archaeological incursions into central-Huarochirí burial caves apparently started informally in 1907. The curator of Hrdlička-Tello holdings at Harvard, which include the material the two removed in 1913, reports that holdings do not include khipus or reports of any such in their context.[42] Tello is remembered in a good many oral traditions of San Damián, and although memories emphasize his aggressive emptying of burial caves—still shocking to local sensibilities—they do not mention quipocamayos, the village of Tupicocha, or any reinvention lore.

Second, Tupicocha's specimens hugely overshoot the mark of "reinvention." Compared with most archaeological specimens, they are not sketchy likenesses but a remarkably complete high-quality corpus. They show a maximal and accomplished knowledge of khipu technology. One may tellingly contrast them with known or suspected reinventions: the showy but coarsely made pseudo-khipus used for indigenist pageantry in Cuzco, or the simulacra that schoolteachers and students make for pageants, or the embarrassingly crude specimen proffered by Carlo Animato, Paolo Rossi, and Clara Miccinelli (1989) as a purported remnant of a royal khipu.

Third, Tupicocha's specimens include materials and techniques not known from ancient examples and not in accord with modern notions of Inka material culture (e.g., use of handmade flat-wire metallic windings). Such features would be pointless for a reinvention since they would disagree with popular notions of "authenticity."

Fourth, indigenism is itself so closely linked to writing—indeed it first arose as a literary and social-scientific project, and always advocated "alphabetization"— that it is highly unlikely such a dramatic, indigenist change of events as the inauguration of new ayllu insignia would fail to leave a written trace, especially in a village where writing already abounded. By the indigenist years even very minor Tupicochan events were written up locally. Quite apart from glorification, by the 1920s such a large venture would have needed intravillage documentation if only because villagers expected proofs of work done for civic purposes, or payment for services. Those ayllu actions which appear related to the official indigenism of President Augusto Leguía's regime (1919–30), such as reformed ayllu constitutions, did take written form, and do bear verbal traces of indigenist ideology. But they do not mention quipocamayos.

Could a weaker version of a reinvention thesis explain the facts? As for how the remarkably conservative technology of Tupicocha's khipus survived, we cannot discard the possibility that the living khipu tradition was at some phase renewed in a dialogue with archaeological sites themselves. In pre-Hispanic times, khipus were placed with the venerated dead. In 1561 Polo de Ondegardo saw the great Inka Pachakuti, mummified, with his cord records still on his body (Julien 2000:129).

Since mummies periodically came out of their shrines to be feted by living descendants, it is entirely possible that a folk "archaeology" — that is, a cultivated attempt to interpret the past on the basis of that past's own codes — was part of the routine ritual competence of early- or mid-colonial Andean peoples. It is true that in the middle seventeenth century, when the extirpationist church so infamously busied itself with killing the dead, Huarochirí suffered the burning of thousands of mummies.

But even today intact ones are occasionally found, and they are still respected. We do not know the last date at which proper local ancestor cult was practiced. (In other parts of Peru, it still occurred clandestinely c. 1750.) Since ayllu consciousness was expressed around the motif of faithful descent from ancestors, it is worth considering the possibility that at some probably remote date, ancestor veneration formed a "school" in which the ancients reminded their descendants of the art. Urton has made a strong case (2001) that colonial villagers used khipus in mummy-cave context as sources of benchmark data. In 1994, a villager suggested that the mode of donning quipocamayos was perhaps inspired by the fact that mummies are often wrapped with cordage: "The *gentiles* . . . had bands or sashes on their chests as government officials do."

In making this remark, the villager was likening the ancient milieus and techniques of khipu curation to modern ones. The modern ones are Tupicocha's peculiar claim to importance in the history of Andean media. It is to this tradition of quipocamayo curation, and to the material patrimony it protects, that we turn next.

THE PATRIMONIAL QUIPOCAMAYOS

OF TUPICOCHA

THE PATH toward context-enriched khipu study begins at the civic ritual plaza (Collca), where cord records go on public view once a year. Once we have sketched this display, we will "zoom in" on the objects themselves, studying typology and physical characteristics. At the close we will "zoom" back out to ask how material properties of the cords are related to the social agenda which they dignify.

This chapter begins the analysis of specific features. The next two chapters also concern relations between social practice and specific features. To prevent the exposition from becoming confusing, a general schematic or Key Figure of these attributes, above and beyond the Lockean model, is presented as figure 26 (shown later in the chapter). Readers may want to bookmark the Key Figure for continuing reference.

Huayrona and Modern Quipocamayo Display

Chapter 3, in particular the closing section, mentions the 2–3 January huayrona, or civic plenum, when citizens hold outgoing officers responsible for the past year's work, install newly elected officers, and listen to reports by visiting dignitaries. (Since 2000 it has been compacted to a single day.) We are concerned only with one aspect of this intricate spectacle, namely, its function as the hinge of articulation between ayllu/parcialidad and communitywide authority.

The meeting takes place at a ceremonial complex called the Collca, also called the Casa de Costumbre, or "House of Customary Law." The name comes from

Quechua *qullka*, meaning "storehouse." It really did function as a storehouse until into the twentieth century. Ayllus used to bring quotas of their harvest there for storage until it was time to cook and brew for communitywide feasts. The actual deposits were two strips of rooms with doors opening onto a ceremonial plaza from opposite sides (see fig. 17).

In this respect the Collca reminds one of the ceremonial and storage centers known from Inka archaeology (Morris and Thompson 1985:97–108; LeVine 1993). The act of displaying the khipus to higher political authority while standing between the two strips of storage rooms brings strikingly to life Guaman Poma's famous drawing of an Inka cord master doing something similar (see fig. 18).

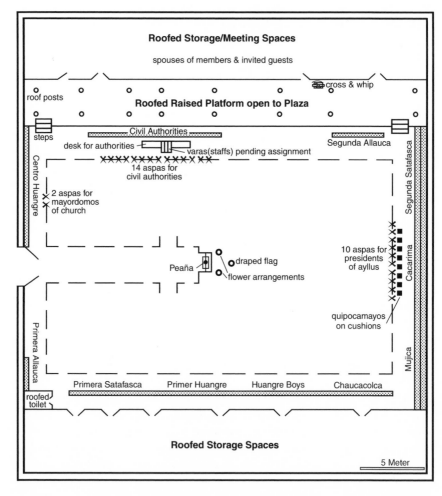

FIGURE 17 Schematic ground plan of the Collca ("Storehouse") or Casa de Costumbre ("House of Customary Law") in Tupicocha, 1995–97. From personal collection of author.

FIGURE 18 Felipe Guaman Poma de Ayala's famous drawing of an Inka *qullka* shows an "administrator" displaying a khipu to his ruler between two rows of storehouses (Guaman Poma 1980 [1615]:309). Tupicochan practice bears a resemblance in conducting political inspection of cords between two lines of storage cells. By permission of the Royal Library of Denmark.

In architectural detail the storage resembles what Guaman Poma de Ayala (1980 [1615]:754, fig. 19) called "comunidad o sapçi," that is, a colonial-indigenous deposit for common welfare. Despite its resemblance to certain ancient ceremonial-cum-storage structures (Topic and Chiswell 1993:214–17), Tupicocha's Collca (see fig. 20) is far from ancient. In fact the Collca is frequently modified, most recently by the addition of a hangarlike roof and steel gates in 1998. This modern Collca is actually a replacement built circa 1937 to replace what is now called the Collca of Santa Clara, a similar but smaller structure adjoining the civic plaza. Tuna, Pacota, and other villages have roughly similar collcas.

When the huayrona assembles, the three main hierarchies of local officials sit shoulder to shoulder in a long line down the *tribunal*, or head table, which is set up along one row of warehouses, facing the plaza. The tribunal thus consists of three subarrays: the community authorities, the national and municipal authorities, and the vara (staff-bearing) lesser officers. The church mayordomos, sacristan, and catechist sit close by to one side. Representatives of the Ministerial agencies (the health post and the school) are also supposed to attend. The raised platform behind the officers' shoulders (i.e., the same platform on which one line of storage cells is built) is available to out-of-town guests, and also to wives and daughters of the officers, whose bright-striped shawls and wide straw hats add splashes of color to the sobersided tribunal.

The great plaza has a sacred center: a peaña or small pyramid-based cross adorned with the national flag and the whip of civic discipline. On New Year's Day, vara officers demarcate the sacred space around it with bunches of fresh grass from the puna (*guayllabanas, catahuas, uywanes*) laid out as a series of rayas (lines) and aspas (X's). The lines, X's, and peañas are the same signary used on the staff insignia which chapter 4 details, and could be taken as a summation of their authority. Only staff-bearing officers may step into the sacred space. Everyone else must enter the huayrona by advancing to the cross along the grass-demarcated middle avenue. Each curtsies on one foot while tipping the hat (a gesture called *venia*), then retreats along the avenue and tracks along the outside of the sacred perimeter to his or her seat. Each entering comunero goes to the seating area reserved for his or her ayllu, as shown in figure 17. Ideally, ayllus sit in their standard order of precedence, but in practice they exchange benches so as to fit attendance.

On the afternoon of 2 January or the morning of 3 January—that is, in the interval between huayrona sessions, a liminal period between the extinction of the old hierarchy and the inauguration of the new—each ayllu meets formally to choose its incoming officers. When the huayrona reconvenes, each ayllu separately marches in procession to the Collca amid as much pomp and musical fanfare as it can muster. The ten kin corporations wind in and out of the village's streets in a tangled dance of processions, each following its hypnotically repeated anthem to houses whose owners have pledged or provided gifts. When these benefactors of the ayllu have enjoyed their honors with a dance, and have reciprocated with

ADMINISTRA DORES

TINEEN TEIPROTETOR

capac apo suyoyoccona

depocito
delacomuni
uadysapci-

enes de reyno   capac

FIGURE 19   Guaman Poma drew a colonial community welfare deposit, or *sapçi*, similar in design to the storage areas of today's Collcas: a secured cell on a raised platform inside a larger structure (1980 [1615]:754). By permission of the Royal Library of Denmark.

FIGURE 20   In 1998, the Community put up a new, overarching roof onto the Collca plaza, which entailed removing the old roof of the "House of Customary Law." Construction revealed warehouse cells of the Collca. From personal collection of author.

rounds of drinks, the ten corporations snake their way to the Collca gate. Staff-holding officers usher them to their customary seats. The outgoing and incoming presidents of ayllus, however, do not sit with their ayllu mates. They head instead for a special bench along the wall opposite the gate. There they wait for their moment of glory while the plenum grinds through its long agenda.

The morning of the second huayrona session is the moment at which the quipo-camayos are taken from safekeeping to greet the public. Each outgoing president of a quipocamayo-owning ayllu works with at least one senior man to prepare it for display.[1]

The mode of preparation, which involves twisting the quipocamayo into a spiral, shows startling continuity with the pre-Hispanic and the colonial record. It exactly matches that which Conklin documented in a pioneering 1982 study (see fig. 21). This preparation served the Inkas for storage and transport (Conklin 1982: fig. 2). The Tupicochan method also exactly matches Guaman Poma de Ayala's drawing of a khipu (fig. 22) coiled for Inka use. And it likewise matches the superbly conserved Inka example Arellano (1999:224) reproduces.

Today villagers do not coil quipocamayos for storage but store them loose in bags (to their detriment) and only coil them for the huayrona. In plates 2 and 3 and in figures 23 and 24, members practice the technique. These men are not familiar with any studies of khipus or museum holdings and report learning quipocamayo practice only from their elders. The persistence of the technique suggests that active khipu use skills survived into a relatively recent generation.

First, one takes the quipocamayo from its storage bag and untangles it. This takes considerable patience as one must be careful not to tug on the often frayed pendants. Unlike museum curators, Tupicochans never lay quipocamayos out on tables. Some appeared surprised to see me do so. This has to do with a social habit of handling the cords. Laying a khipu out is the only way for a single person to

FIGURE 21   An Inka khipu rolled for storage. By permission of William Conklin (Conklin [1982:264]).

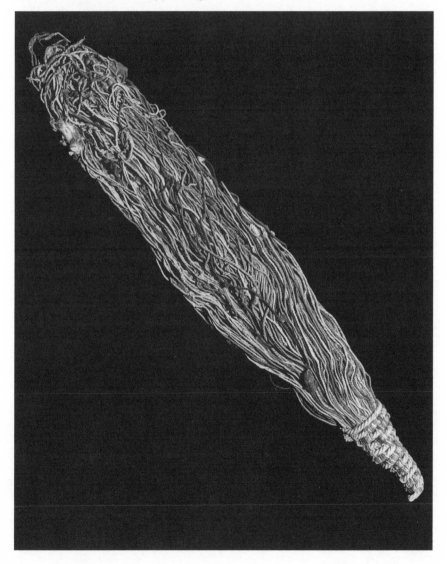

FIGURE 22   Felipe Guaman Poma's "Provincial Administrator" carries a pair of khipus with matching end knobs. One is still in rolled storage position, but with its binding released for use (1980 [1615]:320). By permission of the Royal Library of Denmark.

FIGURE 23   The long "tail" of the main cord serves to bind the pendants. From personal collection of author.

FIGURE 24   The rolled quipocamayo (2SF-01) is tied into a single huge overhand knot. From personal collection of author.

study it. But Tupicochanos never do handle them in solitude. Quipocamayo work is always done four-handed: one person holds the ends of the main cord while another arranges the pendant cords. If this continues ancient practice, the practice seems a testimony to the profoundly social, rather than individually authorial, work of the quipocamayo master.

When all pendants hang parallel from the horizontally extended main cord, the quipocamayo is said to be *peinado* (combed). Again in four-handed partnership, the handlers now coil the main cord into a spiral from which all the pendants hang parallel, in a close column (see plate 2). The long "tail" of the main cord is helically wound downward about the outside of the columnar bundle, so as to make a sort of floppy fasces. The main cord's end is then tucked into itself on the last turn, so as to stabilize the bundle (see fig. 23).

Up to this point, the quipocamayo matches ancient storage and transport configurations. Arellano (1999:226) synthesizes findings of Alberto Bueno, Carmen Beatriz Loza, and Carlos Radicati to suggest that the plumed bulb of the wound khipu that projected from its storage bag—for example, in the "archive" of khipus attested as existing in houses of Andean lords—functioned to identify the khipu. I would suggest further that the helix of main cord visible below the plumed bulb, but above the pendants, served as a table of contents. The attachment loops (and perhaps to a trained eye their directionality) are visible without unwinding. By noting colors and other cord qualities, the user could tell what materials were on the khipu, and in what order, so that he could turn to the relevant part immediately when the cord was unrolled.

The final stages of modern practice, however, do not resemble archaeological practice. The two handlers, each holding one end of the rolled quipocamayo, twist the whole thing so that the pendants become a single thick cable.[2] This cable is called a *culebra*, or serpent, and snake metaphors are half-jokingly applied to it when torque causes it to writhe: "It's fighting back, it has plenty of life."[3] The last stage is to tie the entire "snake" into a single giant overhand knot. The presumption is said to have come out well if the large knob of the main cord protrudes pointing vigorously upward at the top. This positioning is called *cerro* (mountain) or *peaña* (see fig. 24). The quipocamayo is now ready for display. The handlers place it on a colorful cushion or pad of folded cloth, often a woman's carrying cloth or a mantle embroidered by a woman. It rides in a place of high honor as the ayllu troops off to the civic meeting. On entering the consecrated square, each ayllu places its quipocamayo at the spot corresponding to ayllu rank, as marked with grass X's, or *aspas* (see plate 3).

On the mid-afternoon of the second huayrona day, when the plenum has finished its agenda, the tribunal of officers signals the outgoing presidents of sectors to invest their successors with their regalia of office. These regalia are the quipocamayos themselves. Like the staff rituals described in chapter 4, this procedure is wordless. The outgoing president lifts the displayed quipocamayo, unknots and uncoils it with a cohandler's help, then stands behind his successor. He drapes it over the new president from left shoulder to right hip with the knob end at the shoulder. He then ties the other end up the back to the knob end. As of this moment, the political apparatus is renewed (see plate 4). The act of donning the quipocamayo has performative force. As an outsider, I found it quite striking that this most revered legacy is accompanied by no verbal cues or formulas at all, much less by free commentary or metalanguage, even though the meeting as a whole is verbose to an extreme. This is as one might expect if segregation between inscription and speech applied to khipus.

As the new officials parade past the tribunal, the ritual context dissolves. First the presidents, then all the celebrants pick up bunches of the auspicious grass that marked the huayrona, and carry them out to the "family reunions," actually ayllu-sponsored feasts,[4] which bring the day to a convivial close. The quipocamayos will make a few other brief appearances during the New Year ritual cycle: at the first meeting of the Community Directorate (see color plate 5), and at the occasions when the directorate receives visits from the curcuches, or sacred clowns, during 5–8 January. In 1999 quipocamayos came out for the Patriotic Festival, 28 July, but I was told this was done mostly to please me. Sunday-supplement journalism which promotes Tupicocha as a touring venue usually shows the quipocamayos, and this is creating incentives for more exhibition. Normally and traditionally, however, they rest in safekeeping at secure places chosen by the respective ayllu presidents.

What do modern Tupicochans think about the global import of the ceremony? All know that their quipocamayos are a peculiar local treasure. No nearby village has similar objects. The former sense of the term *quipocamayo* as the title of a cord master (from khipu "knot," plus the Quechua *kamayuq*, meaning a person having a special area of responsibility and mastery) is no longer remembered. No living person in Tupicocha claims ability to read or make quipocamayos. If one asks what quipocamayos mean, common answers are, for example, "They contain the laws; they say what the camachico [ayllu president] must do." "They're like an almanac. The days, the harvests are in there, everything. Whether it will be a good year or not." "They're writings. Every knot is a letter. They have an alphabet." "They're our Magna Carta. The foundation, the Constitution." Other glosses are "a credential," "an insignia," "a [law] code." Some say that the reading of quipocamayos is or was an art of augury, like telling fortunes with a deck of cards (see chapter 8). Although Tupicochans learn in school that the Inkas made cord records, they do not regard their quipocamayos as Inka artifacts. Far from recalling the glories of Cuzco, these objects stand emphatically for local autochthony. No one is allowed to alter them except for preservation purposes.

The future of the patrimony looks uncertain. A few people say such things as "This will all come to an end when we get electricity," because they think nobody will want to spare TV-watching time for the intricate regimen called "custom."

Faced with this self-fulfilling pessimism, one political faction wants to take the quipocamayos away from the ayllus and put them in safekeeping in the municipality, releasing them only for the huayrona. Others say such a breach of customary law would lead to their disactivation and expose them to theft.

The meeting's name, huayrona, poses an interesting question. Locally, it is considered etymologically opaque. Until 1935 — the year of state recognition, which brought changes toward modern bureaucratic forms — a ritual game called *huayra huayra pichcamanta* used to follow the act of investiture. Tupicocha's annex of Pacota inherited the game and still plays it at the end of its huayrona (see fig. 25). Huayra Huayra (or Huira Huira) Pichcamanta is a variant of the pre-Hispanically rooted,[5] pan-Andean game known as *la pichca* or *wayru* (Gentile Lafaille 1998; Salomon 2002a). In Pacota, the opposing teams consist of the incoming and the outgoing officers. Teams take turns throwing two large dice in the form of truncated pyramids, called "male" and "female." The thrower tries to make the die come to rest in a standing position. As he pitches or bowls the die, he shouts, "Huayra huayra pichcamanta!"[6] The way the dice stand or fall gives an augury about where the divine "owners" of rain will send it during the coming agricultural cycle. The name huayrona is probably a Hispano-Quechua variant of *wayruna*, which by normal Quechua morphology would mean 'huayru-playing occasion.' Until 1935 the quipocamayos apparently formed part of the regalia associated with this game. For reasons explained in the next section, the ritual opposition of incoming and outgoing officers echoes the former functioning of paired quipocamayos.

Physical Characteristics and Local Terminology of Tupicocha's Quipocamayos

Radicati di Primeglio (1979[?]:52–56) wrote a blanket verdict of irrelevance on ethnographic khipus, which he considered so deviant from ancient norms as not really to be khipus at all. Works postdating Mackey (1970) generally abstain from ethnographic comparison. Urton (2003:48–53) judges Tupicochan specimens and colonial examples from Sacaca (Bolivia) unlikely to be relevant to pre-Columbian record keeping. But the Tupicochan specimens do embody nearly all pre-Hispanic conventions, as well as some others. In the Conclusions chapter, I will return to their possible use as heuristics for archaeological decipherment.

By looking at the parts of Tupicochan specimens, one can identify likenesses to, and differences from, Lockean or classically Inka constructions. Performing this job in the presence of Tupicochans makes it possible, additionally, to do a little bit of what Locke could not do at all, namely, learn how quipocamayo owners classify the parts of quipocamayos. Key Figure 26 is an ideal-type schematic synthesizing the observed features and, where known, local terms of Tupicochan quipocamayos.

FIGURE 25 Don Gregorio Javier, an elder of Pacota, throws the "male" die in the New Year's game of huayra huayra pichcamanta for 2000. Throws by incoming and outgoing teams of officers provide the augury of the new year's rainfall. From personal collection of author.

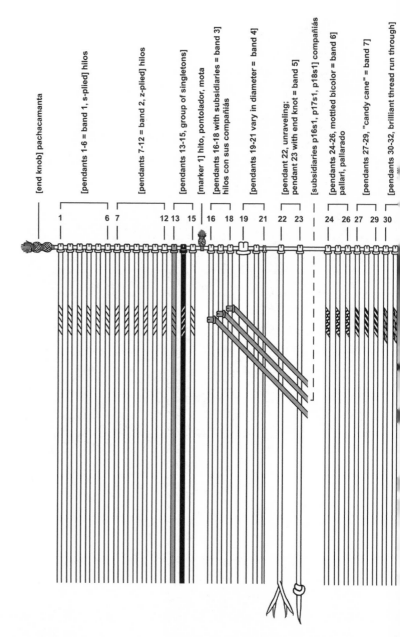

FIGURE 26 (Key Figure) Schematic structural features of Tupicochan quipocamayos. From personal collection of author.

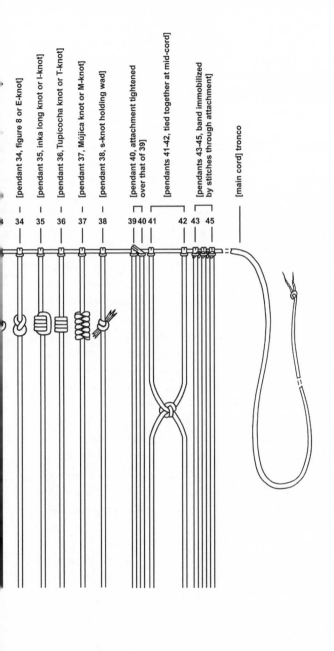

34   [pendant 34, figure 8 or E-knot]

35   [pendant 35, inka long knot or I-knot]

36   [pendant 36, Tupicocha knot or T-knot]

37   [pendant 37, Mújica knot or M-knot]

38   [pendant 38, s-knot holding wad]

39 40   [pendant 40, attachment tightened over that of 39]

41   [pendants 41–42, tied together at mid-cord]

42 43 45   [pendants 43–45, band immobilized by stitches through attachment]

[main cord] tronco

Tupicochan specimens are made wholly or almost wholly of wool (see color plate 6). The vast majority of museum khipus are made of cotton, although a few woolen museum specimens exist. At least one, specimen VA66811 of Berlin's Ethnologisches Museum, bears some likeness to Tupicochan specimens. Colonial sources (Betanzos 1987 [1551]:96; Molina 1959 [1573]:35–36) almost always describe khipus as woolen, probably implying alpaca wool. Exceptions include hair of the brocket deer (Wassén 1990 [1931]:206) and even human hair (Pereyra 1997:194). Tristan Platt (2002) associates the wool of Aymara chinu cord records with Aymara primacy in herding. Mackey too (1970:26) suggests that woolen cords may have been prevalent in the highlands (Arellano 1999:226) and that cotton prevails in modern collections only because of bias in preservation and collecting. All of Mackey's forty-two modern specimens of "herder's khipus" are woolen (Mackey 1970:133). Prochaska (1983:105) personally inspected alpaca-wool herders' khipus from Taquile Island and summarizes a perhaps unreliable description by Brauns-berger Solari of older Taquile specimens using dyed wool. The modern "confessional" khipus which some southern Bolivian girls showed to Gisbert and de Mesa (1966) were likewise of wool. When Cuzco-area highlanders speak of khipus in oral tradition context, they routinely mention wool (Valderrama, Escalante et al. 1996:57). All told, it seems that cord records by and for highland communities, including royal ones, were made of highland fiber, namely, animal fiber.

What kind of wool do Tupicochan specimens contain? An analysis of fibers found in the storage bag of Chaucacolca's second quipocamayo (UCH-02), which is not displayed in the January cycle because of its poor condition, was performed by fiber microscopist Richard Bisbing at McCrone Laboratories. It shows that the fiber is almost entirely camelid wool, more likely alpaca than llama. Cordage of varied color consists of naturally different-colored wool, but the samples also contain dyed fibers of a faintly bluish red and of a bright blue. Dyes have not been chemically identified. The blue is said by local *hilanderas* (women experienced in wool technology)[7] to be a now-disused flower dye called *azul tiñi-tiñi*. As noted above some strings on some quipocamayos look like sheep wool, notably on Mú-jica ayllu's specimen M-01, and these are discussed in chapter 9 with reference to recent curation, repair, or replacement. The only clearly cotton cords are ones attached within living memory to facilitate ceremonial draping.

GROSS DESIGN FEATURES

Tupicochan specimens are remarkably akin to Inka and other archaeological specimens in their gross features: construction of main cord, construction and attachment of markers, pendant and subsidiary attachments, relationships among component cords, construction from spinning to plying to multi-ply cordage, composition of color elements, and, with exceptions noted in the "Knot types" section, knotting. In large collections, seeming prehistoric congeners are not hard to find.

Museum specimens labeled "Inka" range in size from a few centimeters of yarn with four or five pendants up to giants with over a thousand. Within this spectrum, Tupicochan specimens are of medium size. Their main cords vary from 35 to 189 cm, but much of the variation is due to long "tails" and in one case a long "neck" (i.e., a long space between knob and pendants) rather than to the number of pendants. Complete data-bearing pendant cords (i.e., those which still have their end knots) are usually 60–80 cm. Some are as short as 40 cm, and a few are as long as 90 cm. Pendant cord lengths vary greatly within individual quipocamayos.

However, nonstandardized dimensions and other variations occur within a basically common overall design. Nine of the ten specimens are of essentially similar design, containing single-color groups, which I will call bands. The tenth, M-01, is of fundamentally different design. M-01's groups consist of sets of cords in a repeating cycle of colors. The two kinds of design are compared in detail in chapter 9.

Pendants number from 70 to 125 and average 98 if one includes the dissimilar M-01 or 101 if one excludes it.[8] Subsidiaries are usually attached at cm 0 but sometimes farther down pendants. Subsidiaries are found on 10.6 percent of pendants. Subsidiaries are completely absent on Cacarima's C-01 and Mújica's M-01.

Wool artisans today call the main cord of a quipocamayo its *tronco*, 'trunk,' and pendants its *hilos*, or 'threads.' Artisans call subsidiary cords the *compañías* ('accompaniments') of their pendants (Key Figure 26, pendants 16–18 and 16s1–18s1). The point of attachment of subsidiary to pendant is called its *empate* ('junction' in a local usage).

MARKERS

"Markers" (as they are called by the Aschers) are noncord constructions attached to cords (Key Figure 26 between pendants 15 and 16). Usually they are bound onto the main cord by lashings around it. Tupicochan quipocamayos bear markers of striking complexity, clearly indicating that the designers intended these quipocamayos to be precious objects, and also perhaps that they meant them to be identifiable when viewed from a distance, as in public ceremony. Markers utilize a different palette of colors from data cords: crimsons, yellows, greens, and blues — which are almost never found in the structural fiber of main cords or pendants. Crimson, yellow, and blue are, however, found as colors of what the Aschers call "run-through" threads: "underline" threads which parallel one or more plies of a pendant cord (Key Figure 26 pendants 30–32). The existence of two separate palettes of color suggests two levels of symbolic registry, one "meta" to the other.

The most striking markers are ornamented knobs marking one end of main cords, namely the end where the plies make their "U-turn," or in other words the end opposite the finishing knot (left extreme of Key Figure 26, and color plate 7). Some villagers think the knobbed extreme marks the end, not the beginning, of the cord document (see chapter 8). Large museum collections contain pre-Hispanic examples similar in construction to Tupicochan knobs, though usually smaller. There is as yet no study of these ornamented bulbs. Guaman Poma drew both Inka

FIGURE 27   Pachacamanta of Primer Huangre's quipocamayo 1G-01.
From personal collection of author.

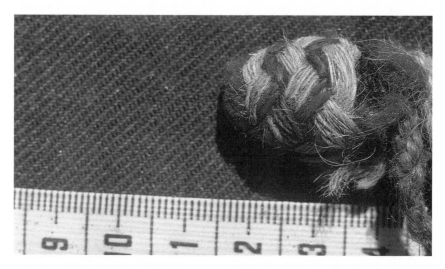

FIGURE 28   Pachacamanta of Mújica's quipocamayo M-01.
From personal collection of author.

and colonial khipus with bulbous, tufted end ornaments (see figs. 18, 22) like the
ones illustrated here.

An elder with a long-standing enthusiasm for ritual identified such knobs as
pachacamantas (see figs. 27–29). If this word is, as it seems, a Hispano-Quechuism,
its etymological sense is "about the hundred." This is an important clue to the organizational significance of quipocamayos. It suggests that ayllus formerly counted

FIGURE 29   Pachacamanta from Mújica's lost specimen M-0x attached to quipocamayo M-01. From personal collection of author.

as the "hundreds" (*pachaka*) of which the Inkaic "Checa Thousand" was composed, and that the ayllu khipu was its record.

Another word for such a knob is *sostén*, 'support,' because one grasps it at the beginning of display procedure. Villagers say that originally all quipocamayos had them. The designs differ markedly from ayllu to ayllu and more than suffice to tell, even from a distance, which quipocamayo one is looking at. Sometimes knobs are called 'heads' (*cabezas*) or 'crowns' (*coronas*) of quipocamayos.

Tupicochan pachacamantas are among the most richly ornamented known specimens. The pachacamanta of Primer Huangre's quipocamayo (see fig. 27) is decorated with two 6-bight, 7-strand Turk's heads made of cordage wrapped in flat wire of copper or a copper alloy or compound,[9] a cordage slightly resembling a guitar string but flattened-oval in section. Segunda Satafasca also used this material. The overall concept of "guitar string" winding seems to imitate sixteenth-century European designs (Farr 1994:68). The wrapping wire appears cut from a flat sheet, perhaps suggesting native Andean manufacture.[10] Pachacamantas seem to have an inner armature of some harder material, perhaps wood, cane, felt, corncob, or rawhide. They are decorated with windings of brightly dyed thread in various patterns. They are usually topped with tufts of dyed wool reminiscent of feather cockades.

The smaller ornaments, similar in color scheme, which occur along the main cord (see color plate 8, fig. 48, and Key Figure 26 between pendants 15–16), are known today as *motas*, a term also applied to tufts and pom-poms on church banners and altar cloths. In other families they are called *pontoladores* ('punctuators'). Another term is *hito*, more usually meaning 'landmark,' 'boundary stone,' or 'milestone.'

As for the meanings of markers, two opinions were voiced. First, geographical metaphors are occasionally used in discussing the shape of the rolled-up quipocamayo. The ascending spiral of the main cord is compared to a "road" with "steps." The markers along any road are called *hitos*. One elder uses the form *hitun*, which apparently retains a Hispano-Quechuism opaque to modern monolinguals, namely, the third-person possession marker -*n* ('its landmark'). The whole conical shape is occasionally referred to metaphorically as a 'hill' or a peaña (step-pyramid, as in chapter 4). The usage suggests that a quipocamayo is seen as having a geography of its own. Elders speculate about possible likeness to the larger political geography with whose integrity folk-legal processes are intensely concerned. Chapter 8 discusses a village interpretation which advances the idea of iconic relation with land features in further detail.

Second, chronological metaphors vie with topographic metaphors in folk explication of quipocamayos. Some villagers say that the bright tufts signify important times of the year such as the major festivals. In chapter 9 this hypothesis is further developed.

We turn now to the run-through threads (Key Figure 26 pendants 30–32). In pre-Hispanic khipus, some pendants have one or more threads of a contrasting bright color laid in alongside a simple thread or a ply for part or all of its length, so that the cord as a whole seems "highlighted" or "underlined." The Aschers abbreviate the feature "thread run through" as "td rt," and they record numerous examples. In Tupicocha it is common for brilliant colors to run through, but the construction may not be a true match for what the Aschers describe, because the brilliants occur in multiple threads and may be constructed like mottled bichromes. (A few are visible near the knob end in fig. 48, and details appear in plate 16.) Run-throughs share their dyed color palette with "markers" and not with monochrome cordage. All but one of the hues found on pachacamantas and hitos also occur as "td rt." (One borderline case is a brownish yellow which can be "run through" contrastingly dark pendants, but is close in hue to some structural cords.) Colors that are run through are likely to be "meta" in relation to the main body of data cords, and together with pachacamantas and hitos they may form an integrated metacode or commentary orienting users to data which the cord embodies (see chapters 8–9).

Artisans say of a cord with "td rt" that it is made *con su hilo* or *con hilo* ('with its thread'), or that it has a *cantito* ('little edging'). Today, people who make their own rope from agave fiber sometimes run a colored "cantito" through it as a sign of ownership.

A form of accentuation or annotation which must have been added at a later stage of construction — the knotting stage — consists of small wads of unspun fiber tied inside data knots (see fig. 30 and Key Figure 26 pendant 38). The tying of small objects onto data cords is one of the most important enigmas of khipu study. The giant patrimonial village khipu photographed by Ruiz Estrada appears heavily laden with tied-in objects. The image is too coarse to show detail and is not accompanied by complete description, but Ruiz says, "at various points hang figures of human appearance: little dolls made from a corncob nucleus and dressed in modern cloth of varied colors" (1981:21). Wiener (1993 [1880]:826) drew a khipu from Paramonga, on the coast north of Lima, whose knots hold pieces of fibrous material that might be wood and/or wool or cotton, and Prochaska's Titicaca islander respondents told her tied-in wooden emblems identified livestock (1983).

CORD CONSTRUCTION

The pendant cords themselves are of varied diameter (about 1 mm to over 3 mm). Most are constructed of two plies, each of which is itself composed of two simple threads. The usual construction is alternating directionality, namely, S-spin of thread, then Z-twist of thread into ply, followed by S-ply of plies into cord (see Key Figure 26 pendants 1–6), or the inverse (pendants 7–12). Tupicochan specimens have a markedly higher incidence of Z-plying than ancient specimens, in which S seems to be the default. A few exceptions to alternating torsion occur with no evident regularity. They tend to unravel and may be subject to selective loss. Some plies have three or rarely four threads, and some cords have three plies (see fig. 31).

The great majority of cords are of a single color each. The major color range seems to be that of undyed camelid wool. Villagers often comment on the fine quality of cords, particularly admiring those which are spun and plied tightly and have a glossy finish. Finishes range from glossy to nappy, but it is hard to tell whether nap results from design or from wear. Mid-brown cords appear more subject to both napping and fraying than black or pale cords.

Two of the three kinds of bicolor design which the Aschers described from museum specimens occur in Tupicocha's cordage. The more common kind of two-color construction is the sort called *moteado*, or "mottled," in the literature (Ascher 1997:21, 1978:18; and Key Figure 26 pendants 24–26). It results from making each ply by twisting together threads of dissimilar color, for example, if ply A contains colors 1 and 2, and so does ply B (several examples are visible in fig. 30). "Mottled" bicolor cords are called *pallari* or *pallarado* or *pallaradito*, alluding to speckled beans (*pallares*).

A rare "bichromy" type is the "candy cane" or "barber pole" design (Key Figure 26 pendants 27–29), in which whole plies of dissimilar color form paired helices. It occurs on two quipocamayos (Primer Huangre's 1G-01, and Mújica's M-02). In the Aschers' third type of bichromy, a cord begins with one color and switches to another. This is the only naked-eye feature of basic prehistoric cord design never seen in Tupicocha.

Not all deviation from monochrome construction is due to multicolor plies or the "thread run through" construction. Another source of variation is the inclusion of multiple fiber colors at the stage of spinning the simple threads. Many cords have a multicolor look which, on closer inspection, is not due to differentiated

FIGURE 30   Pendant 66 of quipocamayo 1SF-01 has a tuft of wool tied into its knot (near main cord, below and right of the tufted marker). From personal collection of author.

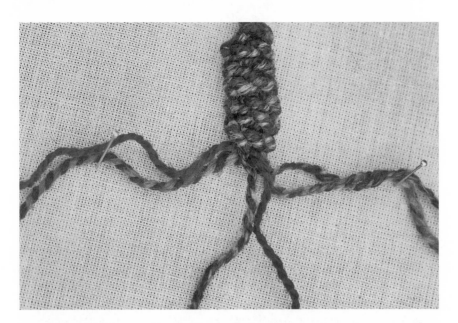

FIGURE 31   A complex cord unraveling at end of pendant 77 of Segunda
Allauca's quipocamayo 2A-01. From personal collection of author.

threads or plies, but to heterogeneous fiber throughout. Since the colors involved
do not stand in any structured relation to each other, one may guess that such
cords are monochrome from the "emic" viewpoint. That is, fiber mixing might be
a device for creating a wider palette. Artisans call cords like this *jerga*, "tweed."[11]

No artisan spontaneously pointed twist direction out as an interesting feature,
though it is an obvious variable to those who work wool. When asked, villagers say
that anyone can spin, twist, and ply in either direction (often citing their respective mothers' practices), but they think it is only a matter of personal habit. Yet in
at least one Tupicochan case, it is likely to have been a meaningful feature. The reason for thinking so is that the originally paired set consisting of specimen 1SF-01
and 2SF-01, that is, the pair which belonged to undivided Ayllu Satafasca until the
1920s, contrasts in cord directionality. The specimen 2SF-01, which now belongs
to the junior segment, is mostly Z-plied and its counterpart 1SF-01, of the senior
segment, is mostly S-plied. (The other pairs, in Allauca, Mújica, and Chaucacolca
ayllus, do not show this opposition.) Key Figure 26 shows an S-plied band in pendants 1–6 and a Z-plied band in pendants 7–12. Across all specimens, many bands
have nonuniform plying.

CORD COLORS
Pendants on quipocamayos are usually grouped by color, as discussed in chapter 9. The range of actual colors present in any one band is not standardized. In

fact, it varies enough to cause doubt about whether a given cord belongs to the group or not. In fieldwork I used Munsell Soil Chart colors so as to document physical variation in hues and saturations. However the actual object of study is, of course, the "emic" or locally understood categories of color, of which cords are performance variations. Several local people experienced in textile work were consulted. All disclaimed specific quipocamayo expertise, saying it was a lost art. However, three were willing to collaborate: Vicenta Javier Medina, Justo Rueda, and Dominga Antiporta Medina, all experienced wool artisans. Sra. Javier and Sra. Antiporta have experience in dyeing, spinning, and knitting, and to some degree weaving (which is not much practiced in Tupicocha now). Sr. Rueda is expert in tailoring, knitting, and mending men's clothes, and he also makes liturgical textile objects.

Each person was asked in a separate session to sort the cords of a given quipo-camayo, "putting similar threads together" (juntando hilos similares). I listened to them name the colors while sorting, which all did spontaneously. After sorting, I sought confirmation by asking for the name of the color of each sorted group. The sortings were internally consistent with small exceptions, but not mutually consistent. Antiporta tends toward "splitting" small differences, perhaps because her work with industrial dyes stimulates interest in color accuracy. Javier and Rueda do not work with industrial dyes and are more willing to "lump" small differences.

However, if one is willing to lump small differences, a common implicit color scheme (Von Bischoffshausen 1976:22) does emerge. The color terms which all three know are given below. They are understood to overlap by shades, allowing binomials like "café-mortaja."

blanco	pure white through pale yellowish browns and sandy or tawny tones.
rusqui, lusqui	range of mid-grays, including brownish, bluish, and olive tints, perceived as neutral.
oque	grays, especially pale gray to charcoal gray, and grays with bluish or silvery tones.
ancarri	blue.
chacua	brownish-yellows.
calhua	pale browns.
chumpi	browns, broadly. Some persons include only beige to middle browns. Others include dark browns also (von Bischoffshausen 1976:59–63).
café	dark brown.
mortaja	('shroud') very dark grayish brown to brownish black.
prieto	very dark reddish brown to brownish black. *Mortaja* and *prieto* are not consistently differentiated.

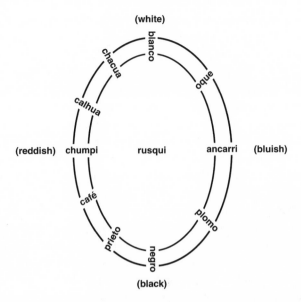

(white)

blanco

chacua

oque

calhua

(reddish) chumpi   rusqui   ancarri   (bluish)

café

prieto

plomo

negro

(black)

FIGURE 32   An interpretation of "emic" color terms as perceived by Tupicochan fiber artisans. From personal collection of author.

plomo	deep charcoal gray to black.
negro	very dark blackish grays or blackish browns and true black.
azul tiñi-tiñi	near-primary blue, slightly grayish.
rosado	slightly bluish strong pink to slightly bluish red (also rarely called *anaranjadus* [*sic*])
granate	strong slightly bluish red to wine red or maroon.

To the best of my understanding, the colors sort out into a pattern consisting of two families of shades, the brown, or chumpi, range and the gray, or oque, range, meeting at black and at white. A small list of "lively" (*vivo*) colors, perceived as isolates, is used for accents (see fig. 32). People perceive reddish or bluish shades of black. They apply the general term for black (*negro*) only when they cannot detect either tint, however slightly. The elusive term *rusqui* or *lusqui* is applied to a range of middling grayish-browns and brownish-grays, including tweedy complex colors, and it might best be glossed as "neutral middle tone."

In the discussion of cord groups throughout this chapter and later ones, the cords are described and grouped using the above scheme, following as best I can the set of color discriminations taught by these three artisans.

KNOT TYPES

Locke's typology of knots on putatively Inka khipus has been used with some variation by most later authors. The knotting of Tupicocha's quipocamayos includes all the common Lockean Inka types. But there are also knots unknown in the typical Inka khipu canon. The traditional canon appears in figure 3 in the introduction. These are the simple overhand knot, coded "s" in the Ascher database; the figure eight, or "E"; and the Inka long knot, or "L" (Key Figure 26 pendants 33–35). Since Tupicocha has plural long-knot types, I call the Inka long knot "I" to avoid confusion with the noncanonical long knots described next.

The noncanonical long knots are of three types. Are they allomorphs of the Inka long knot? It is hard to see why the extra complexity involved would be introduced unless it carried some emic significance. Also, they are of very unequal difficulty, so that if they were allomorphs one might expect the easy Inka long knot to displace harder types. It is rather common for Tupicochan pendants to have two long knots, and when they do, they almost always have two of the same sort. But every quipocamayo has more than one kind of long knot. There are only two unambiguous exceptions to whatever rule or habit inhibits the coexistence of I-knots and T-knots on single cords.[12] Both Inka long knots and the noncanonical ones occur in denominations over nine in Mújica's quipocamayo m-01. Quipocamayo m-01 is a singular instance, explored in chapter 9, and possibly subject to different organizing rules.

Urton (1998) notes "anomalies" such as values over ten and non-Lockean knot placement in about one-third of ancient khipus. He argues that they indicate the presence of what he calls "narrative" material. While Tupicocha research does not confirm narration as such, it does confirm a range of functions outside the numerical (see chapters 8–9).

The first of the noncanonical knots is what I will call the Tupicocha knot, or T-knot (see figs. 33–35 and Key Figure 26 pendant 36). It is the commonest long knot in all ten specimens. At first glance it resembles a hangman's knot, but it is actually more closely related to an unnamed hitch which the incomparable knot expert Clifford W. Ashley registered for attaching fish hooks. It also resembles one variant of the monkey's fist stopper knot (1944:53, illus. no. 324, 88 illus. 535 left). Modern Tupicochans remark that it is puzzling, because no actual knot is visible. When perfectly executed, it looks as if the vertical pendant were encased by an unsecured cylinder made of cord circling it in a tight spiral. Actually, the knot is a

FIGURE 33   A variant of the "monkey's fist" knot. (From *Ashley Book of Knots* by Clifford Ashley, copyright 1944 by Clifford W. Ashley:354, illus. 2203. Used by permission of Doubleday, a division of Random House, Inc.)

FIGURE 34   A Tupicocha long knot of quipocamayo 2SF-01 from
one side looks like a "4." From personal collection of author.

FIGURE 35   The same knot seen from the other side
looks like a "5." From personal collection of author.

close relative of the Inka long knot. Both are begun by bending the free or working end of the cord upward in a "U," but, whereas one makes an Inka L by passing the descending spiral turns that signify integers only around the descending
axis of the knot (let us say, the left vertical of the "U") leaving the ascending axis
visible, the Tupicocha knot has turns bound tightly around both (Ashley 1944:354,
fig. 2203, fig. 6.31).

There are two ways to construct the Tupicocha knot. One is by making a "U"
with two axes first, then winding turns downward from the top around both and
finishing with a pass through the bottom of the "U." The more difficult way, the
proper way according to Don Martín Camilo (fig. 33), begins with a downward

axis only, then makes the turns around it going upward, and finally constructs the second axis by a second downward pass, running the working end through the turns and parallel to the first axis. This produces the "knotless knot" effect more consistently, but it is difficult.[13] As we will see below, one other Tupicochan knows how to do it.

Theoretically, there is a third and perhaps significant way to make a Tupicocha knot, namely, by modifying an extant Inka long knot. One must slacken its exposed or ascending vertical axis, and, by winding it around the already existing turns in a contrary direction, exhaust them. The effect of this surprising "rope trick" is to replace the turns with a series of oppositely spiraled turns lacking an exposed axis (Ashley 1944:94, illustration 566). Such a transformation might have expressed a transvaluation of the long knot's value (such as, postulating a speculative example, negative to positive). However nobody in Tupicocha demonstrated this trick.

In the majority of examples, the Tupicocha knot is difficult to interpret (as R. Ascher, who has probably counted more khipu knots than any living person, confirms).[14] The reason is that the bend forming the bottom of the "U" is visible from one side but not from the other, so a knot that looks like, for example, a "4" from one side will look like "5" from the other (see figs. 34–35). I noted such knots, as, for example, 4/5T. Assuming turns do encode integers, "4" is probably a better gloss, because the bottom of the "U" is not topologically similar to the turns. This attribute seems to have bothered the makers of the quipocamayos too, for they took pains to hide the bottom of the "U" as much as possible. In data registry, I used the lower of the two possible readings for this reason.

Although most villagers think this knot mysterious, at least two know how to make it. One is young Nery Javier, discussed in chapter 8. The other is an elder of Mújica ayllu, Don Martín Camilo, who serves as the village's unofficial "priest" and folk healer (curandero). He has a reputation for arcane knowledge of all sorts. He makes a Tupicocha long knot by using his index finger as a spindle (see fig. 36). He winds the working end once around the fingernail while holding the other end still with his thumb against the base of the index finger. He then passes the working end n times around the index. He delicately removes the coil from the finger, holds it, and passes the working end through the coil to emerge from the original loop. Then he tightens from both ends. This yields a close likeness to many knots on the patrimonial cords.

Two other long knots escape the Lockean typology. One is Ashley's "multiple figure-eight knot" (1944:85, illus. 523 center, 94, illus. 568; see figs. 37–38). It occurs only twice, and only in ayllu Mújica's quipocamayo M-01, so it is labeled the Mújica, or M, knot (Key Figure 26 pendant 37). It is made by weaving the successive descending turns around both of the axes of the "U" that begins the knot, while crossing over back and forth in a figure-eight movement. A finished Mújica knot (fig. 37) looks like two separate stacks of turns. We do not know whether they are

FIGURE 36   Don Martín Camilo makes a Tupicocha long knot, by using his index finger as a spindle to stack the turns. From personal collection of author.

to be counted separately (i.e., seeing each "8" as containing two turns), summed (each "8" as one), or read as a tens and a units place.

The last of the three noncanonical knots might be called a reversing Tupicocha knot, because it is made like the Tupicocha knot but reverses directionality in mid-descent. That is, the first few turns spiral counterclockwise and the last few clockwise, or vice versa. A few other types occur rarely or only once, and it is not clear whether they are errors, repairs, allomorphs, or meaningful variants, so they are omitted from the Key Figure.

The unusual knots may be influenced by cursive writing. If one examines the flourishes (*rúbricas*) that distinguish signatures from ordinary script, one finds forms that can be executed as knots. Perhaps Peruvians noticed this long ago, when first becoming familiar with European script. The signature rubrics of Francisco Pizarro and that of Alonso de Riquelme, signatories to the act founding the city of Los Reyes (Lima), can be read (if one imagines a third dimension) as respectively forming diagrams of a Tupicocha knot and a figure-eight knot (see fig. 39, José María Córdoba y Urrutia (1992 [1839]:22). Like Peruvians in general, Tupicocha's peasants have long had the habit of signing with complex flourishes.

TURNS OF LONG KNOTS

Some people call the turns *vueltas*, "turns," but others speak of them as *nudos*, or knots, in their own right. This is confusing to the outsider, but it is likely to be a calque from the Andean technical lexicon, since we know that the turns of an Inka long knot are best considered allomorphs of simpler knots (E, s) in their role of representing a unit.

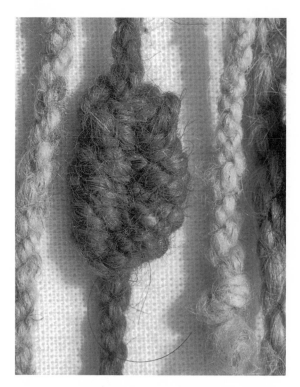

FIGURE 38   The multiple figure-eight knot according to Ashley. (From *Ashley Book of Knots* by Clifford Ashley, copyright 1944 by Clifford W. Ashley: 85, illus. 523. Used by permission of Doubleday, a division of Random House, Inc.)

FIGURE 37   A Mújica knot or multiple figure eight on pendant 11 of Mújica's quipocamayo M-01. The cordage appears to be sheep's wool. From personal collection of author.

FIGURE 39   Rubrics of signatures of Francisco Pizarro and Alonzo Riquelme, 1535 (From Córdova y Urrutia 1992 [1839]:22.)

When counting turns of a long knot, one comunero, Julio Javier, uses a distinctive series of numerals whose first four members are

mikchu pikchu
makchu makchu
makchu pakchu
makcha makcha.[15]

He said the series continues but that he cannot remember it. The terms are not Spanish nor in any obvious way Quechua. They appear cognate to number terms in Kauki, the nearest relative of Huarochirí's extinct pre-Quechua ethnic language. In Kauki the word for "one" is *maya*, and "two" is *paja* (Belleza Castro 1995:235, 300). I never heard the terms in any other context. The usage strongly suggests that quipocamayos were in use before the ethnic language was lost, and it also suggests the khipu art was common enough in non-Inka contexts to have a localistic lexicon.

Javier regards these words as esoterica, and he chose not to say what he thinks they mean translationally. The noticeable thing about them is that each binomial is a name for a number marked as odd or even. Odds have initials MP and evens MM. The first odd (1) and the second odd (3) are differentiated only by their initial vowels, the first and the second evens (2 and 4) only by their second vowels. Perhaps they formed part of a secondary numeral system emphasizing the properties "first odd," "first even," "second odd" and so forth. This would seem to be connected with the esoteric use of quipocamayos described in chapter 8, which takes as its initial step the reckoning of odds and evens. It may suggest latent relations with Urton's reconstruction of a code variable *chulla* ('unpaired') and *chullantin* ('paired') (2003:89–97).

GROUPING OF PENDANTS

Most Inka khipus contain groups of pendants separated by spaces of bare main cord. They are so neatly delimited that the Aschers and Radicati used groups as their usual initial framework for description and analysis.

Tupicocha's quipocamayos do not exhibit spaces separating groups. Key Figure 26 is drawn so as to indicate this difficulty. (Stretches of bare main cord do exist, but they do not separate homogeneous groups. Moreover, spaces may not be stable, since pendants are hitched to main cords loosely enough to move perceptibly in the course of a use cycle. In any case, some pendants are lost.)

But quipocamayos do ordinarily (i.e., in nine of ten cases) exhibit grouping of pendants sorted by color, including groups of *pallaris*, or bicolors. These quipocamayos will be called "banded" (see fig. 26). Some bands consist of pendants of one color, all having subsidiaries of a different contrasting color (pendants 16–18 in Key Figure 26). This feature too was common in antiquity.

Is a Quipocamayo a Text?

At many points, this book's argument posits alteration of extant quipocamayos. I have taken as a working assumption the idea that decisions on what kinds of cords to make, how to assemble them, how to knot them, and when to add features posterior to main construction, like wads, occurred in mimesis of the changing social process by which ayllus made ritual, political, and economic choices.

This does not seem a far-fetched supposition, but it goes against the grain of khipu literature. The Andean functionaries who persuaded early-colonial Spaniards that Andean data records were credible did so by doing what conquered cultures always do, namely, transculturation of rather than translation of their knowledge. Andean experts persuaded the text-making *letrados* and clerics that khipus were something Europe already knew — accounts — and in courts they encouraged a presumption that cords were analogous to account books or ledgers. Similarly, chroniclers who wrote of dynastic khipus took them as analogous to annals or chronicles. By this route khipus were assimilated to an imported concept of the document. To Spaniards, documentation meant an array of symbols in a finished and unvarying state. Indeed some scribal conventions, such as drawing flourishes on blank spaces lest someone later try to add text, are meant to insure fixity.

From this process a further unexamined inference was added, namely, the supposition that the function of a khipu is lodged in its legibility ex post facto. This assumption is an overgeneralization from Locke's otherwise valid observation that quipocamayos are not good calculating devices, because knotting lags behind reckoning. It may be true that they are not as good as the abacus for arithmetic, but this hardly proves they were not operational devices.

Specimens from Tupicocha suggest that the functional strengths of khipus include operability. In the next few paragraphs I will argue that a quipocamayo was an assembly of movable parts, and that the moving of parts was a simulation or mimetic device used to represent changing properties and problems of ayllu and community. More precisely, I suggest that in its normal use, each ayllu-level quipocamayo seems to have cycled between a role as *operable semasiograph*, when the group deployed tokens of its members' performance and as legible record, when, at the end of a cycle, the sum of operations was viewed as documentary totality.

This is not to dispute the existence of khipus made for fixity, nor to deny that the "time-binding" function was key to Inka political arithmetic. One can hardly doubt it after looking at museum collections. But it is reasonable to ask about the relation between imperial and local levels. Inka recording technique, as an apparatus of imperial bureaucracy, would necessarily use standardized and simplified notations with common denominator devices to cover the diverse on-the-ground practices of Andean populations. Otherwise, there would be no way to create aggregate statements on which to base policy, or to share data among functionaries with different cultural backgrounds and jurisdictions.

The ayllu quipocamayo, on the other hand, was a ground-hugging medium. It would work best when most able to match the changes and unforeseen peculiarities of ayllu- and community-level work in progress. So it makes sense that it shows greater variety and complexity of detail than higher-level khipus, but lesser consistency of structure. It also makes sense that it included easy means to change records so as to simulate changing realities or plans.

These assertions are only worth as much as the physical evidence that quipocamayos actually did serve as operational devices. Hernando Pizarro and Garcilaso Inca both said that Inka accountants updated accounts by adding and removing knots. But the first scholar to show materially that ancient khipus actually have changeable—and changed—parts was Radicati di Primeglio, in his 1979(?) book on "the Inka system of accounting" (97–102). He later summed this up: "A quipu with knots removed from its cords and re-knotted is, strictly speaking, a palimpsest, which can be reconstructed. . . . It is amazing with what facility one can remake the knots, based on the traces which they leave marked on the cords. Unknotting is usually found on isolated cords, pendants, and subsidiaries, but sometimes also on a whole section of the quipu" (1990 [1987]:91).[16] By "traces" Radicati was alluding chiefly to cuts, kinks, and/or color discontinuities visible where a knot was removed. A removed overhand knot does leave a characteristic kink (like a letter "C" with an angle in it), but in museums it is not easy to differentiate kinks of former knots from kinks caused by accidents of preservation. Radicati, a master khipu examiner, was convinced that ghost knots occurred in patterns related to regular data knot positioning. Because data knots in Tupicocha occur in irregular positions, I do not feel able to tell which kinks are former knots. Nor do Tupicochan specimens have snipped cords like those Radicati examined (1979[?]:98). But Radicati's model of a "palimpsest" (a surface with superimposed multiple inscriptions) can be demonstrated by other means.

First, if a quipocamayo served as an operational device over various cycles, it is likely to show heterogeneity of manufacture (see color plate 9). We have already mentioned in the discussion of banding some details that show "emically" grouped cords to be "etically" dissimilar insofar as they are made of unlike cordage. When I asked modern wool-workers in Tupicocha to group quipocamayo cords by color, I found that "emic" colors each comprise Munsell color taxa that vary by two or (rarely) more grades of saturation and of hue. There are disparities in the "handwriting" of similar knots (i.e., equivalent number and knot type) on single quipocamayos, or even within a single color band. Pendants 19–21 of Key Figure 26 show how cords which belong to a single band and "emic" color vary in diameter by ratios of up to 3:1. This makes it unlikely that they were made as parts of a uniform batch such as the neat batches Mackey (1970) found in a prehistoric khipu master's kit. Pendants in a single band also vary in texture, tightness of spin, ply and twist, and degree of wear. It would take a true fiber technology expert to study these differences at the level of, so to speak, "handwriting analysis," but some cordages are distinctive enough to trace across different contexts. In studying the Satafasca pair, I found myself giving the mental nickname "hard gold" to cordage of Munsell color 7.5YR 4/4–4/6, which has a slightly bronze-like sheen in a dominant yellowish color, and which stands out for its very tight spin and ply, and its absence of taper. "Hard gold" appears on both Satafasca quipocamayos (1SF-01: p12s1 [Z], p14s1 [Z]; 2SF-01: p29 [S], p79 [Z])but not on other specimens. Similarly, one nicknamed "bright-in-matte" appears in both (1SF-01 p35 [S], p36 [S], p108 [S]; 2SF-01 p27 [S]). "Bright-in-matte" is an easily recognized unreflective yellowish-brown cordage that has glossy yellow and red threads running through; it is of thick upper diameter but tapers sharply. Several manufacture types can be distinguished within given bands. Artisans agreed with my guess that these idiosyncrasies seem to be the traces of individuals.

As for time of attachment, any given quipocamayo contains cords in uneven condition. Villagers point out the fresher looking ones as "new." Because different colors and cordages have different wear characteristics, it is not easy to guess which ones are actually newer. The interesting point is that villagers unhesitatingly assume that these putatively ancient objects are composed of parts made or added at different times.

If a quipocamayo was the product of successive action by multiple hands, all of which belonged to ayllu peers who knew each other well, then it seems probable that "handwriting" features would be seen as authenticating information. Insofar as they registered identities, and with them the history of composition of the document, they were probably considered as data or content. In using paper documents today, peasant readers are very attentive to the history of the composition of the document, noting successive secretaries by their handwritings, replacement of rubber stamps, and so forth. Weavers too say they can recognize each others' work.

This matter is of theoretical interest insofar as it connects with Roy Harris's concern for writing, in the wide sense, as the legible concretion of achieved social integration—a concept which refuses the Saussurean boundary between langue and parole. We know that demonstrating interaction is precisely what quipocamayos did at the level of civic ideology. Quipocamayos' ability to concretely fuse the parole or performance of many members, then, is likely to have stood even higher in public consciousness than do performance variables about modern legal text. (It is relevant that when reading their ayllu books, as discussed in the next chapter, villagers tend to look first at the most performatively individual parts, the signatures and rubrics.)

Second, if the default is operability—that is, if the working assumption of quipocamayo makers was that quipocamayos would change—then an operational quipocamayo would have technical characteristics allowing easy movement, removal, and attachment of elements. It seems nonaccidental that the standard attachment of pendants, the half-hitch, is the optimal one to allow either removing and reattaching a pendant individually, or repositioning it by sliding, without disturbing the rest of the quipocamayo. One can slide a pendant by loosening its attachment loop and carrying it past adjacent pendants, pulling the extremes of intervening pendants through the moving loop until the desired position is reached, then retightening. While this might be difficult in the tightly attached cotton Inka khipu, it would be easier with Tupicocha's specimens. Some Tupicochan specimens show stretches of bare main cord and a number of attachment hitches so loose that cords slide randomly in storage. The bare main cord spaces along which they slide may reflect loss of pendants, but they may also reflect removal of cords. Other specimens, notably Chaucacolca's uch-01, have jammed main cords. They seem to be carrying more pendants than they were designed for. This may reflect demographic factors, since Chaucacolca is the biggest quipocamayo-owning ayllu.

Third, if the hallmark of an operational device is movability of sign-bearing parts, those parts which are not to be moved, or to be moved jointly if at all, should bear signs or mechanical devices that impede mobility. Several such devices are in evidence. One is an irregular attachment in which the attachment loop of one pendant is tightened over that of an adjacent one, apparently signaling that the two are to be taken together; the latter cannot be loosened and moved without also loosening the former (see fig. 40 and Key Figure 26 pendants 39–40). Another device which falls outside the conventional canon of khipu literature is the tying of pendants to each other by attachments at mid-cord, allowing them to be readily moved but only if moved together. In Tupicocha only two cords (not necessarily adjacent) are tied to each other, but at least one case of multiple bundled pendants occurs in museum collections (see Key Figure 26 pendants 41–42).[17] A third technique, indicating the highest level of immobilization, is the binding of a group of pendants to each other with stitches right through their attachment loops (schematized at Key Figure 26 pendants 42–45). This makes it impossible to move the group nondestructively, because the affected cords cannot be loosened from the main cord or from each other (see fig. 41).

Fourth, if quipocamayos used cords made on separate occasions by separate hands, and perhaps used pendants that were modified before attachment to the main cord, one could expect a low degree of positional standardization of knots relative to the main cord. Unlike Inka specimens, whose knots usually lie in parallel rows representing decimal places, multiauthored or reshuffled khipus might exhibit knots difficult to identify as belonging to a tens or units places. Tupicochans themselves notice the nonparallel alignment of knots in most of their specimens, but do not have an explanation. Figure 42 shows a representative example. In this respect also, Tupicochan knots resemble the ones Urton has typed as "anomalous."

Those modern Tupicochanos who retain elements of quipocamayo knowledge consider operability too obvious to require explaining. This idea is latent in the norm that because they no longer know how to update correctly, they may not make substantive changes at all. Nery Javier (see chapter 8) is a young man once tutored by the reputed last cord master. He made a likeness of his own ayllu's quipocamayo and gave it to me. Since it is not "real," he feels free to change it. When I greeted him in 1999, after six months' absence, he asked if I had brought his

FIGURE 40 Overlooping on 1G-01. The attachment loop of the dark cord is tightened over that of the adjacent lighter one so that the light could not be moved without slackening the dark. From personal collection of author.

FIGURE 41 A series of pendants on quipocamayo 2SF-01 have been sewn in place with binding thread. From personal collection of author.

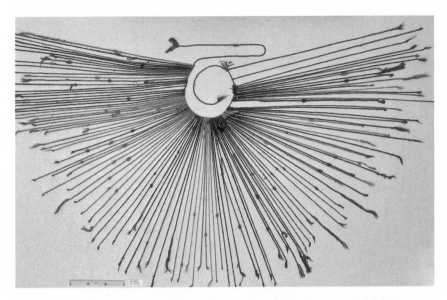

FIGURE 42 Quipocamayo 1A-01 shows little or no standardization of knot placement. From personal collection of author.

simulacrum quipocamayo because it needed to be "corrected." He began removing "wrong" cords, then installed replacements. While doing so, he commented on how authorities updated quipocamayos in former times: "Yearly they would change the knots. They'd remove the knots and put on new ones. On the third of January they would bring up to date everything they'd gained or lost."[18]

We conclude that officeholders did use cords to document the completion of current social agenda during their mandates of office, updating them continually and, in doing so, introducing new parts or immobilizing and remobilizing parts. Quipocamayos were current records, which, as an ensemble, were recycled. To recognize their importance as records or time-bound data resulting from recent operations, one might call them annals, but if so, they would need the qualifying title of rotating annals. It was probably some similar arrangement which Garcilaso Inca meant when he said (notwithstanding his belief that royal khipus contained multicentury records of royal history) that "their [i.e., khipu masters'] records were annual, and they never referred to more than a single year" (Harold Livermore's translation, 1966:1:330; Garcilaso 1991 [1609]:344, cf. Blas Valera in Garcilaso 1991:344).[19]

Operable Semasiography and Social Articulation

We turn now to the question of what these findings might mean for the informational makeup of ancient Andean empires, and more broadly for the theories of writing sketched in chapter 1.

Perhaps the most prominent debate of recent decades concerning the origins of writing is the one which Pierre Amiet (1982) and A. L. Oppenheim (1959) set in motion by their discoveries of Mideastern "tokens" older than writing. Schmandt-Besserat (1980) has developed an argument that a shift away from operable use of clay tokens—a tendency toward summary labeling, and then labeling with signs for words that designate categories—generated the Mesopotamian transition to "writing proper." The gist is that preliterate agropastoralists kept track of herds and crops with small clay pieces in easily made geometrical shapes. These stood for animals or measures of foodstuffs. Like the token potatoes that Andean harvesters use today to represent every hundred or thousand potatoes, they could be used to keep track of inventory. This is an operational or simulative use.

But tokens were also used as signs for agreement in transactions. This implied a "time-binding" function, that is, a means to insure a graphic representation against change. In order to guarantee the integrity of a transaction (e.g., a shipment), a sender would send along a clay sphere containing tokens for the goods, that is, a sealed bill of lading. Since the contents of the sphere were invisible, it was convenient to make the sphere identify the transaction it "contained" by stamping on its outside imprints of the tokens inside. Since clay is not erasable, labels summarizing the tokens inside made the original tokens redundant. Impressed marks on clay changed the vector from envelope to tablet. One could then improve efficiency by eliminating the "token-iterative" repetition of n tokens for n objects by the crucially innovative practice of impressing a simpler symbol for the checking off of five objects—in other words, for the concept "five." "Five sheep" could then be impressed as a speech-independent numeral, such as "5" and a shape meaning "sheep" semasiographically. Such signs, closer to spoken language, came to be interpreted as representing verbal phrases. This opened the way to the "rebus mutation" and thus toward "writing proper."

This allegedly happened because from the traders' viewpoint, efficiency in time binding—the creation of a message invulnerable to change during the transaction—was all that mattered. The quest for easy fixity trumped the operability which had been the token system's original advantage.

The overall Schmandt-Besserat thesis has become the target of archaeological critiques impossible to ignore (Michalowski 1993). The argument that a mutation in numeracy produced lexigraphic literacy is not universally accepted. But it is not disputed that such tokens existed prior to writing in their area, nor that manipulability—their operability as analogue simulators of work and property—was their first function. Amiet, Oppenheim, and Schmandt-Besserat hit on something important in noticing that elementary graphic behavior entails a tension between operability and textual fixity. It is this point we need to follow. In doing so, we question the idea that fixity succeeds operability, that text replaces simulation.

Philological grammatology has generally ignored the operable agenda, not for any forceful theoretical reason, but because in the European division of labor it fell outside the humanist mandate. Simulation and operations research became the concern of applied mathematicians, accountants, and engineers. Scribes and scholars, predisposed by the fact that their professions were beholden to the idea of a sacred and unalterable divine scripture, tended to see themselves as retrievers and preservers of fixed texts, and as creators of such texts. Accountants and engineers became manipulators of purportedly different and more labile stuff, today called data. The latter have inherited as their guild language the most powerful of semasiographs—mathematical notations—and in recent times augmented them with an astronomically expanding yet minimalist sign system, binary code.

But a moment's reflection shows that the distinction between functions of operability and functions of fixity occurs as much within lexigraphy as within semasiography or binary code. Yes, a text is a text insofar as it is fixed for a period. But the value of a collection of texts also lies in its mutability. For example, to say that the school registrar's files derive value from their permanence is no truer than saying that they derive value from their impermanence. We scholars feel delighted to find old papers that contain fossil discourse. But that preference is an attribute of our vocation, not an inherent function of literacy. When Jack Goody, Harold Innis, and others make much of the time-binding quality of writing, they are manifesting an "error of the tribe" of historians. Writing systems can just as well minimize fixity as maximize it. Both writing and cord records alternate between poles of operability and fixity. I will suggest that this is a key fact for understanding their interplay.

	Semasiography	Lexigraphy
Fixity	Pecked petroglyphs	Maya stela
	Icon-instructions on appliances	Legal contract
Operability	Abacus	Slate and chalk
	Spreadsheet	Word processor

From the viewpoint of graphogenetic theory, the khipu art presents an interesting "road not taken" by Old World cultures. Suppose that the users of tokens had applied their art more widely and consistently; that they had developed flexible "emblematic frames" (in Harris's term) suitable to hold tokens in arrays representing the integration of complex social action. Suppose that they developed a lexicon of labels and "meta" devices or markers, showing how to put various sorts of data into correlation. In that case, could they not have accomplished by other means much of the work that the Old World learned to do with lexigraphy? This, I suggest, is approximately what happened in the khipu-using orbit.

This thesis is neutral on the question of whether cords could stand for words or other verbal artifacts. There is no inherent reason why the structured code properties of a cord could not stand for a morpheme, and so on. Likewise, there is no reason to suppose that what happened so many times elsewhere—the rebus mutation, in which a sign for a nonverbal entity is taken to stand for the sound(s) of the name of that entity in a given spoken language—could not have occurred with cords. However, in Tupicocha I found no evidence that this had happened. I therefore abstain from such hypotheses in the explanation of cords from here onward.

For what it may be worth, at a level of gross probability, a Quechua- or Jaqaru-speaking environment is not the kind of linguistic setting in which the invention of visible signs for speech segments tends to occur easily. As Daniels (1996a:585) notes, the typical linguistic setting of this mutation is one where many freestanding morphemes (words) are single syllables. Quechua and the Jaqaru group do have some meaningful monosyllables, but most roots and many suffixes are polysyllabic. Both are strongly agglutinative languages.

But, it may be objected, isn't discourse mimicry at the gross level inevitable anyway, simply because the rules of syntax and rhetoric dictate the order in which people expect to have things mentioned? Yes, and to this degree we should expect that the cords will have speechlike properties even if they involve no true lexigrams. In chapter 9, I propose an analysis which takes its form in part from the rhetorical frame of work records, as discussed in meetings and verbalized on paper. But I lean to the opinion that once discourse yields authoritative solutions, Andean practice tends to invest the solution in media maximally separated from discourse: muted media, in the sense of chapter 4. Knowing that it might be possible to verbalize khipu content does not necessarily mean that the words they matched were taken as their "real content." It is a significant fact that although villagers compare cords with scripts, none ever mentioned reading out or reading aloud as a part of cord use in the days when the huayrona used them actively.

What other sources of formal regularity or irregularity must we expect? Pure token-iterativity pulls in the direction of simplicity and regularity (because the more tokens are standardized and aligned, the easier they are to use). But the irregularity and idiosyncrasy of social events to be represented would pull in the opposite direction. A set of tokens can admit quite a bit of secondary elaboration via iconic usages and so forth, serving to anchor it more securely in unique context, without sacrificing the token set's logical intelligibility. This sort of proliferation of meaning would make a set less interpretable to outsiders, but perhaps more so to insiders. For as the contents of an emblematic frame come to bear idiosyncratic signs (of their makers' hands, of material available at a given time, of "exceptions" noted by metasigns and so forth), its parts come to have gestalt recognizability.

In practice, one uses both regularity and irregularity. Looking at a tree-ring database, which is a nonhuman token-iterative record, a scientist in search of information about a drought can locate a given date via regularity, by counting back to the nth ring from a ring of known date, or via irregularity, by eyeballing for a stretch of about j thin rings close together, which form a visual gestalt. This sort of irregularity, occurring in the course of routine simulation and modification, might also occur in khipus and even provide a positive incentive to "anomaly."

Suppose, now, that in this environment an imperial state wished to take control of many such systems and coordinate processes of simulation and fixity at a higher level of inclusivity. We know that khipu technology existed in various language communities. If properties of local spoken languages did not govern methods of notation, the problem of translation would be eliminated, or at least limited to learning local variants of all-empire conventions. The Inka state could generate a seamless web of data from ayllu up to sovereign level. Perhaps this is one of the reasons the Inka state, which was more linguistically diverse than its colonial or republican successors, maximized cord use. Likewise, far-flung Andean "insistence" (Ascher and Ascher 1997:37–57) on using fiber technology as a medium for "diagrams" of cultural order (Parmentier 1985; Arnold 1997) made cord recording a suitable vehicle for schemata crosscutting intra-Andean cultural differences.

The fact that Tupicochans regard quipocamayos as garments offers a potent interpretative clue. It also brings up hard methodological questions: given the fact that khipus and textiles share a common technological base at the micro-level, how far should we extend the comparison between them as we ascend upward toward the more aggregated levels of textile structures, motif analysis, and whole-garment design? *Tuqapu* (heraldic-like modular designs on fine Inka textiles) and archaeological caps bearing what look like small thread-wrapped khipu pendants of Middle Horizon type certainly need to be accommodated in a model of Andean fiber-based semiosis. Arnold (1997), Gail Silverman-Proust (1988), and Verónica Cereceda (1986) argue that textile technology all the way up to whole-garment design implements a "textile code." This gross oversimplification may bring useful partial insights. Textile figures, they hold, represent general prototypes (e.g., the symmetry of living bodies) and meaningful variants of them (e.g., the lightening or shading of the "heart"). While nothing in Tupicochan evidence bears on their specific hypotheses, the local interpretations presented in chapter 8 support Cereceda's suggestion (1986:171) that cord representation is not so rigidly aniconic as it first appears. Rather it "is located somewhere between the two extremes" of the arbitrary sign and the iconically or even indexically motivated sign.

Life Lived like a Khipu?[20]

As we begin developing a context-enriched idea of how quipocamayos fitted into the local informational order, and some notion of how that fit differs from the conventional image of the Inka khipu system, we improve our position for thinking about what sort of a "literacy" the cord art was. We will do so in two steps. First we will bring together chapter 4's findings on vara inscription as a code functioning separately from verbal processes, with this chapter's hypothetical reconstruction of cords as the operable data matrix of political life. We join these arguments using the broad definition of writing provided by Harris. Then, in the hopes of providing a better account of what cord media accomplish than the Lockean legacy alone provides, we close with a return to Goodman's semiology.

A QUIPOCAMAYO IS, IN SOME WAYS, AN "EMBLEMATIC FRAME"

Chapter 4 argued that staff inscriptions do not operate by recording someone's verbal log of the ritual action through which authority reproduced itself. Rather, authority reproduces itself by interacting to make material objects which become "correct," that is, politically acceptable and therefore authoritative, only when the symbols upon them mimic in abstract pattern the parameters and relationships of power that their directors work with. The ritual acceptance of these has performative force. It brings a new hierarchy of officers into being. The making of an intra-ayllu quipocamayo may have had a similar character. Imagine, for example, that the task consists of arranging and stringing pendants representing members' respective rights to a certain service by the collectivity. Assembling them for prospective use would not be so much a matter of documenting decisions ex post facto, as of actually deciding—that is, of "according"—social interaction by trying out simulations. Quipocamayos do also seem to have been produced for retrospective use, for example, at the huayrona. But their ontogenesis, like that of staffs, seems to have involved "impressing" acts of integration themselves, rather than "expressing" discourse about them. In this respect they—and how many other Andean objects?—enjoyed an ontologically distinctive status.

A Tupicochan quipocamayo was likely to have been used at a typical ayllu meeting, in which members were expected to take a position by adding their part to a proposed planning arrangement, or by checking the correct placement of their respective cords in a performance record. In a work context, cords were worked so as to document compliance or absence. This is today the "atomic" act of documentation contributing to ayllu books. Such tasks might well involve moving and modifying preexisting components. Chapter 9 provides a detailed example.

In other words, a set of cords in the ayllu tradition was, in my opinion, a simulation tool: a "deck" of tokens by which a group could "play" possible representations of the future, or mimic past performance. Much of the intellectual effort of modern ayllu and community affairs concerns deploying the "deck" of resources in an optimal way. In chapter 7, a study of the papers that replaced quipocamayos, we will explore how this has been done in recent decades. But quipocamayos differed from papers in an important way. The basic cord structure (main cord, markers) were not intended as archival records but as reusable "game boards" cycled over and over, handed on to new officeholders, and "rewritten" in successive cycles. It is clearly recorded that the correct number of quipocamayos per ayllu used in the huayrona was two and only two, and that they were used year after year. So these must have been updated rather than replaced. And therefore they must also be seen as rotating annals with a fixed chronological horizon, rather than as accumulating archives.

The initial stages of cord work might thus have been "symbolic" in an archaic sense harking all the way back to the Greek expression *sym-bolos*. "Symbolism" in Greek meant the putting together of tokens (e.g., to count votes or cast lots). Signaling proposals by positioning cords visually would help clarify logical alternatives while minimizing waffling and vagueness, the marginalization of the tongue tied, and other defects of verbal process. Also, like the ultraspecialized lexicon of vara signs, a specialized lexicon of tokens for other civic attributes would focalize only those "strands" of multiplex ayllu relationships which were germane to the immediate issue. Although simulation through cords is not practiced today, ayllu meetings do retain a rule unknown in state parliamentary procedure, namely, formal periods of silence. If asked why this admirable rule is enforced, modern villagers say it is important for members to "contemplate" and "find" choices. Perhaps visual signs displaying the situation at hand formerly helped people "find" solutions.

In sum, an operable quipocamayo had most of the attributes of Harris's "emblematic frames": it contains a finite inventory of emblems which stood in relations of equivalence or priority to each other. It therefore had qualities of internal or intrinsic order irrespective of "functions each may acquire when the frame [was] integrated into" a specific round of structured communication. So, for example, the cards of a deck have a constant internal structure irrespective of whether they are being used for poker, cartomancy, or three-card monte. We know a few elements of these orders where quipocamayos are concerned, such as numerical seriation, the hierarchy of pendants and subsidiaries, and perhaps the cardinality of the center cord in certain applications (see chapter 9). We are only now coming to see an order of attributes, "non-Lockean" variables such as wadding, stitching, interknotting of pendants, and overlooping of attachments, which seem to point out attributes of specific "plays" made using the members of the emblematic frame.

However, it is hard to avoid suspicion that quipocamayos were emblematic frames so complex and flexible that they begin to escape from Harris's definition. The number of data states any true "emblematic frame" can convey is finite (even if very large, as in chess). Quipocamayos, by contrast, seem at last to jump the boundaries of the "game board" analogy, because they accommodated openended numbers and combinations of signs. That is, like a spoken language, but unlike a board game, they can without damaging intelligibility produce an unlimited number of combinations. To account for this, Goodman's concept of "notation" may be more powerful.

NOTATION, DIAGRAM, AND MODEL
We noted in the section "Operable Semasiography and Social Articulation" that all sorts of graphic behavior apparently have a common functional ancestry, rooted

in the integration of exchange and other transactions. But we also suggested that whereas the tendency to mimic speech became the uppermost logic of information technology in the Old World, the Andes pursued an option rarely used elsewhere — one in which codes which were not necessarily keyed to speech segments became a core "technology of intellect." This road branches off from the lexigraphic one at the same analytical point where Goodman's semiology of notation branches off from his semiology of representation and description.

Let us take a moment to review the core of Goodman's idea of notation (or the reader can turn to fuller summary in the last part of chapter 1), then move on to its khipu application.

A notation in Goodman's sense differs from all other sign systems by establishing two-way determinacy between the exterior referent and the "written" product. That is, a notational sign ("character," in his special usage of the term) does more than refer to one and only one exterior entity (as, for example, a certain note on a musical staff refers unambiguously to a sound of x pitch and y duration). It also guarantees that within the referential scope of the system, there is only one possible character corresponding to any given entity. (That is, a given musical sound can be represented by one and only one sheet-music sign.) In order for such a scheme to work, the "exterior" field — the notation's referential scope — cannot be the whole formless flux of experience. It must be a specialized world with special attributes. In other words, in addition to making rules about the set of characters that can denote referents, we impose some rules about the set of potential referents that can comply to characters (pitch, duration, scale . . .). Notations, unlike representations (e.g., in pictures) or descriptions (e.g., in so-called natural language) achieve two-way determinacy at the expense of imposing on the user a peculiar "contract." The contract is that whatever will be recorded, will be recorded under three very constricting assumptions that prestructure the experienced reality. These are (1) unambiguity, meaning that the compliance relation (what x is referred to by symbol a) is invariant; (2) compliance-class disjointness, meaning that no two characters may have a compliant in common (no two symbols a and b can refer to the same x); and (3) semantic finite differentiation, meaning that any two potential referents must contrast, and never shade into each other, lest it become impossible to decide whether an a or a b should stand for the entity.

Goodman notes that "we" (he is best versed in European traditions of art and science) tend to use symbol schemes this way "if the subject matter is antecedently atomized." How widely such schemes can be used obviously depends upon how many domains a given culture is disposed to treat as antecedently atomized. Treitler (1981) reminds us there is no musical need to perceive musical sounds this way. The need arose historically from composers' desire to control choruses. That is, it is the graphic trace of a way of integrating social relations. But neither is insistence on discreteness necessarily a jump into arbitrariness. The reason is that condition (3) can best be met, and social control can best be exerted, through discriminations that are culturally obvious, systematic, sensually compelling, and easy to learn.

How well do khipus or quipocamayos fit the basic idea of notation? The Spanish bureaucrats who worked with cord masters before 1600 apparently thought they were seeing an almost perfect fit with a European notion, since all three conditions are indispensable to the European notation called accountancy. (I refer to accountants' actual data registry, not to the final product in archives, which is often muffled in prose.) Khipu "readouts" in colonial records decidedly refer to "antecedently atomized" referents (e.g., numbers of coca fields, per household, per ayllu). In the case of Tupicocha's cords, the formal resources of the sign system are suitable to meet "character" ends of the three conditions.

As we saw in describing the faena (workday) and ayllu complex (chapter 3), recent Andean practice embodies many devices that "atomize" the social flux by punctuating it with frequent ritual breaks, reducing levels of performance to simple discrete evaluative "grades" (fulfilled, excused, fined), bracketing material contributions in stereotyped ideal numbers, setting tasks in putatively discrete stretches, dividing topography into named sectors, and similarly bracketing personal attributes and statuses. The extreme bureaucratization of relations among close kin within ayllus—the imposition of artificially precise grids on relations which, in other contexts, are informal, continuous, improvised, and fluidly intimate—appears keyed to this imperative. The practice of community social control through mechanisms such as review of attendance and ledgers is predicated on reducing questions to highly schematic yes/no or discrete-interval values.

If asked why they insist on these rigors, villagers answer that "formal" practices cut down on disputes by clarifying cases. Tupicocha looks as though its practices have undergone a selective pressure favoring those which produce clear "factual" entities and distinctions—in other words, toward antecedent atomization. One test of this idea is to observe what conditions strain the system. A frequent cause of anxiety is improvisation in which performance fails to allow segmenting and measuring of resources. For example, the normal program for festival dancing is that dancers should form discrete troupes, which each make a circuit of "devotees" houses in a sequence of discrete "visits." In 1997 certain dancers combined troupes into an improvised conga line and snaked around the village ad lib. The dancers thus made it impossible for women of host households to schedule their cooking beforehand, and check off those groups already served so as to apportion enough for the remaining ones. In discussion over the next few days, some said the dance should be redefined, by written statute, as a series of discrete points on an itinerary.

Can Goodman's model accommodate code change? Chapter 4 detailed the likelihood that superficially "uniform" results are actually produced by continually redesigning control structures. Since the creation of these structures' visible tokens is itself their performative implementation, the notation representing the "uniform" order is not a constant code. When one takes into account the enormous modifications of the ayllu's functions from pre-Inka times to the end of the khipu-using era, it is hard to imagine that the appearance of "constancy"—for example, the durable corporate structure of the six-ayllu village until the 1920s—was achieved without analogous alterations in the media which achieved these functions. Formal deviations from the pre-Hispanic norm have already been discussed. Nothing in Goodman's position prohibits altering a notation. It is possible to imagine that the successive ways of implementing the purportedly invariant "round" of faenas under actually changing conditions would leave in cords signs of code inconsistency not unlike those of the staffs.

Goodman has something interesting to say about total notational products. He calls the assembly of notations representing a whole object (e.g., the sum of the sheets representing instrument-specific parts of a whole symphony) the *diagram* of that object. Goodman holds that although diagrams superficially look pictorial (as notes mimic the flowing contours of sound), and are therefore often taken as analog media, their analog components are usually minor. A wiring diagram resembles its object, yet a wiring diagram or a molecular model is digital in the sense of being "discrete throughout." Every sign in it falls in one slot of its paradigm, regardless of whether that is a two-slot paradigm, that is, a binary code.

In this way, as chapters 8 and 9 will argue, a Tupicochan quipocamayo seems in some respects analoguelike, diagrammatic, or even pictorial in the sense that a map is. In however schematic a way, it resembles its object. In chapter 8 we will discuss how some Tupicochans perceive certain cord features as being "like a diagram" or "like a map." If quipocamayos worked as suggested above, "diagram" in Goodman's sense appears a good characterization of their functioning when considered synchronically.

However, since analytical clarity is his only goal, Goodman sets aside what others might want to accent: the fact that a sign-bearing object may at once belong to plural sign systems. A moment's thought shows that in fact most do. Even the barest numerical ledger printout has lexigraphic and even prose components. There are reasons for supposing that not only arbitrary notational, but also iconic (representational) and even indexical (metonymic), object-relations played parts in the making of khipus.

Even if we were to suppose that Tupicocha enforced the arbitrariness of the cord sign with Saussurean severity, still, as long as individual cords were associable with individual members or acts, quipocamayos could go beyond pure diagrammatic function to become multiply constituted "data graphics," or as modern journalists call them, "infographics." Data graphics are images with properties beyond notation proper, as discussed in the works of Edward Tufte (1983:9). The reason data graphics (e.g., pie charts, quantified flow charts, and histograms) are more useful than bare data printouts is that they give the user multiple simultaneous cognitive toeholds on patterns in the data. Quipocamayos give the impression, too, of being data *displays* (see chapter 8). Tabular presentation, to which khipu readout in colonial texts is sometimes converted, does not help us notice this property.

The terms *notation* and *diagram*, then, have been of heuristic use in developing a less far-fetched concept of the khipu art than "cord writing" implies. Yet they do not capture the actual symbolic complexity of which cords are capable. In the end, one might consider the notion of *model* as the best accommodation for all these properties. "Models . . . are in effect diagrams . . . in more than two dimensions, and with working parts; or in other words, diagrams are flat and static models. Like other diagrams, models may be digital or analog or mixed" (Goodman 1976:172–73). The quipocamayo was apparently a model of a special sort: (1) it was a model functioning to effect control, (2) by making the rules of symbol assembly congruent to the rules of social practice, and (3) entrusting the acts of assembly to many participants (simultaneous, sequential, or both), (4) so that the product became an authoritative "collective representation" in the fullness of both Goodmanesque and Durkheimian senses. The remainder of this book is an attempt to reconstruct how this was done.

AYLLU CORDS AND AYLLU BOOKS

T UPICOCHA ABOUNDS in written archives: not just its community archive, which holds the colonial titles and modern business of the state-
recognized peasant corporation, but archives written by each individual
parcialidad or ayllu, spontaneously, outside state supervision.[1] Ayllu books allude
to the quipocamayos, without actually telling what information the cords contained. However, since books and cords belong to overlapping periods and were
presented as records at the same gatherings, where books gradually replaced cords,
the two media probably covered overlapping functions. (On vernacular accounting in general, see Enrique Mayer's *The Articulated Peasant* [2002].)

This chapter concerns nothing other than correspondences between manuscript
books and khipu structures. It is an admittedly dry topic. The eight section head-
ings are propositions derived from book-khipu comparisons, which will each be
put to the empirical test. For the nonspecialist reader, it will suffice to understand
the gist of each proposition, as summarized in the first paragraph of each section.

First, we will begin by interrogating archives for clues to cord content in their
relation to the huayrona-quipocamayo complex. In each of the eight following
sections, we comment on eight general rules of data handling. Finally, in the section "Quipocamayo Lessons from Audit Observations," data-handling practices
are examined for formal likenesses and functional analogies with the cord records.
As in chapter 6, references to Key Figure 26 aid comparisons with visible khipu
forms.

Intra-Ayllu Writings as Clues to Contents
of Tupicocha's Quipocamayos

Since the blurry 1650–1945 radiocarbon record cannot assign quipocamayos to any specific moment, it is too soon to discard the possibility that they record colonial institutions. These might include mitas or forced labor levies. Chapter 5 showed that the Tupicocha area managed its contribution to Lima-area forced labor through cords. It seems less likely that the cords were sources for visitas, the field inspections on which colonial governance based tribute levies. The cord basis of visitas up through the 1580s is undisputed, but the Tupicochan specimens hardly resemble the khipu format which Rostworowski (1990) reconstructs by working backward from a visita text.[2] It is easy to list other possibilities, from grazing fees to religious devotions, which are not unique to any period, but harder to square with any observed quipocamayo properties.

However, in view of the radiocarbon interpretation that nineteenth-century dates are more probable than earlier ones, and oral-historical evidence pointing the same way, it is the postcolonial ayllu which deserves priority in the search for khipu analogues.

The century-long run of books which ayllus wrote about their own doings fortunately do give a clear idea of what activities ayllu members felt bound to put on record. Comparisons among modern accounting practice, intra-ayllu writings, and the cords themselves warrant eight working propositions. They are discussed in a convenient expository order but are of equal heuristic standing.

1. The contents of quipocamayos are probably ayllu-internal.
2. Documentation consisted of planning and performance proofs (constancias).
3. The unit of account in books, and probably in cords, is the household.
4. Household sequencing may be relevant to quipocamayos.
5. The internal authority structure of ayllus governed the use of quipocamayos.
6. Prominent concerns of ayllu books are likely to continue concerns of quipocamayos.
7. Vernacular accounting may reflect khipu methods in data registry.
8. Vernacular auditing may reflect khipus' social uses.

The subsections which follow explore each hypothesis in relation to attributes of the quipocamayos.

The Contents of Quipocamayos Are Probably Ayllu-Internal

No entity other than an ayllu/parcialidad owns quipocamayos or ever claimed to in extant local writings. This section argues that they record the kinship corporation's internal self-management, and it suggests that since each ayllu had some

TABLE 8 Ownership of Tupicocha's Quipocamayos, 1999

AYLLU OR PARCIALIDAD	QUIPOCAMAYOS
Primer Allauca	1A-01
Primera Satafasca	1SF-01
Primer Huangre	1G-01
Unión Chaucacolca	Uch-01
	Uch-02
Mújica	M-01
	M-02 (in care of municipality, 2001)
	M-0x (fragment, apparently lost)
Cacarima	C-01
Segunda Allauca	2A-01
Segunda Satafasca	2SF-01
Centro Huangre	none
Huangre Boys	none

autonomy in how to do that, quipocamayos of differing ayllus utilized slightly different variants of the khipu art.

Table 8 shows the distribution of extant quipocamayos in customary precedence order.

Oral tradition holds unanimously that cord work was an ayllu-internal responsibility. No members ever comment on a quipocamayos other than their own group's. Members seemed uneasy when I probed for comparisons among different groups' quipocamayos. Not a single person was willing to compare them, or even reply to my own cross-ayllu observations. No recorded occasion includes auditing of parcialidades by authorities other than their own. Book practice is just as sharply segmented, with the same implicit rules. Community authorities accept without challenge the lists tendered by ayllus in establishing the membership database as well as in checking compliance with labor levies, grazing fees, and so on.

All this implies two questions. First, if ayllus did their cord work separately, as they do their book work, to what degree did the results form a uniform medium? The great bulk of cord technique is common to all ayllus, but there are distinctive features. The following features are each restricted to one ayllu: the color bluish-green, the color pinkish-beige, the color pale oque (bluish-gray), the Mújica knot, the placement of the start knob at the center of the main cord, and a variety of rare knot variants. If ayllus were separate documentary communities, they may well have evolved idiosyncrasies in cord conventions, thus drifting from Inka norms.

Second, we have already seen that the kinship corporations partake of an indispensable supra-ayllu sphere which manages canals, water turns, pasturage, and community-level ritual. If ayllu quipocamayos were such inward-looking documents, did they also hold outward-looking content, that is, information about the ayllu's participation in the wider sphere? Clues to the question, all pointing to a "yes" answer, are found primarily in the written register. Books profusely document ayllu contributions to the whole.

Documentation Consisted of Planning and Performance Proofs

The 128-plus volumes of internal proceedings which the Checa ayllus have compiled since the 1870s — that is, the accumulation of paper that grew as the cord complex receded, and which is in all likelihood its functional replacement — give a good index to what ayllus expected documentation to achieve. We hold that in the face of the bewildering scheduling problems that characterize polycyclical agropastoralism, books, like cords, achieved rationality by laying out plans to reconcile household with group needs. To deal with potential conflict, they sought equity by tracking each household's contributions to executing plans.

The early ayllu books are not extensions of municipal record keeping. From its spotty beginnings and inconsistent initial format onward through its genre evolution, the intra-ayllu paper record has two underlyingly consistent themes: *planning* and *performance*. Entries either record (1) a group commitment to do something or (2) group or individual fulfillment of a recorded commitment. The performance of a commitment is frequently noted by cancellation, that is, overwriting the obligation with *cumplido* (fulfilled) or *no vale* (invalid),[3] or by crossing it out.[4]

There are scattered exceptions such as protests about unrecognized paternity and the occasional *aide-mémoire* list of persons excused from one duty because they have incurred a conflicting one. The tendency to treat books as omnibus registers, strong at the beginning, steadily decreases.

The local books have a highly unified pragmatic intent: first, they ratify plans and thereby illuminate the future (allowing members to fit their separate household plans around the collective agenda), and second, they stand witness to the completion of plans (establishing each household's standing in regard to the group). Asked why everything must be written, villagers answer unanimously: "There must be proof" (Tiene que haber constancia). Apparently unlimited demand for "proof" derives both from functional anxieties — how to best deploy resources? — and group dynamics in a system where everyone demands equity and everyone suspects cheating.

As chapter 2 illustrated, the demands of irrigation, infrastructure building, private labor, vertical diversity, and out-of-town business have faced highland villagers with labyrinthine scheduling problems for a very long time. The functional point of documenting so many variables is not idle perfectionism, but the fact that exact planning and documentation are the sine qua non for rational action at household as well as collective level. Every villager threads his or her working days in and out of an intricate calendar of obligations at varied ecological and organizational levels. This is by no means a specifically modern imperative. As Stephen Brush (1977) and Jürgen Golte (1980) noted long ago, precise allocation of time is the heart of "polycyclical" rationality, which allows productivity in an ecologically heterogeneous setting. (Polycyclical systems are those in which producers manage multiple assets with dissimilar cyclical input demands.) It is likely, therefore, that prealphabetic systems of reckoning served this purpose, whether in the idiom of "regulative ritual" (Stanley Tambiah's phrase, directed to Andean cases by Gose 1994:4) or in frankly economic idiom.

The Unit of Account Is the Household

What unit was held accountable in vernacular accounting? It appears that the household rather than the person was the protagonist (Mayer 2002). Quipocamayos are therefore unlikely to have had censuslike properties.

An ayllu is an association of people called the "sons/daughters," "brothers/sisters," "fellows" (*socios*, also meaning business partners), or "citizens" of the group. In signed documents the household is represented by its usually male head, who is an inscribed member. The household's inner conduct is not the ayllu's business (officially). No ayllu document reckons numbers of individuals, only of members. Any right or duty of a member may be performed by, or privately assigned to, any able member of the household, or even to a nonkin designee, as in sending a peon to carry out an ayllu duty. Ayllu-internal functions have never included censusing, so it would be strange if quipocamayos turned out to be censuslike or individual-oriented records. Whatever they account for, the account is likely to be in terms of households. This convention matches an Inka practice (Murra 1978 [1956]:148) left in place by later regimes except when villages were captured by private estates.

Household Sequencing May Be Relevant to Quipocamayos

A record is not very useful unless its parts stand in an easily searched order. In addressing the data retrieval potential of quipocamayos, this section argues that Tupicocha in the last hundred years has used three methods, all visible in books, to array households. These may be clues about how quipocamayo parts are ordered.

The first is "ordinal number" (número de orden) by seniority. The most common practice today in ayllu-internal paperwork is to seriate by seniority as members (not by birth date). A person's ordinal number decreases as his seniority increases. Socios know their ordinal numbers like they know their own names. In early ayllu books, there is some tendency for members to sign in a regular sequence which probably reflects ordinal number. The system is simple and useful but has one defect: it fails to segregate people with handicaps (physical limitations, single parenthood, widowhood) so as to assign them adjusted duties. It is for this reason that ayllus supplemented it with functional bracketing (to be discussed below).

For the purpose of quipocamayo analogy, one must bear in mind another limitation, which may or may not be a defect. One's ordinal number of seniority is fixed only for a short interval (possibly as short as a semester, since retirements and inductions can occur on the "half year"). A person can be identified synchronically with an ordinal number, but diachronically, his ordinal position is only relational: "I am junior to member X, senior to Z." Provided people know each others' seniority—and it is among the readiest items of social knowledge, since one's immediate seniors and juniors are sure to be close lifelong associates—there would be no advantage in knotting ordinal numbers onto cords as numbers. Provided that (a) everyone knows that a given sequence of cords is a seniority sequence, (b) every member is represented, and (c) there is a way of knowing whether the sequence is current or relates to a specific past time, the sequence alone would suffice. This method would produce a series of elements (e.g., pendants or groups) equal to the number of members, but not labeled with numbers.

On the other hand, if a data set about members were arrayed in some sequence other than seniority (e.g., a series of work dates assigned to members on a non-seniority basis), ordinal numbers of seniority might serve as member labels. That would produce a series in which each ordinal number occurs, but not in numerical sequence.

Despite all limitations, "número de orden" sequence is congenial because it fits those micro-macro homologies so central to Andean ideology. The seniority idea saturates models of order among peers, from the mythic kindred of Paria Caca Mountain (whose Checa branch was a group of demes or clans ranked by birth order of founding sibling-heroes), through political ideology (*kuraka*, "ethnic lord," derives from *kuraq*, "firstborn"), through the seating of ayllus in the huayrona, to relations among living siblings.

The second method of sequencing, no longer in use, is "family order" (*orden de familias*), that is, patronymic grouping. Chapter 3 showed that although the ayllu is considered the indivisible political unit for public purposes, ayllus now as in 1608 internally analyze themselves as consisting of multiple "families," that is, predominantly patrilineal surname clusters. In ayllu books it was a recognized (though by no means uniform) procedure to have all the members of one family,—that is, patrilineage-by-surname—sign, then those of another (e.g., AP1A/SAT_01: 1955:18–20, 1959:36–37). The details of family order are not now clearly remembered. Nowadays Tupicochans consistently hold that all families have equal standing within their respective ayllus, so that the order of surname blocs is supposedly not significant. Certain families enjoy eminence as founding stock, without claiming ritual precedence. Looking back on old surname signature clusters, modern Tupicochans are unsure about whether (a) each bloc contained all the members of a patrilineage, or (b) each bloc contained a surname cluster consisting of one father and his sons, or, after the father's death, of a fraternal group. The latter hypothesis is more likely because (at least in Tuna) one may find nonadjacent family signature clusters with the same surname. The fact that some ayllus differentiate lineage segments with a shared surname by adding oral nicknames reinforces this second hypothesis. Sequence within family sets is likely to be seniority.

We do not know whether this overt equality of "families" was assumed at the time of quipocamayo manufacture or not.[5] If the quipocamayo makers still recognized the pre-Hispanic notion of precedence among families, family sets should occur in regular sequence. If one assumes on the contrary that families lacked hierarchy, one cannot assume family sets would occur in any repeating sequence.

For the purpose of quipocamayo analogy, one can assume that sets of a given feature representing a "family" (yumay, 'patrilineage') would have a visible attribute in common (e.g., a color). The various family sets within a given ayllu would have unequal, perhaps grossly unequal, numbers of members. The overall number of such sets would be small, because Tupicochanos think an ideal ayllu has no more than two or three surnames.

The third method for seriating members is the one which Guaman Poma de Ayala reports as Inka practice in his remarkable pages on the Inka census (1980 [1615]:168–209). Its principle is to sort people by their potential contribution to the polity. First comes a series of brackets running from prime tributary age upward to the retiring brackets; then comes an interlude concerning persons with modified responsibilities because of handicaps, regardless of age; and last comes a series of brackets running downward toward infancy. A few *padroncillos*, or registries, particularly in the Allauca ayllu (AP2A/SAT_02 1932:28–29; AP1A/SAT_01 1955:18–19), follow this system in a simplified form. Segunda Allauca used a system of numbered brackets for its 1932 membership list:

1. "Citizen tributaries" or persons under "obligation," that is, fully active members. This list is internally ordered by family clusters, and within each family by ordinal number.
2. "Elders" (mayores), that is, semiretired people.
3. Those who are "widowed or alone" and therefore unable to fulfill "tributary" obligations. (The words are marked with feminine gender.)
4. "Forthcoming" or "young" persons,[6] that is, those beginning to assume responsibilities in preparation for induction (AP2A_02 1932:28–29).

In 2000, Primera Satafasca worked similarly, handling the business of active members in the first of the paired sessions (horas de costumbre) and both past (retired) and future (próximo, that is, postulant) members in the second.

For purposes of quipocamayo analogy, one might look for the following as indicators. First, since the component sets are conceived as qualitatively dissimilar, they might be marked by some emphatically nonquantitative sign, such as colors, a "marker" tuft, or a "separator" cord. Second, in all the historic Tupicochan examples studied, the sets had a characteristic numerical profile. The first set was much larger than the last three, and the last three had successively declining numbers of members.

The Internal Authority Structure of Ayllus
Governed the Use of Quipocamayos

Early alphabetic records make some reference to the cord art in the context of ayllu office holding. They partially clarify how paired quipocamayos served paired officers in leading the ayllu. This section argues that the parts divided as paired responsibilities of office were (1) the semesters of the year and (2) inward- versus outward-looking duties.

References to these practices obey a logic of unequal duality. Like so many Andean structures, the two chief offices were arranged as counterparts, but not twins. Rather they were similar in form, complementary in function, and unequal in rank.

A first step in reconstructing this order is to note that before the wave of fissions which increased the ayllus from six to ten, quipocamayos were held in pairs (see table 9). In its internal records from 1914 until 1925, when a schism led to division of the goods, Satafasca made this explicit by inventorying "un par de quipo camayo con sus motas curiente" ("a pair of quipocamayos with its markers in OK condition"; AP1SF/SAT_01 1914:5, 1915:7, 1916a:9, 1918a:17, 1919b:24, 1921:30, 1922:35, 1923:38, 1923b:40, 1924:43, 1926:48). For other objects that number two but are not seen as counterparts, inventories use the numeral "2" and not the word *pair*. A very aged widow of a past camachico said that there were twelve quipocamayos in her husband's lifetime, as one would expect if undivided Huangre and Cacarima had held pairs.

The second step is to sort out the relation between dual quipocamayos and office hierarchies. Today the ayllus have elected hierarchies that are miniatures of the Community Directorate. But up to varying dates in the early twentieth century, each ayllu's directorate was topped by a pair of officers who stood in a relation of unequal precedence, as "diarchic" Inkas apparently did (Duviols 1979), or moiety lords of some non-Inka polities before 1532 (Murra 1968).

The day-to-day conduct of intra-ayllu policy was entrusted to a camachico, later renamed presidente. The camachico had as his complement an officer called mayor (Quechua equivalent unknown). In Leguía-era reforms, ayllus sometimes redesignated the mayor as vice president or as officer-at-large (*vocal*). The mayor was supposed to be a person of higher seniority than the camachico (AP1SF/SAT_01 1919a:23), and would typically be the outgoing camachico or a former one. Mújica in article 17 of its 1913 Constitution assigned the mayor the task of "maintaining the list of people who do not fulfill faenas" (APM/SAT_02 1913:5), which exactly matches the role of ayllu khipu knotting in the 1608 Quechua source.

AYLLU OR PARCIALIDAD	QUIPOCAMAYOS		
Allauca	1A-01	2A-01	
Satafasca	1SF-01	2SF-01	
Huangre	1G-01	?	
Unión Chaucacolca	Uch-01	Uch-02	
Mújica	M-01	M-02	M-OX
Cacarima	C-01	?	

The dual officers were responsible for work acts as far back as ayllu books reach (APM/SAT_01 1900: f. 16v, 15 April). Their two signatures sufficed to ratify political resolutions. When the ayllu authorized a cash expense, each of the two apparently held half the cash (APM/SAT_01 1906b:f. 30r, 1912:f. 39v).[7] Cacarima and Segunda Allauca still had the dual authorities signing off on faena records of the 1920s–1930s (AP2A/SAT_01 1932:113; APC/SAT_01 1925:98). Through the 1920s, each ayllu's mayor was explicitly required to be present when the camachicos attended all-village meetings (ACCSAT/SAT_02 1901:6, and similarly in the next five years). In practice, mayores often seem to have been treated as retired eminences attending optionally for the sake of gravitas. The mayor, people remember today, was expected to act as the conscience of the ayllu and speak out about matters on which a prudent president with hopes of higher office might keep silent.

A similar principle of dual leadership held at community level until approximately 1919. In the 1890s, before the Peruvian state recognized comunidad as an entity, it treated Tupicocha as a submunicipality, where a state-mandated agent exerted the authority of San Damián town (agencia municipal). Tupicocha responded by naming "customary" officers to sit alongside the municipal agent and cooperate with him.[8] The village had two *principales*, and not one but two "mayors" (*alcaldes*): a "municipal mayor" in charge of state-governed matters, and a "customary mayor" in charge of folk-legal matters. It is not clear whether the two mayors were the same individuals as the principales. It is certainly striking that their duties were, respectively, outward oriented and inward oriented. This offers one possible model of complementarity between mayor and the camachico at ayllu level (ACCSAT/SAT Folder "Irrigación" 1893; ACCSAT/SAT_01 1904:unnumbered; ACCSAT/SAT_02 1901:6; ACCSAT/SAT_04 1864:unnumbered; ACCSAT/SAT_05 1897b:25, 1897a:45–46).[9] From 1920 onward, camachicos continued in the same role as ayllu delegates / community constituents, but the twinned alcaldes and/or principales dropped out of the community-level record when single-apex "constitutional" arrangements took hold in the Leguía era.

(Anyone who has troubled to digest these intricacies will have noticed that the pattern of governance held constant in one way but was changing in another. A constant norm upholds microcosm-macrocosm homology between different levels of governance. But the direction in which homology proceeds has shifted, from upward to downward. The 1890s system, though it grew under a state regimen still unsympathetic to the comunidad concept, embodied an attempt to make the state's local agency mimic ayllu institutions. In today's system the community has a modicum of state power, and, as if by way of emulation, the internal structures of both the community and the ayllu have introjected state patterns of hierarchy.)

Thus far, we have treated the duality of authority in atemporal structural terms. But the actual use of dual authority followed a pattern of flip-flopping alternation through time. This temporal structure, like duality itself, uses a deep-rooted cultural template. It needs to be understood in its deep chronological context. A detour illustrating uses of alternating dualism will clarify the relation between paired quipocamayos and alternating duality of offices.

The Quechua Manuscript of Huarochirí, circa 1608, contains examples of ritual cycles that do not simply repeat, but alternate in a pattern of turns: cycle A, then cycle B, then A again. Pre-Hispanic Tupicocha had conceived of itself as a symbiosis between the aboriginal yunka ayllus, associated with the deities of the coast including the fivefold "Center Goddess" of the Rímac Valley, Chaupi Ñamca (let us say ayllus A[10]) and invading ayllus protected by Paria Caca Mountain (let us say ayllus B). In the pre-Christian regime, a two-year cycle presided by the aboriginal A lineages climaxed in the Machua Yunca fertility festival, when the ayllus competed in spearing giant male and female dummies. It alternated with a two-year cycle presided by the invading B lineages, climaxing in a warlike festival evoking conquest. At this event, the children of Paria Caca danced with masks made of war captives' flayed faces.

Paria Caca's modern children still use flip-flopping schemes, but for other purposes. In neighboring San Damián, where a Checa jurisdiction shares the village with a Concha community belonging to a different "Thousand," tradition has it that "One year Concha Sica used to come to Llaquistambo (for a certain festival), and the other year, Llaquistambo would attend at Concha Sica."[11] In Tupicocha, patron saint festivals are organized in an alternating cycle. The male patron, Saint Andrew, is feted on November 30 of each uneven year, and the female patron, the Virgin of Asunción, is feted on 15 August of each even year. This "biennial" system started in 1940, showing that alternating dualism is still a cultural recourse ready at hand. In the January festival cycle, when sacred clowns, or curcuches, descend from the mountains to bless the village with curative plants, two large urban-rural voluntary confraternities likewise alternate in leadership. Neighboring Tuna village uses a similar scheme, except that the alternate sponsors are the moieties known as "high neighborhood" and "low neighborhood." The lay officers of Tupicocha's church, too, cooperate by alternating: the first and second majordomos take turns holding the key, and the two sacristans take turns carrying the censer in processions. Each bulletin board used for posting irrigation turns is organized in two columns, which are read alternately in left-to-right order during odd months and the reverse in even months. The divining game of huayra huayra pichcamanta, discussed in chapter 6, limelights duality-in-alternation as the very core of political process and even of historicity.

We can now return to the question of paired officers, paired quipocamayos, and the ayllu books. It was noted above that the regime prior to the current one rested on dual ayllu authorities (camachico and mayor) as well as dual community spokesmen (the two principales). How did the duality of authorities relate to the duality of quipocamayos?

An oral tradition from Ayllu Chaucacolca holds that one quipocamayo belonged to the incoming, and one to the outgoing Ayllu president (camachico). The late Dionisia Alberco, who gave her birth date as 1900, remembered that in her youth both the new camachico and the outgoing one wore quipocamayos at the huayrona. This begs a further question: What would the outgoing or ex-camachico be doing with a quipocamayo of office?

In the old regimen the camachico held one quipocamayo and the mayor held the other. Ayllu Mújica's oldest book (APM/SAT_01 1900:p.16v) and still-undivided Satafasca's second book (AP1SF/SAT_01 1913:1–2) both affirm that dual officers headed ayllus into the twentieth century. Later, when the hierarchy had changed to a presidential system, inventories included "two quipucayos [sic] and one belongs to the President and the other to the Vice President"[12] (APUCh/SAT_03 1945:226). No record explicitly says which of the two offices absorbed the old mayor post, but it seems to be the vice presidency, because people today say that "president" means the same as "camachico." Mújica went on for decades inventorying two cord records as respectively "the president's" and "the vice president's."

If paired quipocamayos belonged to paired officers, then one may assume that their registered data concerned rules which the respective officers were responsible for enforcing. What data did the two offices have to maintain, and on what schedule? The scheduling part of the question is the less difficult of the two. There is ample evidence that Tupicocha's scheduling used (and still does use) a "six-month" or semester system as well as an annual one. The year, like so much else, is organized in terms of halves. This is reflected in the ayllus' core function of organizing faenas or workdays. In the 1910s and 1920s, Satafasca met yearly in February to organize "work until the June six-month for the potato planting . . . for all of us who have need" (AP1SF/SAT_01 1916b:11). Segunda Satafasca audited its treasurers on the semester system (AP2SF/SAT_02 1929:20–21, 1945:89). Early Mújica records of the 1880s (APM/SAT_01 1889:f. non num. 3v) show the same pattern, and also a system of loaning funds on six-month terms. Every major festival cycle still includes "the six-month" (el seis-mes), that is, a planning session one semester before the climactic day.[13]

The semester system intersected with the quipocamayo system insofar as semesters structured the camachico-mayor relationship. In 1913, still-undivided Satafasca set down in its new Constitution the attributes of its top dual authorities. The language is somewhat elusive, but it can be translated approximately as follows: "The Mayor's right to this parcialidad to accompany six months from the first of January until the month of June thirty without any grounds or pretext to having the same attributes of the camachico they will associate [*se conjergaran*] and coordinating equally [*y cordonandose*[14] *ygualmente*]"(APISF/SAT_01 1913:1).[15] The admittedly obscure 1913 passage seems to mean that during the first half of the year, the mayor was to enforce his domain but not to try to override the camachico responsible for the ayllu's primary function. The statute seems designed to correct a tendency for the mayor to usurp.

Both offices were elected at New Year, so one may assume their respective quipocamayos were updated concurrently and that both served for a year. The respective domains of the two offices are not pinned down in any document. Elderly experts on customary law are unsure of the details of the old dual regimen. Some suggest that the camachico was responsible more for ayllu-internal affairs and faenas, while the mayor was responsible for those looking outward to all-community interests. Others suggest that the differentiation of jurisdictions might have been chronological, with the mayor responsible, in the first semester, for enforcing overdue obligations from the cycle ending at New Year—leftovers that should definitely be seen to by the half year. This would explain the usurpation problem. If the mayor came into office honor-bound to clear backlogs (perhaps registered by cords stitched into place as a caution against false clearing, like the band seen in fig. 41 and Key Figure 26 pendants 43–45), he might be tempted to strong-arm the new camachico's agenda—the more so if the deficit had accrued during his own camachico term.

Prominent Concerns of Early Ayllu Books Are Likely to Continue Concerns of Quipocamayos

This section argues that the main administrative duties of the two officers holding quipocamayos were to organize members' "round" of mutual-aid workdays, to mobilize the ayllu for building communitywide infrastructures, to support the major fiestas, to manage the ayllu's collective assets, and to attend to several less pressing matters which may nonetheless also have stamped their formal properties on cord records.

The words *camachico* and *principal* both crop up much earlier than the first ayllu books, in mid- and late-colonial papers. Since we do not know for certain that Tupicocha's quipocamayos postdate the colonial era, it remains possible that they connected with the functions for which ayllus were responsible to their "natural lords," the kurakas. The cords could also have concerned the responsibilities of kurakas to the Spanish state, namely, the supplying of forced-labor quotas to the Lima labor market and to the tambos, or way stations, of the Cuzco highway. The fact that the old titles survived through the early Republic suggests that after the end of *kurakazgo* (O'Phelan 1997) and after the (frequently phony) transformation of tribute to citizen taxation, local people continued to perceive a continuity with Inka-derived colonial office. This mentality—the disposition to meet the demands of supra-ayllu authority but meet them on terms reserving for ayllus the status of preexistent polity (Platt 1982)—continued on into a time when outside demands no longer included colonial levies.

Early ayllu books show some of the results. Books at first planned and recorded many sorts of activities ad hoc, typically concerning monetary and bureaucratic matters outside the ayllu tradition. But as the habit of keeping books became consolidated after 1900, entries become orderly, and they began to cover the uppermost ayllu priorities.

As regards ayllu-internal duties, chapter 3 emphasized the fact that until about 1930, the chief obligation and the chief benefit of belonging to an ayllu was labor reciprocity through internal faenas or collective workdays. In each ayllu Constitution, the first duty of membership was to "andar faenas entre los ciudadanos" (to walk workdays among the members)—that is, apply collective labor to each member's household by turn, and receive in return certain ritual tokens in sign of commitment to reciprocity. A complete cycle of mutual-aid faenas was called a vuelta (round) of faenas. The round, as I will call it, was only one of the scheduled labor obligations, since both intra- and extra-ayllu officials also had the right to call out ayllus as teams to accomplish tasks on the larger, communitywide infrastructure. But it was certainly the most important one.

Here is a representative entry from a Segunda Allauca book of faenas, standing for one day in the round:

> List and fines of the Allauca parcialidad in the faena that Don Marcos Vilcayauri carried[16] to thresh wheat in the place of Cancasica on the date 10 of October of 1923 and the absentees were
> Saturnino Cajañaupa, paid
> Elías Cajañaupa sick
> Ysidro Capistrano, paid
> Celestino Llaullipoma, paid
> Domingo Cajañaupa paid
> And he [D. Marcos Vilcayauri] owes on the work 1 sol
> [signed with flourish] Higinio Cajañaupa
> [Whole entry overwritten:] not valid (AP2A/SAT_02 1923:12).[17]

As in the Quechua manuscript of Huarochirí, and also as discussed below, the way of record keeping is to mark negatively, that is, to register the absent.

Although books elaborate the faena theme and pick up additional themes, nothing rivaled faenas for central importance. But as the twentieth century passed, outward-looking or supra-ayllu obligations gradually became the dominant concern of the books. Little by little, the former beneficiaries of the round came to feel that despite all its advantages (low risk, low cost, incremental benefits in the form of solidarity beyond labor), the round's rigid demands of formal reciprocity made it less convenient than flexible hired labor. Since quipocamayos belong to the age when the round was the first order of ayllu business, faena administration seems a good clue to what quipocamayos are likely to have encoded.

The second most frequent order of ayllu-internal business is limandas, that is, pledges on loans of portable sacred objects. Pledges, as explained in chapter 3, were the leading way for the ayllu to generate a welfare and ritual fund. Pledges and cancellations also take up a substantial share of early paperwork. The history of limandas is obscure. It seems that they were few around 1900; Cacarima ayllu only had four in 1905. They seem to have reached their present massive popularity in the twentieth century, perhaps in step with the rising importance of cash. But that does not prove they are a novelty. The possibility that they figure in quipocamayos cannot be discarded. Similarly, loans from the fund thus generated are a possibility.

The third most frequent order of ayllu-internal business is the election and installation of officers, and especially the handing over of the current expense fund and the welfare-ritual fund. It seems a reasonable hypothesis that for formality's sake — and ayllus are nothing if not formal — the ayllu-internal cords included information on office holding, even though in practice nobody would have to look up such obvious facts.

What about ayllu-external functions? The general rule during the first few decades of ayllu book-writing was that it was primarily the community's job to keep books of supra-ayllu work. From the 1920s on, however, ayllus became more and more punctilious about writing "work acts" documenting their respective labor quotas and performance, at first to provide a basis in case of dispute, and later for commemorative purposes too. For example, the Segunda Allauca book cited above regarding the "round" of faenas also records annual communitywide champerías, or canal cleanings, as well as pasture-wall work and the construction of the Community Hall. To communitywide obligations, Leguía-era state authorities added still another level: increasing levies for highway building and other national public works. From 1926 on, supra-ayllu duties began to outweigh the "round." This trend has accelerated ever since.

For recent decades ayllu books provide a clear idea of ayllu contributions to the community whole. Usually, each ayllu keeps one book for each of the major water systems (or other villagewide enterprises) in which it is active. For example, Primera Satafasca keeps a book on its work in the Lanzasa canals, a group watering the lower-lying fruit groves (AP1SF/SAT_07 1948–84). The bulk of records concern the canal-cleaning season, that is, the second quarter of the year. The record has, as noted above, a planning section and a performance section. The planning section in turn has two parts: acts of "installation" (estalación), which constitute an intra-ayllu agenda, including the names of the sponsors who will conduct the work rituals, the quotas of coca, and so on; persons stationed at each node of the system; and sanctions for absence. The other planning act is called "Plan for shares of labor and supplies," which contains the detailed schedule. The performance record also has two parts: reports of compliance with the plan, namely, lists which are compiled into multiday charts, and, later and less regularly, "historical reports" narrating the project synoptically in prose. The formal makeup of ayllu-external task records would seem likely to resemble that of ayllu-internal ones.

As for the patron saint ritual cycle, a major piece of the economy, ayllu books do not break down contributions of crops or labor. They only identify ritual sponsors. It is likely that quipocamayos once contained accounts of goods and services for communitywide festivals, perhaps quotas delivered to the Collca. Some elders think brilliant run-through threads were earmarks referring to fiestas. But as noted in chapter 2, actually staging these festivals was mostly a task of the community-wide Directorate.

The actual division of water-use turns, the most urgent of all agricultural worries, has not been under ayllu control in the era documented or remembered, as explained in chapters 2–3 and is not likely to be reflected in quipocamayos.

Vernacular Accounting May Reflect Khipu Methods in Data Registry

Today, exhaustive public audits scrutinize each member's and each group's standing. Auditing is the theater of social responsibility. This section argues that quipo-camayos evolved as the infrastructure for Tupicocha's "social audit" procedure. Drawing admittedly high-risk ethnographic analogies, we argue below that still-extant technical issues in summarizing people's records clarify the technical alternatives that quipocamayo makers faced. For example: Did one record the default or the exception? Did one include or omit blank records?

The best-documented theme of khipu recording in Huarochirí for the colonial-to-modern khipu era is labor registry (and not herd records, as in the Cuzco-Titicaca regions). We have already seen that labor is also the uppermost theme in paper records. The atoms of labor registry are attendance marks, mostly for faenas and business meetings and occasionally for production. But the implications of this fact for cord interpretation depend on working assumptions about how these marks work: What, exactly, is each mark the mark of? Ayllu books give a warrant for studying four models.

Method 1, *negative listing* or the marking of absentees, is the method mentioned in the 1608 Quechua source. It also was by far the commonest way to record attendance from the first signs of alphabetic registry until the 1930s, and it predominated in some ayllu books through the 1940s (e.g., 1A_01, belonging to the ayllu reputedly most conservative of khipu customs). The Segunda Allauca act translated above is a typical example. This example reminds us that to say a record is negative is not merely to say it contains "no" answers to "yes/no" questions about attendance. A "no" demands explanation. For the universe of absentees, a negative labor registry deals with four or five variables: date, place, identity of absentee, and status of absence (unexcused and fined, excused, sick). The fifth variable is the beneficiary or function of the work. Why these items? They are the ones indispensable for intra-ayllu equity. They are the same items audited in parcialidad proceedings up through 2000.

These variables are strong candidates to have been core data in quipocamayos. In fact, it is simply impossible to imagine an ayllu maintaining coherence without accurate and consensual knowledge of them. Such knowledge would quickly outrun memory. Early in the 1920s, Segunda Allauca began a "book of lists and fines," which contains long continuous runs of such data. Most are in negative format, and will be analyzed in more detail below.

Method 2, *positive listing*, or listing of those in compliance, is less common in early writings. It was used at first for mandatory contributions other than faena labor, usually those demanded by outside state authority. Examples are mitas or turns of messenger service (APM/SAT_01 1914:f. 56v), service in directorate offices, or payment of "porratas," i.e., quotas of structural materials (e.g., APISF_01 1918b:19).[18] However, in the 1920s and later, scribes did occasionally render faena service positively, sometimes for unknown reasons and sometimes to highlight a certain day's work as deserving of remembrance, for example, because it marked the kickoff of a new project. It may be significant that positive listing, unlike negative listing, is useful for the later production of *historias memoriales*, or commemorative narratives, a festive genre sometimes found in ayllu books.

Method 3, *negative-positive reckoning*, in which all members are listed and marked as to whether they complied or not, is a relatively recent innovation. It did not become common until tabular reckoning in grids was popularized, in the later 1930s. Today, labor records usually germinate as unofficial lists of absentees or compliant persons in secretaries' private notebooks, and they may become prose-format negative records in daily "work acts." They are prepared for audit by compiling lists into negative-positive multivariate charts.

Method 4, not witnessed, but attested elsewhere in the Andes, is *double-entry*. A Tupicocha youth, remembering that an old herder on the heights had shown him his khipus, said, "When an animal is lost, he unties one knot and ties another." This is a striking datum insofar as it matches the earliest of all European observations on khipus, Pizarro's observation that cord workers noted a transaction as both debit and credit. However, there is an obstacle to believing intra-ayllu records were double-entry. From the 1890s on, ayllus bought ledgers preprinted for double-entry bookkeeping, but not one officer has ever adopted the method. Either nobody saw the analogy with double-entry khipus, which seems unlikely given the prestige of bookkeeping as a form of cultural knowledge, or else double-entry was seen as less useful than charting in tables (the padroncillo method).

Bringing all this together for quipocamayo analogy, one may make two inferences. The first is based on the fact that negative reckoning was the more habitual or "default" method at the time when paper media were just coming into intra-ayllu use. In that era, positive reckoning was used for more marked or special occasions. One may therefore suspect that cord media would show a preponderance of negative reckoning in routine affairs but more instances of positive recording in nonroutine items.

Second, it is important not to assume that compliance implied the absence of a cord. The 1608 source says that the Concha authorities recorded absence by "knotting" (*quipuspa*) absentees, that is, making a knot in a putatively already-extant cord. It does not say, and neither does any other known source, that one created a cord to signal absence. So a cord record which makes heavy use of negative notation would not necessarily contain fewer cords for any given recording task than one which reckoned otherwise — only fewer knots on them.

Vernacular Auditing May Reflect Khipus' Social Uses

The previous section suggested that ayllus' peculiar internal audits echo ancient practice in techniques for reckoning. This section argues that they also clarify the broader practices of "social accounting." These include the organization of ayllu wealth into two nonconvertible spheres of exchange; a concept of total social audit, of which money is a subset; a concept of collective authorship; the targeting of zero; the ritual framework of quantitative rationality; and the open-endedness of the "social audit" mandate.

Andean accounting has been studied by Enrique Mayer, who, like his collaborator Fonseca, characterized it as a method for guaranteeing reciprocity in multiple spheres of exchange (2002:205–37). One Tupicochan ayllu wrote down a statute for audit procedures in 1905, a date probably within the last era of quipocamayo usage (APC/SAT_01 1905:1–4). Its basic rules to some degree parallel Mayer's characterization.

The fundaments of ayllu auditing are

1. The money of the ayllu consists of two funds or accounts, which are separately audited: a fund called the "work funds,"[19] which are the proceeds of work sold and of fines for work undone; and the "income of limandas"[20] fund, which contains the proceeds from pledged donations and other ritual income. The former covers routine expenses and infrastructures, while the latter functions as credit union and also as financier of ritual functions. Terminology varies over time and between ayllus, but the retention of separate accounts which may never be cross-transferred and which might therefore be considered "spheres of exchange," is enduring.

2. Unlike metropolitan accountancy, peasant accountancy does not depend on money as a universal common denominator. It is a *social* audit, covering every member's contributions, whether monetary or not. In 1905 the treasurer was to be audited for money, the camachico for ritual objects, and the collectivity for tools. Related modern procedures are still in place. The items audited in 1997 in Segunda Satafasca were

a. Attendance at faenas and business meetings.

b. Payment of fines for nonattendance at these. The analysis of performance is carried out with the household-heading member, not the faena (or other group) as the unit of account. That is, first John Doe must stand audit for his absences and fines in all the events of the term, then Richard Roe, and so on.

c. Other "work"-related income.

d. Expense of the "work" account.

e. Balance and liquidation of this account.

f. Inventory of the *enseres*, or moveable corporate property, with tools, ritual objects, and books as the main subcategories. All objects must be actually present and inspected (see fig. 43).

g. Income to the ritual fund account, that is, audit of ritual promises made at the ricuchico, and charging of overdue promises.

h. Expenses of the ritual fund.

i. Balance and liquidation of the ritual fund, and decisions on future applications.

3. The audit is a ritual occasion. It is punctuated by music and circle-dancing. It is sanctified in the usual fashion with "enflowerment" and rounds of coca, tobacco, and liquor at the appropriate break times.

4. The audit targets zero. That is, for any given category, the default correct outcome is to have neither assets nor debits at the end of the cycle. Just as each individual wants a zero balance of labor/fines due, the collective expense fund is either to be brought up to zero by pro rata donations, or liquidated down to zero by dividends (see fig. 44).

5. The ayllu has the option of carrying forward a balance or a debit, but this must be decided by sense of meeting. This option is used when some part of the ending cycle's agenda remains unfinished and the new cycle therefore cannot be a fresh start. The foregoing also applies, separately, to the ritual fund.

6. The audit has no individual author or authority. All members are equally responsible for calculating all items (see fig. 45). It is an "audit" in the most literal sense, that is, an oral-aural event. Each member brings a pad and pencil, and calculates or lists every item as it is stated aloud, without consulting peers. There is no such role as authoritative accountant. Calculation continues for as long as it takes for all to agree. The directorate presides without itself deciding anything except the order of business. Indeed when the members of one ayllu offered their incoming 2000 officers a motion of confidence to leave some overdue accounting

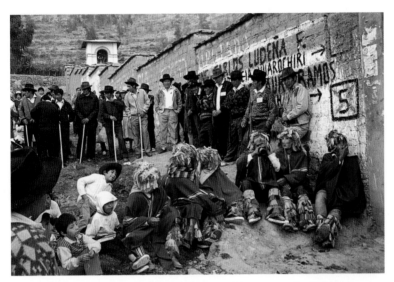

PLATE 1 Staff-holding traditional authorities of the community (left rear) gather with quipocamayo-draped presidents of ayllus (right rear) and sacred clowns (foreground), 7 January 1997. From personal collection of author.

PLATE 2 Rolling up ayllu Segunda Satafasca's quipocamayo 1SF-01 in the ancient way. From personal collection of author.

PLATE 3   Quipocamayos on display at the Huayrona or civic plenum, 1995.
From personal collection of author.

PLATE 4   The newly
invested ayllu presidents
of 2000. From personal
collection of author.

PLATE 5   Signing the minutes after installation of 2000 ayllu presidents. From personal collection of author.

PLATE 6   Pendants of ayllu Segunda Allauca's quipocamayo 2A-01. From personal collection of author.

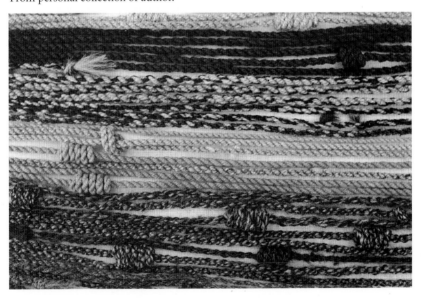

PLATE 7 The pachacamanta or end knob of ayllu Primera Satafasca's quipocamayo 1SF-01. From personal collection of author.

PLATE 8 Hito, or marker, on quipocamayo C-01 of Cacarima ayllu. From personal collection of author.

PLATE 9 Pendants of Cacarima's C-01. Note variety of diameters, designs, and finishes of cordage. From personal collection of author.

PLATE 10 Nery Javier Rojas and his former teacher with his simulacrum, in 1999. From personal collection of author.

PLATE 11 Amancio Javier lifts
cords seeking relevance to a
numerological reduction of a
name. From personal collection
of author.

PLATE 12 Close-up of 1A-01. Note color bands, using combinations of natural wool
colors, and their unequal numbers of pendants. From personal collection of author.

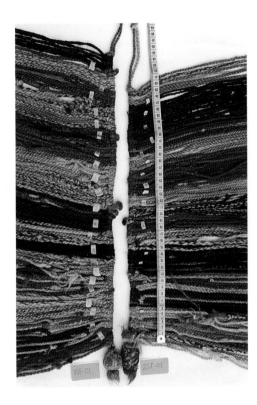

PLATE 13   The formerly paired quipocamayos 1SF-01 and 2SF-01. From personal collection of author.

PLATE 14   Primer Huangre's quipocamayo is almost empty of knots. From personal collection of author.

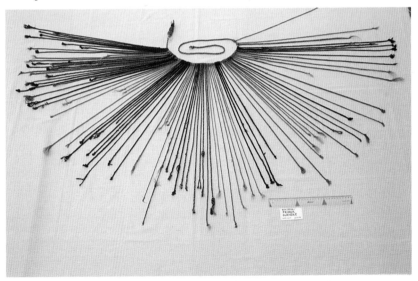

PLATE 15   To observe M-01's quartet structure, look for the pale gray cord forming the third member of each quartet. From personal collection of author.

PLATE 16   Pendant 39 of quipocamayo M-01 is exceptional in its multiple bright threads and in its knotting. From personal collection of author.

in the officers' hands, these wisely refused on the grounds that any number not reckoned in the plenum would eventually become a bone of contention.

7. Since the unit of account is the household, a member's spouse or grown child can substitute in any function and is co-responsible for debts. Wives are frequent proxies of male members in handling cash. (Women are considered better fiduciaries since, unlike men, they are not expected to drink during audits. But because they are considered worse workers in hard labor, a member who often has his wife stand in at faenas may hear grumbling or even challenges to his compliant status.)

8. The audit is open-ended and flexible in format. Since it is a plenary meeting, any timely business can be enacted. Examples include the induction of new members or retirement of old, debate on policies of the community, resolutions of appreciation or of censure, and proposals for changing rules or beginning new projects. The record created at an audit is therefore not necessarily limited to the above-mentioned accounts. It is entirely possible that quipocamayos also treated a miscellany of agenda.

Quipocamayo Lessons from Audit Observations

For the purpose of quipocamayo analogy, these observations must be used cautiously, because two major changes separate current practice from that of pre-1900 quipocamayo makers. One is the drastic monetization of many kinds of transactions. The other is the learning of metropolitan bookkeeping techniques by schooled villagers. Nonetheless, one can entertain a few inferences.

1. The unity of a quipocamayo resides in its correspondence to the unity of the social event that generated it, or the single class of similar events that generated it (e.g., huayronas, cuentas, or audit days), rather than in unity of subject matter. I would hazard a guess that local-level quipocamayos group together disparate subjects which are socially audited in the same forum, rather than grouping together conceptually related subjects. Since the quipocamayo is the precipitate of transactions in a meeting of wide scope, it too may be of wide scope.

2. The ethnographic observation of recent audits confirms what the study of old written records indicates: the single greatest concern is faena duties. The intracommunal commoditization of labor has relocated the "readout" of faena debts as part of the "asset" audit for the corporation's running expense fund (because the delinquents' fines are important income to it). However, at the time when quipocamayos were made, their cords may have been organized in terms of workdays due rather than monetary fines incurred. Extant records do not clarify when ayllu duties and cash became convertible.

3. In asking what works are recorded, it is important to note that the ayllus' current audit deals with both duties of the inward-facing, ayllu sphere and the outward-facing duty to attend faenas for the whole community. The need for faenas in the overarching interest is as old as communitywide governance of water

FIGURE 43   On audit day, each ayllu inventories its *enseres*, or collective property, with detailed inspection—here a flower vase used to adorn its chapel. From personal collection of author.

FIGURE 44   Distributing the balance of ayllu treasury on Segunda Satafasca's 1995 audit day. From personal collection of author.

infrastructure. That is, it may well be pre-Hispanic. Nowadays, with the round of mutual-labor faenas obsolete and the supra-ayllu demand for faenas accentuated by state and NGO levies, the outward-facing faenas have become the lion's share of them. The ayllu does not originate them; nor is it corporately sanctioned if any of its members fail to serve, but ayllu members must make up for absent peers' labor. Moreover, ayllus feel ashamed if they lag, and proud if they lead, in multi-ayllu jobs. Therefore service to the larger whole, and not just to ayllu mates, is on the minds of ayllu auditors and on the pages they produce. It is likely equally to have concerned the makers of quipocamayos.

4. There remains a chance that ayllus in the past recorded collective land use, namely, grazing fees on ayllu lands as well as management of those sectors of community cropland apportioned by parcialidad. Ethnographic analogy is not a powerful tool on this score, because ayllus today do not generally govern pasturage. But the lands which the community won in its "war" with a neighboring village (see chapter 3 in the section "Ayllu and Land") are apportioned to parcialidad, and its crops are accountable within the ayllu. Certain crops (perhaps those of special plantings earmarked for festival use) are a plausible quipocamayo content.

FIGURE 45   At community and ayllu levels, auditing requires every member to calculate the entire year's transactions as they are read out from records. From personal collection of author.

5. After faenas, the most important focus of the modern audit is the segregated ritual fund, that is, data on ritual income (pledges, etc.) and expenses. (The 1608 Quechua source, too, mentions ritual donation—namely Inka subsidies to huacas—as the only other khipu subject matter besides hydraulic faenas.) Records of ritual income abound in paper records. Unlike faenas, however, pledges are never grouped in khipu-like columnar or tabular fashion, but rather documented in prose paragraphs. Since ritual funds are sharply segregated from the labor record today, they may have been so in cord-using days. If pledges appear on quipocamayos, they may appear as groups of pendants out of proportion to the numbers of pendants in labor-related bands or groups, because the number of persons pledging in any given year does not covary with number of members obligated in faenas. Pledgers may be non-members, and their cords may therefore have atypical features. They are possible referents for "groups of singletons" discussed in chapter 9 and illustrated as pendants 13–15 of Key Figure 26.

6. The third most important focus of the audit is inventory of collective property, consisting of tools, ritual objects, and books. An inventory of tools and ritual objects would also probably look quite different in quipocamayo from faena or ritual registries, because not all belongings have a per-capita dimension, that is, a proportion to demography. Because it consists of a list of heterogenous items, it might contain strings that look a "hodgepodge." Inventories are also possible referents of the "groups of singletons" discussed in chapter 9.

7. Since the audit targets zero, a large number of unknotted, that is, zero-value, strings would be expectable for the data state immediately after audit. All Tupicochan specimens have large proportions of knotless pendants and subsidiaries.

8. If the ayllu quipocamayo was made and maintained by processes similar to the ayllu audit, then it must be considered a collective artifact. Presumably, a single person in any given audit did the actual job of working cords, and might be called a khipukamayuq, or khipu master, for that given context, just as today the immediate scribes of auditing are the secretary and treasurer. But the authority of the audit depends on the fact that everyone made it. Given the fact that quipocamayos were not annually replaced, it is likely that this also means everyone made it physically, or at least modified it. Composite construction, alteration, replacement of parts, heterogeneity of material, and so on, as discussed in chapter 6, are therefore expectable attributes of the physical record.

9. If quipocamayos were worked at functions resembling the audit, they may embed additional agenda besides the above. The quipocamayo analogue of a complex meeting might be one containing cords in regular data array (i.e., bands of cords with regularities proportionate to the faena regimen, etc.) but also miscellanea such as rate setting, inductions and retirements, changes of policy, etc.

10. Under the same assumption, quipocamayos are *not* likely to record the following:

    a. Calculations ancillary to major obligations, such as calculations of "stretches." These calculations do not occur in early paper records, and at later dates, though written, they are not integrated with audits.

b. Calculations outside ayllu control. Water turns, while of vital importance, were not under ayllu control in recent times. They connect the supra-ayllu sphere to the consuming household, with the ayllu mediating in the supply of labor but not the distribution of benefits.

Taken together with chapter 5's argument for a long khipu chronology, this chapter's discussion may well provoke debate about how and when the transition from cord to paper record-keeping took place, and whether it entailed cultural shifts in thinking about the nature of inscription. This question is separable from khipu decipherment as such. It will be treated in a forthcoming work. For the moment, it is interesting that until villagers learned to make multivariate tables in the 1930s, they had no compact data registry system comparable in power to the khipu art. This fact may have much to do with the long survival of a technology ignored and occasionally banned by state and church.

Having gathered what is known about vernacular data-managing and administrative process, we now ask whether extant quipocamayos may be understood as related to these practices.

THE HALF-LIFE AND AFTERLIFE OF AN ANDEAN MEDIUM: HOW MODERN VILLAGERS INTERPRET QUIPOCAMAYOS

LIVING MEMORY in Tupicocha connects with the quipocamayo legacy too tenuously to offer any breakthrough. Yet time has not completely obliterated khipu culture. The present chapter gathers folk exegeses obtained through elicitation and relates them to the structures identified in Key Figure 26. Because this entails working with fragmentary, semicompetent testimony, it requires pondering how to approach media that are not "alive" but are still the objects of folk interpretation. We present elements of apparently conservative khipu knowledge retained in "half-life" today. We also consider a secondary occult lore of quipocamayo interpretation. Finally, by a route which involves considering the "death" of media in terms of Andean death concepts, we ask which local ideas about the nature of lost inscription appear firm enough to be of interest for decipherment research.

The Half-Life and Afterlife of Dying Media

Bruce Sterling, a science fiction writer, has mounted an Internet project on "dead media."[1] In its 1995 inaugural speech, he asked his peers to momentarily set aside the canon of decipherment methods, and engage each "dead" medium through "an act of imaginative concentration":

> I think it's quite a good idea to go into a quiet room with a *quipu*. Go to a room and shut off the electricity. Don't look at the quipu with scorn or condescension. Just hold it in your hands and try to pretend that this is the

only possible abstract relationship, besides speech, that you have with the world. Really try to imagine what you are "missing" by not comprehending all economics, all governmental business, all nonverbal communication, as a network of colored yarn. Think of this as a discipline, as an act of imaginative concentration, as a human engagement with a profoundly alien media alternative.

As an exercise in clearing away extraneous assumptions and meditating on unfamiliar ones, Sterling's suggestion makes some sense. But the "dead media" approach itself involves a hidden extraneous assumption, insofar as it assumes that media death is analogous to Western folk ideas of death: a moment of expiration followed by an eternity of absence. This is misleading. In the first place, the cord medium did not expire at a particular moment, but rather waned slowly, leaving some traces of competence. Second, insofar as the medium actually is dead (i.e., competence for the original civic function has disappeared), its status is still not exactly what we usually mean by the word *dead*. In ways which I believe to be nonaccidental, the status of the quipocamayos resembles the standing of the ancient Andean ancestors: immobile, everlasting, socially "present," and forever interrogated for meaning. In treating their "dead" medium somewhat as Andean peoples formerly treated defunct human beings, Tupicochans seem to have retained some old interpretative habits which may fittingly be collated with traces of "living" knowledge.

THE DEATH PROCESS OF AN ANDEAN MEDIUM

"Birth" versus "death" metaphors governed by commonsense ideas of mortality, as well as "invention" versus "abandonment" metaphors governed by the history of Western technology, can easily put us off the track of what might be dissimilar trajectories in inscriptional history.

In chapter 1, we noted that there is something arbitrary about choosing any particular point as *the* moment when a practice of social problem-solving through signs begins to be a script. "Writing-ness" is better seen as a gradually emergent property of simulation practices, not an invention. Likewise at the other end of a sign system's trajectory, one can rarely put "RIP" to any particular date of abandonment. Students of "language death" (Dorian 1981; Kahane and Kahane 1979) have identified certain processes and landmarks in waning speech communities, such as abandonment of certain contrasts, endemic uncertainty about correct usage, and retreat to highly specialized contexts. Just after the present study was completed, Stephen Houston, John Baines, and Jerrold Cooper published the first systematic attempt to compare script obsolescence with "language death" (2003).

I suggest that for Andean purposes the end of the cord-inscribing age should be imagined not as death but as a fading half-life, like radioactive decay or the decreasing activity of a drug dose. Half-life serves only as a gross heuristic metaphor, since the concept was invented for quantitative tracking of continuous variables, while the components of a symbolic code competence are not additive quanta but functionally interlocked parts. The actual path of decay may therefore be more stepwise than continuous, falling of successive "cliffs" of incompetence as functionally vital principles are successively forgotten. The half-life metaphor serves rather to evoke the quality of khipu knowledge as Tupicochanos experience it: ever-receding, and yet never quite gone.

There are ethnographic reasons to think of Tupicochan khipu competence as a sign system far into decay, but one that still has a way to go before reaching a de facto vanishing point. Quipocamayo competence seems to have fallen off the cliff of widely shared productive competence almost a century ago, and off the cliff of shared passive competence some decades later. An individual, even esoteric and unshared, competence seems to have lingered longer, past 1950 in incomplete form. In the opinions of the few people focalized throughout this chapter, fragments of this last competence still cohere. Their exponents believe themselves possessors of an incomplete but still meaningful skill. Their readings, however incompatible and speculative, may yield some clues about older cord usage.

In the next section I examine a young villager's attempt to recover the systematicity of cord and knot patterning by mobilizing half-forgotten lessons from a dying cord expert, his great-grandfather. This youngster's procedure is an attempt to climb back up the downward path of code half-life, emulating what is remembered by making a simulacrum, and using the simulacrum to clarify memories about how parts once fit together.

However, his effort at conserving patrimonial knowledge is far from the only thing that has been happening along the quipocamayos' way to dusty media death. The fact that inscriptions, unlike speech, have material incarnations outliving their actual usage, allows a second process, quite different from half-life, to take over as the original competence recedes.

This second process could be called afterlife. A far-decayed or unknown symbol system gains as well as loses putative legibility, as long as its physical inscriptions endure and are taken to be signs worth noticing. Some "dead" inscriptions become opaque metonyms, as when one finds factories marketing Sigma lenses or Beta camcorders, not because customers can read Greek, but because Greek letters are emblems of the mathematical rationality putatively underwriting the merchandise. Other lost codes acquire aesthetic or even sacred meanings: Mayan glyphs and Southwestern U.S. petroglyphs multiply as jewelry motifs, or icons of regional loyalty on banners and bumper stickers, among populations now lacking the original competence. Lost codes are vessels into which new meanings get poured, by rules alien to the original code rules. This happened when seventeenth-century Neoplatonists claimed to see in Chinese or Egyptian glyphs a "philosophical language." Their heirs took khipu in the same way in the eighteenth century (Sansevero 1750).

The quipocamayos of Tupicocha enjoy an afterlife partaking of metonymic, aesthetic, and reinterpretative processes but notably the third. We have already underlined their unique vigor as metonyms of folk-legal authority, when we mentioned villagers' pride in them as the "Constitution" or "Magna Carta" of the ayllus. Cords are also aesthetically appreciated as treasures of a vanished craftsmanship. What remains to be studied is their esoteric afterlife: a system of beliefs that attributes to them, as Neoplatonists did, the standing of a superior language, that is, a code of signs standing in a special, nonarbitrary relationship to reality itself. The notion that inherited signs incarnate a prototypical and supratemporal knowledge partakes of what Ernest Gellner calls "generic platonism," a family of notions common to many agrarian societies (1988:85). But the way it is worked out seems to owe something to specific Andean notions about the dead, to local ideas about relations between the eternal and the transitory, and, I will suggest, to genuine attributes of the past cord-using system.

Half-Life Phenomena: Oral-Traditional Interpretation of Cords

The different ayllus or parcialidades are on unequal footing regarding oral traditions of cord media. For example, Unión Chaucacolca, even though it owns an unusually intact pair of quipocamayos, is also the ayllu most sympathetic with ideologies of modernization. Its elders tend to disclaim khipu interpretation, referring to Tello's scientific authority as the proper inquiry. The corporation that engages most actively in inquiry about its own quipocamayo is Primera Satafasca. Its tradition is highlighted in this chapter.

THE QUIPOCAMAYO KID AND HIS PATRI-KIN

In 1997 Tueda Angélica Villaruel Gómez, who teaches in Tupicocha's secondary school, assigned her second-year (early teenage) students to do a project on khipus. Some of the products showed misunderstanding of basic cord structure, while others faintly resembled local quipocamayos but bore random overhand knots or none at all. Then one student, Nery Javier Rojas, twelve years old, plopped onto her desk a plump, colorful woollen quipocamayo as big as the originals, with knots that seemed to match the ones she had seen in the huayrona (see plate 10).

Surprised and impressed, Villaruel asked Nery how he had managed to make such an elaborate likeness. Nery told her that his father, Juan Javier, happened at the time to be the president of parcialidad Primera Satafasca, so an original quipocamayo lay close at hand. It was Nery's idea to imitate it. He started by gathering some loose bits of gaudy acrylic yarn from his mother's work area. His mother liked the project and offered to let him use some natural-colored (brownish-black and near-white) sheep wool yarn which she had been spinning for children's sweaters. Nery added to the yarn some bits of white cotton commercial string. Unsupervised, with the original before him, it took him about six hours to make the simulacrum.

Nery says he had not paid much attention to the cords before, but almost as soon as he picked up his father's regalia he got interested in the enigmatic Tupicocha knot and soon became absorbed. He loosened or even untied some of the quipocamayo knots and retied them, so as to learn how they were made. (This probably accounts for some changes in its physical state, which I observed between 1995 and 2000.) He now knows how to duplicate all the knots in it.

In 1999, Nery was kind enough to give an explanation of his simulacrum. He felt diffident at first, but after testing me on whether I had also worked out the Tupicocha knot, he warmed up and explained that a much earlier family experience had paved the way for the simulacrum project. In 1992, when he was seven, his patrilineal great-grandfather Tobías Javier lay ill and bedridden at the age of eighty. Nery's father was at that time absent in Lima, so it became Nery's job to care for Tobías. To relieve boredom, Don Tobías talked at length about "custom," urging his boy to learn and preserve arts that other people undervalued. Among these was the art of the quipocamayo, which he tried to teach Nery. Shortly after that, Tobías died. Nery did not at that time discuss the teaching with anybody.

Tobías Javier is the common root of the traditions discussed in this chapter. A past camachico and patriarch of a core Primera Satafasca "family," he had the reputation of being the last master of the old art. He transmitted it to Nery in a different and later context than that which conveyed his legacy to other, older descendants. Nery is the patrilineal grandson of Tobías's deceased son Cornelio. Cornelio's also-deceased brother Víctor had three sons, discussed later in this section, who each claim to have learned from the patriarch. The two lineage branches occupied different social niches, and these differences are relevant to their shares of the quipocamayo patrimony. Víctor's branch lives almost entirely on the remote heights. It specializes in herding and shuns village-centered functions. A reputation for secretiveness, reclusiveness, or even magic hovers around it, and certain members are considered troublesome because of faena nonattendance. Nery's three uncles apparently learned the cord art in this typically pastoral climate of standoffishness toward village-centered "custom." Nery's own parents, on the other hand, are notably active townsfolk. They run a business marketing meat and cheese to Lima and travel weekly to the city. They take active part in town governance. It was this branch which cared for the aged Tobías. For them, the quipocamayo legacy was part of a public and civic role.

Nery remembers Tobías vividly and, in 1999, still talked animatedly about him. "He used to tell me things when he was feeling a little ill, to keep from falling asleep. He had a quipo [the pronunciation Nery picked up in the classroom] and it was his own [i.e., not ayllu property], but they buried it together with him, because he used to say, 'Why should I leave it behind if they won't know how to read it?'"[2]

When I asked Nery what the old man had made his personal khipu for, Nery replied: "He also made a quipo for his own household, accounting [*financiando*] for everything he had in his house. [That happened] when he was young, and he used to write with quill pens. He said, 'For me, it was easier to make a quipo than to write with quill pens.'"[3] Tobías must have been born around 1910, so the time at which he would have begun accounting for his own household could hardly have predated 1928. Since his preference for cords was at that time already, in his own view, atypical, we can envision his young manhood—the 1930s—as a time when the cord art had already lost official standing but not evaporated from public knowledge. (This fits the independent evidence reviewed in chapter 5.)

I asked Nery whether in his great-grandfather's youth, people were officially trained in the art and whether most then knew it. Nery thought not. Rather, "His [Tobías's] friend had showed him what all the knots of the quipo were useful for, and he knew what each knot was for, and how many knots."[4] Nonetheless Nery also thinks that at that time some women could handle the cords, namely "wives of the *amautas*." *Amauta* is a Hispano-Quechua version of the Inka term for a court adviser or state intellectual. It was already a favorite word of indigenists in the 1920s, and since then public school popularizations have made it a commonplace. I asked whether Tobías himself used the term about himself, and Nery said he did. It is hard to guess whether Tobías picked the term up from then-current ideological discussion, or whether Tupicocha had preserved it as old local lexicon.

Nery's simulacrum is not a facsimile of 1SF-01, his ancestral quipocamayo. He concentrated on working out the knots, rather than copying their placement on cords. He preferred to place the cords he calls "blacks" and "whites" in alternation or near-alternation (and not in bands, as in 1SF-01). He found no other natural colors in his mother's basket. Bright acrylic pendants punctuate the series singly or in clusters usually close to markers.[5] Nery is interested in the figure-eight, or E, knot, which is in fact frequent on 1SF-01. He identifies it as the authentic single knot, as opposed to overhand knots. Once he figured out the Tupicocha long knot (T knot, Key Figure 26 pendant 36) and the Inka long knot (pendant 35) by slackening old knots, he enjoyed mimicking them; he put more of them on pendants than the original has. Asked whether he attached any significance to tying leftward or rightward, he said, as other Tupicochans do, that it is only a matter of personal habit. Nery made few subsidiary cords (Key Figure 26 pendants 16–18), but he did notice and emulate them. Sometimes he did so attaching cords with attachment loops either overlapping or running through attachment loops of adjacent pendants (Key Figure 26 pendants 39–40). He identifies these as "two coming out of one" (dos salen de uno), and says Tobías taught him that the "two-out-of-one" construction has a specific significance. This mechanism is found in at least one patrimonial specimen.

It would take a tortured interpretation to represent Nery's simulacrum as anything more than a demonstration of general methods for making a quipocamayo.

Nery describes his work as "imitating" the patrimonial model, not duplicating it. But the discrepancies cannot all be accounted for by the limited material at hand. He was also influenced by the need to satisfy his teacher's expectations as he understood them. These in turn were influenced by archaeological generalities as transmitted in national curricula. (Ms. Villaruel comes from another region, has no obligation at the huayrona, and has never closely inspected patrimonial cords.) So what Nery made was a culture-brokering "pidgin" demonstration, rather than a facsimile likeness. It served to show his teacher that by studying patrimonial cords, one can match and even supplement the technical resources of officially "known" (i.e., taught) Inka culture.

INTERPRETATION OF KNOTS AND CORDAGE CONSTRUCTION
We turn now to Nery's substantive understanding of cords. Great-grandfather To-bías called the figure-eight or E-knot (Key Figure 26 pendant 34) the "simple" (*sencillo*), and the rest "long knots." Within the latter, he perceived Tupicochan and Inka types of long knot (Key Figure 26 pendants 35, 36) as variants of one class. He saw the variance as representing "bound" or centralized versus "distributed" or free entities. There is an element of iconicity in the distinction. The Inka type, as noted in chapter 6, has an exterior ascending member that visibly "binds" the turns signaling count value. It is locally called a "ring knot" (*nudo con argolla*) because the turns appear contained by their binding, like keys on a key ring.[6] Nery demonstrates this with cords which he takes to be records about tools belonging to the ayllu. If the cord bears an Inka-style long knot "with a ring," it means the tools "are guarded in a storage deposit." But if it bears a Tupicochan style long knot, the tools are released for use.

Nery raised the matter of cords without knots without prompting. "A cord without a knot. A member of the community fulfilled all his duties as member of the ayllu, [including] three times [as] president [of ayllu], three as secretary, three as treasurer, one term as alguacil ["deputy"] and another as member-at-large. He's up and out."[7] The basic concept of an unknotted cord as sign of discharge is persuasive in view of the "negative reckoning" convention (chapter 7) which treats compliance as the default or unmarked feature.

Asked about cords with a bright color run through, locally called cantitos (Key Figure 26 pendants 30–32), Nery said he was not sure about them. At first he said they indicated completion of a task. Later, in 2000, Nery expressed an idea, which his uncles also share, that cantitos identify corporate affiliations. The bright-colored threads "run through" are interpreted by the senior men of the Javier lineage as metacommunications with regard to the main information burden of a cord, identifying the jurisdiction to which the referents belonged. For example, according to Julio Javier, the run-through of yellow or yellowish-brown signifies that the cord concerns an item belonging to the community (as opposed to the ayllu, which is noted in red), or the unmarked option, the household.

Nery's estimate of the number of data-bearing traits, that is, khipu-code variables, is closer to a maximalist than a minimalist estimate. He recognized his ayllu's quipocamayo (1SF-01) as made of heterogeneous fiber, as do other villagers: "llama, alpaca, vicuña, also sheep." He considers type of fiber a meaningful variable. He recognizes the Lockean variables of color, knot type, and numerical value. He sees several previously unstudied kinds of variations as data bearing. Throughout our discussions, he asserted repeatedly that diameter of cordage (Key Figure 26 pendants 19–21) and tightness of twist are data-recording variables. He gave some examples of their values (see the next section). He also includes as a data-bearing variable the unraveling of plies (Key Figure 26 pendant 22), which he takes to be intentional in certain cases. Mackey's ethnographic work on Cuzco-area ethnographic khipus, which took place when competence was less eroded (1965–67), confirms that both thickness of cordage and the unraveling of plies could carry data values (1970:121, 150–51). In Inchupalla, an Aymara community near the city of Puno, Nicanor Apaza Suca also attested diameter as a data value: if a single thread means a unit, ten parallel threads knotted together overhand represented the next higher decimal bracket (Villavicencio et al. 1983:32–33). Each time such a thick cord accumulated ten tens, it was overknotted to represent a hundred. Such overknotting seems reminiscent of the way Tupicochans overknot the whole khipu into a single giant knot, described in chapter 6, as a way of suggesting finality and totalization — the presentation of the quipocamayo as, for the duration of ceremony, an accomplished constancia rather than a simulation in progress.

After Nery had explained everything that occurred to him spontaneously, I asked him about some variables discovered by Conklin and Urton, including directionality of spin, ply, twist, and knotting. Nery says he does not remember Tobías's commenting on directionality in regard to making cord (Key Figure 26 pendants 1–12) or knotting it. His patrimonial quipocamayo would have exposed him to only slight plying variation, as 1SF-01 is overwhelmingly S-plied, with just one short series of Z-plied pendants. He knows experienced spinners can easily reverse but does not know any reason for doing so. Neither did Nery comment spontaneously on knot directionality.

BANDS AS FUNCTIONAL GROUPS IN TEMPORAL ORDER

In January 2000, Nery studied the original cords of his ayllu (1SF-01) in my company. I started by simply watching him handle them as he saw fit. He sorted the cords according to their color groups or bands (see fig. 46). He associated the bands with functional domains of the ayllu. His explanations had the sound of ready and confident recall. He spoke in a steady voice, running cords through his fingers and occasionally demonstrating features, without noticeably racking his brain or contradicting himself. If asked to repeat, he repeated consistently. He again affirmed that he was voicing what he remembered of Tobías's lessons. These can be summarized in a few principles.

FIGURE 46   Nery Javier studies 1SF-01 by sorting it into bands and interpreting them. January 2000. From personal collection of author.

1. "The khipu was the statute and the order of his parcialidad."[8] That is, as inferred in chapters 6 and 7, these cords constituted a corporate policy document. Nery saw them as official at the ayllu-internal level rather than the higher communitywide one.

2. Nery's perception of the varicolored bands is that they refer to different subjects, with colors coded to subject. I asked him if one might compare them to chapters of a book with multiple subjects. He nodded vigorously: "like foodstuffs, collective workdays (faenas), jobs like the reservoir."[9] Nery's uncle Toribio Javier put the same idea a bit differently, explaining that it is as if one were keeping accounts of pasturage on paper of darker color and other things on papers of lighter colors.

3. Nery is ready to suppose that some cords have metonymic reference or an attribute of consubstantiality with their referents—or, in the terms of chapter 1 and the Conclusions chapter, indexical properties. Looking at a photo of quipocamayo c-01, he pointed to a pair of dark gray pendants. "It's twisted with [a hair of] a cow's tail. It might be that [the khipu] has a cow to the parcialidad's credit."[10]

4. Nery takes the sequence of pendants along the main cord to be chronological. This is implicit in his explanation of a group of pendants on his simulacrum, which he said could refer to a distribution of goods. "When they carried out [the distribution] is known by counting these [indicating attachment loops] from the beginning."[11] He is much intrigued by the idea that the sections of main cord de-

marcated by tufted or other main cord ornaments (motas) indicate a fixed term, either a semester or a year. But he does not claim to know what the term was.

5. Nery said he knew something but not everything about code values of colors. Lifting several black cords from his simulacrum, he said: "the livestock they [the parcialidad] had."[12] Lifting white ones, he said: "varieties of seed. Various places that they sowed in common"[13] (i.e., sowed for the parcialidad's collective harvest). On some of the cords, "the knots explain that there are potatoes or there's *mashua*."[14] (*Mashua* is a tuber crop, *Tropaeolum tuberosum*.)

6. Nery specified the following as substantive contents of quipocamayos as recalled by his great-grandfather:

a. The use of cords, Nery mentioned initially with a "first-things-first" tone, was inventory of collective property. "They [cord keepers] used to count how many sacks of foodstuffs were in the parcialidad's storehouse."[15] (It will be recalled that the civic meeting ground called "the Collca," i.e., storehouse, does in fact include chambers identified as former storage deposits.)

b. Second, he mentioned that "they used to leave the date for the meeting fixed by knot."[16] When I commented that the most important meetings do not vary in date and questioned the need to record such dates, Nery replied, "no, any meeting," including routine and ad hoc meetings too. His uncles confirm reference to "assemblies."

c. Third, Nery mentioned faenas or collective workdays. "They [cord keepers] fixed the days on which there were going to be faenas during the year."[17]

d. Nery was at his clearest and most emphatic in explaining his fourth topic: how a pendant records the usage of a given cultivated field (*chacra*) for the benefit of the parcialidad (see fig. 47). A cultivated field is classified as *ladera* ('slope') if it is a hillside and *andén* ('platform') if it is a terrace. A terrace or irrigated field has parts named according to its hydrology. A field is made up of one or more *llanchas* or *tablas*. A llancha or tabla is an area watered by a single minimal branch of a canal. This terminology applies whether the field is an andén or a ladera, but in all the examples he volunteered, Nery referred to *andenes*. This suggests that the old land tenure (including collective harvests) was associated with the old technology of terracing. The area abounds in apparently pre-Hispanic terraces, many of which are now neglected.

In his view, the whole length of the pendant represents the whole area of the chacra. The portion of the pendant defined by a space between the main cord and the uppermost knot, or between any two knots, or the last data knot and the end or stop knot, represents the proportion of the chacra making up a given llancha or tabla. Therefore the number of knots on a pendant (excluding the end or stop knot) would be one less than the number of llanchas. One could infer that if the length of field-representing pendants were totaled across the quipocamayo, one could estimate the total planted area under a parcialidad's control. One could also derive subtotals regarding llanchas and

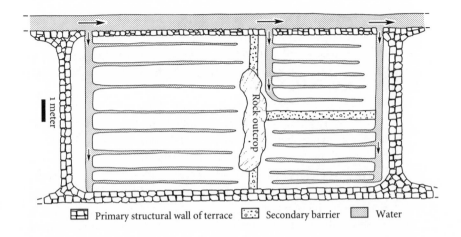

Primary structural wall of terrace   Secondary barrier   Water

1e knot   1e knot   1s endknot

FIGURE 47   "A khipu is like a map," said Nery Javier. He interprets a cord with two E-knots as recording the use of an agricultural terrace as one field with three irrigation subdivisions called llanchas. From personal collection of author.

their respective crops. This would add up to a fairly complete agricultural forecast. The thickness of the cord, according to Nery, corresponds to the quality of the seed potatoes. Thick cords refer to superior varieties such as *yungay, tumasa, peruanito, chaucha*, and *wayru*. Nery was sure that the knots which separate the "llanchas" indicate the crop, but he was not sure how. Examining a pendant with three evenly spaced knots (on his simulacrum), he said that they respectively show three small llanchas, one with potatoes, one with oca, and one with mashua. But the three knots appeared alike to me (E-knots). Perhaps specific knot forms identified specific crops, but Nery did not demonstrate any such code. Nery regards unraveling as a data-bearing variable in at least some field-describing pendants. A "chacra" cord with plies separated means the water in it is "diverted" (*desviado*). This means, if a llancha has, for example, a rock outcrop in it that would keep water from flowing smoothly all the way to the end of a furrow, some water from the next higher-lying waterway is diverted downward to moisten the part of the llancha that the rock obstructs.

e. Nery, like his uncles Toribio and Julio, named as a fifth topic of cords "the tools that they had."[18] This neatly matches the numerous references in ayllu books to sets of tools which parcialidades bought collectively, such as crow-bars, shovels, and so on. Nery did not mention dishes, but on the analogy of books I would guess "tools" topics also include the vessels that ayllus bought in large sets. In these cords, as in field-representing cords, the distance between the main cord and first knot (or end knot) is taken by Nery to signify quantity, in this case "the quantity of tools."[19] He said the number of turns in the long knot means the "number of kinds of tools."[20] This phrase might make more sense if we take it to mean "number representing a kind of tools."

f. Nery raised as a sixth topic the likelihood that some cords described statuses or phases of ayllu members' family cycles. Here is his discussion, made while pensively handling his simulacrum. "Each member of the community has his family. The [people of] the parcialidad were [in Tobías's time] more abundant. For each member it was noted who he was and who his wife was."[21] At this point, Nery picked out one white cord. It has a long interval between the main cord and the first knot, which is an E-knot. Then after a shorter interval there is a second E-knot, and finally plies separating at the end. Indicating the first, long interval he said, "a couple. For a long time they were lovers."[22] Then, touching the uppermost knot, "the couple married."[23] "But [indicating interval down to the second knot] the couple is distancing itself from their children. The grandmother has the couple's children."[24] How Nery derives the information about the grandparents is unclear. After the second knot, the plies separate. "They are two adults, and each has gone his own way."[25] One reason why ayllu-internal record keeping might require such information is control of eligibilities for potential future members. However, such use is not corroborated by any other evidence, and indeed Nery did not offer any such remarks when commenting on his ayllu's patrimonial quipocamayo.

g. Nery's seventh topic is related to the first. Pointing to the cords near the large knob (Key Figure 26, left extreme), he says, "on one of the cords, the date of the huayrona is fixed. I believe it's at the beginning. The new presidents. New authorities, right at the beginning that's already stated."[26] As he said this, Nery pulled aside a group of pendants at the knob end of the simulacrum, as if isolating these as the ones containing the new officials. The interpretation is plausible, since most quipocamayos do contain a group of cords of heterogeneous color and style at this point, as if setting some baseline information.

h. Nery's eighth topic was financial. "Then, [after the "officers" group] are the cords of the parcialidad's savings."[27] By "savings," he meant earnings in donations accrued to the welfare/ritual fund. The example he chose was a black wool cord with a white cotton subsidiary. On the pendant below the subsidiary's point of attachment, he indicated two s-knots. He said of these, "two persons," then moved his hand back up the pendant and down the subsidiary tracing its knots, which were three s-knots. He said, "they're responsible for three *cajuelas* [dioramas] which they are going to place with different people [as pledge tokens]."[28] Noting six loosely tied s-knots at the end, he said: "plus six pictures"[29] (referring to the framed oleographs which are tokens for minor pledges). The term of pledges is standard (one year) and therefore may not be expressed.

i. Nery's ninth topic, also discussed by his uncles, was the use of cords to record collective-labor faena performance. He was sure this was a matter of content but unsure how it was expressed, except that the quipocamayo recorded absences, not compliance, and that it mentioned punishment. Separating a white cotton cord with an Inka long knot with eight turns, he says, "for arriving late at a faena [someone] is punished."[30]

j. Nery also mentioned "customs" as a tenth topic. I asked what that meant. "Customs are things you do the same year after year,"[31] he replied. Guessing this category corresponded to ayllu book entries on fiestas, which have annual schedules, I asked whether "customs" meant ceremonies such as the work and ritual of canal cleaning. He agreed. He also said the Festival of the Crosses belongs in this category. He did not know how pendants record them.

One of the most important properties of Nery's system is that it uses distance between knots as an analogue variable. To implement it, one would need a way to key the length of each internode with units of measure such as meters or the currency unit. When asked about this, he had no ready answer. He may have provided an unconscious clue in emulating Tobías's cord-handling habits. In demonstrating a distance along a cord, Nery ran his right index fingernail along the surface of the cord so that it ratcheted in the small grooves that separate turns of the spiraling plies. It would not be difficult to count turns, if there were a convention about their correspondence to a unit of measure. Only a few cords are too slackly plied to allow this.

OPERATIONAL MODIFICATION OF CORDS

Without prompting, Nery explained that quipocamayos are made to be easily updated and modified. He described the following techniques:

Sometimes, he said, a cord keeper would want to carry over a datum from one khipu to another. He calls this "uniting" them, that is, combining data. He demonstrated by manipulating his simulacrum as if adding a datum to it: "Here something's missing about tools." He loosened an attachment loop and pushed one pendant aside. "He [the cord keeper] opens another space and puts in what's missing, one more cord."[32]

Continuing with the above example, he showed how the cord keeper reknots. "They would open the knot [untying a stop knot at the bottom of the pendant, so as not to create an obstruction for the passes of the new knot]; they would make a big space. They'd complete it according to the orders of the other khipu."[33]

If, after adding cords, a particular band or khipu became too full, the cord keeper could put in a cord with a long knot "indicating that five [pendants] have gone out to the other khipu."[34] That is, khipus may be cross-referenced. Perhaps some "singleton" cords on otherwise banded khipus may be cross-reference markers.

DUALISM OF QUIPOCAMAYOS

Chapters 6 and 7 emphasized that quipocamayos worked in pairs, and that the dismemberment of pairs, which tended to coincide with the fission of certain ayllus from the 1920s onward, may have become possible precisely because their official data usefulness had ended. It may also have hastened the obsolescence of those pairs still undivided, because all ayllus were and are expected to maintain mutually commensurable procedures at the aggregated level of responsibility to the community. Their dual operation is not well understood in "half-life" memory.

Nonetheless, some relevant concepts survived into recent times. One was the idea of quipocamayo as prospective inscription of a plan, which forms half of the prospective-retrospective pairing sketched in chapter 7. The notion of prospective inscription became manifest in a conversation with Toribio Javier, a scion of Víctor Javier's family, when he likened the role of the quipocamayo to that of the specialized guides he uses in his hobby, fixing broken radios.

> How can I explain?—it's like a circuit diagram, haven't you studied them? You can buy them in Lima. Like those little signs for components [bobinitos], it tells it there. The brown [icon for component], what number [of ohms, etc.] it corresponds to. This [quipocamayo] is just like that circuit diagram. Because a circuit diagram has . . . little signs for components some with additional lines: it has black, red, green lines. So you have the brown, what number is its value, and the black, what number is its value, and you add them, add them, and sum them up—zas! So much. Then you find the one with the right capacity [grado] and that's the one to solder in.[35]

Toribio's point is not necessarily that knots function as component icons, or lines as circuits, but that by studying the relation among the parts of the complex sign, one knows what action to take in constructing the signs' larger analogue—in this case, communal activity rather than a radio.

ORIENTING QUIPOCAMAYOS AND DELIMITING THEIR SEGMENTS

Most researchers, including the Aschers, treat the end of the khipu at which the original cordage of the main cord was doubled back to create its final plying as the start, and the other, tied-off, end as the finish. So did I, in making cord descriptions. I was additionally influenced by the tendency of people in huayrona ritual context to treat the knobbed end as the start. But there are contrary arguments both local and otherwise. In his 1982 article on Middle Horizon khipus, Conklin argued that this is not the criterion, though it may agree with the outcome. The specimens he studied have main cords with one end left very long and bare (dangle end, in Ascher terminology). The dangle end was used to wrap the artifact into a

FIGURE 48   Quipocamayo 1SF-01 has a loose end and a knob end. Some elders of the ayllu see the former as its starting end. Note that the size of main cord markers "grows" in ascending order from it. From personal collection of author.

spiral cone for handling or storage. This, too, is still the practice in Tupicocha (see chapter 6). To Conklin (1982:270), the long bare extension of the main cord "is probably the beginning of the recorded information, since it would have been the first portion seen when the quipu was opened."

Some older quipocamayo consultants agreed with Conklin. For them, the long loose "tail" is actually the beginning (see fig. 48). Looking at their patrimonial quipocamayo (1SF-01), all three of the senior Javieres argue that one can see the directionality of the main cord by looking at its pontoladores (punctuators, i.e., markers; Key Figure 26 between pendants 15–16). They say 1SF-01 has four markers of increasing size and visual salience, as sequenced from the tied-off end toward the large ornamental knob. These men liken increasing size to the growth of crops and the maturation of social activity as the year advances (see fig. 48). Asked about this, Nery said he remembers that Tobías told him that the number of ribs or chain-stitches making up the surface texture of a marker is part of its meaning. This is compatible with the growing-plant analogy because the larger markers have more such stitches.

Many villagers vaguely associate markers with the calendric festivals that divide the year, but nobody was willing to specify the correspondences of specific markers. Plausible candidates would be the canal-cleaning period (usually late April), the "half-year" business meeting (usually near 1 July), and perhaps the Assumption of the Virgin (15 August) or the patron saint's day (30 November). If it is also correct that the group of pendants right next to the knob signifies the 2–3 January meeting for choosing officers, then this meeting would be taken as the end as well as the beginning of the political cycle, and the occasion for beginning a "circuit diagram" of the coming year. The wearing of quipocamayo at the civic plenum then puts on public view the legible proof that the respective ayllu has fulfilled its past commitments and is ready for new ones. It may be relevant that markers are less readily detached and reattached than pendants. (However, in order to avoid destructive handling, I did not test whether they can be slid along the main cord.) Perhaps they indicated benchmark fixed dates (deadlines?) to which other actions were keyed.

The direction in which khipus should be read remains uncertain, but these memories perhaps add weight to Conklin's and (independently) Radicati's opinion that the ornamented bulb marked the end, not the start, of the document (Radicati di Primeglio 1979[?]:66).

Afterlife Phenomena: Khipumancy

A difference in attitude separates young Nery from his patrilateral uncles. Nery feels himself engaged in reconstruction of a dormant or lost system of meaning, and readily admits to incomplete knowledge. His uncles believe themselves to be vessels of a system that has enjoyed continuity as esoteric practice even though it died out from the public domain. They do not admit in principle that the overall meaning of cords is lost, although they do admit to personal failings in applying the system. They are secretive, claiming the overall meaning is not publicly available. As will be seen in the next section, there is reason to think some of their technical operations partake of older competence, but their overall canon of "reading" seems to have altered radically in the transition from civic to private and even esoteric context.

While eliciting modern opinions and recollections about quipocamayos, I was often told that Tobías Javier and other less-clearly remembered sages not only understood what the khipus recorded about the past but could use them to foretell the future. Tobías's older patrilineal descendants showed various practices that, taken together, might be called "khipumancy" by analogy to cartomancy and like practices, because they use the cords as oracles.

The social framework of khipumancy is confidential. An aura of occultism hovers over the whole practice. Those associated with occultism tend to have disturbed relations with their ayllu and community. The New Year's rite is so public that villagers eagerly invite tourists, but khipumancy is so private—even shady—that few are even willing to concede its existence. It seems to have become rare before 1990, so it is described here in past tense. Only once did I learn the name of a purported recent client (a man from a Rímac valley town). Other people from outside the ayllu and even outside the village are said to have requested readings, but nobody admitted to having done so. Since all members of an ayllu have rights in its quipocamayo, the "khipumancer" needed not be the current president, but the khipumancer would certainly need the president's consent for access to the quipocamayo.

Clients consulted khipumancers about lost objects, causes of mysterious illnesses, the identity of thieves, and good or bad outcomes of future herding or planting. The most often-mentioned use of quipocamayos was weather prediction, as with the augury game of pichcamanta (chapter 6) once played in the presence of quipocamayos. One person said Don Tobías sought out songs (*cantos*) in the cords. "Just like looking for 'Amancio' [his own name] or 'Tupicocha' I can look for a song," said one descendant.[36]

Khipumancy was based on the notion that cords have inherent correspondence with reality, reaching beyond the data humans encoded in them. They were seen as a concretion of dialogue between human input and superhuman power. Pendants were seen as "pathways of memory and power," in Abercrombie's (1998) phrase. "Pathway" is a prototypical general idea of which trailways, genealogies, pilgrimages, and khipus are all specific instantiations. Like other such lines of knowledge, khipus in their esoteric meaning had known nodes and unknown, but spiritually accessible, implications (much as cards have known icons such as the queen, and magically accessible "cartomantic" implications). Modern khipumancy seemed to have originated in an analogy between khipus as paths of knowledge and widespread European popular occult ideas about ancient inscriptions with mystical capacity for truth. A likely local prototype for khipumancy occurs in an anonymous paperback, of which a copy exists in Tupicocha, called *Oráculo novísimo*. Stationery stores all over urban Latin America sell uncountable copies of this evergreen favorite under varied titles. Tupicocha's newsprint *Oracle*, like most congeners, claims to transmit the legacy of Hermes Trismegistus. (This Hellenized legendary personage was in Renaissance and baroque times identified with Egyptian Thoth. Apocryphal Hermetic works have been perennial occult best sellers throughout and beyond Europe since the seventeenth century.)

According to the *Oracle* (Anonymous 1997), the diviner should begin by rapidly and spontaneously drawing five lines of "sticks," each line numbering over twelve sticks, at a speed precluding counting. After this automatic, spirit-guided writing the diviner counts the "sticks" line by line. If their number on one line is odd (*non*), he marks that line with one asterisk. If their number is even (*par*), he marks two. This operation yields an "oracle" such as, for example,

||||||||||||	*	"non"
||||||||||	*	"non"
||||||||||||||||	**	"par"
|||||||||||||	**	"par"
||||||||||||||||	**	"par"

The diviner then opens the chart, or *rollo escrito* (scroll).

The client and diviner identify a row beginning with a question the client needs answered, such as "Do I have one or many enemies?"[37] The diviner then reads across the top of the chart until he identifies a column headed by the oracle (the sequence of *nones* and *pares*) just obtained. Where the column headed by the oracle meets the row containing the desired question, he finds a "glyph," for example, the "pyramid." He then goes to the section of the book which deciphers pyramid and finds under pyramid the entry beginning with the non-par sequence obtained. He reads the answer, which in this case (Anonymous 1997:84) is "Seek the help of one wiser than yourself."[38]

It is easy to imagine the "Hermetic" oracle as a way for unlettered people to putatively benefit by a powerful and mystified knowledge system, namely, writing. Khipumancy afforded khipu-illiterate clients something of the same mystagogy.

In khipumancy, a consultation also began with numerological operations. But here it began with the names or terms involved in the question rather than with an aleatory process. This operation required at least one party to be literate in the alphabet, since one could only do it if confident about spelling. The first step was to spell the name of the person concerned. The number of letters the person's name was then decomposed into *pares* and *nones*, that is, evens and odds. Amancio Javier, demonstrating with his first name (see plate 11), analyzed it as having 3 pares and 1 non (2 + 2 + 2 + 1 = the 7 letters of his first name). He used a sign like an "H" to mean par (two verticals joined) and a sign like an "I" to mean non. He transcribed his name, then, as HIHH. Any combination of three H's and an I would have been alternative formulations, but he preferred to work by reckoning alternate H's and I's until it was no longer possible. (For example: Tupicocha =

HIHIHI, but Sunicancha = HIHIHH.) He then sought cords whose knots match this pattern (see plate 11). Cord matches for HIHH would be, for example, a long knot of value 2 (or 2 overhands side-by-side), an overhand or figure-eight knot, and two more of value 2. But a long knot of value 4 could also equate to HH. Any cord making a match in terms of digital value of any odd-even rendering of the name was deemed relevant to the consultation. At this stage, one had established only the criterion for which cords would be deemed relevant to the question's key word.

Sometimes adepts spoke of the search for cords to match a word as being "like a dictionary": one had a word, and needed an increment of meaning about it; one did not know where the word was, but one did know a procedure to find it, together with its increment. But the likeness stopped there, for the finding method is partly aleatory. The khipumancer picked up a bunch of cords and let them drop without looking. This act was called *tijear* (to scissor), because in lifting the selected cords, one angled them apart like an opening scissor. Guidance was felt to come from the quipocamayo itself. Dropping the cords was called *jugar los hilos*, "to play the threads," in parallel to the phrase "play the cards" in cartomancy.

The khipumancer then scrutinized the swirled cords as they had fallen, looking for conjunctions between cords with the relevant oracle-numbers, and others. If relevance did not appear from knot counts, the khipumancer might force it by counting plies as well as turns of whole cord, or by counting across multiple cords. A cord without knots was called a *camino largo* [long road, another instance of the path metaphor] and was taken to mean distance or duration separating the person from the object being referred to.

Toribio Javier explained that "playing" the cords, for example, to find out who stole something, involved jotting down the runs of odd and even results that accumulate from successive "plays" of the relevant strings. One detected relevance by lifting and letting the selected pendants fall, and observing which other cords they touched. These runs could then be used to narrow down suspects among suggested names, because names incompatible with the resultant odd-even patterns were eliminated. The outcome was termed the *juego*, or "play," and its interpretation was called the *estudio*, or "study."

Nobody was willing to verbalize the reasoning involved in applying this principle. I think the obstacle may have been a matter of mute inscription such as that explained in chapter 4: once one put a matter to the cords, one was putting it out of discussion in words. Words would not again become relevant until after the divinatory process was completed.

A wordless demonstration occurred when I asked how a quipocamayo would clarify performance in a group faena. The khipumancer thought I was saying that as a future faena sponsor, I wanted a forecast of how my work party would turn out. The answer was to select a group of like-colored cords exhibiting a numerological-key affinity to the question "faena" (pattern HIH). The pendants of the band were then taken as members obligated to do the faena. The khipumancer held up the group as a bunch and let them fall. The fall of the cords, with its multiple curves, crossings, and disjunctures, as well as odd-even clues to names, would reveal who would be absent.

The details of the fall in khipumancy were closely examined for numerological properties, that is, conjunctions of odds and evens. In an example about crop forecasting, where a band of a certain color represented the rows of a field, a single cord (i.e., an odd cord) which did not fall with the rest meant that the set as a whole "played odd," that is, predicted a shortfall. A pattern that "fell out" with dark cords followed by lighter ones was taken to forecast improving weather. When a khipumantic consultation was finished, the quipocamayo had to be twisted and tied back into the single giant knot, which was its display or locked position. If the pachacamanta, or knob, stood straight up at the top of the tied object, it was taken as a sign that the "study" came out trustworthy. In many such ways, khipumancers behaved as if imputing knowledge to the quipocamayo and not to themselves.

In my opinion, dissenting from Radicati di Primeglio's guess about pre-Hispanic "magical khipus" (1965:175–77), this system for establishing reference between words and cords was a recent back-formation influenced by cartomancy and alphabetic literacy, not an element of pre-Hispanic or Republican khipu competence. One may object that letters were not necessary, because unlettered persons could readily "numerize" words by counting syllables. However, this measure would make the system even more underdetermined than it already was, to such a degree as to lose "predictive" plausibility. A given combination of knots serving only to indicate reference to a $\{1 \ldots n\}$ syllable word would be hugely ambiguous unless further specified by additional variables. One would be hard put, too, to explain knot values exceeding ten, since words over six syllables are exceedingly rare. (Greek-style or Gothic-style names, common among peasants now in middle to old age, e.g., Hermenegildo or Aristóteles, tend to be the longest words in ayllu books.)

Chronology also supports the hypothesis that khipumancy modeled upon letters, numerology, and cartomancy was an afterlife and not a half-life phenomenon. Those familiar with khipumancy say that they learned it at a time when nobody any longer updated quipocamayos. "This was in the 1930s, the 1940s, this equipo [i.e., quipocamayo] was already formed. Nobody could add or take away any knots then."

In interviews with the khipumantic experts, many minor discrepancies of testimony arose, but one firm consistency overlies them, and in my opinion outbalances them for heuristic purposes. The consistent tendency is this: when asked to work from words toward cords (e.g., how will my faena turn out?), they hewed to khipumantic aleatory techniques, but when asked to work from cords toward words (e.g., what do these brown cords say?), they followed the functional-grouping approach which Nery also prefers. As an overall judgment, it seems most believable that the half-life of quipocamayos is a fading readout of color-bands as functional areas.

A KHIPUMANTIC SESSION

When I asked Julio Javier for an interview about quipocamayo 1SF-01, he interpreted it (to my surprise) as a khipumantic request and opened the session as a sacred occasion. He placed the storage bag on the table, and before opening it, removed his hat and mumbled an invocation. In the course of the consultation, I asked him to comment upon the cords as such, but he drew the discussion into khipumantic directions by explaining, for example, how particular bands—bands which he identifies in much the same descriptive terms which Nery uses—are used to divine particular kinds of questions. For example, in a group of black and white mottled cords (Key Figure 26 pendants 24–26) supposedly useful for weather forecasting, the cords which the client causes to fall out would be evaluated by the position of their knots as predicting better or worse weather.

Other khipumantic values included knots with uneven numbers of turns, *nones*, as predictive of dissension in social matters or of poverty in natural resources. A large knot in a band which generally has small ones is taken as an icon of dominance; for example, the single long knot (9T, that is, consisting of nine turns) in a band explicated as concerning herds, purportedly stands for the stud of the herd. Although some of Julio Javier's dominantly khipumantic associations between bands and functional areas disagree with those of Nery Javier, the two agree quite accurately on the idea that a cluster of off-white pendants with brown subsidiaries represents pastoral activity, the former standing for pasturage users and the latter for their animals. This suggests, although it is far from conclusive, that the "afterlife" groupings and associations exploited for augury in some measure reflect the functional associations created in the productive competence of which "half-life" readings are remnants.

Since I did not steer the interrogation of cords to the degree that a normal client would, Julio engaged in guesswork about my interests and came up with the notion that I was surreptitiously searching for clues to metal veins or hidden mines. (This is a common rural opinion about the motives of urbanite or foreign visitors.) The guess stimulated a round of examining certain cords for "metalismo."

Another band was taken as indicative of underground water flows and the future yield of springs. The curve of the fallen cord is taken as a shaped watercourse. Knots on it are taken to signal surface outflow. The numerical values of knots are taken as water yield. Another band was taken as referring to "lakes and their roots," meaning lakes with the upper snow slopes and the melt-off streams that feed them. This interpretation has affinities to the chacra/llancha interpretation of space-measuring cords by Nery in its iconic or even maplike method, as well as its pathway structure. Interpreting the vitally important, but hard-to-predict movement of water is a permanent focus of folk science and myth, from the Quechua

Manuscript of 1608 to the present (Salomon and Urioste 1991:136–44). Susan Niles (1999:230) hypothesizes an inverse relationship when she comments that "the physical design of the terracing system at Yucay looks a bit like a quipu, with a main road (Hatun Ñan), which even has the fluid, curved shape of a cord, from which other roads descend."

Still other groups of cords were linked to the various hills with their respective pasture lots and *chafnales* ('water meadows,' elsewhere called *bofedales*), to the dead and their influence upon the living, and to the titles and boundary inspections of lands, which may or may not "cause" villagers to prosper in litigation. (Titles and inspections are considered "vital" documents in a strikingly literal sense; they are felt to be almost alive, endowed with ability to favor or fail one's interests.)

It is an interesting sidelight on khipumantic ideology that in khipumantic context (never in other contexts) the knots on such cords are termed *hítolos*. This portmanteau word combines *hito*, 'landmark,' with *ídolo*, 'idol,' the colonial Spanish term for non-Christian deities. In general, khipumantic discourse includes archaisms and nonstandard usages. One is the outdated use of *naturales*, or 'natives,' as a self-reference to the local group. Another is *comunidad indigna* [*sic*; 'unworthy community'] for *comunidad indígena* 'indigenous community.' The latter was the official term for the collectivity up until the agrarian reform laws of the Velasco Alvarado presidency (which in 1969 replaced indigenist terms with campesino rhetoric). Survivals in this context typically use lexicon of the 1920s to 1950s. Khipumantic discourse also makes reference to rare or extinct social institutions, such as pasture lots held in common at the ayllu level. These facts favor the likelihood that the khipumantic art took form when such usages were still common — not much later than the 1940s.

Toward the end of my khipumantic session, Julio Javier said the cords were making reference to my own person, presence, and future: "This here, this [pendant] for example, is testifying about your trip that you're making on this day, studying. This is it, look. . . . With nothing [i.e., no knots]. It's your fortune. It's your fortune, that you have gone out with good faith, that you are on a journey. [Next cord:] It means, it says, a sojourn. Sojourn with two turns [in a knot], I'll loosen it for you. [Loosens, then tightens.] And one with one turn, this is one turn. This is [the fact] that you approached me, and I'm here, getting to know and respect you." [39]

I then asked about a third knot, located between the two he had just explicated. "Bigger, yeah. With four. [Counting with thumbnail:] one, two, three, four. This is from where we met each other yesterday [by chance, in the plaza], where we conversed. This is your fortune. . . . That you had faith enough in my person to convince me [laughing] to work [i.e., conduct the present session]. Here it is. This is it. . . . Here's the payment you've given me yesterday, this is the payment. That's the end of it. Mission accomplished." [40]

Conclusions from Folk Exegesis of Quipocamayos

In reviewing the encounter with Tupicochan observers of the cord legacy, we will quickly retrace a path from the esoteric reading called khipumancy back toward the more public reading oriented by memories of their political functionality, or, in other words, from afterlife effects back toward half-life effects. For a related inquiry in Bolivia, see Denise Arnold and Juan de Dios Yapita (2000:350–76).

THE AFTERLIFE OF QUIPOCAMAYOS AND THE ORIGINAL COMPETENCE

The afterlife of quipocamayos is inseparable from their standing as sacred objects: objects which humans have lost the ability to make but retain the need to interpret. One difference between profane and sacred inscriptions in many cultures — apparently regardless of their degree of current legibility — seems to be that the sacred object is no longer seen as containing "meaningful" versus "meaningless" layers of structure. The notion of the arbitrary, that is, of convention imposed by humans, is overridden by the notion of sacred signs as signs beyond current human ability to create, and therefore saturated with meaningfulness in respect to the superhuman process that putatively did create them. The domain of the superhuman, authoritative in all respects, is putatively "legible" throughout and not just at a given code level. Everything about it would be legible if only readers were sufficiently inspired.

Interrogation of inscriptions takes place within the cultural canons of interrogators, and canons produce diverse interpretative "sciences" (just as diverse interrogations of nature produce varied "ethnosciences"). If the "afterlife" reading of quipocamayo cords described above depended on the "overheating" of reading principles genuinely inherent in the older productive competence (as, e.g., Kabbalah depends on an "overheated" extension of realistic knowledge about Hebrew lexigraphy and numeracy), then afterlife phenomena may be more conservative of the original manner of inscription than one might first guess. We interpret the khipumantic reading of quipocamayos as embodying overextensions of legitimate principles of semasiography and "mute inscription."

The idea that the fall of cords, that is, their observation in variable array, provides dictates for human conduct resembles the way in which the mutable array of staffs, which like cords are inscriptions of collective process, provides dictates for politically organized work (see chapter 4). Like the reading of a given array of staffs, the "study" of fallen cords is a matter of detecting relational combinations among sets of signs that are each, as a set, already physically fixed. The detailed interpretation of knots seemingly "overheats" attributes of the old productive competence, for example, by numerizing without consistent distinction among levels of cord and cord-component (whole cord, ply, simple thread). The same might be said of widely extended metaphors based on a maplike iconographic reading. As far as one can tell—it is a shadowy matter—khipumancy errs by extending principles of legibility beyond their original range of relevance, and not by inventing principles fancifully.

The logic by which cord legibility is made to connect a public but opaque inscription (the quipocamayo as regalia of ayllu office) with an esoteric but legible inscription (the same quipocamayo as khipumantic tool) depends on a specific Andean ideology. That ideology is the family of Andean ideas about what happens after death. For what people think a writing can do after it has passed out of "ordinary" life depends in part on ideas about the meaning attached to "writers" who have themselves passed on.

DO ANDEAN MEDIA DIE AN ANDEAN DEATH?

Andean death concepts were, and to some extent still are, more like the "half-life/afterlife" contrast than they are like the vernacular English or Spanish "life/death" contrast. When the Huarochirí Quechua Manuscript was written (Urioste 1981; Salomon 1995:328), and wherever Quechua is spoken today, people use a single word, wañuq ('die-er'), to designate both a person on the deathbed, and one who has already died but recently enough to be mourned rather than venerated. The concept behind this usage is the "death continuum." In dying, a person is passing through one of several gradient changes which connect initial, immature, temporary stages of life with final, mature, eternal ones (Allen 1982). Initial, temporary ones (babies, seedlings) are soft, moist, mobile, and fast-changing. Until Christian clergy forcibly replaced the mummy cult with underground burial, the drying, stiffening, and slowing of old age, punctuated but not ended by the loss of respiration, only presaged further change in the same direction, toward the completely mature dryness, immobility, and eternal existence of a mallki, or mummified ancestor.

Most khipus in museums were extracted from tombs. But why were they in tombs in the first place? They are said to be funeral wealth of old khipu masters, and some cases do seem to be such, as in Puruchuco (Mackey 1990:136–40). The 1997 Laguna de los Cóndores discovery includes mummies entombed with khipus. Adriana Von Hagen and Sonia Guillén (2000:53) take these mummies to be Inka bureaucrats. Whether or not all the cord-bearing dead were Inka functionaries, however, the reason for entombment is less than obvious. Why must the medium "die" with its curator?

Perhaps mummy shrines were the "libraries" of old khipus. Urton (2001) has termed the Laguna de los Cóndores cords "messages from the mallkis," that is, from enshrined ancestors. Since visiting and feting the dead were a normal part of social life in prehistoric Andean societies, entombed information would not necessarily lie out of "reading" reach. Combining the "death continuum" with the model of khipu operability espoused in chapters 6–7—a model of cords as the ever-updated doublet of ongoing life—one might say of cords, as of the person holding them, that the end of modification (updating) marked the beginning of eternalizing. At least some burial khipus may refer to the individual's performance in his group, or the group as it performed under his leadership. Once he became mallki, they would have become information of a different status: information with the permanence of the sacred. "Benchmark" data is the term Urton prefers. The khipumancer's conviction that khipus know and decide what the petitioner cannot resembles the older Andean conviction that ancestors know and decide the future of less mature generations (Gose 1996).

Like the mallki her- or himself, a being who has reached the extreme of life's transit, the immobilized, no-longer-updated khipu has shifted from the status of current co-agent of society to that of eternal source of society. The information the dead bore would then have become subject to reading in a different light. Their cord information, like their oracular voices, might have been taken as stating the relation between transient or contingent events (e.g., should a certain marriage take place?) and the putatively transcendent, permanent, and "real" virtual entity called society (ayllu, etc.) with its baseline norms and recurring calendric schedules. Since Andean people regarded themselves as existing in continuing social relationship with mallki ancestors, including verbal conversation, they could reasonably regard already-ancient khipus as in some sense addressed to themselves, and relevant to the current, ongoing conduct of society. This is already the basic premise of khipumancy.

Obviously, Tupicocha did not have a working mummy complex within the chronology of this study. Nonetheless, the logic of enshrinement applies. When quipocamayos were still productive media, the New Year's festivities of Tupicocha implied a process almost inverse to that of khipu entombment. The everlasting life of the collectivity was vested in a pair of khipus which never ceased to be updated, never stopped changing, and therefore never ceased to be of "live" interest. As long as the Tupicochan khipu complex had full operational capacity, the invested khipu-wearer was, so to speak, the inverse of a mummy: a mummy was an eternalized person with the record of his transient lifetime, but an officer is the transient person bearing the record of eternally recycling community time. The fact that like all others he was embarked on the personal transit toward individual death was metaphorically canceled by superimposing on his body the ever-changing "body politic" of an immortal collective enterprise. By this route, what seems the "wrongest" use of the ancient cords may point us back toward a realistic vein of interpretation.

MEMORIES OF FUNCTIONAL ORGANIZATION IN QUIPOCAMAYOS

Tupicochans tend to offer different representations of khipu legibility, depending on which end of the problem one introduces. When asked to work from words toward cords, with questions such as "do these cords speak of Mayani?" or "what is the name of the thief?" afterlife phenomena predominate, because Tupicochanos think they are hearing an appeal to khipumantic techniques. When they are asked to work from cords toward words, with questions such as "what does the band of black-white speckles refer to?" half-life phenomena predominate. In the latter case, villagers timidly and uncertainly but more or less consistently follow the functional-grouping approach of which Nery's summary in the section "Half-Life Phenomena: Oral-Traditional Interpretation of Cords" is the most assertive expression.

The findings from folk interpretation which appear relevant to future interpretation are, in order of descending level of structure, the following:

Duality of Quipocamayos. A preponderance of evidence from both written and oral sources indicates that each ayllu maintained two quipocamayos related to each other as rotating annals on a finite cycle, as explained in chapter 7.

Directionality of Main Cord and Segmenting of Quipocamayo. Directionality is not an easy matter to settle. The large knob called pachacamanta seems, to Nery, a sign of beginning, but for the more senior consultants, the quipocamayo runs from the long pendantless extension of the main cord to the pachacamanta, which signifies fruition or completion. Both Nery and his seniors think that the markers along the main cord mark temporal segments, without being able to identify the periods marked consistently. On specimen 1SF-01, they are said to divide the year roughly into quarters. Senior men take them to represent the "growth" of the ayllu's work cycle to maturity at the annual meeting.

The meaning of bright-colored "run-through" threads is likewise less than consensually understood. The most-supported opinion is that they signify corporate ownership of a function. For example, a faena or workday for the community would be "underlined" with yellow and one benefiting the ayllu with red. Alternative explanations suggest that they signify the culmination or end of a process, edge of a space, and so on.

Color Bands as Functional Domains. Consultants agreed that the color bands which organize all but one of the Tupicochan specimens correspond to functional domains for which the ayllu had responsibility. (Some of these functions are now handled otherwise, not at ayllu level.) They are aligned along a temporal axis because they were administered at different times of the year.

Toward the end of our first long interview, I asked Nery to sum up the subjects (*materias*) of quipocamayos. He ticked off the following:

andenes ('terraces')
chacras ('fields')
siembras ('plantings')
cosechas ('crops')

almacenes de alimento ('storage deposits of foodstuffs')
herramientas ('tools')
obras ('works')
faenas ('collective labor')
castigos ('punishments')
costumbres ('customs')
acomodos ('sacred pledges')
cónyuges ('spouses')
fechas de reuniones (meeting dates)
autoridades (officers)

In this list he omitted a matter on which he and his elders usually insisted, namely pasturage.

Nery does not claim to be listing these fifteen topics in khipu order. Yet perhaps they are organized by some habitual typology, and if so, it might be one which in earlier times influenced cords. (One thinks of the ranked "ethnocategories" which seriated early colonial khipus; Murra 1975b.) The topics are clustered by large areas of interest. The first four concern agricultural foci in chronological order, the next two capital resources, the next three the collective labor regimen, the next two the ritual cycle, the following one kinship and/or membership, and the last two political administration.

The sequence of Nery's fifteen functional topics may reflect their successive salience in different parts of the productive round. It begins with matters associated with the first-semester planting season, followed by harvesting, storage, and the turn toward political affairs at year-end. It would be unrealistic to expect that this list constitutes an actual khipu table of contents. But even allowing for blurring of memory and the effects of association in arranging remembered items, it remains interesting that the number of topics and the structural scheme roughly fit the band pattern of Tupicochan quipocamayos. As we will see in chapter 9, the number of bands per quipocamayo is not constant, but varies within a narrow range with fifteen as central tendency.

Consultants did not agree on what colors of band correspond to each agenda. An exception is that of pasturage, which seems to be consensually remembered as reckoned on off-white pendants with brown subsidiaries.

Operationality. Here we see divided opinion. "Half-life" oral traditions states, as the study of material traits also suggested, that the quipocamayo was routinely subjected to removal and modification of cords by way of updating or correction. Local people think operational modifications also included removal of the end knot and perhaps intentional unraveling, which would have signified division or dispersal of the items referred to. On the other hand, those who discuss cords in the rhetoric of afterlife credit them with supratemporal validity. Consequently, they deny the legitimacy of any alteration, and they claim the present data-state is relevant to any and all contingencies — even though they themselves slacken and tighten knots to study them.

Diagrammatic Spatial Representation. It is a common ground between "half-life" and "afterlife" interpretative styles that both interpret some cords as icons about the distribution of space or geographic features. These features are the surface area of fields or terraces (sometimes specifying crops), the inflow and storage of water in lakes (reservoirs?), and the quantity and distribution of water from springs. In such reckonings, the total length of the cord is taken as representing total extent, unequal internodal distances as proportionate to functional sectors, and the knots themselves as indicative of the function to which the sectors were applied. Cords studied this way were sometimes said to be "like maps."

Indeed there is some tendency to regard the quipocamayo in its totality as a single all-embracing image of social totality at ayllu level, with the long main cord as an "x axis" representing time and the vertical extent of cords as a series of "y axes," many of which correspond to physical space. However — importantly — there is no presumption of universal commensurability across bands.

Knotting. The interpretation of knots is an area of low consensus, but scattered insights were gained. First, a contrast between the T-knot and the "ring knot" (Inka-style long knot) (Key Figure 26 pendants 35–36) is taken to signify the contrast between dispersed (distributed) and centralized (stored) assets. Second, the absence of knots on a cord is taken to signify discharge of obligation or null balance. Third, for some purposes knots were read arithmetically in Lockean fashion. The odd-even reckoning which forms a dominant motif in khipumantic interpretation would be suspect of conveying only an "interference" from Old World cartomancy and related occult arts but for the fact that it also resonates strongly with the pre-Hispanically rooted Huarochirí emphasis on alternating duality and the chulla/chullantin contrast Urton derives from Bolivian evidence. For the time being, the relation between the two systems must remain an unknown.

This chapter's conclusions may be partially articulated with "exterior" study to suggest synthetic interpretations. This is the agenda of the next chapter.

TOWARD SYNTHETIC INTERPRETATION

THE PREVIOUS four chapters followed four converging evidential paths: external historical documents, physical traits of the quipocamayos, ayllus' internal record-keeping, and memories about the cord patrimony. Taken together, how far do they bring us toward a context-enriched interpretation? They yield no certain decipherment of any one quipocamayo. They do suggest a model of the quipocamayos' overall functioning as a suite, and about the integration of the community through khipus.

Because this chapter is complex, it is useful to foresee where it is going. The first section, "Banded Quipocamayos: Historiographic Artifacts?" compares the nine banded quipocamayos across ayllus, demonstrating a common profile in terms of major information blocs. The second, "A Precedent from the *Huacsa* Priests circa 1608?," argues that this profile derives from a multipurpose template of pre-Hispanic origin. The third section, "Forms and Functions of Banded Quipocamayos," argues for a "function-band hypothesis," namely, that each band of pendants is a bloc of data about performance of a specific ayllu task (the ones discussed in chapters 3, 7, and 8). The fourth, "Possible Functions of Cantitos, or Threads Run Through," concerns the "meta"-code of brilliant colors which apparently guided use of bands. The fifth section, "Mújica Ayllu's Quipocamayo M-01: A Planning Device?," suggests that the one specimen with color-cycle format (specimen M-01) relates to banded format as planning relates to performance. The sixth, "A Hypothetical Reading of M-01," offers a detailed interpretation of how M-01 enacted and recorded a plan, based on fit between cord structures and extant ayllu planning documents. The seventh section, "The Quipocamayo Suite," sums up how planning and performance khipus jointly mediated group rationality through both operational and documentary functions. Throughout, quipocamayo features are referred back to Key Figure 26.

Banded Quipocamayos: Historiographic Artifacts?

If bands (Key Figure 26 pendants 1–6, 7–12) are the largest units within the quipocamayo, what could they represent? This question demands a look at some methodological hazards. The makers took care to give bands contrasting colors (see plate 12). Nonetheless, on close inspection it is often quite difficult to define band boundaries, for three reasons.

First, a given band often contains one or more pendants resembling the rest but differing by a hue or two, so one is forced to judge whether a boundary exists within the band. Two of the three village fiber workers consulted favor a more "lumping" approach, treating only obvious color differences as band discontinuities. I follow this counsel. Likewise, I follow all three in assuming that a pendant with a brilliant "run-through" thread is a member of the same band as adjacent and otherwise similar ones lacking this feature.

Second, not all pendants on banded quipocamayos are members of bands. One must either admit the category "singletons," meaning pendants that have no adjacent pendants of like color, or else allow "bands of one." The former is more believable, because singletons not only occur sporadically but also gather in sectors where several dissimilar singletons are attached side-by-side, as in Key Figure 26 pendants 13–15. (Some sets of singletons hang adjacent to the pachacamanta knob.) This suggests that cords not located in bands were meaningful in a distinctive way. Singletons also occur frequently as "separators" between differently colored bands. In eleven cases,[1] singletons have as neighbors cords of one color, for example, a brown singleton among black pendants. Is such a case a "separator" of two like-colored bands, or an interrupter of one band? In cases where both sides contain more than one pendant of the given color, we take the former interpretation. However, in nine of eleven cases, the singleton comes between a band and a lone outlier of the band's color. These lone cords then are ambiguous. They could be taken as outlying band members, or as singletons. I chose the latter interpretation because it is more parsimonious in using one category (separator singleton) instead of two (separator vs. interrupter). If one accepts the "interrupter" idea, the number of bands in 2A-01 and 2SF-01 falls by one each.

Third, in Tupicochan examples, unlike many prehistoric examples, intervals of bare main cord never separate groups.

The banded quipocamayos use a common repertoire of colors, cordages, and knots. Yet no two quipocamayos obviously resemble each other in color array of bands. Just as the modern books of various ayllus have similar formats and conventional parts, but array them in different orders of business, numbers of pages, and

TABLE 10 Comparison of Quipocamayos in Terms of Major Structural Blocs

QUIPOCAMAYO	NUMBER OF GROUPS	AVERAGE NUMBER OF PENDANTS PER GROUP	NUMBER OF PENDANTS, INCLUDING SINGLETONS BUT NOT SUBSIDIARIES
1A-01	15 bands	6.1	106
2A-01	16 bands	5.2	100
1SF-01	17 bands	6.2	114
2SF-01	15 bands	6.4	116
1G-01 [1G-02 destroyed?]	15 bands	5.7	88
Uch-01	12 bands	9.1	125
Uch-02	13 bands	4.5?	70 (some lost)
M-01	16 cycles	4.4	70
M-02	16 bands	4.4?	90
C-01 [C-02 lost?]	20 bands	3.9	101
Totals	155	55.9	980
Averages	Number of groups = 15.5	Number of pendants per group = 5.6	Number of pendants (excluding subsidiaries, including M-01) = 98

so on, so the nine banded specimens display some component bands that resemble each other across ayllus but do not match in sequencing or in knot content. Whatever the "somethings" that bands represent, they were somethings which ayllus had liberty to deploy dissimilarly.

We are no longer wholly in the dark about the identity of these somethings. We have reason to think that many or most bands represent the ayllus' internal duties and their respective duties to the community over a fixed (annual?) cycle, or functions ancillary to these duties like inventorying tools or registering pasture use. A plausible sort of regularity to seek in examining quipocamayos, therefore, is a rough congruence between the number of bands that each quipocamayo contains, and the numbers of such duties which its respective ayllu had to perform during annual cycles in the relevant historic period. Ayllus had, and still have, some autonomy about how they fulfill their duties, so dissimilarity of detail, such as color sequence of duties (bands), is expectable. And things that just happen to happen — weather, fluctuating numbers of people available, political choices — are also likely to have left their marks in the record.

As a starting point, therefore, we need a guide to the major structural blocs. This is given in table 10. Some relationships worth watching, then, are the following. First, we will consider relations between number of collective functions per ayllu and the number of bands per quipocamayo (average 15.5), or the number of bands per pair of quipocamayos, considering only reasonably complete pairs (i.e., Allauca and Satafasca). With one exception (Chaucacolca), banding seems to cluster around a pattern of about thirty-one bands per pair and about fifteen-sixteen bands per quipocamayo. If one removes M-01 on the grounds that it has cycles instead of bands, the result is an average of 15.4 bands per quipocamayo, a median of 15, and a mode of 15.

The average number of groups per quipocamayo, 15.5, has a standard deviation of 2.1. The standard deviation amounts to 13.5 percent of the mean value. The number of groups per quipocamayo appears somewhat constrained across ayllus, a fact which we may take to mean that the number of "somethings" they record was also constrained by some supra-ayllu convention.

As a second structural bloc, we will be considering relations between the function represented by a group and the number of pendants per group. The average number of pendants per group across all quipocamayos varies more widely than the number of groups. The average number is 5.6, with a standard deviation of 1.5, which is 26.7 percent of the average. If one introduces median and mode to control for effects of extremes, one finds that the median number of pendants per group is 5.5 across all quipocamayos, and the mode 6 across all quipocamayos. If one eliminates M-01 (because it has a special kind of groups, namely, cycles), the average number of pendants per band is 5.7, the median 6, and the mode 6. So bands were packets of loosely constrained size, containing six or slightly fewer pendants. These pendants represent components commonly numbering near six per ayllu function.

As a third structuring element, we will consider the number of pendants per quipocamayo. Table 10 shows an average of 98 if we include M-01. The median is 100.5, and the mode, pulled down by the double occurrence of 70, is 70. If we exclude M-01, the average is 101.1, and the median 101, with no mode because no number occurs more than once. The scatter around the central number is wider than that of the number of bands per quipocamayo but less than that of the number of pendants per band. The standard deviation equals 17.65 (M-01 included), which is 18.0 percent of the mean. There appears a central tendency in the neighborhood of 100 pendants per quipocamayo. Such a number forcefully calls to mind the fact that the main marker is called pachacamanta, which, if it is Quechua, could be glossed "concerning a hundred." The pachaka, or "hundred," it will be remembered, was a common Inka administrative grouping.

Are singletons similarly constrained? Singletons are distributed very differently in different quipocamayos. It may be relevant that the two most complete pairs of quipocamayos (Primer Allauca and Primera Satafasca) contain, respectively, 32 and 28 singletons, but singletons are not as equally apportioned between members of the pair as bands are.

In sum, then,

1. Banded quipocamayos occurred in pairs.
2. Each banded quipocamayo contained about 15–16 bands plus a variable number of singletons. Each pair had about 31 bands.
3. The lone color-cycle quipocamayo also had 16 groups.
4. The number of pendants per bands loosely centered around 6.
5. Quipocamayos on the average had about 100 pendants.

What social organization could correspond to this profile?

A Precedent from the *Huacsa* Priests circa 1608?

Recent decades' findings about colonial and Republican transformations warn Andean specialists against comparisons that leapfrog intervening centuries. But the numbers just demonstrated show an almost embarrassingly insistent likeness to the Quechua Manuscript of 1608 and related sources. It would be evasive to ignore it. The likeness concerns a recurrent 15/30-fold structure with tendency to ceremonialize the midpoint. It was administered by the hereditary priests called *yanca* and the annual officiants called *huacsa*.

The most overarching example appears in a 1609 Jesuit Annual Letter describing the Tupicocha-San Damián region and signed by P. Juan Sebastián de la Parra. Influenced by Avila, Parra gives a detailed Spanish viewpoint on Paria Caca's cult. Fifteen days dedicated to him were to begin on a certain day in April (with an apparent reference to *yanca* priests' decision—on the equinox [?]—by gnomon).[2] At that time, certain "officers" (*oficiales*) ordered men to sleep ten days away from their homes in rough shelters corresponding to their ayllus, for celibacy's sake. During these ten days, they prepared the offerings. They kept vigil until the dawn of the eleventh day, blowing conch trumpets (*huayllas*) and bringing llama sacrifices to ancestors. On the eleventh day they set out in pilgrimage. On the twelfth, the yanca priest would assign penitence. On the thirteenth day, they made climactic confessions and gifts to Pariakaka [*sic*]. On the fourteenth they chose the officers for the incoming year. Once the [outgoing?] officers had distributed coca, everyone returned home and danced "until they fulfilled the fifteen days that the fiesta had to last" (Polia Meconi 1999:275–77).[3]

Forty days later, they performed the corresponding ceremony for Paria Caca's female counterpart, Chaupi Ñamca, "and it lasts almost the same amount of time" (Polia Meconi 1999:278).[4]

A second such schedule occurs in the great Quechua source's descriptions of Paria Caca's huacsa priesthood, a corps of dancers who impersonated pre-Christian deities. Information about huacsas was gathered close to Tupicocha or even in it, to judge by places mentioned. In each Checa village, one or two hereditary yanca priests would name a troupe of huacsa and initiate them to dance at three annual occasions: the June rites for Paria Caca, a paramount male deity; the immediately following June rites for Chaupi Ñamca, a paramount female deity; and the November Chanco, or ceremonial hunt, around low and high landholdings.[5]

The 15/30-fold organization stands out in chap. 18 of the Huarochirí Quechua Manuscript, which tells how the Inka reorganized the huacsa priesthood under imperial patronage. "The Inka himself decreed, 'Let thirty men from the Upper Yauyos and the Lower Yauyos serve Paria Caca in the full moon and in the waning moon.' In obedience to that command, thirty men served him in shifts of fifteen days, offering him food." (Salomon and Urioste 1991:96, 198).[6] The Quechua original (anan yauyo rurin yauyomanta quinça chunca) does not clarify whether he meant thirty from each half of Yauyos Province or from both jointly, but later passages of the same and the next chapters say Paria Caca's retainers numbered thirty all told. Either way, it seems a corps of thirty served in shifts organized around a rotation at mid-month. The source does not explain whether the teams worked on a strictly lunar cycle of 29.5 days, or in adjusted lunar-solar months of 30 or 31 days (which would suggest exposure to Christian calendrical systems). Either way, there is a residue to be covered. The radiocarbon intervals for the specimens, like the texts just cited, fall entirely within the era when the European solar-lunar calendar had come into rural ritual use.

Another relevant passage tells how "all the Checa" served a deity named Maca Huisa, whose cult also enjoyed Inka subsidy. In post-Inka times, the Checa served Maca Huisa "ayllu by ayllu, in the [moon] called waning and in the [moon] called full" (Salomon and Urioste 1991:100; see also Taylor 1987:289).[7] The chapter on Maca Huisa reports specifically that ayllu-by-ayllu cultic service survived into colonial times as part of the cultic reorganization designed to protect deities in clandestinity (Salomon 1998b). This would suggest an organization much like the above, with the lunar/solar discrepancy no better clarified.

Let us consider these three textual sources in relation to khipus. In the Jesuit source, periods of fifteen days were assigned to paramount male and female deities. In the Quechua source, two teams of fifteen corresponded to the waxing and waning moon within the cycle of worship for the male one.

If we imagine paired khipus corresponding respectively to the Paria Caca and Chaupi Ñamca pilgrimages as described in the Jesuit letter, they would show approximately similar gross divisions into fifteen, with something to differentiate the ten preparatory days from the five consummatory ones.

If we imagine khipus corresponding to the team of thirty which served within the cult of Paria Caca, it might well take the form of paired khipus, each bearing about fifteen bands, and each band corresponding to a day's service. If we take the match between number of men and number of days to imply that a different man led the corps on each day, we might guess that each band would represent one day's cult, including the day-leader's record of those absent, or particular deeds such as sacrifices or auguries. The bands would not necessarily be alike in format, because different days had different agendas. Some might, for example, require subsidiaries and others not. This would yield a khipu resembling the Tupicochan specimens.

The Quechua source shows that in colonial times, the focus shifted to smaller-scale cultic organization. The gist of the post-Inka reform of Maca Huisa's cult, responding to Christian persecution, is not only a shift to clandestinity, but reduction of priestly leadership from regional to local management. Small organizations were more viable because they were easier to hide. Within the newer, clandestine system we find clear testimony on two important points. First, the pattern of organization by half months was continued. And second, this pattern was executed "ayllu by ayllu."

Is it possible that the pairs of Tupicocha quipocamayos are surviving records of service to huacas? Their radiocarbon dates overlap the latest part of the "extirpation" era. Could each pair be an ayllu's record of how it carried out its duties to some postextirpation cult in the waxing and waning parts of one month? In the era when quipocamayo competence last played a part in governance, that is, the late nineteenth century and the early twentieth, the ayllus numbered six. So a round of "ayllu by ayllu" action would have equaled a half year. This seems inviting, because as was noted in chapter 7, the half year is a recognized ayllu-governing principle.

A whole community-year, then, could have been seen as the magnified homologue of an ayllu-month, with its waxing and waning halves being semesters and the divine month of June its fullness. If ayllus took part in their usual order of precedence, spread through the solar half-year, January and July would have belonged to Allauca, February and August to Satafasca, and so on.

But this model has problems. First, *n* hours of service in a peak labor month would have weighed heavier than *n* hours in a lighter month, an inequity that modern ayllus would never tolerate. Second, the model works if ayllus constantly numbered six, but as we know from chapter 3, this has not been the case in all post-Inka periods. Third, no function verified in ayllu or community books is described as being organized in month-long stints assigned to ayllus. Fourth, while the khipus have an overall tendency toward fifteen-bandedness, it remains to explain why only one ayllu's pair has the exact combination (15 and 16 bands) which would match an ordinary month.

It is more likely that Checa ritual complexes, and Republican-era civic-ritual complexes, both partook of a common multipurpose organizational scheme — a versatile 15/30-fold template for getting many things done. This matrix was observed elsewhere by Rufino Chuquimamani and Natalio Choquehuanca, who collected from a Quechua settlement in Azángaro Province (Puno) a testimony that a circuit-riding "khipu" supervisor was responsible for "14 to 16 'kiphus' [*sic*]" and that "each herder or colonist was responsible for two sets" (Villavicencio et al. 1983:35–36). Unfortunately the report does not reveal how fifteen-fold and dual traits interacted.

Should we think of the 15's in Tupicocha as half months, or as sets corresponding to half years? Ayllu books allude to the fact that the first and second officers of ayllus had roles keyed to the first and second semesters. They say nothing at all about month-long or half-month cycles. So the longer-period (semester/annual) duality is a better documented clue to nineteenth- to twentieth-century khipu pairing than is the seventeenth-century monthly cycle. If so, the fifteen or so groups per quipocamayo would reflect a fairly standardized number of events or duties to be completed in each semester.

Forms and Functions of Banded Quipocamayos

Chapters 6–7 argued that quipocamayos were coordinated to the internal authority structure of ayllus. We demonstrated that the two major offices of each ayllu formerly were symbolized by one quipocamayo each. The definite former pairs are 1A-01 with 2A-01, 1SF-01 with 2SF-01, and UCh-01 with UCh-02. Plate 13 shows a restored former pair on the study table.

THE RECORDING OF PERFORMANCE

To what division of labor does this duality correspond? The ayllu books and living memories discussed in chapter 7 indicate two distinctions. First, the camachico (later president) concentrated on the prospective, executive work of governance: carrying forward the faena "round" and duties to the community, while the mayor's (later vice president's) regime was more retrospective and judicial, enforcing arrears and judging results. Second, the camachico was more responsible for daily intra-ayllu administration and the mayor more an outward-facing, ambassadorial figure.

Knowing that the paramount work of these officers was to manage group resources and duties, I think the most secure judgment of content is that bands documented performance of duties. But how did they do so?

One immediately faces a difficult choice of models. On the one hand, one might hypothesize that each band represents the record of a given duty (a faena, a meeting, a group purchase and redistribution, etc.). Its component pendants signal attributes of the task or function, for example, the supplies used and compliance of members. I will call this the *function-band hypothesis*. On the other, one might hypothesize that each band summarizes the record of one member, with pendants representing his household's participation in successive tasks. I will call this the *member-band hypothesis*.

Both hypotheses present difficulties, but the member-band hypothesis has more serious ones. The member-band hypothesis predicts that the ways of ordering members should match the ordering of bands. In chapter 7 we documented three manners of ordering members: (1) by bracket of duties in Guaman-Poma–like order (active, semiretired or disabled, probationary), (2) by seniority, and (3) by "family" cluster. Do the quipocamayos match these? Order 1 is governed by a top-level tripartition. This predicts that in all specimens, we should find bands grouped into three top-level, supraband brackets, delimited from each other (by markers?) or else each defined by some structural uniformity. Following demography of the relevant era, they should be of descending size. We do not find this. Neither do we find the predicted pattern of "adjectival" specification about duties. Suppose, for example, that probationary members needed an "adjectival" specification such as a subsidiary telling how much of their entrance quota they had paid. We should then find a series of bands each bearing such an adjective (presumably only one) at one end of the main cord. But we do not. Instead we find on several specimens bands each of which has a characteristic adjective repeated on most or many of its cords, for example, each bearing a whitish subsidiary. If a quipocamayo has more than one such band, these bands are not gathered but occur at scattered locations along the main cord. As for order 2, seniority, it shows a similar predictive failure. If each band represents a member, its pendants must represent the member's attributes or actions. We know that in all ayllus, activity requirements were and still are differentiated by seniority, with members of highest and lowest seniority subject to different duties. This suggests that irrespective of markers or delimiters, bands near either end of the main cord should be regularly different from mid-cord ones in size or format. No such pattern appears. As for order 3, family cluster, it predicts that bands in a single "family" should lie adjacent, and should share a common marking trait. The clusters they form should be of unequal size and there should be very few of them. I found no such clusters.

A function-band model (such as what Nery Javier suggested) handles the heterogeneity of bands better. Functions as diverse as inventory of tools, attendance at faenas, and management of endowed fields would have given rise to diverse forms within the bands that respectively reflected them. For example, some tasks and functions do entail additional data-variable attributes such as porratas (quotas) of raw material, or tools, or a number of animals involved. These need "adjectival" statement while others do not. These would correspond to bands with subsidiaries. We also saw in chapter 7 that the range of functions ayllus had to document was wide and that the set of variables recorded itself varied with the type of function.

IMPLICATIONS AND TESTS OF THE FUNCTION-BAND MODEL

If banded quipocamayos are performance records organized around a series of functions, they should show the following properties:

1. The number of bands in a pair of quipocamayos should correspond to a plausible number of functions for the institutional scope of a given quipocamayo within a one-year cycle.

    a. The portion of a given pair of quipocamayos addressing ayllu-internal functions should have at least enough bands to match the number of faenas and other functions that fulfilled the mutual-aid "round" in a relevant historical era.

b. The portion of a given pair of quipocamayos that addresses supra-ayllu functions should likewise have at least enough bands to cover known numbers of levies the community made on its component ayllus.

c. Whether we assume these two kinds of functions to have been recorded on separate quipocamayos, or whether we assume each khipu to contain material of both kinds assembled in chronological order for first and second semester respectively, the banding patterns of pair members will not closely resemble each other. Conversely, if members of a pair mirror or otherwise mimic each other's banding, they probably had overlapping or shared scope, and a double-entry or otherwise mutually dependent makeup.

2. Within any given band, it should be possible for a competent user to associate pendants with particular members' compliance, or with other facts about a task, meeting, etc.

The function-band hypothesis does not imply that bands within one quipocamayo or across various need be of like design. Since workdays involve many different sorts of work, they might well create records as diverse as the forms which the Primera Satafasca respondents suggested in chapter 8. For example, a faena for working a terrace to benefit the welfare-ritual fund could well include a cord of the field-mapping design shown in Figure 47. A band recording a day of roofing likely included cord subsidiaries about the quotas of straw members were to bring. The collection and warehousing of a harvest for collective use might include Lockean yield quantities and so forth. The observed irregular distribution of format properties among bands is expectable under a function-band hypothesis but anomalous under a member-band hypothesis.

Let us now try the function-band hypothesis against numerical data from sources exterior to the cords:

Test 1a: Do the figures given in table 10, which average close to fifteen per quipocamayo and thirty-one per pair, accommodate plausible "rounds" of faenas for ayllu-internal cord records, that is, records which covered an ayllu's duties to its members?

Apparently they do. Cacarima ayllu troubled to make explicit the basic agenda of labor planning for members' own benefit in 1919: "They [members] will carry the said faenas under the list which will make the round in 14 parts [and] when the works [i.e., the 14 parts] are fulfilled the session [i.e., business meeting] will be reopened to pay works and fines" (APC/SAT_01 1919:59).[8] In 1919 the number of members was also fourteen. Thus a cycle of the "round" would indeed be likely to yield a record consisting of membership plus one: work sessions plus a planning session at the start or end. In practice, an elder attests, the "round" was not necessarily fixed at one meeting, because in the course of one faena a member might ask for rescheduling of another. For such uses, an easily revised medium such as moveable cords would work well.

Would such a magnitude fit ayllus in general, at relevant dates? Chapters 5 through 7 argued that the likely last updates of quipocamayos took place in the early twentieth century, with perhaps some minor reworking later. Satafasca numbered nineteen households in 1913, before its division (AP1SF/SAT_01 1913:2), Mújica was in the neighborhood of fourteen-sixteen through the 1880s and 1890s. When Guangre split, 7 signed the Constitution of the "first" faction and it stabilized at 9, so the undivided ayllu might have been 14–18 members (AP1G/SAT_01 1930:5).

So it is likely that at relevant dates, the "round" by itself would occupy a number of bands in the mid-teens. It is plausible that this series of bands filled one quipocamayo of each pair, such that one of the two was specialized in mutual-aid functions and the other in suprahousehold functions. But it remains possible that each quipocamayo covered a half year, with intra-ayllu functions like the "round" interspersed among other supra-ayllu functions in chronological order.

This finding leaves a doubt as to whether the ancient ideal number of 15 (a half-month team of huacsa priests) has anything to do with the de facto number 15 which is attributed above to demography. The improbable coincidence is not necessarily a pure coincidence. An ideal number such as 15, regardless of astronomical fit, is hardly ideal if it flies in the face of demographic practicality. Fifteen or so faenas of the internal "round" may have been a normative number not just for astronomical and ritual reasons, but because the demands of agropastoralism set a ceiling on the number of days a household can conveniently give to such work. To be a member of a large ayllu — let us say one much above fifteen — would have been troublesome, because it would mean giving up more days of household work. The additional workers present on the day one's own household hosted the faena would hardly compensate unless one happened to have so many capital goods as to absorb them efficiently — and the pressure of demographic growth on resources makes it all the less likely that an average peasant would.

Although villagers today attribute the ayllu fissions of the 1920s to moral faults, it may be significant that they occurred in a period of rising demography. (Indeed a deep stratum of Huarochirí culture sees the two issues as connected. Some myths in the Huarochirí Manuscript imply that people become morally vicious when overpopulation causes fierce competition; Fuenzalida Vollmar 1979.) A too-small ayllu would incur the inverse defects, and these indeed became prevalent problems of the 1990s. Perhaps the ancient schema of half-month teams was functionally strong precisely because it naturalized a sociologically optimal levy — a scale at which households could realize the moral bond of reciprocity without undue economic stress.

Test 1b: If the sum of bands in a pair of quipocamayos equals the sum of mutual-aid functions plus functions for the benefit of suprahousehold units, then the number of bands above and beyond the fifteen-odd turns of the "round" should be similar to independently attested numbers of suprahousehold levies. The sum of the two classes in any given ayllu's non-khipu records should come out around thirty.

In the cases where evidence suffices, this prediction is verified. In the 1920s ayllu Segunda Allauca had the habit (alas, not 100 percent consistent) of recording all its collective obligations on paper, not just its internal ones as most ayllus did at that time. Levies above the ayllu level included jobs such as cultivating fields to subsidize festivals, roofing the Community Hall or church, improving the road, or building the school. This record enables us to tell what obligations an ayllu was responsible for enforcing on the whole community's behalf, above and beyond its own needs.

If one sums all the items which this group annotated as collective obligations owed to the larger collectivity, including faenas and other sorts of business, for the period 1925–30 the average is thirteen items per year. For 1925–33, it is twelve per year. These can only be accepted as order-of-magnitude estimates, because records are not equally well written for all years.

Such numbers are compatible with the function-band hypothesis. They also match Gelles's findings in another Huarochirí village (see chapter 2) that the average annual total number of faenas was thirty. The likeness of band numbers within each quipocamayo pair is closer than the likeness between intra- and supra-ayllu functions in books of the subsequent 1919–30 oncenio era and after. This seems a reflection of the higher jurisdictions' increasingly numerous demands after oncenio-era reforms retired quipocamayos from official use.

If this reconstruction is correct, the pre-1919 quipocamayo regimen embodied norms about labor equity between intra-ayllu and supra-ayllu levies. In no ayllu does the number of bands on one quipocamayo deviate by more than two units from its mate. If the respective quipocamayos of the pair represent semesters, collective work was loaded equally on each. If they represent inter-ayllu versus supra-ayllu functions, there may have been a norm (long since upset) that the two burdens should be about equal.

But how could bands have conveyed the execution of tasks — especially such heterogeneous ones as the folk memories in chapter 8 attest? One plan would be for each of, say, fifteen bands to represent a task and each pendant a different member's compliance or absence, so each band should have a number of pendants similar to that of households. This guess is refuted by the small number of pendants in average bands.

The method which appears most believable would be for each band to represent a single household's leadership or host role in executing one function, and the outcome of that function. These leadership positions need not be guessed at because they are recorded in ayllu books. The task leader in an ayllu's major annual irrigation work was called *gastador*, or 'spender'. The gastador had the job of rallying his peers to a community task and conducting "enflowerment" plus the usual ritual gifts of liquor, coca, and tobacco. When a person became the beneficiary in a "round" of faenas, he was said to lead it by "carrying" it, and he too incurred ritual expenses. As was noted in chapter 7, it was considered important to document ritual expenses. They may well have been coded onto cords. We will consider below, under the subsection "Intra-band Properties," how a pendant could be coded to a member.

INTRA-BAND PROPERTIES

We hypothesized that quipocamayo usefulness would seem to depend on a competent user's ability to associate pendants in a given band with particular members, and/or with particular facts about a function. The ability to do so is test 2 for the function-band hypothesis.

Let us begin, then, with the question of how cords could be associated with identity. Knots are usually regarded as the "guts" of khipu data technology, and Tupicocha villagers occasionally compare them to letters. But if so, one has to answer for knotlessness. Conklin (2002) makes a strong case that unknotted cords are data rich. They abound in Tupicocha, probably for the zero-targeting reason discussed in chapter 7. Primer Huangre's quipocamayo (88 pendants and 10 subsidiaries) has only 6 knotted pendants and 4 knotted subsidiaries (see plate 14). Ten of its fifteen bands have no knots at all.

The presence of some zeros in any data register can be expected, but the dominance of zeros in this specimen, and the presence of whole knotless bands on six of nine banded specimens,[9] suggests that knotlessness was not the "blank slate" condition of an unused band but a meaningful value of "cleared" khipus. Radicati di Primeglio (1965:133–38) describes a khipu resembling Tupicochan ones (including yellow end-tuft), whose ninety pendants hang in thirteen groups. Groups 10–13 bear no knots but show traces of knot removal. A completely knotless band may be taken as a function completed, with no pending residual business. The function remains recognizable by nonknot properties of the band's pendants, with perhaps no reference to members as such.

But in cases of noncompliance, etc., members did need to be referred to. Many knots on the pendants are likely to be individuating label numbers, that is, ID numbers such as the "order" or seniority numbers used today on paper. The nonstandardization of knot placement suggests, as does the total absence of topcords and summation cords, that computing across cords was not a common objective. Nonstandardizing, diversity-increasing features fit well with "identifier" rather than "quantifier" use of knots. Also, the knot system contains contrasts seemingly superfluous for quantifiability. Tupicocha had two separate kinds of long knots, the Inka, or I-knot, and the Tupicocha, or T-knot. The fact that both kinds can occur on one cord (though rarely) suggests they are not interchangeable, not allomorphic. Here too, non-Lockean norms suggest that what is to be made recognizable may be uniqueness or identity, not commensurable quantity.

The existence of many unknotted cords does not by itself call the ID knot hypothesis into question, because (under the "negative reckoning" convention described in chapter 7) if a knotted pendant represents a member's deficit, for example, his pending fine or debt, then unknotting would clear the member but leave in place a record of payments or goods received. This would be a necessary element for the "social audit." The knotting observed does show enough different data states to cover a plausible number of members. (See the analysis of M-01 below in this chapter.) Nonetheless, the mode of correspondence between knots and persons or households remains the least-intelligible part of the Tupicochan record.

Possible Functions of Cantitos, or Threads Run Through

Chapter 6 observed that a palette of brilliant colors in nonstructural fibers occurs in markers and in the threads that "run through" some pendants. Villagers suggest that main cord markers could signal major festivals and that bright "underlining" of certain pendants with colors that also occur in markers might associate a person or a function to its institutional "owner"—the festival, the ayllu, the community, the patron saint, or the state.

Those bands whose member pendants are all marked with such "underlinings" could be faenas performed for the benefit of a special event, for example, sowing a field whose harvest is earmarked to support a festival or a community project. (Such functions are attested on paper.) Some bands contain a series of pendants with cantitos and a few without. These might represent work on assets (e.g., plots of ayllu land, herds) partly earmarked as donations. Cantito construction seems to be a way of running a parallel tally of variables intercalated with the functional series but separately accountable.

Yellow, red, and brown cantitos show dissimilar distributions along main cords, with red being by far the commonest. Across all specimens, red is concentrated in bands from the midpoint to the pachacamanta bulb. Brown, much less frequent, tends to occur at the opposite end. Yellow, also uncommon, is distributed more evenly throughout. If the succession of pendants along main cords represents the passing of time, these distributions might reflect supra-ayllu coordinated contributions to rituals or peak functions, such as the canal cleaning and visit to the divine water-owners (near 1 May), or the patron saints' days (August, November). We will not be able to key them to a calendrical system until the direction of reading, still uncertain, becomes clear.

Mújica Ayllu's Quipocamayo M-01: A Planning Device?

We now turn from the rule to the exception. The exceptional case is quipocamayo M-01. Mújica ayllu displays it in the normal way at the huayrona, but its design differs from the other quipocamayos. It is not organized in bands. Rather, it displays a repetitive sequence of four differently colored pendants, a design Mackey called "color cycles."

M-01 is also deviant in its dating and pedigree. Fiber shreds in Mújica's storage bag yielded a "bomb carbon" date—a firm date of the post-Hiroshima era, probably 1979. Of course, it is possible that somebody had stored modern clothes in the same bag. But some M-01 pendants do look new. These are thick nappy pendants which look and smell like sheep wool yarn.

M-01 has a third peculiarity. It formerly bore one cord which was not a legitimate half-hitched pendant. Instead it was a portion of main cord from another, lost quipocamayo. From this fragment dangled the beautiful pachacamanta or ornamental knob of the lost specimen, which we will call M-0X. The piece of main cord was tied onto M-01's main cord with a coarse overhand knot. Between 1995 and 1997, this fragment disappeared.

A MÚJICA MYSTERY: THE CURATION OF M-0X, M-01, AND M-02

These peculiarities need to be examined in light of Mújica ayllu's curation history. In 1958, an ayllu book reported the accidental loss of the "Vice President's" quipocamayo (APM/SAT_03 1958:53). This is remembered as a scandal. Nonetheless in subsequent years, Mújica presidents did appear draped in the usual way at the huayrona. What did they wear? Never having fissioned, Mújica must have held another quipocamayo in reserve, perhaps in bad condition, just as the also-undivided Chaucacolca ayllu withholds its decrepit quipocamayo UCH-02 from view now. Probably it was Mújica's reserved quipocamayo, namely, the originally "presidential" one, that came forward in huayronas after 1959. I think this was M-0X.

At an unknown time, which I believe close to the 1979 radiocarbon date of fiber in the M-01 bag, M-0X was apparently judged too far gone for public use. Someone then retrieved M-01 from an unknown source. This restorer prepared it for substitute service by tying the symbolically potent remainder of M-0X, namely, its main cord and knob, onto it. This was when the recent sheep wool cords were added. The result of the restoration, in my judgment, is a historic main cord bearing historic pendants and also new pendants perhaps made to replace lost or broken ones. The restorer may also have transferred pendants from M-0X to M-01.

From about 1978 through 2002, restored M-01, actually a non-huayrona quipocamayo, was designated to carry the symbolic essence of the vanished M-0X "presidential" quipocamayo.

But when least expected, the lost "vice presidential" quipocamayo turned up again. In 1998 a crew clearing garbage from a disused latrine found it in a shopping bag tucked under the tin roof. Villagers recognized it without dispute as the missing Mújica one. I termed it M-02. Mújica has left M-02 in care of the municipality (which owns the latrine) without making any claim, allegedly to avoid incurring a community sanction for negligence. A banded quipocamayo, M-02 figures among the ones discussed above.

Mújica members feign ignorance about how M-01 was remodeled to serve as M-0x's substitute. One elder referred to M-02 as the "old quipocamayo, the Vice President's" as opposed to the "new one, the [current] President's" (i.e., M-01), thereby unguardedly conceding that M-01 is at least in part a replacement.

From all this a question arises about whether M-01, seemingly reconstructed after the extinction of quipocamayo competence, has any value as a sample of the art. It is certainly compromised. Yet, the present pattern of cords is unlikely to be a pure fabrication because M-01 closely resembles various pre-Hispanic "color cycle" khipus registered in museums. Specifically, it looks like the Musée de l'Homme's specimen 64.19.1.7. (The Parisian specimen's pattern number is 5 compared to M-01's 4.) It can also be compared to V.A.66830 of Berlin's Ethnologisches Museum. The chances of direct imitation are vanishingly small. The Ascher database and European museum records are locally unknown. I think it likely that the reconstruction reflects a good-faith effort to restore an older design by reworking an old quipocamayo that was not banded and was not originally part of the pair used in the huayrona. The main cord and pachacamanta of M-01 match historic specimens. Both pachacamantas and main cords of the historic main Mújica pair are already accounted for, as M-0x and M-02. So M-01 is almost certain to be structured on a genuinely historic main cord which never was part of a banded pair. It is likely that restoration differently affected different components. The new sheep wool cords appear usually to fill first and third positions of the cycle structure explained in the following subsection. First cords in each cycle are brown, and brown camelid fiber is more fragile than other colors, so the apparently nonrandom refilling of position 1 could be a good-faith restoration. The M-knot, or Mújica long knot (Key Figure 26 pendant 37), also seems to belong to the restoration. If these components were made to replicate regularities in the original, we have an M-01 partly "transliterated" from its original. If not, there remains a possibility that the restorer merely added cords in a regular pattern to pad out a sparse number of rescued original cords. This would call the meaningfulness of its present structure into question.

A further question then arises: what sort of quipocamayo was M-01 in the first place? How was Mújica able to come up with a khipu from outside the inventory of paired civic specimens? I see two possibilities: it may have been illegally obtained from another ayllu, which would be an almost unthinkable transgression. It would surely have caused an unforgettable uproar if not combat or prosecution. Otherwise, M-01 may be a specimen from, or replication of, a genre which supplemented the paired and banded genre. I believe this latter to be the case.

THE "COLOR CYCLE" STRUCTURE OF M-01
The basic structure of M-01 is evident to the naked eye (see fig. 49 and plate 15). M-01 consists of sixteen iterations of a sequence of four pendants. I will call

each iteration a quartet. Each quartet contains two fixed-color pendants and two variable-color pendants in the following order:

Ch (chumpi, i.e., brown)
v1 (first variable color)
O (oque, i.e., silvery or bluish gray)
v2 (second variable color).

Only one anomaly in quartet structure occurs. It concerns four pendants near the beginning of the khipu which seemingly violate the above pattern.[10] The fact that they all occur in v1 and v2 positions allows one to conserve the "quartet" rule by positing that categories v1 and v2 may redouble. (The alternative is to import the singleton category from banded format.) Given this amendment, the khipu yields up a range of regularities:

Ch pendants   Are always knotted.
               May be knotted with Tupicocha (T), Inka long (I), or Mújica (M) knots.
               Value of knots ranges 2/3T to an "anomalous" 12/13T. N.b., T-knots appear ambiguous in number and are valued at the lower of two apparent numbers.)
               Pendant may bear two long knots.
               Do not have dyed threads run through.
               Vary in color within range beige to mid-brown.
               Seem to be of sheep wool in some cases.
               Are always Z-plied.

v1 pendants   May or may not be knotted.
               Are knotted with T-knots dominantly.
               Values range from 3/4T to 5/6T, with two apparent exceptions.
               Pendant may bear two long knots.
               May have dyed threads run through.
               Vary widely in color.
               Seem to be camelid wool always or almost always.
               May be Z- or S-plied.

O pendants   Are always knotted.
               May be knotted with T-, I-, or M-knots.
               Values range 21 through an "anomalous" 11/12T.
               Pendant may bear two long knots.
               Do not have dyed threads run through.
               Vary moderately in color, light gray to darkish or olive-gray.
               Seem often to be sheep wool.
               Are always Z-plied.

v2 pendants	Are only rarely knotted before group 9, which bears as its v1 a conspicuous tricolor that might be a place marker.
	Are always knotted after group 9, with one exception.
	Are knotted only with T-knots.
	Values vary from 2/3T to 4/5T.
	Have one long knot maximum.
	May have dyed thread run through.
	Vary widely in color.
	Seem to be camelid wool usually or always.
	May be Z- or S-plied.

Generalizing, one can say of M-01 that

1. It contains two kinds of pendants, to be called type A and type B.
2. Type A consists of Ch and O pendants, elements 1 and 3 of each quartet (counted from the left in Figure 49). These encode variation on a smaller number of data variables than type B. Many are recent in origin.
3. Type B consists of v1 and v2 pendants, elements 2 and 4. They vary on all the variables noted in the study of banded quipocamayos.
4. Meaningful differences among type-A cords are apparently restricted to the type and value of knot(s).
5. Within this restriction, variation is "anomalously" wide. Type and value of knots on type-A cords vary considerably beyond the Lockean canon.
6. Variation among type-B pendants is about as wide as variation among pendants on any given banded quipocamayo. Variables include
   a. Color of structural cordage.
   b. Presence or absence of threads run through.
   c. Color of threads run through.
   d. Ply direction of cordage.
   e. Knotting versus nonknotting of pendant.
   f. Type and value of knots.
   g. Number of cords occupying the v1 or v2 position.
7. Type and value of knot(s) on type-B pendants vary within the Lockean canon, but knot position is weakly standardized.
8. Knotting, as opposed to nonknotting, of v2 cords is characteristic of quartets toward the end of the quipocamayo.
9. Type-A cords are Z-plied. Type-B cords are sometimes S-plied though usually Z-plied.

Despite the above-mentioned doubts about the trustworthiness of restored type-A (Ch and O) pendants, the resemblance with the above-mentioned pre-Hispanic specimen at the Musée de l'Homme (and other ancient color-cycle speci-

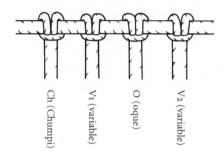

Ch (Chumpi)   V1 (variable)   O (oque)   V2 (variable)

FIGURE 49   The quartet structure of quipocamayo M-01. From personal collection of author.

mens) is too close to ignore.[11] Reservations notwithstanding, the coexistence of banded and cyclical designs deserves further thought because it is also a pre-Hispanic fact.

Although M-01 is richly structured, arithmetical relations across cords, if present, are inconspicuous. The positioning of knots on pendants seems all but random. The fact that type-B pendants obey the Lockean canon better than type-A ones do suggests that type-A knots may convey "labels" or nonnumerical signs, while type-B pendants may carry numerical signs which might be intended as quanta.

Let us now further refine the descriptive picture of type-B data. First, M-01's type-B cords have three colors of threads run through (Key Figure 26 pendants 30–32). None of them occurs in type A. All three occur in V1. Only one occurs in V2.

Second, V1 and V2 both vary in color, but not in the same way. Pendants in V1 position are of many colors in both the grayish and brownish series. Pendants in V2 position tend to be near white, near black, and light-dark mottled. The distribution of their colors shows no particular trend.

What Mújica ayllu information set could fit this profile? M-01 and M-02 may be closely related, even of the same year, because both consist of sixteen segments. Are they likely to be related renderings of the same or similar household rosters? The sixteen iterations of the Mújica quartet and the bands of M-02 match early ayllu book data quite well. Around the turn of the twentieth century, on the three occasions when all the members were to sign, the numbers were 14, 16, and 17. When Mújica elder Román Antiporta reminisced, he said that "the fifteen men of Mújica were like a Congress"—even though I had not even asked him about numbers.

IN THE FOOTSTEPS OF MÚJICA'S QUIPOCAMAYO USERS
We are now in a position to try empathizing with the user of M-01. The user intends to control sixteen "somethings," perhaps keyed each to one member household. We will call these somethings functions. The user is probably interested in com-

paring or coordinating functions, since she or he demands a similar body of information about each function. At the top level of m-01's organization, four items about each function are on record.

The user needed to know two data items about each household that were very salient and may well have been nonquantitative. These two variables are the contents of the two type-A pendants, colored Ch and O respectively.

What might type-A data be? If the sixteen quartets of m-01 represent sixteen member households, they could represent either a general database about the households, or a specific plan deploying them over a period such as a "round" of reciprocal labor.

CH PENDANTS

The Ch, or chumpi, series contains Z-plied, brown-hued, cantito-lacking, unredoubled cords. A Ch is the first pendant of each quartet (if the knob is the beginning). It appears designed to highlight just one variable, since chumpis are uniform on most of the variables that potentially carry data. Chumpis seem to differ saliently from each other only in knotting. Knots therefore might be the identifier telling what discrete item the quartet referred to.

Could Ch pendants be names or seniority numbers (see chapter 7) of household heads? If we assume that each household is referred to once, each "name" should be different. Assuming that only the knot type and value of the lowest knot signify, Ch pendants bear twelve signs. If we assume that the value of the second knot on a pendant disambiguates the first, there are fourteen. If we assume that the direction of knotting is also significant, there are fifteen. If we assume that the nonstandardized positions of knots on their pendants also signifies, there are sixteen unique signs.

The unique-name solution seems reasonable if one is convinced that m-01 is a database of households. Then all households must be mentioned, and for sixteen signs we must accept the maximalist guess at the range of cord-construction variables bearing data. However, if we take m-01 to represent an already planned "round" (or other series of functions), rather than baseline data prior to the planning of a round, there is a good reason why names might recur. The "round of faenas" allowed a beneficiary to trade or sell his turn to a peer, or even (at a higher price) to an outsider.[12] After negotiating, one householder well might "carry" more than one faena, and Ch pendants might not mention every household.

If one sees m-01 as a primary database, another objection damages the "name" hypothesis. Given what was explained in chapter 7 about seniority numbers, a starting-line database for a given year would not need explicit seniority numbers, because one would know what household any quartet applied to simply by noting that it is the nth quartet. Unique or near-unique knotting of the first element would then need a different explanation. But if one accepts the idea that m-01 records a plan posterior to the negotiating of a "round" schedule, then identifiers are defi-

TABLE 11 Mújica Surnames circa 1890 and Gross Knot Configurations on
Ch Pendants of M-01, in Order of Frequency

DOMINANT NUMBER IN KNOT IN DESCENDING ORDER OF FREQUENCY	NUMBER OF INSTANCES	SURNAME IN ORDER OF FREQUENCY	NUMBER OF INSTANCES
4, all types	5	Antiporta	6
5, all types	3	Adbincula	2
6, all types	2	Miranda	2
8, all types	2	Romero	2
2/3T	1	Camilo	1
10/11T	1	Urbano	1
12/13T	1	Ymaña	1
[unknotted]	1		

nitely needed, because the principals would come to the fore in a negotiated sequence different from their seniority.

The latter, or postnegotiation interpretation, has an additional edge in cogency because of a value-added argument. The postnegotiation khipu does not sacrifice any of its value as a general database. It is merely the general database sorted on an additional variable — and that variable is precisely the one which might often need "looking up" or renegotiation, as opposed to the purely obvious matter of seniority. This affords reason to think that the quartet is the record not of a household's durable attributes but of an event in context of the household that owns it.

If the knotting of Ch cords is an identifier, it might be possible to tell how Ch knots encode identity. Tupicochans occasionally liken khipu knots to "initials" or remark that "these [quipocamayos] have letters." How literally should we take this? In the earliest document with a full list of signatures, Mújica housed seven surnames which began respectively with A_1, A_2, C, M, U, Y, and R (APM/SAT_01 1897:f. 3 non num.). If identifier knots include surname identifiers, and the list of knotted surnames largely overlaps the ones in the written record, one would expect seven grossly distinguishing knot forms on Ch pendants with a distribution grosso modo comparable to that of surnames. The distribution is seen in table 11.

The anomaly of one unknotted cord in a class whose other fifteen members are long-knotted occurs on pendant 1. It is usual for the pendant next to the knob to be anomalous, perhaps because as a "title page" or label it has a "meta"-function with regard to the rest of the artifact. In M-01, as the start of quartet 1, it may label quartet 1 as referring to the ayllu as a whole and not to a household. For example, the function it recorded might be a business meeting, ritual expense, or work on common infrastructure.

Could these be, alternatively, calculable numbers? Perhaps Ch cords represent some parameter of faenas for which 4 and 5 are common values. The possibility is hard to foreclose, but it entails a great difficulty: Why should knot makers go out of their way to record similar values by means of knots that are so conspicuously dissimilar, and, in the cases of the T-knots, numerically ambiguous? When Inka khipu masters knotted summands, they were careful to make them formally and positionally alike. It seems much more likely that differences in ways of tying knots let the user know their values are not commensurable, and perhaps not numerical at all.

The v1 cord which follows the Ch cord varies in more ways. In this regard v1's and v2's, the type-B cords, are much alike. Presumably v1's and v2's are data sets of similar order. But they probably have different referents, because they do not work in quite the same way. Assuming that the knob end is the beginning, the v1's work as follows:

First, each v1 signifies by choosing among a palette of widely varying colors, some belonging to the gray gradient and others to the brown gradient. Nonetheless, v1 colors do not vary randomly. The colors seem arranged to represent some sort of crescendo-decrescendo pattern. If one leaves aside the first two and the last two v1 cords, the twelve v1's darken as one follows them from the start to the middle of the quipocamayo and then lighten toward the end.

If we continue to assume that progression is annual, one might look for a category of monthly phenomena that is internally varied, and also related to a zenith or a nadir about halfway through a "round." One possible interpretation is types of labor—the "verbs" for whose clarification Urton (1998) appeals.

Ayllu books fortunately do tell us what the faena verbs are. In connection with the "round" they mention planting tubers, hilling, harvesting, threshing, fencing, making adobes, transporting construction material, building, thatching, and a few infrequent tasks (AP2A/SAT_02 1923, 1932 being the fullest listing). These fit our expectations about v1 insofar as they are qualitatively heterogeneous.

These types of labor have nonrandom relations to the annual cycle. By recording the "round" and also collective labor for suprahousehold units on paper, ayllus left records of the relation between faena demand and seasonality. Tuber work comes with and after rainfall, and seems related to a peak demand for faenas as rainfall ends, that is, April–June. The grain harvest follows a longer dry interval and is reflected in a second and lesser peak demand for faenas in August, September, and possibly October. Construction is also best done in dry weather and may be the source of the October demand.

The early twentieth-century "round" functioned for the most part in the second and third quarters of the year, with a lull occurring at midyear between the tuber and grain labor demand peaks. As discussed in Chapter 7, the midyear date 31 June was also ritualized as the date for the "half-year" audit and officer turnover, held in the first week of July. If we interpret M-01 as a "round" in this pattern, we might well expect (1) a marker somewhere near the center, (2) substantial numbers of faenas on both sides but slightly more on the earlier or second-quarter side, and (3) a major feature keyed to seasonality.

The pendant which appears marked as a center—hypothetically, as midyear—is pendant 39 (discussed later in more detail), that is, the v1 component of quartet 9. It is black, but spectacularly marked with bright yellow and red run throughs, so it jumps out to the naked eye. The v1's before it get darker, while those after it get lighter. (Quartets 1–2 and 15–16 carry anomalously dark v1's.) Possibly, the darkness of a cord represents closeness to midyear.

The second component of the v1 parcel is knotted data. Five v1's are unknotted, so, unlike type-A knotting, v1 knotting must answer a question to which an unstated default, or value zero, or "no information" or "inapplicable" are admissible answers. Those v1's that are knotted bear only one kind of long knot, the numerically ambiguous T-knot. They lack positional standardization. Two v1's have second knots. The only exception to T-knotting is an s-knot on the center-marking (midyear?) pendant 39. One can read the T-knots as unique by taking cord position and second knot into account, but the clustering of values at 4/5 and 5/6 (which appear eight times as lowest knot), as well as the five unknotted, suggests dominant values rather than individuation. The unique outlier value 8/9T occurs in quartet 1, the same segment which bears an abnormal knotting (o) in the Ch series.

Going by the ayllu book precedent, there appear at least two evident possibilities for what variables v1's record. One would be a dating referent, with absence of knot meaning an unstated default. The default day for faenas of the "round" in most ayllus during most periods was Wednesday, day 4. The number of days "off schedule" (Thursday, etc.) here would be higher than the written record shows.

The other possibility is specification of task. Roughly, the numbers would be compatible with some such formula as "unstated default = planting potatoes," which, as one might expect, occurs mostly in the early quartets, and the other knots corresponding to other tasks. Or else unknotted cords might mean a faena with task "to be announced" (as was a member's right). A 4/5T might correspond to potato harvesting, which occurs mostly but not entirely before midyear, and a 5/6T to a task occurring mostly after it, perhaps a part of the grain cycle. Any agropastoralist would know an average sequence of tasks by heart and would find it easy to learn them as mnemonic ordinals (as hospital staff or police have no trouble remembering, e.g., that "Code 6" calls for a certain class of emergency responses). The v1's show seven discrete values at the grossest level of knot construction, which is within range of the different tasks (the above-mentioned verbs) appearing in a given year's paper records of the "round." The use of the T-knot, which is ambiguous in regard to absolute number, but clear in regard to ordinal number vis-à-vis other T-knots, would also become less problematic. Perhaps T-knotting means "ordinal"—like the "th" in "seventh."

Another possibility regarding knots as task markers is that knots on v1's tell what tools a worker must bring. This was among the cord attributes Nery Javier recalled from his great-grandfather and it is among the items specified in work-planning resolutions of the community. Members were often sanctioned for forgetting tools, and it is recalled that town criers announcing faenas were expected to mention tools. Tool knotting would result in a small number of categories, and would neatly explain the unmarked (unknotted) category as "no tool needed." If correct, these interpretations would fit with Martti Parssinen's Inka-oriented (1992:36–43) hypothesis about categories with numbered members.

The third component of the v1 package is a binary variable, with values S- and Z-ply. The S-ply occurs only in the first, sixth, and thirteenth quartets. Urton (1994:292) suggests binary variables possibly associated with directionality. Since v1 may be the part of the khipu concerned with scheduling, it might have been the appropriate point for entering whether the faena was internal or "sold" to an outsider as an aid to setting priorities. In the paper record, "sold" faenas were entered in the record together with the "round" because they had to be coscheduled with it.

The fourth component of the v1 parcel is thread run through, or cantito. It appears only twice in v1's, and one of these is in pendant 39, i.e., the midpoint indicator. The more normal v1 pendant with a thread run through is that of the fifth quartet. It has a cantito of blue, not used anywhere else in M-01. Quartet 5 is also the one whose Ch cord is apparently copied in quartet 10. And it has a third peculiarity: it is one of the three with a redoubled v1 cord. So the blue thread followed by a redoubled v1 might have something to do with doubled scheduling, with "belonging to" another quartet, or perhaps with a special status (e.g., a major festival sponsorship) which triggers these attributes.

Since the midpoint indicator pendant 39 is a v1, this is a good moment to examine its spectacular combination of red and yellow threads combined in a glossy black cord (see plate 16). Pendant 39 is knotted anomalously with regard to the v1 series, bearing 1s. Its knot is irregularly positioned compared to all other knots on M-01, being tied right up tight against the main cord. This might be an immobilizer (as in chapter 6) to inhibit slackening this attachment and moving the pendant — as if to say, this is the fixed point around which others are located. Pendant 39 might not represent a task like any other task. It might be associated with the midyear business meeting. Pendant 39 might also be designed to help a user orient use. It is reminiscent of the singular blue pendant which separates group 10 from 11 (of 17) on the Musée de l'Homme's specimen 64.19.1.7. There, as in M-01, differences appear in the knotting of pendants depending on which side of the special cord they hang from. Such "special cords" might make a fruitful theme for study in museum collections.

The fifth and last component of the v1 parcel has already been mentioned in connection with quartet 5: redoubling of v1 cords. In this hypothesis, the "owner" of quartet 5, that is, the person who "carried" faena 5, has apparently also acquired faena 10 and affixed his or her identifier (Ch pendant) to it. In addition to quartet 5, redoubled v1 occurs in quartets 1 and 4. We hypothesized above that redoubling of v1 meant something like "more pending," such as an additional faena to be scheduled for the same household. The redoubling of v1 in quartet 1 is less likely to be interpretable, since irregularities in initial groups (or final ones, depending on one's theory of orientation) are common and relate to some special function of groups at main cord extremes.

O PENDANTS

The third member of each quartet is of a silvery gray (oque or O) color, unseen in banded quipocamayos. In this series, we come back to the simpler type-A registry. Series O is a suite of pendants which resemble each other closely in everything but knotting. They presumably register just one variable, rather than a parcel of variables such as type-B cords impart.

All O's are knotted, and always with long knots. So perhaps zero, 1, or a tacit default were not useful values. We know that O is close in meaning to the Ch series because O and Ch alone in the whole quipocamayo corpus use the multiple figure eight, or M-knot. At the grossest level, knots on O cords register six numerical values (2–6 and 11). If one adds knot type to numerical value of knots,[13] there are 12 signs. If one takes a second knot as disambiguating the first, there are 13; if one adds knot directionality, there are still 13; if one adds knot position, there are 14. Even if one thus maximizes differences, one pair of true knot-identicals remains (in quartets 7 and 10).

The forms of O, then, resemble those of Ch but have a narrower range of knot variation. If one looks in paper records about faenas, a variable with comparable range is the site of labor. It is not redundant to Ch (ownership), because each household works multiple sites. Site is one of the indispensable data (one cannot comply with a scheduled faena until one knows where to go), but the information itself is compact (because Andean toponymy is so detailed that one term specifies locale down to a single field). The item "site" consists of a set of proper names, which we suggested may be the domain in which M-knots are admissible (again, assuming they are more than an empty flourish of a restorer c. 1979). The number of sites is somewhat less varied than the membership of the ayllu. In the best-documented faena years, 1923–27, the number of named sites in which Segunda Allauca performed faenas of its "round" numbered from 8 to 15 and averaged 11.6, yielding a degree of repetitiveness similar to that of O-cord knots. The more or less repeating nature of knots on O pendants might be compared to the repetition of the more important toponyms in given faena cycles.

V2 PENDANTS

The last member of each quartet is again a type-B pendant, that is, one which varies widely in structure. The v2's vary upon the same axes as v1's and will be discussed in comparison to them.

The first way v2's vary is in cord color. The v2's have a color range comparable to v1's, but without any naked-eye tendency toward clustering of darks or lights. The v2 shows one conspicuous exception to v1 in terms of type of color, namely, a mottled bichrome cord, pendant 49 in quartet 11. The other colors of the v2 series do not match v1 colors, so they are not a reshuffle of the same referents. The v2 is likely, therefore, to have a referent independent of the crescendo-decrescendo v1 chronology. This referent seems to vary unconstrained by sequence. If the v2 series admits both various degrees of lightness and darkness (both brown and gray, but mostly brown), and also admits an entity which combines the extremes of lightness and darkness, namely, a mottled cord (found nowhere else on M-01), one may ask what variable can be visualized as a gradient but also as a discontinuous classification.

In chapter 7, we noted that seniority is treated both as a gradient ("order number," that is, years of service) and as a discontinuous variable (brackets of "active," "semiretired or infirm," and "probationary"). Seniority is something that a member has more or less of (in "order number") but at the same time experiences as a discontinuous set of brackets (in level of obligation). Certainly seniority was and is a major concern of ayllu record-keeping. Perhaps the point of including it here was to "weight" various members' requests for dates according to their entitlements.

A second way v2's vary is in knotting. As in v1, unknotted cords occur, indeed more commonly than knotted ones. Knotting of v2's is not without pattern: a clump of knotted v2's occurs toward the "tail" of the quipocamayo, namely those of quartets 10 through 14. Only two quartets prior to quartet 10 bear knots (2 and 7). So the variable to which v2 knots refer was more likely to have nonzero values toward the end of the cycle. The numerical values of the knots may be clues. Like v1 knots, they are long T-knots with one exception. Their numerical range at the gross level is spread over just 4 values, namely, 1 + 1 (two adjacent s-knots), 2, 3, and 4. Taking knot directionality into account would produce six values.

As to their meaning, if we recur to major recording preoccupations of the ayllu books, we are reminded that pending debts to the treasury were an impediment to receipt of ayllu services. If we assume that M-01 as we see it reflects some particular moment in one particular cycle, it is likely some people owed but not others. Early twentieth-century fees and fines came in one-peso increments (less commonly, fifty centavos). One to four pesos are not unlikely sums for householders to owe. People would be disposed to pay off debts prior to their faena dates lest they lose eligibility, then start reaccruing debts afterward. So if we assume the data state of M-01 reflects a moment corresponding to approximately the midyear audit, it is fairly believable that some upcoming faena hosts still owed—and that some who had already been served (quartets 1 [?], 7) already owed again. It makes sense that fines might be coregistered with seniority since fines were adjusted to seniority brackets.

A third way in which v2's vary is S- and Z-plying. Quartets 5 and 7–9 have

S-plied v2's. If we try to gather what v2 so far seems to contain, the common-denominator concern is standing of the faena holder, and this may be another aspect of it: gender. An ayllu could well have three female heads of household.

A fourth way in which v2's vary is bright thread "run through." The v2 position has three of these, all red, in quartets 9, 10, and 12. It was suggested in chapter 8 that cantitos meant "belongs to" or "earmarked for," as with faenas for the community or for festival *cargos* ('role of responsibility'). Ayllu bylaws sometimes state that any household about to sponsor a major communitywide festival is excused from faenas within a certain interval because it is already carrying an overload in the common interest. One of Tupicocha's two patron saint days, the Virgin of the Assumption, falls on 15 August. So it would not be unreasonable for persons about to carry a cargo to have that fact noted in their intra-ayllu records, particularly when the records concern duties close to the festival date. The red-marked cords would in this hypothetical schema correspond to dates after the midyear (again, assuming sequence starts at the pachacamanta). The red cantito might remind people of fiesta service due to the cargo holders, or of exemptions they enjoy as festival sponsors.

A fifth and last way that v2's vary is, as with v1's, redoubling. Quartets 2 and 7 have redoubled v2 pendants. In the case of quartet 7, the knot on this group's Ch pendant is almost identical to that on another quartet. In the case of quartet 2, it is not known what the "extra" v2 might be relevant to. In some way redoubled v2 may convey an attribute of the faena holder relevant to entitlement in a different faena.

A Hypothetical Reading of M-01

Our hypothetical reading is intended to exemplify the *kind* of reading M-01 can bear if we assume (1) that the covert restoration process did not grossly falsify its makeup, and (2) that its content resembles alphabetically documented intra-ayllu administration. True decipherment, that is, a reconstructed native-competence view, is not claimed.

[Ch cord]: *Beneficiary*	
"For the *n*th faena,	ordinal position
member *R*	knotting?
[v1 cord]: *Task*	
in *w* part of the agropastoral cycle	color
is to have *x* task performed (with specified tools)	knotting
as a 'round' or as a 'sold' faena	ply
according to *y* set of negotiated arrangements,	redoubling; run throughs?
z weeks before or after midyear	number of quartets before or after midyear

[O cord]: *Location*	
at *j* site.	knotting
[v2 cord]: *Eligibility*	
R's eligibility is affected by *a*	
seniority/disability status,	color
b fines-pending status,	knotting
c gender status	ply
d festival-cargo status	run-through threads
and *e* special arrangements."	redoubling.

We may ask how planning quipocamayos were made. If an analogy with staffs (chapter 4) obtains, cords would supposedly have been new, but many of them would really reenter the pool by disassembly from a previous cycle. Member *R* would prepare by bringing, or making, or recycling, or taking from a common stock, appropriate cords: not just any four cords but four unknotted, unattached cords whose attributes included the colors, plies, colored cantitos, and other details appropriate to his or her standing and project. An initial stage, conducted with type-A cords alone, might consist of attaching a sketch of the negotiated gross schedule to the main cord. At a later stage, with type-B data inserted, there may have been a step of checking whether the ensemble covers all attributes of interest to the collectivity: For example, are all major festival functions mentioned? Are pending fines an impediment to any immediately upcoming beneficiary?

In modern ayllu and community meetings, negotiated scheduling is carried out in a caucus of murmured proposals, quickly bargained toward consensus. Nothing is recorded until consensus emerges. The scheduling and negotiating phase is not silent, but it is hushed. It produces no public discourse, that is, no speech directed to all, and no record that imitates speech (as prose). In one case, the scheduling of irrigation turns, bids are made in the form of visual tokens (paper tickets) which the Irrigators' Committee shuffles to optimize.

Knots as opposed to cordage structures seem reserved for variables which might change during the course of a cycle. A person might revise plans about what task to have done, or where, or pay a pending fine before her or his turn arrived. Even Ch, putatively the identity of the faena holder, could change, because faenas were alienable. Major changes of plan would require more obvious alterations. Since pendants (except the middle indicator pendant 39) are attached by nothing more challenging than half-hitches, it would be possible to alter more fundamental variables but only by relocating whole pendants.

A given quartet, then, might mean something such as Ch: "the Martín Ricsi Ramos household will 'carry' the *n*th faena." v1: "It is to be potato digging, done five weeks before midyear, with a 'bought' faena to follow later." O: "at Cuñanche." v2: "This is a male-headed, active household with a two-peso fine pending and a festival obligation pending."

This hypothesis covers all the variables about faenas which ayllus recorded in writing. In talking about faena practice of the past, Mújica elder Martín Camilo mentioned that at dawn the alguacil or deputy constable of the ayllu would go out and announce house by house four parameters: the date of the next faena, the location, the name of the person "carrying" it, and the kind of tools needed for the kind of work. It is not out of the question that before making these announcements, the crier would check a khipu. Camilo did not volunteer the idea that quipocamayos served this function but agrees it is a likely interpretation. Camilo is proud of his knack for duplicating quipocamayo knots as we observed in Chapter 6. He was active at the suspected date of M-01's restoration.

On the hypothesis that ayllus kept separate records of their internal and supra-ayllu duties, another color-cycled quipocamayo could have embodied planning of the latter. If Mújica held banded quipocamayos in pairs, it is quite likely to have held paired color cycle ones. Mutatis mutandis, the scheme explained above could cover the whole range of tasks discussed in chapter 8 as ayllu or communitywide business.

The Quipocamayo Suite

What constituted one ayllu's complete set of quipocamayos? I have hypothesized that the unbanded M-01 was a programmatic or planning device. "Color cycle" design was, I suggest, a way to simulate prospective agenda. As the agenda was realized, execution was recorded on banded quipocamayos. Quipocamayos M-01 and M-0x had pachacamantas of like design (red/white chevrons) and perhaps formed such a complementary set. Banded quipocamayos were the ones presented to the huayrona because the execution, not the plan, was the point of interest to the whole community. If the two quipocamayos were differentiated between one for intra-ayllu works and one for service to the larger whole, the latter would be the one presented. If not, the two banded quipocamayos may have been presented in alternating terms.

A dialogue between two sorts of cord artifacts seems, then, to have generated the overall rationality of the community. As executed, works would be progressively attested on banded cords, displacing records of the previous cycle as they advanced. The pair of banded khipus would thus constitute rotating annals within the span of a short (one- or two-year) cycle. In highly ritualized work practice, which requires recording work as part of the modules of sacred action that performatively ratified work, the adding of performance cords would itself constitute the hinge between structure and practice.

Would this process be inhibited toward speech, as staffs are (chapter 4)? Of course, realistically it would not be silent; ayllus are talkative groups. But conversation attending cord adjustment might have been hushed and "backstage" to the primary matter of integrating action through emblems or multivariate tokens.

(Chapter 3 noted that intervals of silence are still "parliamentary procedure" for ayllus.) Authority inhered in the nonverbal product. By incrementally adding constraints as assembly progressed, and by forcing attention onto relevant variables while filtering out the "noise" of rhetoric, rivalry, and so on, the khipu operation would have helped villagers arrive quickly at a collective minimax rationality reconciling the interests of member households and the group.

The overall ensemble message, like that of the staffs in their ensemble, would be a unique expression of a putatively constant message: "This is how Mújica ayllu provides each of its members with rotating collective labor benefits in a cycle of parts equal to its membership, taking productive needs and social standing into account, and meeting its community obligations." Like the vara details, cord details show how this was done. Indeed, they may be nothing other than the direct material precipitate of the process deciding how it would be done, and of the ritual ratifying that it had been done.

To turn cords into verbal assertions is possible. Perhaps the ayllu deputy constable actually did verbalize a particular quartet in some such way as the one suggested above, as he made the rounds announcing the next faena. Verbalizing would constitute a constrained task with only one correct answer, plus or minus some phraseology. But in a different sense, the fact that data can be formulated as speech is not the point. The quipocamayo process would have compacted social process into an impressively data-dense medium whose clarity did not depend on expansion into words.

W E CONCLUDE with three overviews: a summary of findings, a reflection on whether they are relevant to Inka khipu studies, and a
return to the theoretical-methodological problem of how the "ethnography of writing" can help with decipherment of radically unfamiliar inscriptive systems.

Findings: Quipocamayos in Their Village Context

Central Huarochirí, whose heroes were the protagonists of the 1608 Quechua book
of pre-Christian divinities, is one of the three areas known to have preserved into
modern times a political-civic khipu complex (as compared to herding and confessional khipus, which exist elsewhere). The other two cases are Casta [Tello and
Miranda 1923] and Rapaz [Ruiz Estrada 1981]). Tupicocha village's corporate descent groups have inherited the names of the ancient ayllus, and they hold ten
patrimonial khipus as their regalia. Although this unread legacy remains unread,
its past and present uses reveal quite a bit about how the cord medium worked in
political institutions to reproduce the ongoing project of a segmented agropastoral
society.

Today villagers curate but do not decipher or update cords. Nonetheless, fieldwork does help attack our core weaknesses with regard to khipus, namely, (1) ignorance of the semiotic and pragmatic means by which cord signs "hook into" social functions, and (2) lack of links between known specimens and known social
functions.

Regarding the first weakness, there remains one live example of productive inscription in a nonalphabetic code: the carving of insignia on the staffs of minor officers. In preparing them, officers register information about the hierarchy by inscribing symbols that form an independent signary, not representative of, and not even locally translatable into, "primary" verbal signs. Staff inscription is a minimalist "parallel language" whose expressions resemble Urton's algebraic "ligatured expressions" (described in chapter 4) insofar as they express a calculus of social articulation. Signs are systematically kept out of the verbal arena, and they gain some functional advantages thereby. The way they function apart from speech shows how action and organization could be mimetized, and how inscription can aid complexity, without writing in the philological sense of the word.

The quipocamayos, however, were a much richer system. What historical path led to their long survival and relatively recent extinction? Against the common opinion that Spanish love of letters implied a quick death sentence on knot records, Huarochirí history reveals a postconquest khipu complex long intertwined with the history of rural alphabetic literacy. In Inka times, cord competence was already diffused though Huarochirí's non-Inka local priesthoods. In the early days of Spanish invasion, native elites parlayed khipu expertise into political advantage through mastery of logistics. During the inchoate colonial era (1532–69), indigenous lords already made compelling use of khipus in lawsuits. From 1569 on, in Toledan times, khipus articulated forced labor levies but also underlay "everyday resistance" in the form of independent accounting. Some evidence in the trial of Francisco de Avila, which gave rise to the 1608 Quechua book, was khipu based. When a short-lived anti-Spanish rebellion shook Huarochirí 142 years later, khipus played a part in the counterinsurgency campaign. Cord notation remained a widely diffused, versatile medium in the late colony, but unlike the alphabet it was sharply restricted to indigenous context.

We come now to attacking our second weakness, that of matching specimens with social functions. First of all, to what period of action could given specimens refer? The Tupicocha quipocamayos have been partially radiocarbon dated. Results are ambiguous because they fall within the time of fluctuating atmospheric isotope ratios (1650–1945). Within this range, however, dates of the late nineteenth century are the most probable, both for radiocarbon-related reasons and because of independent evidence. Independent evidence includes inventorying of quipocamayos in the internal records of ayllus. Oral testimony suggests that the generation born after the War of the Pacific (1879–83) was the last to fully understand and the first to relinquish the art. It was apparently before or during the Leguía oncenio (1919–30), when the folk-legal community became a part of state apparatus, that villagers stopped treating quipocamayos as a recording system and started seeing them as insignia of indigenous—later, campesino—legitimacy.

We can further specify match between specimen and function by studying the modern political-administrative context of Tupicocha's quipocamayos. They come into play at the New Year's town meeting, called the huayrona. In the liminal period between the first session, which interrogates outgoing officers, and the second, which installs incoming ones, each ayllu selects its new leaders. When the huayrona reconvenes, each outgoing head of an ayllu drapes his successor with the quipocamayo. This sacred occasion reproduces an intricate political structure, in which the kinship corporations can be seen either as the prior constituents of a political whole, or as segmentary components—"teams"—within it. Quipocamayo recording constituted the exact hinge between kinship organization and the articulation of kinship units into an emergent politically structured whole. When cords still functioned as documents, they were brought to the plenum to prove that each ayllu had performed all its community duties and thereby helped reproduce the totality. Knot recording was not only *about* the community—a controlling simulacrum, and important as such—but was itself the means of *producing* the community performatively.

Quipocamayos are overwhelmingly of camelid wool, probably alpaca. They are mostly undyed, but dyed fiber appears in markers and "run-through" markings. A substantial, mostly Spanish vocabulary of terms for khipu parts is remembered. Nine of the ten specimens have single-color cord groups (bands). The tenth has pendant groups patterned in a cycle of repeated colors.

The Tupicochan specimens show signs of having been made by multiple hands, and altered at various times. Some techniques appear designed to inhibit or facilitate moving, adding, or removing pendants. They differ in this from Inka "bureaucratic" khipus, which seem to have been assembled on single occasions by one person using standardized materials and techniques. Tupicochan traits reflect functioning as periodically updated simulation devices. Each ayllu possessed two khipus usable for the huayrona. These seem to have been updated and recycled year by year.

Intravillage paper documents provide independent evidence about the relation between specimens and functions. Although handwritten books contain no explanation of quipocamayos, they do contain many references to them. Such books show what it was that ayllus needed to document. The contents of quipocamayos are ayllu-internal, as those of books are. But books document ayllu work of interest to the overarching community as well as mutual service within the kinship corporation, and we think quipocamayos do too. Writing generated two major kinds of documents: planning documents and performance records. Khipus too probably served both functions. Performance was most frequently recorded as listing of absentees with details about amends to be made. The unit of account is the household. Systems of household sequencing may be relevant to quipocamayo design.

Quipocamayos were coordinated to the internal authority structure of ayllus. Dual officers ruled, one called camachico (later *presidente*) and the other mayor (later *vice-presidente*). Paired khipus were associated respectively with the camachico and the mayor. It is not known whether records of ayllu-internal functions, such as the "round" of mutual aid, and of overarching village functions were segregated on the two quipocamayos, or whether they were interspersed in both.

Ethnographic scrutiny of the "writing events" which produce records today, at work sites and audits, yields clues to data-handling habits which may have influenced the khipu art. Constancia, or "proof," starts now as in pre-Hispanic times with the on-site checklist of attendance. Data are redacted into ever more synthetic documents of performance. The review of overall ayllu performance is a social audit, covering all duties both monetary and nonmonetary. The audit is strictly collective, with all transactions scrutinized by all members. The audit is also a ceremonial function including rituals, music, and dance. Two funds support the ayllus: a running expenses fund and a reserve fund for ritual and relief. The latter may be a continuation of what Guaman Poma called "comunidad y sapçi." Ayllus usually prefer to close cycles with a zero balance. The targeting of zero as a default value at certain times of year is apparently reflected in the high incidence of unknotted cords on quipocamayos.

Another vein of ethnographic evidence is popular remembrance about the cord art. Villagers voice both topographic and chronological theories about the meaning of main cords. Markers are called by terms meaning "landmark." But those who interpret chronologically see markers as corresponding to landmarks in time, namely, festivals or other annual occasions. The chronological model appears more productive. Descendants of an elder who was reputedly the last competent cord worker recall some specific parts of the cord art. Their interpretation of knots and cords suggests elements of diagrammatic representation. They define color bands as chapterlike sections referring to sequential functions of the ayllu. Cords about lands are allegedly legible in terms of node and internode, with internodes signifying llanchas, or irrigation sectors. Popular memory confirms that users inserted and removed cords to update, but is inconclusive about directionality. Markers are taken as benchmark fixed dates around which other functions were scheduled. There is some tendency to regard the quipocamayo as a single all-embracing image of social totality at ayllu level, with the long main cord as an "x axis" representing time, and the vertical extent of cords as a series of "y axes" some of which correspond to physical space. However, there is no presumption of commensurability across bands. Tupicochan quipocamayos show few if any "Lockean" arithmetical regularities and have no topcords or totalizing cords. They are taken as internal, heterogeneous, holistic models (in Goodman's sense) of the ayllu's conduct within a finite stretch of time, namely, a year.

An "afterlife" of the khipu art takes the form of oracular consultation of quipocamayo cords, which might be called "khipumancy." Like the popular derivatives of the Hermetic oracle in Europe, khipumancy begins with a numerological operation (using odd and even letter counts in words of the query), then interrogates the cords for the "found" odd-even patterns. Attributes of the cords where these patterns appear are deemed relevant to the answer. As dissimilar as it seems from practical cord use, khipumancy may be grounded in the Andean ideology of death, which encouraged the people to consult ancestors whose voices (through mummies and oracles) expressed the collectivity's power of decision over the affairs of the living. Cords taken out of simulative function — "dead" cords — formed the baseline for ongoing decision in social action, much as ancestor shrines formed a baseline for ongoing construction.

As long as quipocamayos were still productive media, the New Year's festivities of Tupicocha implied a process almost inverse to that of khipu entombment. The everlasting life of the collectivity was vested in a pair of khipus which never ceased to be updated, never stopped changing, and therefore never ceased to be of "live" interest. As long as the khipu complex had full operational capacity, the invested khipu-wearer was, so to speak, the inverse of a mummy. The fact that like all others he was embarked on the transit toward individual death was metaphorically canceled by superimposing on his body the ever-changing "body politic" of a collective enterprise bound for no such destiny. Modern rhetoric treating quipocamayos as living things reflects a trace of this attitude.

How can the four sources of information (historic written sources, traits of the cords, vernacular data-handling practices, and local interpretation of cords) be integrated? We begin by noticing gross structural profiles which may connect facts observed in different sources.

On the average, quipocamayos occurred (1) in pairs (2) with each quipocamayo containing about 15–16 bands plus a variable number of grouped singletons. Each pair therefore had about 31 bands, (3) with bands having numbers of pendants loosely centered around 6, and (4) each quipocamayo having about 100 pendants.

The above numerical profile closely resembles the quotas which non-Christian priesthood required of Tupicochans around 1608. We hypothesize that the priesthood and the ayllus' civil regimen both reflect an underlying multipurpose model, namely, first and second terms each requiring about fifteen services. It could be adapted to monthly or annual schedules. Annual quipocamayo functioning is well documented, but monthly use is not. We hypothesize that the paired quipocamayos were either affiliated with semesters, a well-attested unit, or else each one covered a year's work, with one specialized in intra-ayllu and the other in supra-ayllu work. Neither model can be discarded yet. If the latter model is correct, the quipocamayo specialized in supra-ayllu duties would be the one displayed to the huayrona. The units represented by bands are more likely to be tasks (or other specific collective functions) than members. The overall favored model (by villagers and by the present writer) could be called a function-band hypothesis.

The numbers of bands per quipocamayo are close to the numbers of members per ayllu recorded in the early twentieth century. It is likely that a "round" of mutual aid workdays around fifteen would correspond to the content of one khipu (or, if dispersed across two quipocamayos, about half the total bands). The numbers of bands are also similar to the attested numbers of tasks performed for the supra-ayllu sphere (village, municipality, state) per year. Summing these with the tasks of the "round" would yield a number of workdays roughly commensurate with the thirty or so bands on a pair of khipus.

Within the function-band interpretation, different tasks apparently entailed cord notation of different variables. For example, sowing would entail a cord regarding use of llanchas or irrigation sectors, while roofing would require data on quotas of straw. Dissimilar demands of functions seem related to dissimilar design of cords in different bands. For instance, a function requiring participants to bring quotas of materials might yield pendants with subsidiaries. The function-band hypothesis demands ability to match members with deficits or other performance variables. How this was done is not clear. Knots may have identified member households by their seniority numbers, or by correspondences between knot and "family." Signature knotting is within possibility. "Run-through" threads of brilliant color may have served to earmark certain tasks as benefiting collective functions, possibly the major festivals.

The exception to banded structure is M-01. Although Mújica ayllu displays it in the normal way, it is not a normal specimen but one with a repeating cycle of colors in quartets. A main cord fragment of a lost specimen, M-0X, formerly hung from M-01. Quipocamayos M-0X and M-02 probably formed the original pair, comparable with other ayllus' pairs. Specimen M-02 was missing from 1958 to 1998. During this interval (c. 1979 [?]), with M-0X too damaged for display, a third specimen from a different genre was refurbished and installed as M-01. In this way a surviving member of a different class, normally not public, was legitimated for public viewing. The abnormally late radiocarbon date of M-01 reflects this restoration. M-01 must be taken as a compromised specimen because we do not know how heavily the restoration altered the source. However, M-01's striking resemblance to pre-Hispanic specimens offers some reassurance that its structure is meaningful.

It is hypothesized that each ayllu's apparatus consisted of a suite divided between cyclical and banded specimens. Cyclical format would represent planning, and banded format execution. Specimen M-01 consists of sixteen iterations of the four-pendant group here called quartet. Each quartet contains two fixed-color pendants and two variable-color pendants. The interpretation most compatible with other sources is that the quartets record a negotiated schedule—a semester or a year, perhaps—of the "round" or perhaps of services to the community each led by one household.

As they were executed, works would be attested on banded cords. Each inscription would displace earlier and now cleared records. Today, the highly ritualized work practice of Tupicocha requires recording the work during modules of sacred action that bracket periods of labor. Such acts of inscription ritually keyed to work may have created performance cord records in the past.

Both banded and color-cycle quipocamayos bear traces of alterations over time.

Cords made by different hands in different materials, as well as knots added and removed, and devices for immobilizing or restraining certain pendants—all these things strongly suggest that unlike texts, but like simulation devices such as abacuses or molecular modeling kits, quipocamayos were basically operational devices. The Tupicochan evidence suggests that in the planning stage, participants used cords as tokens to try out alternatives and assemble a plan—subject to further revision—and thereby rationally deploy labor and other factors of production to meet the complex demands of household/suprahousehold work in polycyclical scheduling. In execution of the plan, too, cords were used to register the completion of obligations as they were fulfilled. Updating, accounting, and (ideally) closure of accounts would bring an end to the finite diachronic horizon of ayllu quipocamayos. The system, however, also provided a method for carrying over residues, and this sense did provide a means for open-ended diachronic record-keeping. It is not asserted that this suite of records represents any more than a single variant within the broad possibilities of cord technology.

Did these practices involve verbal readout? Perhaps people actually did verbalize cord contents, in auditing. Verbalizing the kinds of input so far adduced would constitute a constrained task with only one correct answer (allowing a margin for phraseology). And is this "writing proper"? Chapter 1 noted that in a monolingual context, a sematogram (e.g., knot encodes absence, irrespective of speech), if "read out" by pronouncing the name of its referent (the word *absent*), would be in practice hard to distinguish from a sign for that word, that is, a logogram. If the quipocamayos constituted "writing proper," I suggest it would be such in the sense of "semasiography in, lexigraphy out." Semasiography of composition (via diagrammatic simulation, etc.) combined with lexigraphy of recitation (via "virtual logograms") would account for Tupicochans' conviction that the cords themselves *generate* newly spoken truths and do not merely encode speech heard before. (Khipumancy seems a belated memory of this *grafismo*, a useful term in various romance languages that seemingly lacks an English equivalent. Grafismo means a manner of employing writing, as opposed to the characteristics of any particular writing as a sign system.) Such a procedure could, hypothetically, yield the rebus mutation and transition to "writing proper." Yet in one sense, verbalization would be a side issue. The khipu process apparently compacted social process into an impressively data-dense medium whose clarity did not depend on expansion into words.

Are Tupicochan Quipocamayos Relevant to Inka Studies?

Tupicochan specimens resemble Inka-era museum specimens far more than they do recent herding or confessional khipus. Assuming their role in community life was as reconstructed in the preceding section, does this imply relevance to Inka imperial usage?

Carlos Radicati's 1965 study of what he called "seriation" (*seriación*) in pre-Hispanic khipus, like the present work, is a study of khipus that formed an ensemble. It concerns an apparently pre-Columbian set of six khipus which, together with some disassembled pendants, came from a single burial at an unrecorded place in the Santa valley (113). Radicati is convinced enough of their functional interdependence to call them an "archive," based chiefly on the fact that all are designed around a modular group of six uniformly colored pendants (which he calls a series). The module of six is clearer than the blurry central tendency of six-to-a-band prevailing in Tupicocha. Radicati demonstrates regularities across khipus, such as the tendency for the initial cord of the sextet to bear a constant knotting across the khipu in which it occurs. Radicati's specimens differ from Tupicochan ones by having spaces of bare main cord between groups, by conforming more to Lockean conventions, and by having more widely varying numbers of groups than Tupicochan ones.[1] But there are interesting likenesses. Three of Radicati's six have knobs or tufts of yellow wool or red and yellow wool at the redoubled end of their main cords, reminiscent of similarly colored tufted knobs in Tupicocha. Two of his specimens (numbers 2 and 3) markedly resemble Tupicochan specimens in numerical profile (90 and 108 pendants in 13 and 16 groups) and in showing exceptional groups (of 12, 18, 10, and 4) as well as sextets. Perhaps the band, which chapter 9 treats as a modular data-set to describe a social function, was employed in Santa by entities of more widely varied size to inscribe their respective, nonuniform rosters of functions. If the Santa valley system resembled that of far-distant Tupicocha, the six khipus might be the paired documents of three federated ayllus.

The two basic data organizations described here, namely, color cycle and banded array, are both fairly common in museum collections. It is not known if they occur in any systematic association, because provenience information is almost always lacking. But nothing in the known parts of Tupicocha's cord complex seems incompatible with the Inka data system as attested in chronicles or as exemplified in museums.

Just as a thought experiment, let us suspend historical caution and imagine the reconstructed Tupicochan system as if it were part of the Inka state, Tawantinsuyu. In this scenario, Inka administrators treat corporate ayllus as "hundreds" within an all-empire decimal record system. Ayllus and/or heads of federated-ayllu polities (*llahta* for internal purposes and *waranka*, or "thousand," for external ones) make internal-use khipus of planning and of performance, perhaps in pairs. Ratification of records, demonstrating equity among ayllus, is the act constitutive of suprasegmentary polity. Perhaps using these, but more likely using an all-community aggregate khipu, they also tender proof of external compliance and entitlement to state authorities. Inka officials consult the village database in formulating their more standardized, more synoptic, less operable record, which will get attention at higher levels. At all levels, ceremony functions to structure modules of recordable action.

The architecture of ceremonial spaces is keyed to display of records. A politically apt space brings together in formal closure and renewal three things: the actual people or representatives of social segments, their records, and products which the record attests. A suitable space therefore is one with storage facilities, but also with space for assembly of people and a focal place for display of records. Redistributive celebration using the goods documented is a likely concomitant. Without taking comparison to levels of spurious detail, this outline seems a plausible image of the drama for which both Inka-era ceremonial plazas, such as Huánuco Pampa, and colonially derived local assembly places, such as the collcas of Huarochirí, formed stages.

Urton (2003:49–53) questions the relevance of Tupicochan data to Inka usage (as suggested in Salomon 2002c) on two main grounds. First, he holds that khipus made of movable parts and susceptible to reshuffling would not be functional for local governance, much less imperial, because such a medium would not provide firm enough documentary constancy to enforce compliance. Urton is right to emphasize that *comuneros* as much as state functionaries demand authoritative recording. But the argument of this book does not suggest free or "continuously rewritten" reshuffling. Rather, it contrasts the simulation function (in planning, here associated with the "color cycle" specimen M-01) to the performance registry function (of banded khipus), allotting each a ritually defined and publicly transparent occasion for composition and alteration. Hypothetically, the New Year's and midyear's meetings would have been the occasions for major planning. Incremental changes would occur between these times as performance data accumulated in banded format. All occasions for cord work would have been as hedged with discipline and sanction, as are modern village audits, and as are the designated moments for recording under the "work cross." That the Inka state would have held a data set to supervise and check the records adduced by villagers is not in question. Neither does the reconstruction given here imply (as Urton 2003:52 takes it to imply) that village records would have been illegible to Inka officials.

Second, Urton notes that his study of some 450 pre-Hispanic specimens finds "some evidence [of moved khipu parts], but not a great deal" (2003:52), leading him to conclude that movable simulation was not a major function. This finding admits plural interpretations, needing evaluation through future research. First, it may be that Tupicochan methods are products of a post-Inka evolution. As the colonial state became indifferent to khipu use, it left a growing margin for diverse unofficial development, somewhat as the shift to Spanish as the state language favored Quechua dialect rediversification. If so, Tupicocha is indeed a non-Inka phenomenon, but not by that token less illuminating about the potential of the cord medium. Second, it may be that khipus suitable for tomb preservation and hence archaeologically visible were of a different genre than village civic khipus. Deposited as "benchmark" data, grave-lot khipus may have been specifically earmarked as unchanging, just as the mummified person became a putatively unchanging reference point for social organization. Tupicochan civic quipocamayos were used and reused—the very specimens show it—until parts literally fell to shreds. Earmarked for constant use rather than deposit, any such pre-Hispanic specimens would have been at a selective disadvantage for preservation.

Moving Khipus Toward an Ethnography of Inscription

In the introduction and chapter 1, we noticed that the khipu is often classed with so-called partial or proto writings that form a large and poorly understood share of humanity's "technology of intellect." We mentioned that progress with Inka sign systems may depend on refining our awareness of relations between sign and cultural action through means other than lexigraphy. What does the Tupicochan case contribute to an expanded "ethnography of inscription" which would contextualize the now well-established "ethnography of writing"?

Chapter 1 observed that many South American cultures, including Andean ones, treat some visible things as being legible not because they are codes with regular "stand-for" correspondences (though, from an outsider's viewpoint they may be such), but because they are the marks left by the emergence of a reality and therefore congruent to its features. Villagers understand a still-productive nonalphabetic code, the staff code, in this spirit. Likewise when using alphabetic writing, villagers give emphasis to script as the concretion of a performative act, rather than as a referential statement "about" the act. This is what they mean by constancia, and constancia is the point of inscription. The idea that signs are "of" rather than "about" reciprocal acts is locally axiomatic. It is essential to the way polity is articulated by inscription. The khipu art as remembered seems also to have functioned on this principle. The emphasis on the performative aspect of writing seems to have survived the transition to the alphabet, forming an element of a regional grafismo.

Other traits of Tupicochan grafismo may also be khipu-alphabet commonalities. One is a tendency to distance if not dissociate the sign as visible precipitate of social action, from speech, pushing it toward the status of "parallel language." Staff code (chapter 4) seems an extreme case, but even if khipus went less far, to notice the tendency is to notice that the functionality of inscription does not point pell-mell toward speech mimicry. Another is collective authorship. The khipu art as employed in quipocamayos, like writing "proper" in modern public contexts, has no individual author. More than script, in its physicality it is the work of many hands.

When stepping a level deeper, toward the characteristics of quipocamayos as a sign system, we need to entertain varied theories about systems of representation and referentiality. By showing how visible codes distant from "natural language" work, Roy Harris and Nelson Goodman clarify unfamiliar, non-text-like relationships between script and society.

Roy Harris's "integrationism," which defines signs as coming into being whenever a mark constitutes a social interaction, makes it easier to understand why Tupicocha's local cords are more heterogeneous in manufacture than imperial ones. Harris's insistence that meaning inheres in the particular appearance of a sign, and not just in its purportedly invariant type value as langue, makes it possible to think about cords as code (with, e.g., seven variables) without ditching as "noise" attributes 8 through n (e.g., tension, finish, diameter, shade). Rather, we could think of them as "performance variables" whose inseparability from code variables creates a constancia. The grassroots khipu code was enriched for a range of gemeinschaft meanings. Since it concretized a set of acts among its own physical authors, the idiosyncrasy of their hands constituted for users a retrievable range of data.

Archaeology and ethnohistory tell us that Inka state khipus were not like this. Prepared by outsiders, they were "about" subjects, and concerned the standardization of cases rather than their idiosyncrasy. To envision the articulation between a village's huayrona or Huatancha and Inka record keeping is to envision a process by which Inka bureaucrats leached the local record of its performance variables and packed it into a decimally bracketed, impersonal summary which some functionary far away could integrate with similar state records.

Another local attribute that calls for "integrationist" interpretation is the seemingly wide scope for manipulation of cords—maneuvers such as repositioning, immobilizing, and interlinking. If we think of the ayllus' quipocamayos as an "emblematic frame" with which it was possible to play out numerous arrangements of parts adding up to a putatively constant whole (like the putatively constant varayo establishment in chapter 4), it becomes possible to account for the finite character of the quipocamayos as a set. This, too, may have been a peculiarity of a "grassroots" khipu art as opposed to imperial inscription, which may have had more use for cumulative or archival approaches.

In drawing on Goodman we learned to think about a different non-Saussurean dimension. Even if a khipu was taken as the concretion of performative acts, the relation between cords and acts cannot be indexically transparent, like the relation between the animal and its spoor. Goodman gives us a better alternative than supposing a signary is a culturally designed set of utility tokens just hoping (as it were) to match the haphazard shape of a world "out there." Rather, he tells us, the signs and the things they stand for may *both* be subjected to prior cultural processing, to make them bidirectionally compliant with each other. When people construct a sign system this way, it is a "notation." Sheet music is an example: If we want to use sheet music, we must agree to think of sounds in a certain way, namely, as discrete tones in modular durations. When such rules are applied "anteriorly" to the universe of possible referents (sounds)—that is, when musicians agree to play notes that can each be linked to just one such sign—music can then be notated. "Anterior" cultural processing of some activities, especially labor, made the lived world of Andean action cord-compliant. Pervasive ritualism, as well as the characteristic formalisms of Andean cultures, richly documented in structuralist and poststructuralist ethnographies, confront practical life by means of versatile dualistic and geometrical schemata that easily achieve the code properties needed for notation in Goodman's sense. Tupicochans insist tirelessly on organizing action in sharply demarcated, labeled, and ritually punctuated modules. Work, time, and space are treated as if they came in discrete quanta. The terminology for recordable social acts is strenuously "compliance-class disjoint" and nonambiguous.

The Tupicochan solution, in short, seemed to require that cords and works should be mutually structuring enterprises. The imperatives of accurate recording and politically firm ayllu-community reciprocity were not two different problems. To achieve reliable, rational work was not just a matter of making a khipu mimic life. Life had to be lived like a khipu.

Tupicochans were never Inka, but this habit may belong to a common Andean ground shared by Inka culture and Huarochirí's provincial, biethnic culture. In Julien's important study of the Inka decimal system (1988), she emphasized that decimal units were treated as in principle discontinuous, like those discrete representations of physically continuous variables which Goodman cited as a founding fiction for notation. Inka decimal administration modeled the world as composed of tens (and other ideal numbers), then treated residues through a system of rectification ex post facto. Urton found much the same in modern Bolivian Quechua number systems.

Beyond helping us envision the "atomic" accretion of data on cords, Goodman also provides a second valuable concept: a term for the total assembly of notations, namely, a diagram. Diagrams sometimes superficially look pictorial, because their parts, though constituted in rigorous abstraction, add up to a mimesis of forms also familiar through other senses. Tupicochans occasionally describe their khipus as "like diagrams" or "like maps." The conventions for representing land use and other items remembered by villagers are mostly "notational" in their microstructure, but they derive their memorability from "diagrammatic" clarity. One can even follow Goodman a bit further. Inasmuch as khipus became simulation devices in some parts of their use cycle, and constancias in others, khipus resemble "models" in Goodman's sense: "diagrams . . . in more than two dimensions, and with working parts."

Could this be as relevant to Inka administration as to the village? Here again, the ground-hugging political function of Tupicochan cords may have driven their evolution away from Inka state norms. One divergence may have occurred in applying single khipus to multiple tasks, thereby creating miscellaneous "diagrams" as opposed to specialized bureaucratic ones. The second is that khipus taken to belong to the Inka state often seem to have homogeneous parts and undisturbed fixtures, not "moving parts" suitable for the kind of "models" just sketched. When the work of typologizing museum khipus gets under way, we may learn more about where operativity prevailed in pre-Hispanic cases and where fixity did.

Rural Huarochiranos' demand for constancia exteriorizes the social bond of shared work and is its political affirmation. In my opinion, the local art of inscription was not a matter of sending messages, that is, "communication from" persons. Nor was it finally a matter of "communicating about" society. Rather, it was a matter of making practice itself visible and interpretable. Above and beyond their value as tools for rationalizing an intricate organization, records were and still are the way people seize and hold their awareness of having created and upheld each other. They are reciprocity made visible. They are a moral substance. They are a social fact.

In the above analysis we have argued that the social facts villagers experience, as realized in quipocamayos, are the largest virtual entity of kinship—the corporate ayllu—and the federation of ayllus as a polity—the community. The quipocamayos in their day formed the exact point of articulation between kinship and political levels of organization. What attributes could have realized the higher articulation between village polity and Inka imperial levels? Between living generations, ancestors, and divinities? Museum vaults in Berlin, Lima, New York, and Paris hold many banded khipus, some strikingly like those of Tupicocha with their pachacamanta knobs and their hitos or markers. There are also khipus with cyclical structures such as Mújica's M-01. The Tupicochan specimens seem to be parts of a large and long-lived tradition. How widespread it was in space cannot be judged until scholars systematically sort museum specimens by provenience and design. But we may find that the Tupicochan quipocamayo complex is a colonialized, microscale variant of a scheme once used for greater political structures as well as minimal ones.

Finally one may ask, is it possible yet to answer the insistent question of whether khipus are writing? If we use a broad concept of writing like Gelb's, later Senner's ("a system of human intercommunication by means of conventional visible marks" 1989:2; see also Perri 2001:272), we might find room for them. If we stick to Boltz's or Daniels's definitions of "real," i.e., lexigraphic, writing, then Tupicocha gives little encouragement for a "yes" answer. Nothing in the Tupicochan quipocamayos has been found to encode any segment of speech. Though thoroughly familiar with the alphabet, and prone to say cords "have letters," villagers nonetheless retain as folk memory only non-lexigraphic interpretations. Quipocamayos could perhaps be "read" as words, because signs in them appeared to their owners as "virtual logograms," but that is a different matter from lexigraphy. No "rebus" usages were adduced. No cord sign was discussed in terms of specifically verbal properties such as word order, grammatical gender, clause structure, syllables, phonemes, or alphabetic letters.

The Tupicochan legacy seems rather to belong to a different family of inscriptions, namely, those which deploy signs in ways that obey the structure of a social practice or problem rather than that of a language. Sign systems that are built this way are the ones usually called "proto-writings." Rightly displeased with the Victorian teleology the term implies, some have preferred to rename them semasiographic writings or "writings without words." The point for us, however, is not to invent more pleasing terminologies but to clarify what properties such systems actually had. Some specialists on Old World origins of writing who abstain from giving "proto" scripts newer, more dignified names nonetheless are far ahead in the study of systems that are designed on lines other than lexigraphy.

Proto-cuneiform c.3200–3000 BCE (Michalowski 1996) and Proto-Elamite of the late fourth and early third millennia BCE (Englund 1996) are widely considered the world's oldest writings. They are better understood than khipus, though still obscure. Tablets in both scripts contain accounting records, in which iconic and sometimes aniconic signs link with numerical signs in formats that have little to do with verbal syntax. Proto-Elamite tablets somewhat resemble Tupicochan khipus in their use of a horizontal axis to represent "continuation" and a vertical axis to represent "summation." Although "real writing" did grow from at least the former of these scripts, these "proto-writings" were not embryonic or incomplete versions of "real writing." They were in their own right fully functional systems of a different sort. Although Englund, Michalowski, and their peers continue to use the misleading "proto" terminology, they are far from unaware of this.

Consider Peter Damerow's (1999:2) brilliant summation of proto-cuneiform, the script immediately ancestral to the first clear-cut "true writing." Damerow writes, "It is now a well established fact that the influence of the structures of language on a system of writing becomes weaker the further one goes back in its history. I will call . . . such incipient systems of writing with weak connections to language 'proto-writing'. As might be expected, methods of philology are less effective if the relation between writing and language is weak. It is possibly due to this fact that major corpora of early writing systems . . . have for a long time been widely neglected." Khipus loom large among such corpora. Damerow goes further (1999:6) toward enumerating proto-cuneiform's positive properties. His list will sound familiar to readers of this book:

> The structures of proto-cuneiform are far from matching the syntax of a language.
> Contrary to oral language, proto-cuneiform writing implies only simple patterns of semantic categories.
> In proto-cuneiform, phonetic coding plays only a minor role, if any.
> Proto-cuneiform is not uniformly conventionalized.
> Contrary to oral language, proto-cuneiform is used only in an extremely restricted context of application.
> Proto-cuneiform had precursors in symbolic systems which were used, at least partly, for the same purposes.

There was a co-evolution of proto-cuneiform with certain arithmetical notions.

This summary still speaks in invidious comparisons with what later Mesopotamian scripts achieved, after users had bound the "virtual logogram" closer to language by using it to stand for syllables or morphemes. Yet Damerow's essay does contain the elements of a useful way to characterize the way Andeans wrote before they wrote lexigraphically. This way, I suggest, is more akin to data graphics as Tufte and Bertin conceive them, or to computer "infographics," than to its eventual mutant offspring, "true writing." I would suggest that we simply call the "successful [proto-cuneiform] means of representing knowledge" (Damerow 1999:3) and others like it "data writing," as opposed to the various terms that mean "speech-sound writing."

Damerow is alert to the likelihood that the early processes of representing data, apart from the later process of adjusting representation to properties of language, could have been invented at various times and places: "This anachronistic projection of modern functions of writing into its early use had the consequence that the multiple origins of writing were widely neglected" (1999:5). Andeanists hold an important part of the agenda for rectifying this.

Khipus were an immensely consequential data writing—but one with consequences very different from those of proto-cuneiform. The art of cord inscription lasted longer than proto-cuneiform or proto-Elamite, and grew to cover more functions, becoming the main information armature of a multilingual empire. Tupicocha's quipocamayos help us envision Andean conventions that enabled Andean cord to become perhaps the most complex and versatile of data writings. What enrichments of the basic principle allowed khipus to expand so far? Khipus' singularity as compared to ancient Mideastern accounting tablets seems to be that they allowed users to simultaneously predicate a wide range of information about the entity signified in a cord, not just its numerical measure. The experience of reading khipu may have been somewhat like that of reading a modern "infographic" in which, for example, the segments of a pie chart are given a simulated third dimension of height to signify an additional variable, as well as colors keyed to contextual categories, numbers signifying dates, and labeling icons to trigger "real-world" associations. A multivariate table could convey the same data. So could a prose summary. But both would be harder to understand, because they would not allow one to use different parts of the sensorium for grasping the different variables.

It is too soon to guess why the Andes advanced so far and stayed so long on the Old World's "road not taken" Perhaps sociolinguistic factors like ease of data transfer amid endemic multilingualism gave language-distant writing methods a durable advantage. Perhaps American cultures differed deeply from Old World cultures in their rules about when speech-based inscription (as opposed to inscriptions derived from other symbolic systems) was appropriate. Perhaps cases of a truly independent graphic "parallel language" were involved. Perhaps, as the Aschers, Conklin, and Urton hold, the peculiar kind of reasoning involved in handling the fiber medium itself influenced ideas about the proper structure of information.

Everything now depends on empirical concentration and a long attention span. As the first comprehensive corpus of khipu inscriptions (the Harvard-based Khipu Data Base Project, which will contain the transcripts of Tupicocha's khipus among hundreds of others) takes shape, as archaeological recovery of khipus in context becomes more frequent, and as the ethnographic path toward documentation of patrimonial specimens opens wider, we will be able to inventory the cord signary or signaries. Once the Andes have orderly descriptive resources we may yet identify Andean analogues to those key Mesopotamian readings (e.g., proto-cuneiform's cross-in-circle "sheep" sign) which would complement the broad-stroke "script-in-society" approach this book embodies. If that happens, decipherment of one or more Andean writing systems would become a reasonable hope.

NOTES

The Unread Legacy

1 It also has other historic names: San Cosme y San Damián, San Damián de Uructambo, or San Damián de Urutambo.

2 Hispano-Quechuisms, that is, words of Quechua etymology used in Spanish, are written in Spanish orthography. Quechua words are written using the Peruvian Ministry of Education's graphophonemic conventions (Cusihuamán 1976:13–17). Throughout the book translations of foreign-language quotations are mine unless otherwise noted.

3 To the best of my knowledge, the originator of this phrase is my colleague Sharon Hutchinson.

4 *Huari* denotes kindreds of valley or coastal origin, associated with agriculture, with earth and its deities, and with ancient political legitimacy. *Llacuaz* denotes kindreds of highland origin, associated with pastoralism, with the sky and its deities, and with political aggression. This antithesis is common in central Peru, and implicit in the 1608 Quechua source.

5 Peru's Instituto Nacional de Estadística e Informática maintains a Web site, http://www.inei. gob.pe/, which, in November 1998, distributed these as the latest secure calculations. Lima's annual growth rate is about 2.3 percent per year, while the country's is about 1.7 percent.

6 Chicha music is a hugely popular genre combining Andean lyrics and musical motifs with electric rock instrumentation. Chicha bands shuttle between urban and rural dance dates, and their listeners also often lead bipolar urban-rural lives.

7 According to Gary Urton's reckoning. Address at Colgate University, May 26, 2001.

8 Semiosis: in Peircian terminology, sign action as opposed to mechanical action.

9 "Mechones de lana, figuras humanas y . . . un caracol marino."

1. Universes of the Legible

1 Inkakunaqa manan papelta reqsirankuchu, qelqata, paykunaqa mana noticiasta papelpichu apachinakuranku, sino wik'uña q'aytukunallapi; mana allin noticikunapaq [*sic*] yana q'aytukunapi, allin noticiakunapaqta karan yuraq q'aytukuna. Kay q'aytukunan karan libro hina, pero españakuna mana kananta munasqakuchu hinaspa Inkaman huk papelta qosqaku:

— Kay papelmi riman, — nispa:

— Mayta rimasqan? Sonseras: engañayta munawankichis.

Panpamantaq papelta wikch'upusqa. Inkaqa manan papelkunamanta entenderanchu. Imaynatataq papel rimanman karan, manataq leeyta yacharanchu chayri? Khaynatan Inkanchis wañuchichikusqa.

2 "Lexigraphy" is one of several closely overlapping terms for such inscription. "Phonography" and "glottography" are others. Boltz (1994:16–28) proposes simply reserving the word "writing" to mean systems of this kind.

3 I am indebted to Gary Urton for suggesting Damerow's article.

4 I am indebted to William Hanks for pointing out Benveniste and Goodman as important theorists for khipu studies.

2. A Flowery Script

1 The number is shrinking, a fact harmful to quipocamayo curation. Despite declining death rates and a natural population growth on the order of 2.75 percent per year (Martínez 1996:50), Tupicocha saw a 9.7 percent absolute decline in resident population between its 1972 peak and the last national census (1993). Most years during the 1990s saw declines in the number of households inscribed, usually about 2 percent annually. This produces a very high ratio of retired to active members, making the burden of active membership still heavier and less attractive.

2 One household's March 1995 shipments contained *ajenco* (*Artemisia absinthium*), *asmachilca* (*Stevia punensis*), *cedrón* (*Lippia triphylla*), *chamana* (*Dodonaea viscosa*), *henojo* (*Foeniculum vulgaris*), *huacatay* (*Tagetes minuta*), *boldo* (*Boldoa fragans*), *chupasangre* ([?]), *malva* (*Malva parviflora*), *manzanilla* (*Matricaria chamomilla*), *menta* (*Mentha aquatica*), *muña* (*Satureia boliviana*) *romero* (*Rosmarinus officinalis*), *ruda* (*Ruta graveolens*), and *toronjil* (*Melissa officinalis*; Girault 1984). These are to be distinguished from many rarer and more valuable wild herbs, which are also gathered in small amounts for household and ritual use but rarely sold.

3 Gladiolus, daisies, carnations, dwarf carnations, calla lilies, etc.

4 Because it can be used in lipstick and foodstuffs, as an organic substitute for biochemically suspect dyes.

5 Tupicocha rents from the neighboring village of Antioquía.

6 Theoretically, the committee answers to the water administration branch of Peru's Ministry of Agriculture and Livestock. In practice it upholds local traditional norms as influenced by local political pressures, and it reserves the official forms for occasions when a government work contract brings state-financed engineers to town.

7 Desirable because it is sure to have a good water supply, and also because it maximizes the growing season.

8 The customary cash value of a water turn equals one day's cash wage.

9 At that time, a typical daily wage was in the range of three to five U.S. dollars.

3. The "Book of the Thousand"

1 *Parcialidad* is a multivalent term from the sixteenth century onward. It causes some confusion because it is a context-sensitive, relative term. In a 1940 lawsuit, Tupicocha and San Damián, each a multi-ayllu whole in its own right, were both labeled parcialidades of Checa. On the other hand, in 1939, when a certain ayllu was undergoing fission, it referred to its emerging segments as its parcialidades (AP1G/SAT_01 1939a). Like ayllu, parcialidad seems a general term meaning "sector," applicable within any level (Platt 1986 [1978]:231).

2 Also spelled GUARANGA.

3   The Huaranga has a fascinating place in postcontact culture. After Spaniards invaded Huarochirí (1534), the Inka *waranka* ('thousand') of Checa was parceled out to successive Crown favorites as a component of the *encomienda*, or grant of governance and tribute, which included the approximate totality of Lower Yauyos. Guillermo Astete Flores (1997?) has traced the extraordinary survival of the huaranga as a folk-legal category, long after the decay of the encomiendas and their replacement by other jurisdictional schemes. In their 1933 petition for recognition as an indigenous community (AMAG-UADLC/L 1933-35:leg. 1816), the Tupicochanos copied out eighteenth-century testimonies about the huaranga's rights to common land in the territories that today make up Checa in San Damián, Tupicocha, Tuna, and even Surco, this last being a subtropical outlier down in the Rímac valley which had in reality been lost. All in all, the lands of Tutay Quiri's exploits were still felt to form a moral unit. Tupicochanos feel that the transformation of the Huaranga from a practical to a hypothetical unit is an ongoing tragedy. A Tupicochan well read in the community archive says, "The huaranga was a brotherhood among the four towns. . . . It was all one single land . . . we were one." At that time, the villages could share pastures and did not suffer *minifundismo* ('fragmentation of tenure'). The communities' hostilities began, oral tradition says, when neighboring Tuna began to send the *oidores* ('judge-governors') of the Viceroyalty boxes of peaches as bribes, so as to get favorable treatment of a boundary claim against Tupicocha. Tuna has a bound 1937 paleographic transcription of its 1748 boundary inspection, whose cover is marked "Titles of the Community" but whose title page says "GUARANGA." As the four villages' common interests evaporated, struggles over boundaries became endemic. As late as 1940, Tupicocha physically battled the community called Checa of San Damián on the grounds that Tupicocha was also a "sector" (parcialidad) of Checa and therefore entitled to certain fields—which they did in fact win (APUCH/SAT_03 1940:125-27).

Despite repeated adjudication, there remains a silent consensus that boundaries are only provisionally legitimate, pending an eventual omega point of justice and reconciliation. This ideal is identified with the memory of the Huaranga. Indeed, in its archive, Tupicocha cherishes above all other documents a manuscript volume called *El libro de la huaranga*, or *The Book of the Thousand*, actually a compilation of colonial *deslindes*, or judicial boundary inspections (ACCSAT/SAT_Folder 7 1748). The document legalistically embodies Tupicocha's claim to the boundaries as it sees them, and it morally condenses an enduring idea of the larger, organic unit as a vessel of lost integrity.

4   To Allauca, he gave the shrine of Maca Calla and its lands, to the Sat Pasca, Quimquilla; to the Sulc Pahca, Ricra Huanca; and to Muxica, Quira Raya. Huanri and Chauti, as yunca aboriginal lands, were implicitly left to Caca Sica (Salomon and Urioste 1991:119, 218).

5   The nicknames are as follows:

Primer Allauca   "Frente Limpio": "clear brow," i.e., "clean conscience," because this parcialidad prided itself on conscientiousness.

"Los Tristes": "sad," i.e., reserved and taciturn.

Primera Satafasca   "Los Gallos": "roosters," because of reputation for being eager (early risers) but also proud and touchy.

"Los Cocorucos": same.

Primer Huangre   "La Zapatilla": "sneaker" because they were the first to give up the traditional *llanque*, or moccasin.

Unión Chaucacolca   "Los Mundiales": "world champions" because a certain president of this group sent its people to faenas with a lot of gear "as if they were going to the World Cup."

"Los Discurseros": "orators," "because they're great ones for making speeches, to the community or to each other."

"Los Parlamentarios": "the parliamentarians," for same reason as previous.

"Los Parlachines": "the slick talkers," for same reason as previous.

Mújica	"Los Mujinos": "donkeys"; a pun.
Cacarima	"Los Gualachos": "llama herders," because they are believed to descend from puna migrants.
Segunda Allauca	"Los Zorros": "foxes," that is, astute people.
Segunda Satafasca	"Los Huacos": "ancient or pre-Hispanic" because of attachment to old-fashioned traditions, and also alluding to their alleged pale complexions. *Huaco*, 'prehispanic tomb', implies comparison with mummies.
	"Los Gringos": "blonde" or "pale," because said to be tall and light-featured.
Centro Huangre	"Los Bomboches": "sheep," because they are numerous and supposedly like to travel in big groups.
Huangre Boys	"Los Chalacos": inhabitants of the port of Callao, because they are named after Callao's great soccer team of the 1920s, the "Sport Boys."

6 Just as in the 1608 manuscript (Salomon and Urioste 1991:63).

7 Offspring of the ayllu who opt not to become socios continue to be counted as its "children" as long as they live, even though most of them live in diaspora. Internal documents of the ayllus register them, if at all, in a separate book from membership.

8 "Huc yumay chauincho sutioc," which could more literally be translated "a sperm line possessing the Chauincho name" (Salomon and Urioste 1991:64, 172).

9 Because the culture as a whole is extremely sparing of body contact, this is significant. Social drinking aside, brotherly embraces are seen only at heartfelt ritual moments.

10 In most ayllus, retirement affords continued use of ayllu and community services, in return for payment of money and in-kind levies but with exemption from labor levies. Sometimes aged and arthritic elders show up to rally the rest, or to shame laggards.

11 In Spanish, "para que sepan los linderos de esta parcialidad."

12 Today, young people's need to work or study in Lima is the Achilles' heel of ayllu recruitment. Occasionally, members speculate on reactivating some such flex plan.

13 "Grave situación que atrabiesa en este pueblo . . . una desavinencia muy acalorado. . . . Actos desmoralizados en la reunión pública de la guayrona. . . . Las rentas de esta comunidad lo derrochan como unos tiranos. . . . No reconocemos a ninguna persona nombrada para la directiva de la personería hasta el día de la cuenta de esa personero" (spelling thus in original).

14 "Ni el ayllo menos numeroso aceptó presencia de hijos de otros ayllus. En febrero de 1997 hubo problema para organizar la festividad de Santiago Apóstol de julio 1997. En cinco minutos bastó para solucionar entre sesenta personas que estaban en desacuerdo. Cacarima tenía solo cuatro socios, pero con su sentimiento de iguales, movilizaron sus parientes pudientes en Lima e hicieron tan bien como cualquier." The mayor was Wilfredo Urquizo.

4. The Tupicochan Staff Code

1 Thanks to Regis Miller of the University of Wisconsin Forest Products Laboratory for this identification.

2 "From the crooked timber of humanity, no straight thing has ever been made." Berlin used this for the title of a 1991 book of essays.

3 Slight variations were noticed among 1995, 1997, and 2000 iterations; in such cases, the most recent practice is noted here.

4 These mantles are gifts of love or piety that women make for their husbands and offspring. Crafted for other occasions, they are on loan for the night. This sole, marked female presence always evokes appreciative talk about conjugal loyalty and female artistry.

5 Personal communication, 1997.

6 Tupicochans are justifiably proud of the fact that their village has no police officer and needs none.

7   The term *aspa* is unrelated to the alphabet. Its "literal" sense is the crossing of two beams, or threads crisscrossing along a spool. It can also refer to a Saint Sebastian's cross.

8   In physical reality, the cross is always detachable from its pyramid. Detachment and return is a vital ritual module on several occasions. The word *peaña* strictly refers only to the pyramid. It may be a replacement for the pre-Hispanic term *usnu* (Zuidema 1980). In strictest formality the term is *peaña de la cruz.*

5. The Khipu Art after the Inkas

1   "Cada seis meses el tucuirico envíe memoria por escrito o por quipo de los indios que se han muerto o aumentado o llegado a edad de diez y ocho años, o huídose."

2   "Usaban de una cuenta muy sutil de unas hebras de lana de dos nudos [*sic*], y puesto lana de colores en los nudos, los cuales llaman quipos. Entendíase y entiéndense tanto por esta cuenta, que dan razón de más de quinientos años de todas las cosas que en este tiempo han pasado. Tenían indios industriados y maestros de los dichos quipos y cuentas, y éstos iban de generación en generación mostrando lo pasado, y en pasándolo en la memoria a los que habían de entrar, que por maravilla no se olvidaban cosa por pequeña que fuese." Locke left untranslated the enigmatic phrase *dos nudos*, 'two knots'.

3   In the translation sentence boundaries have been supplied. "Hoy se guarda el uso de unos quypos, que nosotros decimos Libros de Caja, los quales los Indios no los tubieron sino aquellos quipos, que son unos cordeles de lana de varias colores, y en ellos munchos ñudos como aqui se demuestran, diferenciados unos de otros, que por la diferencia conocen y saben las quantidades de lo que entro y salio en la caja, e los pesos de oro e plata que se han dado e pagado e recibido. Este genero de cuenta no la alcanzaron los Espanoles quando ganaron aquel Reyno, ni hasta hoy la han podido apreender, y solo se esta a su buena fee y credito, mediante unos yndios de confianza de aquellos pueblos que les nombran quypo camayos, como Mayordomos de aquellos cuentas y contadores mayores de ellas, a cuyo cargo esta la cuenta de todos los ganados, y frutos e sementeras de las comunidades que aca decimos bienes o rentes concebibles [f. 434v] y estos quipo camayos ante la justicia hacen la cuenta, y dan razon luego verbalmente de todo, y tienen hasta el dia de hoy guardados gran infinidad destos cordeles añudados; y aunque la malicia y habilidad de algunos indios principales se ha estendido ya a aprender en aquel Reyno a leer romance y latin e cantar e tañer varios instrumentos y contar con caracteres de guarizmos: en realidad de verdad no lo usan, ni los corregidores permiten que por nuestra cuenta y guarizmo se les tome y de, sino por estos quipos e los mismos instrumentos eligen los quipocamayos, y ante el Corregidor en su ayuntamiento, y esa orden se guarda hoy, y la otra nuestra sirve de una curiosidad y policia al indio principal que la quiso deprender."

4   Murillo de la Cerda refers to "nuestra cuenta y guarizmo": "our accounting and Indo-Arabic numbers." Indo-Arabic numerals were at that time not yet widely accepted as suitable for accounts of record. He may have meant that Indo-Arabic was used as an off-the-record way of preparing calculations, which would then be legalized in prose or Roman numerals. Understandably, khipu masters, possessing a fully decimal method which avoids this tedium, would regard it as merely ostentatious or curious.

5   If they really existed, Hyland argues, such refunctionalized colonial "royal" khipus might have set in motion an arcane current which reenters the written record in the eighteenth century. At that time, the Neapolitan count Raimondo Sansevero di Sangro (1750) claimed to have a "key" or master khipu for encoding all the syllables of the Quechua language. Documents and purported khipu fragments, many of questionable authenticity, have recently been proffered in support of Sansevero's speculation (Animato, Rossi, and Miccinelli 1989; see also Laurencich 1996). Weighty source-critical rebuttals (Estenssoro 1997; Adorno 1999) and the total absence of corroborating

pieces in the archaeological record weigh against the revived Sansevero hypothesis. Sansevero's work is closely akin to the contemporaneous Neoplatonic guesswork that misled efforts to read Egyptian hieroglyphs preceding those of Jean François Champollion (Coe 1992:14–18). According to Hyland's hypothesis, Valera himself would have been implementing a Neoplatonic scheme.

6 "Ynatacsi yngacunari tucoy ynantin huacacunaman alli ricsisca huacamanca corinta collquinta quipollamanta tucoy ynantin huacacta cochic carcan choc auqui collqui auqui . . . chaymantam choc vrpo collc horpo choc tipsi collc tipsi ñiscacunactas cochic carcan quipollamanta cay hatunin huacacunaca manatacsi huquillanpas pasuccho."

7 Original: "yllacnincunactari tucoytatac quipuspa . . . muchayta callarircan."

8 Excerpts of this lawsuit are printed in Espinoza Soriano 1983–94.

9 Don Gerónimo Cancho Guaman, f. 105v–110r. He figures prominently in chapters 20–21 as the half-idolatrous father of Francisco de Avila's ally Cristóbal Choque Casa.

10 Translated from "quipocamayo y mayordomo de todas las açiendas del ynga topa."

11 Original: "hera camachico de los yndios que guardaban los ganados del ynga y ansimismo tenía cuidado de guardar los cunbis y maizes y papas y demas cossas del dicho ynga."

12 Original: "administrador suyoyoc apo pomachaua."

13 I.e. Tupaq Inka Yupanki.

14 Original: "belicoso y de buen entendimiento."

15 Original: "contador maior i tezorero tavantinsuio quipoc curaca condor chava."

16 "El dicho geronimo pomachagua . . . los mando por la merced que le hizo el dicho marques y abelle rregalado mucho y dado un bestido colorado y una espada y una daga y que como le bian los yndios con aquellas armas y que las traya con liçencia del dicho marques le enpeçaron a temer y a serbir."

17 Original: "bino con brio y enpeço a enseñorearse de este dicho caçicazgo Pero no por que el fuese caçique."

18 Original: "le auia echo merçed de nonbrarle por caçique de las tres guarangas ynclusas en el dicho rrepartimiento de mama."

19 Original: "proveyendo por quipo y por escrito los nombres de los tales indios que en esto sirvieren y de que aillos y cuántos caminos hacen, ansí de ida hacia arriba, como de vuelta hacia abajo con los dichos despachos para que con el quipo y cuenta verdadera se les pueda hacer las pagas de su servicio" (Espinoza Soriano 1960:264–65).

20 The text is ambiguous as to whether this means cords and paper memorandum [memoria] separately, or means the cords were tantamount to a memorandum.

21 Original: "yndios Principales que llaman quipocamayos que toman cargo de Poner por quipo y memoria los yndios que trabajauan y dalles recaudo."

22 Es necesario un quipocama en los obrajes para que también él lleve las cuentas de los días que han trabajado los obrajeros. Tendrá que hacer un quipo grande con cuerdas diferentes conforme a los indios que trabajan también en distintos oficios. Con este procedimiento los trabajadores podrían cotejar lo señalado por el quipocama y lo que había anotado su administrador y de esa manera se podrá encontrar conformidad. (Text modernized by Costales.)

23 Original: "abiendo venido a esta parte a su negocios ocupo quatro mandones quipocamayos que hiziesen mita todo un dia en guardar una mula que dexo con un muchachon suyo—deve estos jornales y seruicio"

24 Original: "esta quenta la tiene el yndio contador destos pueblos en quipo" (f. 3v).

25 Whether the difference is one level or two depends on whether one thinks the witnesses accepted the "town" (pueblo) as a jurisdictional level superior to an ayllu. Given the date, they probably did, which would favor a two-level difference and an overall three-level model of polity.

26 The categories, in their order, are animals and animal products; plants and plant products; shipments involving both porters and horses; personal services; clothing; expenses of hunting; unpaid spinning.

27 "Todo era hazer quipos p.q confessarse aprender lo q. no sabian de la doctr.a confessarse, ayunar, y disciplinarse, y . . . generalm.te attender cada vno ala saluacion de sus almas."

28 Original: "por tassa quipos y padrones . . . por quipos y ayllus" (AAL/L Capítulos 1623:f .2r)

29 "Andaba este indio siempre cargado con un quipo de cordeles, por el cual conocía a todos los de su panaca y sabía por el dicho quipo las personas que debían mitas, sus nombres estados y los ganados y hacienda que tenía cada uno."

30 Cordial thanks are due to Karen Spalding for the chance to consult the transcription of this source.

31 "Cogi papel, y tintero, y me entre solito a casa de Maria Micaela y despues de platicar con ella varias cosas . . . ofreci . . . que le daria cinquenta pesos como ella me echase unos papeles que yo le diese en los pueblos; ofreciome que asi lo haria, confiada en que yo la havia de amparar y que ella llevaria los papeles con achaque de buscar a sus hijos, y que de no cumplir con lo que me ofrecia la castigase" (f. 20r).

32 The implication being, that Spanish authority would give the putative addressees the lands in dispute with adjacent rivals—who would actually be getting this message at the same time.

33 These two villages, both in the crucible of the rebellion, faced each other across a canyon in hostility as heads of rival "thousands."

34 The original Spanish up to this point:
Con esto escrivi veinte y dos papeles para otros tantos pueblos de este repartimiento: pondre el contacto de ellos, porque todo era uno.

[underlined in original:] *Hijos, alcaldes y principales del Pueblo de Langa: Recivi Vuestra Carta En la que me decis soys leales Vasallos de su Magestad, y que solo de miedo de los rebeldes de Lahuaitambo entrasteis en la sublevacion, pero que si os perdono en nombre de Su Magestad este dicho delito, me entregareis muertas o presas las personas de Francisco Ximenez Ynga [y otros cincos líderes rebeldes]; lo que os agradezco y en nombre del Rey Nuestro Senor las recivio, y sereis premiados y os entregare sus tierras . . .*

=este papel escrito a Langa le hizo echar en Lahuaitambo; y el escrito a Lahuaitambo, le hize echar en Langa; y asi en los demas pueblo siempre a la trocada, haciendome el juycio, de que estando ellos tan unidos havian de empezar a recelarse unos pueblos de otros. . . . (f. 20r–v).

35 "Salio mi yndia a cosa de las tres de la tarde, dandome la palabra que en todo aquel dia y aquella noche andaria los pueblos de Tuna, Tupicocha, San Damian, Sunicancha, Lahuaitambo, Langa, y Chorrillos, que al dia siguiente andaria los de la doctrina de Olleros, y que como ella encontrase a sus hijos libres, tenia por cierto que ellos tirarian por otros pueblos a ayudarla . . . Para lo que llevo los papeles amarrados con hilos de diferentes colores hechos quipo, que es el modo conque ellos se entienden; ella me lo prometio, pero los egecuto mejor" (f. 20v).

36 "Vino Maria Michaela de llebar sus papeles, asegurandome que ella y sus hijos los havian hechado, y cumplido con mi orden todos los pueblos y que mis dichas cartas havian causado tal efecto, que todos los rebeldes que estaban en la dirección del traydor, se havian cortado, y levantado vandera un pueblo en contra de otro, tirandose a matar sobre si vosotros escrivisteis a el español minero, o vosotros" (f. 25v).

37 A sample may be as small as a few individual fibers each under a centimeter long, the total sample weighing a fraction of a gram.

38 University of Arizona Radiocarbon Laboratory samples WG451–54 and 521–30.

39 Personal correspondence, July 24, 1998.

40 From the Juan Santos Atahualpa rebellion to the death of Tupac Amaru II.

41 A somewhat arbitrary interval, delimiting the heyday of "scientific" indigenism, from the academic reforms which activated social sciences at San Antonio Abad University in Cuzco, to the publication of the *Handbook of South American Indians*, volume 2 (Mishkin 1946). The latter marked the passage of dominant academic discourse about "Indians" from indigenists to anthro-

pologists. In popular media and arts, the indigenist legacy continues to circulate, as in political pageants such as the 2001 installation of President Alejandro Toledo.

42 Susan Lee Bruce, curator; personal communication.

6. Quipocamayos of Tupicocha

1 The smaller of Unión Chaucacolca's two quipocamayos (uch-02) and the recently recovered quipocamayo m-02 of Mújica are not displayed because of fragility.

2 This maneuver involves a show of muscle power, which is responsible for stress damage such as frayed pendants.

3 "Resiste, tiene bastante vida."

4 This round of open feasting includes celebrations of induction or retirement and circle-dancing in separate male and female rings. Each ayllu prepares a feast to which all are welcome. The general open house and mutual visiting constitute a round-robin renewal of political links. For married women, if they can loose themselves from onerous cooking, it affords a chance to reunite with their ayllus of origin.

5 As early as 1571 Juan Gómez, one of the Jesuits who first missionized Huarochirí, reported an augury named jhanca: "Tienen una piedra pequeña q. se llama jhanca que es ynterprete del ydolo mayor esta piedra tiene vna señal en la una parte. y despues q. adoran. al ydolo mayor q. se llama guaca echan. esta piedra. como quien echa dados. y si sale la señal dizen q. se les conçeden. lo que piden. y si no se les conçede enpiezan a llorar y. entonzes hazen sacrifiçios para aplacar al ydolo" (Polia Meconi 1999:199).

   In 1611 Francisco de Avila reported at length on a similar augury using two stones called *chanca* and *cunchur* (Arguedas and Duviols 1966:156–257).

6 This phrase is no longer understood, but if it is Quechua, *pichcamanta* means "of five" or "from five." The allusion is to the number which consistently stands for productivity in Andean mathematics and for plenitude in Huarochirí mythology.

7 Dominga Antiporta, Vicenta Javier Medina, mentioned later in this chapter's text.

8 Using 1995 data. Rough handling of the quipocamayos in ritual context apparently caused loss of certain cords in the interval 1995–97.

9 For identification of the construction, thanks to Patricia Hilts and Elena Phipps.

10 Elena Phipps, personal communication.

11 A local usage; *jerga* in standard Spanish means "serge." The dictionary term for tweed, *cheviot*, is not locally known.

12 c-01 p33 (pendant 33), m-01 p50.

13 Thanks are due to Patricia Hilts for pointing out this likeness.

14 Personal communication, April 13, 1997.

15 Or perhaps ma'chu, etc., where the apostrophe represents a glottal stop.

16 "Un quipu con cuerdas desanudadas y con un segundo anudamiento es, hablando con exactitud, un palimpsesto que se puede reconstruir . . . es asombroso comprobar la facilidad con que se pueden rehacer los nudos a base de las huellas que todavía están marcadas en las cuerdas. El desanudamiento ocurre normalmente en cuerdas aisladas, colgantes, y subsidiarias, pero, a veces también en toda una sección del quipu."

17 Specimen 87.9.14 of the Musée de l'Homme in Paris.

18 "Al año cambiaban de ñudos. Sacaban los ñudos y ponían nuevos. El tres de enero actualizaban todo lo que habían ganado o perdido."

19 Original: "porque estas cuentas eran anuales, y no daban razón más que de un año solo."

20 With a bow to Julie Cruikshank, author of *Life Lived Like a Story: Life Stories of Three Yukon Native Elders* (Lincoln: University of Nebraska Press, 1990).

7. Ayllu Cords and Ayllu Books

1 Resources are as follows: The archive of the comunidad campesina (ACC) includes the holdings of the former agencia municipal, in which the ayllus were fused onto Republican-era local administration. This unit inherited colonial papers. The modern municipality and Gobernación have papers of their twentieth-century history. The archive of the justice of the peace perished in a fire. All parish archives of the area are unavailable in part due to the earthquake of 1740 and in part to removal by the prelature, which has apparently lost them. Some *cofradía* (Catholic religious sodality) archives exist. Beside the ayllu archives discussed below, all civil-society entities down to and including youth soccer teams maintain archives.

2 The reasons for doubting visita function include (1) limited format standardization across ayllus and (2) absence of typical visita profiles, such as extralarge blocs at the start of the ayllu record (corresponding to privileged households). Totalizing devices over the ayllu (topcords, summation cords) at the end are also absent.

3 "Invalid" not because of error but because it has been neutralized by fulfillment.

4 Early examples of such obligation/fulfillment records include IOUs and their cancellations (transfer of treasury to income officers, vows pending on loans of sacred objects, promises to pay fines, and loans of ayllu funds); inductions (dentradas) and payment of the dentrada or ritual goods owed by inductees; appointments of officers, with cancellations signifying discharge of duties; contracts with receipts for payment; inventories of goods received, which are discharged by transfer of same goods a year later; authorizations of expenditure cancelled by receipts; rentals of lands plus receipts; festival cargos assigned and fulfilled; lists and fulfillments of grazing fees; and, above all, agreements to carry out days of collective labor plus attestations of labor days completed. *Actas de dejación* (resignations) could be considered an exception that proves the rule, since they signify that a person is no longer accountable to ayllu plans.

5 We do know that c. 1608, yumay, the precursor of "family," had the attribute of seniority, because the Quechua source goes to great trouble explaining how a junior yumay could assume the priestly title of a senior one (Salomon and Urioste 1991:136–37, 143). When that rule gave way to the present political taboo on seniority discussions is unknown.

6 *Próximos* or *jóvenes*. Such people were expected to assume partial duties at least a year before their actual induction.

7 An interesting detail: if the amount was an odd number of soles, the sum was not divided using centavos but rather the mayor took the larger "half," as if in recognition of precedence.

8 Municipal agent; lieutenant governor; *síndico personero*, or legal spokesperson; and secretary and justice of the peace (ACC/SAT Folder "Irrigación" 1893:f. 1r).

9 The introjection of supralocal hierarchies downward into local structures seems to occur earlier on the ecclesiastical side than on the civil and may be a prototype for it. A formation of this kind is recorded in the 1860s, on the ecclesiastical side. Much as an ayllu disperses its limandas among couples or individuals and then collects them (chapter 3), the patron saint dispersed his holy objects among the ayllus in December and concentrated them with the ayllus' gifts on his day, in November (ACCSAT/SAT_04 1864:ff. non num.; ACCSAT/SAT_05 1898:44.) As with ayllus' own funds, the saint's treasury functioned as a credit union. It could loan sums over 1,000 pesos in the 1870s. The Virgin of Asunción ruled a parallel organization (ACC/SAT_06). The hierarchies of cargos for the Saints at the whole-community level were even more complex than the civil ones, involving, in typical years prior to 1920, eighteen named offices for the female and a similar number for the male patron.

10 The modern Huangre ayllus are the inheritors of the Yunca, or A, portion, but not consciously so.

11 The quote is from San Damián resident and Concha comunero Roberto Sacramento.

12 "Dos quipucayos [*sic*] i que uno corresponde al Presidente i otro al Vice-Presidente."

13 On the "Six-Month," the main sponsor (*fundador*) has to notify the community and other officials of his or her plans. He or she creates a constancia, or record, by placing a set of sacred tokens (cross, saint image, and three-colored cloak) inside the House of Customary Law, an interesting example of how nonalphabetic objects sometimes have the force of records.

14 One may speculate that this nonstandard spelling of *coordinándose* is influenced by a folk-etymological association with cordón, meaning "thick cord." *Cordonarse* would call up the image of investing each other in office by the draping of quipocamayo.

15 "Tiniendo el mayor su derecho de esta parcilidad á compañar sais mes del primero de Enero hasta el mes de Junio treinta sin pretesto de ninguno que el tendra las mismas atribuciones como el camachico se congergaran [i.e., ¿congregarán? ¿concertarán?] cordonandose [i.e., coordinándose] y gualmente."

16 To "carry" a faena meant to host it and be its beneficiary.

17 Meaning, not that the entry is incorrect, but that since all the debts mentioned in it are paid, it is annulled. Original: "Lista y multas de la parselidad de Allauca en la faena que llevo Don Marcos Vilcayauri para trillar trigo en el lugar Cancasica en Fecha 10 de Otubre de 1,923 y los que faltaron / Saturnino Cajañaupa pago / Elías Cajañaupa Enfermo / Ysidro Capistrano pago / Celestino Llaullipoma pago / Domingo Cajañaupa pago / y debe del trabajo 1 s/ [firma:] Higinio Cajañaupa. [sobreescrito] 'No vale'."

18 The word is a vernacular pronunciation of *pro rata*.

19 In Spanish, "fundos de trabajo."

20 In Spanish, "entrada de la lemanda."

8. Interpretations by Modern Villagers

1 As of April 2000, http://griffin.multimedia.edu/~deadmedia/frame.html.

2 "Es lo que [Tobías] me contaba cuando estaba un poco mal y para no quedar dormido. El tenía un quipo, y era su propio, pero lo enterraron con él, porque él decía, '¿Para qué lo voy a quedar, si no lo van a saber leer?'" [NB, the transitive use of *quedar* is a localism.]

3 "El también para su casa hizo un quipo financiando todo lo que tenía en su casa . . . cuando era joven y escribía con plumas. El dijo, 'Más fácil para mí, era hacer un quipo que escribir con plumas.'"

4 "Su amigo le había enseñado para qué servían todos los nudos del quipo, y él sabía para qué era, cada nudo, cuántos nudos."

5 In 2000 Nery decided the acrylics were wrong—he had used them in the first place just because they were close at hand—and replaced them with new wool yarn.

6 *Argolla* means a ring that constrains something, such as a key ring or one in an animal's nose. *Aro* is any kind of hoop or ring, and is also said of this knot.

7 "Hilo sin nudo: un comunero cumplió todos sus deberes de socio, tres veces presidente, tres secretario y tres tesorero. Una pasada de alguacil y otra de vocal. Ya salió."

8 "El quipo era reglamento y orden de su parcialidad."

9 "Serían de los alimentos, las faenas, las obras como depósito de agua."

10 "Este está torcido con rabo de vaca. Puede ser que tenga res a favor de la parcialidad."

11 "El tiempo cuando se hizo [el reparto] se sabe contando éstos desde el comienzo."

12 In Spanish, "los ganados que tenían."

13 "Variedades de semilla. Varios sitios que sembraban en conjunto."

14 "Los nudos declaraban que hay papa o hay mashua."

15 "Contaban cuántos costales de alimentos habían en el depósito de la parcialidad."

16 "Dejaron fijos en nudo la fecha de la reunión."

17 "Fijaban las fechas en que iban a haber faenas durante el año."

18 "Las herramientas que tenían."

19 "La cantidad de las herramientas."

20 "Número de variedades de herramientas."

21 "Cada comunero tiene su familia. Eran más abundantes la parcialidad. Se contaba quién era y su esposa."

22 "Eran cónyuges. Por largo tiempo estaban enamorados."

23 "La pareja."

24 "La pareja se estaba distanciando de sus hijos. La abuela tiene los hijos de la pareja."

25 "Son dos, son grandes y se han ido cada uno por su camino."

26 "En uno de los hilos está fijado la fecha de la huayrona, creo que está en el principio. Nuevos presidentes. Nuevas autoridades, al inicio lo decía todo ya."

27 "Luego los hilos de ahorro que tenía su parcialidad."

28 "Dos personas . . . son responsables de tres cajuelas que van a acomodar con diferentes personas."

29 "Más seis cuadros."

30 "Por llegar tarde a la faena, es castigado."

31 "Las costumbres son las cosas que uno hace de la misma forma año tras año."

32 "Para unir los quipos . . . aquí hay algo que falta de herramientas . . . abre otro espacio y pone lo que falta, otro hilo."

33 "Abrían el nudo, hacían gran espacio y completaban según sus órdenes del otro quipo."

34 "Indicando que cinco [hilos] han salido al otro quipo."

35 "¿Cómo explicar?—o sea está como que raya técnica, ¿no has estudiado? Se compra ya en Lima ya. Así los bobinitos, allí habla pues. El marrón qué número vale. Este, igualito es este [quipocamayo] al rayo técnico éste. Porque rayo técnico tiene, algunas bobinitas tienen rayas más: tiene rayas negro, rojo, verde. Y entonces el marrón qué número vale y el negro qué número vale, tú vas sumando, sumar, y sumas, zas, tanto. Y así buscas, y ese grado, y ese para soldar pues."

36 "Así como 'Tupicocha' y 'Amancio' puedo buscar una canto."

37 "¿Tengo uno o muchos enemigos?"

38 "Busca la ayuda de uno más sabio que tú."

39 Full transcript, including author's remarks, on tape: "Esto, está por ejemplo, está trasfiricando [i.e., testificando] es esto tu viaje que Ud. estás haciendo en esto hoy día estudiando. Está esto, mira. Sin nada." [Frank Salomon (FS): "El número 4; es un viaje largo. Su color chumpi oscuro."] "Esta es tu suerte. Esta es tu suerte, que has salido con buena fe, está de viaje. Quiere decir que significa, estancia. Estancia—" [FS: "Es el nudo inferior, es un nudo de dos vueltas."] "De dos vueltas, yo te desato. [Loosens.] Y uno a uno vuelta, esta es una vuelta. Esta es que Ud. te dirigiste a mi persona, y ya estoy de Ud. estimándole, conociendo, ahí está." The use of *usted* (Ud.) with second-person familiar verbs is a regionalism.

40 "Más grande, pe. De cuatro. Uno, dos, tres, cuatro. Este es de donde nos hemos encontrado, ayer, donde hemos conversado. Esto es tu suerte." [FS: "¿Ese es?"] "Sí." [FS: "El número 05?"] "Sí. Que Ud. tenías fe con mi persona de hacerme convencer [laughing] de trabajar; ahí está. Esto es. . . . Acá es lo que me has dado de propina ayer, este es propina. [FS: "Es el número 06."] "Ahí se terminó. Servido."

9. Toward Synthetic Interpretation

1 Namely, 1A-01: p12, p54; 1SF-01: p5, p58, p102; 1G-01: p80; UCH-02: p51; C-01: p79; 2A-01: p11; 2SF-01: p81, p91.

2 Yanca was the higher of the two priestly corps in the Huarochirí Quechua source. Unlike the lower, or Huacsa, order, yanca priesthood was hereditary.

3 Original: "hasta cumplidos los quinze dias q ha de durar la fiesta" (277).

4   "Y dura casi otro tanto t.po."

5   The reason for the calendrical discrepancy (April versus June) with the Jesuit source is not known, nor whether the "officers" mentioned there are the huacsas here.

6   "Pay ingatacsi camachircan anan yauyo rurin yauyomanta quinça chunca pariacacacta purapi quillapi siruichon ñispa. Chaysi chaycama quimsachunca runa siruircanco chuncapihcayoc punchaumantacama caraspa micochispa."

7   Original: "pura ñiscapi quilla ñiscapi tucoy checacuna ayllompi ayllompi seruispa."

8   "Que dichas faenas llevaran bajo de lista que dara vuelta en 14 partes complido los trabajos se reabrira secion a pagar los trabajos y multas."

9   There are 2 such on 2SF-01, 3 on UCH-01, 9 on UCH-02, 3 on C-01, and 10 on 1G-01. It is difficult to say how many exist on M-02 because of its many broken cords, but at least two seem to be present.

10 The shortfall between 68 pendants mentioned here (16 quartets plus 4 redoubled V pendants) and the 70 in the full description of M-01 is due to the disappearance of the attached M-0X fragment, and the discounting of a cord which may be a recent addition used to facilitate shoulder-draping.

11 Its modular group is a five-pendant sequence described as yellowish-brown, two whites, a medium brown, and a brown. The khipu consists of an introductory quintet, two nonconforming cords, nine quintets without knots, a nonconforming cord, then eight quintets of which six consist of knotted cords. It resembles M-01 in the following ways: it has similar physical dimensions, contains a comparable number of iterations of the cycle, begins with an untypical instance of the cycle, and contains in its midst a nonconforming cord which seems to divide quintets which are in one data state (untied) from later ones which are in a different data state (tied). There are also nontrivial differences, for example, in ornamentation, subsidiaries (M-01 lacks them), and orderly variation within quintets. The Aschers find weak grounds for taking the initial cycle to sum subsequent ones, but M-01 does not seem to have this property.

12 Reasons for doing so might include a long absence during which one rents out one's land, or else uses it in a way with low labor requirements, such as forestry. Faena sales also result from poverty.

13 And includes in "type" certain variations in the way a given type, e.g., the T-knot, is executed.

Conclusions

1   The number of bands in the Santa set varies from 9 to 48 and the number of cords from 54 to 288.

GLOSSARY

Note on Dialectology

Huarochiranos speak Spanish only. *Hispano-Quechua* designates words of Quechua etymology found in their speech. Some Huarochirí Hispano-Quechuisms are unknown elsewhere. *Regional Spanish* means etymologically Romance usages typical of Huarochirí vernacular. A few words come from a *non-Quechua indigenous language*, probably Huarochirí's extinct Jaqaru-like ethnic tongue. Terms labeled *Quechua* are from the Cuzco-Titicaca highlands, or from chronicles and dictionaries, not from Huarochirí speech. All other terms are *standard Spanish* usages.

acta: minute (of a meeting, etc.)
activo: member with full rights and duties
agencia municipal: submunicipality
alcalde: (1) in folk law, staff-bearing constable; (2) in state law, municipal mayor
ancarri: (Hispano-Quechua) blue
anexo: submunicipal hamlet, satellite village
armada: (regional Spanish) ceremonial redistribution inaugurating meeting or work
aspa: an "X," check mark, or other sign attesting attention
ayllu: (Hispano-Quechua) corporate descent group, defined by preferentially patrilineal eligibility and voluntary membership (synonym: *parcialidad*)
cabildo: town council; open town meeting
cajuela: (regional Spanish) portable diorama dramatizing Catholic theme
calhua: (Hispano-Quechua [?]) light brown
camachico: (Hispano-Quechua) president of an ayllu
campesino: peasant
cantito: (regional Spanish) bright thread run through (abbreviation: *td rt*)
cargo: role of responsibility, political or ritual
chacra: (Hispano-Quechua) cultivated field
chacua: (Hispano-Quechua [?]) brownish-yellow

champería: (Hispano-Quechua) general canal cleaning, with water festival

chumpi: (Hispano-Quechua) brown

ciudadano: citizen, member

cofradía: Catholic religious sodality

collca: (Hispano-Quechua) walled ceremonial plaza with storage areas

compañía: (regional Spanish) subsidiary cord

comunero: community member, defined by local birth eligibility and voluntary inscription

comunidad: (or comunidad campesina) state-recognized self-governing village corporation which controls common holdings

constancia: proof; document of record

costumbre: (regional Spanish) unwritten law

curcuche: (Quechua [?] non-Quechua indigenous language [?]) sacred clown dancer

dentrada: (regional Spanish) debut of new ayllu member; payments for same

devoto: donor

empate: attachment

encomienda: colonial-era trusteeship over indigenous population

enfloro: (regional Spanish) ceremony of distributing herbal or floral cockades

enseres: belongings of ayllu or community

equipo: (1) team, especially regarding an ayllu or its crew as competitive unit; (2) (regional Spanish) quipocamayo

faena: collective workday

familia: (regional Spanish) patrilineage within an ayllu

fundo: earmarked fund or endowment

ganancia: earnings an ayllu receives for selling its collective service

Gobernación: office representing the national state at local level

gobernador: salaried officer of the Gobernación

guayllabana: (Hispano-Quechua) fresh bunch of grass from high puna (synonyms: *catahua, uyhuán*)

hilo: pendant, thread

hito: marker

hora de costumbre: ceremonial break in work or meeting

huaca: (Hispano-Quechua) (modern) prehistoric burial; (colonial) Andean deity

huacsa: (Quechua [?] non-Quechua vernacular?) in 1608 (?) manuscript, a member of the corps of lesser priests or rotating impersonators of huacas

Huaranga de Checa: (Hispano-Quechua) Inka-era "thousand" comprising Tupicocha and adjacent settlements

huari: (Hispano-Quechua) ritual intercessor with the deified "owners"

huayra huayra pichamanta (see *pichcamanta*)

huayrona: (Hispano-Quechua) town meeting or civic plenum

junta directiva: board of officers

khipu: (Quechua) Andean data-recording device made of knottable cord

khipukamayuq: (Quechua) khipu master

lexigraphy: system of visible signs corresponding to segments of speech (after Powell 2002:64)

limanda: (regional Spanish) portable sacred object loaned in token of a pledge

llancha: (Hispano-Quechua or non-Quechua indigenous language [?]) division of a planted terrace or field

mayor: (1) elder or semiretired (synonym: *pasivo*); (2) in former ayllu governance, officer having complementary status to camachico

mita: (Hispano-Quechua) turn, especially of service or irrigation

mota: marker

moya: (Hispano-Quechua [?]) pasture lot, especially walled

municipio: municipality

número de orden: seniority rank number

óbulo: (regional Spanish) donation in the form of a promise

oncenio: the 1919–30 presidency of Augusto Leguía

oque: (Hispano-Quechua) gray, especially with bluish or silvery tones

pachacamanta: (Hispano-Quechua [?]) knob at one end of quipocamayo

pachaka: (Quechua) hundred

padroncillo: chart or table

pallari, pallarado: mottled, speckled

panaka: (Quechua); synonym: panaca (Hispano-Quechua) royal commemorative corporation, composed of a deceased Inka's descendants

parcialidad: (regional Spanish) ayllu, considered as sector of comunidad

pasivo: semiretired or elder member

peaña: (regional Spanish) step-pyramid, usually as base for cross, marking a ceremonial locus (standard Spanish, *peana*)

pichcamanta: (Hispano-Quechua) ceremonial game played as New Year augury

porrata: (regional Spanish) quota for a collective work

principal: in former governance, one of two complementary villagewide officers

próximo: probationary member

puna: (Hispano-Quechua) high-Andean tundra

quipocamayo: (Hispano-Quechua) patrimonial khipu

raya: stripe, bar

ricuchico: (Hispano-Quechua) ceremony at which religious pledges are made and redeemed

rusqui: (Hispano-Quechua) neutral grayish to brownish mid-tones

semasiography: system of visible signs corresponding to culturally recognized entities

socio: member (of ayllu or comunidad); business partner

trecho: (regional Spanish) assigned stretch of work (synonym: tupu, tramo)

tronco: main cord of quipocamayo

tupu: (Hispano-Quechua) (see *trecho*)

vara: (regional Spanish) staff of office

varayo: (Hispano-Quechua) staff-holding officer

visita: inspection for establishment of tribute quota

voluntad: (regional Spanish) goodwill; generalized reciprocity

yanca: (Quechua [?]) in 1608 (?) Manuscript, a member of the corps of greater or hereditary priests of huacas

yumay: (Quechua) patrilineage

yunca, yunga: (Hispano-Quechua) subtropical lower valley and coast, or inhabitants of same

REFERENCES

Notes: These references are divided into two parts: archival references and other references.
Square brackets [ ] indicate titles supplied for documents not bearing original titles.
Ayllu/parcialidad documents are frequently written in nonstandard Spanish. Original spelling is pre-
served.

Archival References

ARCHIVE ABBREVIATIONS (NAME/LOCATION)
In citations of bound manuscripts, the underscore between archive abbreviation and number indicates
number in a series, whether that series is of volumes, folders, or other physical types.

AA/L — Archivo Arzobispal / Lima

ACCSAT/SAT — Archivo de la Comunidad Campesina de San Andrés de Tupicocha / San Andrés de
Tupicocha

AGN/BA — Archivo General de la Nación / Buenos Aires

AGN/L — Archivo General de la Nación / Lima

AMAG-UADLC/L — Archivo del Ministerio de Agricultura y Ganadería–Unidad Agraria de los Depar-
tamentos de Lima y Callao / Lima

AP1A/SAT — Archivo de la Parcialidad Primera Allauca / San Andrés de Tupicocha

AP1G/SAT — Archivo de la Parcialidad Primer Guangre / San Andrés de Tupicocha

AP1SF/SAT — Archivo de la Parcialidad Primera Satafasca / San Andrés de Tupicocha

AP2A/SAT — Archivo de la Parcialidad Segunda Allauca / San Andrés de Tupicocha

AP2SF/SAT — Archivo de la Parcialidad Segunda Satafasca / San Andrés de Tupicocha

APC/SAT — Archivo de la Parcialidad Cacarima / San Andrés de Tupicocha

APM/SAT — Archivo de la Parcialidad Mújica / San Andrés de Tupicocha

APUCH/SAT — Archivo de la Parcialidad Unión Chaucacolca / San Andrés de Tupicocha

BN/M — Biblioteca Nacional / Madrid

MM/BA — Museo Mitre / Buenos Aires

AA/L Capítulos. 1607-9. Leg. 1, Exp. 9. Proceso remitido por el señor dean y provisor al doctor padilla vicario general de capitulos contra el doctor francisco de avila cura y beneficiado de el [sic] doctrina de san damián y sus anejos.

———. 1623. Leg. 4, Exp. 3. Causa de capítulos seguidos por los caciques Diego Lliuyac Mateo Cajauaman, Diego Curamachauai, y Miguel Chinchaipuma, contra el bachiller Andres de Mujica, sobre agravios.

———. 1705-19. Leg. 27, Exp. 8. Causa de Capítulos seguida por los caciques principales de las doctrinas de Pampas, Cochas, Cañete, San Damián, Conchucos, Atabillos, Chincha, Cotaparaco, Canta, Chancay, Sobre los agravios que cometen los curas en la administración de los Sacramentos, llevándoles crecidos derechos parroquiales. Ambrosio de Medina, notario.

AAL/L Visitas Pastorales. 1760. Leg. 10, Exp. 35. Autos de los inventarios de sus iglesias [i.e., de Huarochirí], padrón de sus feligreses.

ACCSAT/SAT_Folder 7. 1748. Folder 7 Testemonio [sic] de la Huaranga de Checa San Damian.

ACCSAT/SAT Folder "Irrigación." 1893. Irrigación. F. 1r.

ACCSAT/SAT_01. 1904. Libro de actas terminados Desojado del año 1904.

ACCSAT/SAT_02. 1901. [Inventario de bienes de la iglesia, s.f. 1901.] Vienes de Iglesia. [1900-39].

ACCSAT/SAT_04. 1864. Libro de actas de San Andres Terminado a 1864.

ACCSAT/SAT_05. 1897a. Cargo de Guardar todos los materiales . . . del techo. Libro de actas Terminado 1892 [1892-1917]. Fos. 45-46.

———. 1897b. Libro de actas Terminado 1892 [sic; includes 1892-1917]. Acta de inventario. 25.

ACCSAT/SAT_06. Libro de actas Terminado 1858.

ACCSAT/SAT_18. 1891. [Acta de sesión.] Libro 18. Actas de 196 [sic] folios año 1891 [sic: i.e., series beginning 1891.] 10-11.

AGN/BA. 1588. Padrones de La Paz. 13-17-5-1. Revisita de Sisicaya.

———. 1588-90. 9-45-5-15. Pleito segundo entre Antonio Guamanyanac y Geronimo Caxayauri. 1588.

AGN/L. 1799. Derecho Indígena, Legajo 29, Cuaderno 556. Autos que promovió Gregorio Medina Sánchez, indio tributario del pueblo de San Andrés de Tupicocha, . . . contra Hilario Rivero y Martín Francisco Pozo . . . [sobre] la huerta de Acochu-Guaylas . . .

———. 1866. Tierras y Haciendas Legajo 7, Cuaderno 53. Autos seguidos por la parcialidad de Cupara con la de Hualcaraya (Huarochirí) sobre el derecho a unos terrenos de sembrar y pastos.

AMAG-UADLC/L. 1933-35. Legajo 1816. Solicitud de Reconocimiento de Tupicocha 1933-35.

AP1A/SAT_01. 1948. Acta de Organización de la Nueva Reforma de la Primera Parcialidad de Allauca [15 julio]. [Libro sin número, no. 1.] Ingresos Anterior Del Año 1960 [1948-60]. 1-15.

———. 1955. [Acta de sesión sobre trabajo del cementerio público, 17 septiembre.] [Libro sin número, no. 1.] Ingresos Anterior Del Año 1960. 18-20.

———. 1958. [Acta de inventario, 3 enero 1958.] [Libro sin número, no. 1.] Ingresos Anterior Del Año 1960. 23.

———. 1959a. [Acta de inventario, 3 enero 1959.] [Libro sin número, no. 1.] Ingresos Anterior Del Año 1960. 29.

———. 1959b. Formulario para rellenar el Censo [i.e., Censo Agropecuario Nacional] de. [sic] La Parcialidad Allauca en de 1º [sic] el año MCMLIX. Ingresos Anterior Del Año 1960. 36-37.

AP1G/SAT_01. 1930. [Acta de instalar] nuevo acuerdo vajo [sic] un reglamento [7 abril 1930]. [Libro sin título, no. 1, de actas y otros documentos de la Parcialidad Guangre, posteriormente Primer Guangre, 1913-73.] 1-6.

———. 1933. [Acta de sesión, 3 enero 1933, sobre] grave situación que se atrabiesa [sic]. . . . [Libro sin título, no. 1, de actas y otros documentos de la Parcialidad Guangre, posteriormente Primer Guangre, 1913-73.] 23.

———. 1939a . [Acta de sesión, 18 abril 1939.] [Libro sin título, no. 1, de actas y otros documentos de la Parcialidad Guangre, posteriormente Primer Guangre, 1913-73]. 81.

———. 1939b. [Acta de nombramiento de dirigentes, 2 enero.] [Libro sin título, no. 1, de actas y otros documentos de la Parcialidad Guangre, posteriormente Primer Guangre, 1913–73.] 71.

AP1SF/SAT_01. 1913. Acta Extrajudicial [i.e., estatuto orgánico reformado de Satafasca indivisa, 3 enero 1913]. [Libro sin título: Actas de Primera Satafasca, 1913–45.] 1–3.

———. 1914. [Acta de traspaso de bienes, 3 enero 1914] [1922]. [Libro sin título: Actas de Primera Satafasca, 1913–45.] 5.

———. 1915. [Acta de traspaso de bienes, 3 enero 1915.] [Libro sin título: Actas de Primera Satafasca, 1913–45.] 7.

———. 1916a. [Acta de traspaso de bienes, 3 enero 1916.] [Libro sin título: Actas de Primera Satafasca, 1913–45.] 9.

———. 1916b. [Acta de] trabajos asta los sais mes de junio trenta [sic] . . . [16 (?) February 1916] [Libro sin título: Actas de Primera Satafasca, 1913–45.] 11.

———. 1918a. [Acta de traspaso de bienes, 3 enero 1918.] [Libro sin título: Actas de Primera Satafasca, 1913–45.] 17.

———. 1918b. [Acta sobre ayuda mutua al techar, 13 enero 1918.][Libro sin título: Actas de Primera Satafasca, 1913–45.] 19.

———. 1919a. [Acta de elección y nombramiento de dirigentes, 2 enero 1919.] [Libro sin título: Actas de Primera Satafasca, 1913–45.] 23.

———. 1919b. [Acta de traspaso de bienes, 3 enero 1919] [Libro sin título: Actas de Primera Satafasca, 1913–45.] 24.

———. 1921. [Acta de traspaso de bienes, 3 enero 1921.] [Libro sin título: Actas de Primera Satafasca, 1913–45.] 30.

———. 1922. [Acta de traspaso de bienes, 3 enero 1922.] [Libro sin título: Actas de Primera Satafasca, 1913–45.] 35.

———. 1923a. [Acta de traspaso de bienes, 3 enero 1923.] [Libro sin título: Actas de Primera Satafasca, 1913–45.] 38.

———. 1923b. [Acta de traspaso de bienes, debido a la muerte del camachico, 4 febrero 1923.] [Libro sin título: Actas de Primera Satafasca, 1913–45.] 40.

———. 1924. [Acta de traspaso de bienes, 3 enero 1924.] [Libro sin título: Actas de Primera Satafasca, 1913–45.] 43.

———. 1926. [Acta de traspaso de bienes, 3 enero 1926.] [Libro sin título: Actas de Primera Satafasca, 1913–45.] 48.

———. 1938. [Acta para que el camachico o presidente fomente el estudio de la] artezanía [y que] siempre sigan esta profecion de oficios profecionales. [Libro sin título: Actas de Satafasca (indivisa) 1913–45 (as Primera Satafasca).] [Libro 2.] 100–101.

AP1SF/SAT_07. 1948–84. [Libro de actas de Lanzasa, 1948–84.]

AP2A/SAT_01. 1932. Lista [de los] . . . que faltaron [en faena de 12 abril 1932]. [Libro sin título de multas y listas.] 113.

AP2A/SAT_02. 1923. [Acta de una faena llevada por D. Marcos Vilcayauri, 10 octubre 1923.] [Libro sin título, no. 2, de multas y listas de Segunda Allauca 1923–32.] 12.

———. 1932. Padroncillo General, de los ciudadanos, del 1º ayllo de Allauca. . . . 3 de Enero, año 1932. [Libro sin título, no. 2, de multas y listas de Segunda Allauca 1923–32.] 28–29.

AP2SF/SAT_01 1921 [–1946]. 1921. [Acuerdo para arar] un tireno [sic] . . . en el lugar de Chamacha. N.d., 1921. Libro [no. 1] y Reglamento de la Parcialidad de Satafasca hecho en el año de 1921 [–1946]. 15.

———. 1928. [Sesión de orden, 6 marzo 1928.] Libro [no. 1] y Reglamento de la Parcialidad de Satafasca hecho en el año de 1921 [–1946]. 48–49.

AP2SF/SAT_02 1927–53. 1929. [Acta de cuentas residenciales, 4 julio 1929.] [Libro sin título de actas de Segunda Satafasca 1927–53.] 20–21.

———. 1945. [Acta de cuentas residenciales, 8 julio 1945.] [Libro sin título de actas de Segunda Satafasca 1927–53.] 89.

APC/SAT_01. 1905. [Estatuto orgánico, 6 mayo 1905.] Libro No. 1 del Año 1905 Perteneciente A la Parcialidad de Cacarima del Año 1905 Al 1989. 1–4.

———. 1912. [Acuerdo para enviar diputación a comprar barretas y lampas en Lima y entregarlos el 5 de julio; 8 mayo 1912.] Libro No. 1 del Año 1905 Perteneciente A la Parcialidad de Cacarima del Año 1905 Al 1989. 29.

———. 1914. [Auto para distribuir] a todos los hermandados . . . la herramienta de una lampa a cada uno sin dejar nadies sin parte. [3 enero 1914.] Libro No. 1 del Año 1905 Perteneciente A la Parcialidad de Cacarima del Año 1905 Al 1989. 35.

———. 1919. [Auto de una sesión para fijar régimen de faenas, enero 1919 sin día apuntada.] Libro No. 1 del Año 1905 Perteneciente A la Parcialidad de Cacarima del Año 1905 Al 1989. 59.

———. 1923. [Escritura de arriendo de] nuestro terreno conocido con en [sic] el lugar "Mayani" [4 febrero 1923]. Libro No. 1 del Año 1905 Perteneciente A la Parcialidad de Cacarima del Año 1905 Al 1989. 85.

———. 1925. [Acta de elección y nombramiento de dirigentes, 10 enero 1925.] Libro No. 1 del Año 1905 Perteneciente A la Parcialidad de Cacarima del Año 1905 Al 1989. 98.

———. 1933. Sesion extraordinaria . . . para tratar con respecto a la disposicion del trabajo de ésta obra [del reservorio de Cosanche] [14 julio 1933]. Libro No. 1 del Año 1905 Perteneciente A la Parcialidad de Cacarima del Año 1905 Al 1989. 158–59.

APC/SAT_02. 1954. [Acta de distribución de vajilla, 24 enero 1954.] Libro No. 2 del Año 1940 de Actas y Otras Actuaciones de la Parcialidad de Cacarima 1940 al 1955. 170.

APM/SAT_01. 1889. [Acta de cuentas de medio año y traspaso de fondos, 19 junio 1889.] [Libro primero de la Parcialidad de Mújica, 1875(?)–1918.] F. non num. 2v.

———. 1897. [Acta de inventario sin fecha.] [Libro primero de la Parcialidad de Mújica, 1875(?)–1918.] [F. non num. 3v.]

———. 1900. Para efecto de Aser un Acuerdo y Recuerdo de la moya del Lugar de tampocaya . . . [Libro primero de la Parcialidad de Mújica, 1875(?)–1918.][F. 16v.]

———. 1906a. [Vale de Silvestre Antiporta, 13 enero 1906, por] una carga de semilla de papas . . . saco del camachico. [Libro primero de la Parcialidad de Mújica, 1875(?)–1918.] [F. 27r.]

———. 1906b. [Acuerdo] que Don Niculas Antiporta deve un camachico como cargo en esta parcialidad de mujica . . . 2 enero 1906.] [Libro primero de la Parcialidad de Mújica, 1875(?)–1918.] F. 30r.

———. 1912. [Gasto. Entrega de 15 soles al camachico para comprar mortaja. . . .] [Libro primero de la Parcialidad de Mújica, 1875(?)–1918.] F. 39v.

———. 1914. [Relación de socios que cumplen la mita de mensajero, c. 1914] [Libro primero de la Parcialidad de Mújica, 1875(?)–1918.] F. 56v.

APM/SAT_02. 1913. REGLAMENTO [sic] De la Parcialidad de Mujica de Tupicocha. Libro de la parcialidad de mojica Reformado un reglamento en el año 1913 [1913–35]. 1–8.

APM/SAT_03. 1958. [Acta de inventario, 3 enero 1958.] [Libro No. 3, de actas de la parcialidad de Mújica, 1947–63.] 53.

———. 1959. Acta de Sedición deluminado de "Hueccho" . . . cuyo fin de hacer una reparticion de los terrenos deluminado "Hueccho," 9 agosto 1959. [Libro No. 3, de actas de la parcialidad de Mújica, 1947–63.] 72–74.

———. 1960. [Sesión. Acuerdo] sobre itos [i.e., hitos] limítrofes convenientes a esta comonidad [6 enero 1960]. [Libro No. 3, de actas de la parcialidad de Mújica, 1947–63.] 92–93.

APUCH/SAT_03. 1940. [Acta escrita en Chupaya, sobre vigencia de los derechos Checas, mayo 1940.] Libro [No. 3] de actas de instalación 1936–52. 125–27.

———. 1945. [Acta de inventario y traspaso de enseres, 3 enero 1945.] Libro [No. 3] de actas de instalación 1936–52. 226.

———. 1951. [Acta para repartir entre los socios] dos docenas de platos [compradas en Lima por el tesorero a pedida de la parcialidad] Libro [No. 3] de actas de instalación 1936–52. 381–82.

BN/M. 1589a. Manuscrito 5938 fos. 433–35. Sobre la escritura de los indios del Perú por el Doctor Murillo de la Cerda.

———. 1589b. Ms 12965 no. 9. Carta de Francisco López al [Virrey] Conde del Villar acerca de los indios que fabricaban pólvora en el pueblo de Santa Inés [de Chíchima] del Perú. Lima.

MM/BA. 1761. Diario histórico del lebantamiento de la provincia de Huarochirí, y su pacificación. Escrito por Don Sebastián Fran.co [i.e., Francisco?] de Melo. . . .

Book and Article References

Abercrombie, Thomas A. 1998. *Pathways of Memory and Power: Ethnography and History among an Andean People.* Madison: University of Wisconsin Press.

Acosta, José de. 1954. *Historia natural y moral de las indias* [1590]. In *Obras del P. José de Acosta.* P. Francisco Mateos, ed. 73:3–247. Madrid: Ediziones Atlas.

Acosta Rodríguez, Antonio. 1979. El pleito de los indios de San Damián, Huarochirí, contra Francisco de Avila, 1607. 23:3–33. *Historiografía y Bibliografía Americanistas.*

———. 1987. Francisco de Avila Cusco 1573(?)–Lima 1647. In *Ritos y tradiciones de Huarochirí del Siglo XVII.* Gerald Taylor, ed. and trans. Historia Andina, no. 12:551–616. Lima: Instituto de Estudios Peruanos.

Adorno, Rolena. 1999. Criterios de comprobación: Un misterioso manuscrito de Nápoles y las crónicas de la conquista del Perú. In *Edición y anotación de textos coloniales hispanoamericanos.* I. Arellano y J. A. Rodríguez Garrido, eds. 15–44. Navarra, Spain: Universidad de Navarra.

Allen, Catherine. 1982. Body and Soul in Quechua Thought. *Journal of Latin American Lore* 8 (2):179–96.

Amiet, Pierre. 1982. Comptabilité et écriture archaïque à Suse et en Mésopotamie. In *Écritures: Systèmes idéographiques et pratiques expressives.* Anne-Marie Christin, ed. 1: 39–45. Paris: Le Sycomore, Actes du colloque international de l'Université Paris, 7, 22–24 avril 1980.

Animato, Carlo, Paolo A. Rossi, and Clara Miccinelli. 1989. *Quipu: Il nodo parlante dei misteriosi Incas.* Genova: Edizioni Culturali Internazionali.

Anonymous. 1916. Idolatrías de los indios huachos y yauyos [1613?]. *Revista Histórica* 6:180–97. Lima.

Anonymous. 1968 [1594]. *Relación de las costumbres antiguas de los naturales del Perú.* In *Crónicas peruanas de interés indígena.* Francisco Esteve Barba, ed. 209:153–89. Madrid: Ediciones Atlas Biblioteca de Autores Españoles.

Anonymous. 1997. *Oráculo o el libro de los destinos el cual fue propiedad exclusiva del emperador Napoleón, traducida por primera vez al castellano de la vigésima segunda edición inglesa habiéndolo sido antes al alemán de un antiguo manuscrito egipcio encontrado en el año de 1864 por M. Sonnini, en una de las reales tumbas del Alto Egipto, cerca del Monte Líbano.* Lima: Empresa Editora Litográfica "La Confianza" S.A.

Arellano, Carmen. 1999. Quipu y tocapu: Sistemas de comunicación inca. In *Los Incas: Arte y símbolos.* Franklin Pease et al., eds. 214–61. Lima: Banco de Crédito del Perú, Colección Arte y Tesoros del Perú.

Arguedas, José María. 1956. Puquio, una cultura en proceso de cambio. *Revista del Museo Nacional* (Lima) 25:184–232.

Arguedas, José María, trans., and Pierre Duviols, ed. 1966. *Dioses y hombres de Huarochirí.* Lima: Instituto de Estudios Peruanos.

Arnold, Denise. 1997. Making Men in Her Own Image: Gender, Text, and Textile in Qaqachaka. In *Creating Context in Andean Cultures.* Rosaleen Howard-Malverde, ed. 99–131. New York: Oxford University Press.

Arnold, Denise Y., and Juan de Dios Yapita. 2000. *El rincón de las cabezas: Luchas textuales, educación y tierras en los Andes.* La Paz: Facultad de Humanidades y Ciencias de la Educación. .

Ascher, Marcia, and Robert Ascher. 1978. *Code of the Quipu Databook.* Ann Arbor: University Microfilms.

——. 1988. *Code of the Quipu Databook II.* Ann Arbor: University Microfilms.

——. 1997 [1981]. *Code of the Quipu: A Study of Media, Mathematics, and Culture.* New York: Dover Publications.

Ashley, Clifford W. 1944. *The Ashley Book of Knots.* New York: Doubleday.

Astete Flores, Guillermo. 1997(?). Anotaciones sobre los Checa del Alto Pachacámac. Tesis de Licenciatura, Departamento de Antropología, Pontificia Universidad Católica del Perú.

Bandelier, Adolph F. 1910. *The Islands of Titicaca and Koati.* New York: Hispanic Society of America. Facs. repr. New York: Kraus Reprint, 1969.

Basso, Keith. 1974. The Ethnography of Writing. In *Explorations in the Ethnography of Speaking.* Richard Bauman and Joel Sherzer, eds. 425–32. Cambridge: Cambridge University Press.

Bastian, Adolph. 1895. Aus Briefen herrn Dr. Uhles. *Ethnologisches Notizblatt* (Berlin) 1:80–83.

Bauer, Brian S., and David S. P. Dearborn. 1995. *Astronomy and Empire in the Ancient Andes.* Austin: University of Texas Press.

Belleza Castro, Neli. 1995. *Vocabulario jacaru-castellano castellano-jacaru (Aimara tupino).* Cusco: Centro de Estudios Regionales Andinos Bartolomé de Las Casas.

Benveniste, Émile. 1985. The Semiology of Language [1969]. In *Semiotics: An Introductory Anthology.* Robert E. Innis, ed. 225–46. Bloomington: Indiana University Press.

Betanzos, Juan de. 1987 [1551]. *Suma y narración de los Incas.* María del Carmen Rubio, ed. Madrid: Ediciones Atlas.

Birket-Smith, Kaj. 1966–67. The Circumpacific Distribution of Knot Records. *Folk* (Copenhagen) 8/9:15–21.

Boltz, William G. 1994. *The Origin and Early Development of the Chinese Writing System.* New Haven: American Oriental Society. (American Oriental Series, Vol. 78).

Boone, Elizabeth Hill. 1994. Introduction: Writing and Recording Knowledge. In *Writing without Words: Alternative Literacies in Mesoamerica and the Andes.* Elizabeth Hill Boone and Walter D. Mignolo, eds. 3–26. Durham, N.C.: Duke University Press.

Boone, Elizabeth Hill, and Walter D. Mignolo, eds. 1994. *Writing without Words: Alternative Literacies in Mesoamerica and the Andes.* Elizabeth Hill Boone and Walter D. Mignolo, eds. Durham, N.C.: Duke University Press.

Brice, W. C. 1976. The Principles of Non-phonetic Writing. In *Writing without Letters.* W. Haas, ed. 30–44. Manchester: Manchester University Press.

Brotherston, Gordon. 1979. *Image of the New World: The American Continent Portrayed in Native Texts.* London: Thames and Hudson.

Bruhns, Karen Olson. 1994. *Ancient South America.* New York: Cambridge University Press.

Brush, Stephen B. 1977. *Mountain, Field, and Family: The Economy and Human Ecology of an Andean Valley.* Philadelphia: University of Pennsylvania Press.

Bryce Echenique, Alfredo. 1984. *Un mundo para Julius.* Bogotá: Ediciones Oveja Negra.

Bueno, Alberto. 1990. Hallazgo de kipu en Pachacamác. In *Quipu y yupana: Colección de escritos.* Carol Mackey, Hugo Pereyra et al., eds. 97–104. Lima: Consejo Nacional de Ciencia y Tecnología.

Burga, Manuel. 1988. *Nacimiento de una utopía: Muerte y resurrección de los incas.* Lima: Instituto de Apoyo Agrario.

Burger, Richard L. 1992. *Chavín and the Origins of Andean Civilization.* New York: Thames and Hudson.

Calancha, Antonio de la. 1974 [1638]. *Corónica moralizada del orden de San Agustín en el Perú con sucesos ejemplares en esta monarquía.* Ignacio Prado Pastor, ed. Lima: Universidad Nacional Mayor de San Marcos.

Castelli, Amalia. 1978. Tunupa: Divinidad del altiplano. In *Etnohistoria y antropología andina: Primera jornada del Museo Nacional de Historia.* Marcia Koth de Paredes, ed. 201–4. Lima: Museo Nacional de Historia.

———, Marcia Koth de Paredes, and Mariana Mould de Pease, eds. 1981. *Etnohistoria y antropología andina: Segunda jornada del Museo Nacional de Historia. [número especial sobre] Ayllu, parcialidad y etnia*. Lima: Museo Nacional de Historia.

Cereceda, Verónica. 1986. The Semiology of Andean Textiles: The Talegas of Isluga. In *Anthropological History of Andean Polities*. John V. Murra, Nathan Wachtel, and Jacques Revel, eds. 149–73. New York: Cambridge University Press.

Cieza de León, Pedro de. 1985 [1553]. El señorío de los incas. Manuel Ballesteros, ed. Madrid: Historia 16.

Classen, Constance. 1991. Literacy as anticulture: The Andean experience of the written word. *History of Religions* 30 (4):404–21.

Cobo, Bernabe. 1964 [1653]. Historia del Nuevo Mundo. In *Obras de P. Bernabé Cobo*. P. Francisco Mateos, ed. Biblioteca de Autores Españoles, 92. Vol. 1:3–427, Vol. 2:7–476. Madrid: Ediciones Atlas.

Coe, Michael. 1992. *Breaking the Maya Code*. New York: Thames and Hudson.

Collapiña, Supño et al. 1974. *Relación de la descendencia, gobierno y conquista de los Incas [1542/1608]*. Lima: Universidad Nacional Mayor de San Marcos.

Conklin, William J. 1982. The Information System of the Middle Horizon Quipus. *Annals of the New York Academy of Sciences* (New York: New York Academy of Sciences) 385:261–81.

———. 2002. A *Khipu* Information String Theory. In *Narrative Threads: Accounting and Recounting in Andean Khipu*. Jeffrey Quilter and Gary Urton, eds. 53–86. Austin: University of Texas Press.

Córdova y Urrutia, José María. 1992 [1839]. *Estadística histórica, geográfica, industrial y comercial de los pueblos que componen las provincias del Departamento de Lima*. Foreword by Rosa Larco de Miró-Quesada; edited with prologue and indexes by César Coloma Porcari. Lima: Sociedad "Entre Nous."

Costales de Oviedo, Ximena. 1983. *Etnohistoria del corregimiento de Chimbo 1557–1820*. Quito: Mundo Andino.

Coulmas, Florian. 1989. *The Writing Systems of the World*. Oxford: Blackwell.

Cunow, Heinrich. 1929 [1890–91]. *El sistema de parentesco peruano y las comunidades gentilicias de los incas*. María Woitscheck, trans. Paris: Imprenta de "Le Livre Libre."

Cusihuamán G., Antonio. 1976. *Diccionario quechua cuzco-collao*. Lima: Ministerio de Educación.

Damerow, Peter. 1999. The Origins of Writing as a Problem of Historical Epistomology. Berlin: Max Planck-Institut für Wissenschaftsgeschichte. Preprint 114.

Daniels, Peter T. 1996a. The Invention of Writing. In *The World's Writing Systems*. Peter T. Daniels and William Bright, eds. 579–86. New York: Oxford University Press.

———. 1996b. The Study of Writing Systems. In *The World's Writing Systems*. Peter T. Daniels and William Bright, eds. 3–20. New York: Oxford University Press.

Dávila Brizeño, Diego. 1965 [1583]. Descripción y relación de la Provincia de los Yauyos. In *Relaciones geográficas de Indias*. Marcos Jiménez de la Espada, ed. Vol. 1:155–65. Biblioteca de Autores Españoles 183. Madrid: Ediciones Atlas.

Day, Cyrus Lawrence. 1967. *Quipus and Witches' Knots: The Role of the Knot in Primitive and Ancient Cultures*. Lawrence: University of Kansas Press.

DeFrancis, John. 1989. *Visible Speech: The Diverse Oneness of Writing Systems*. Honolulu: University of Hawaii Press.

De la Cadena, Marisol. 2000. *Indigenous Mestizos: The Politics of Race and Culture in Cuzco, Peru, 1919–91*. Durham, N.C.: Duke University Press.

Del Río, Mercedes. 1990. Simbolismo y poder en Tapacarí. *Revista Andina* 8 (1):77–113.

Derrida, Jacques. 1974 [1967]. *Of Grammatology*. Gayatri Chakravorty Spivak, trans. Baltimore: Johns Hopkins University Press.

Díaz Pinto, Leopoldo. 1935. *Apuntes monográficos del Distrito de Matucana, Provincia de Huarochirí*. Lima?: N.p.

Dorian, Nancy C. 1981. *Language Death: The Life Cycle of a Scottish Gaelic Dialect*. Philadelphia: University of Pennsylvania Press.

Doyle, Mary Eileen. 1988. The Ancestor Cult and Burial Ritual in Seventeenth and Eighteenth Century Central Peru. PhD diss., Department of History, University of California, Los Angeles.

Duviols, Pierre. 1972. *La Lutte contre les religions autocthones dans le Pérou colonial.* Lima: Instituto Francés de Estudios Andinos.

———. 1973. Huari y Llacuaz: Agricultores y pastores, un dualismo prehispánico de oposición y complementariedad. *Revista del Museo Nacional* (Lima) 39:153–91.

———. 1979. La dinastía de los incas: ¿Monarquía o diarquía? Argumentos heurísticos a favor de una tesis estructuralista. *Journal de la Société des Américanistes* 66:67–83.

———, ed. 1986. Cultura andina y represión: Procesos y visitas de idolatrías y hechicerías. Cajatambo, Siglo XVII. *Archivos de Historia Andina* 5. Cusco: Centro de Estudios Rurales Andinos "Bartolomé de Las Casas."

Echeandía Valladares, J. M. 1981. *Tecnología y cambios en la comunidad de San Pedro de Casta.* Lima: Seminario de Historia Rural Andina, Universidad Nacional Mayor de San Marcos.

Ehlich, Konrad. 1983. Development of Writing as Social Problem Solving. In *Writing in Focus.* Florian Coulmas and Konrad Ehlich, eds. 99–129. Berlin: Mouton.

Elkins, James. 1996. On the Impossibility of Close Reading: The Case of Alexander Marshack. *Current Anthropology* 37 (2):185–226.

Englund, Robert K. 1996. The Proto-Elamite Script. In *The World's Writing Systems.* Peter T. Daniels and William Bright, eds. 160–64. New York: Oxford University Press.

Espinoza Soriano, Waldemar. 1960. El alcalde mayor indígena en el virreinato del Perú. *Anuario de Estudios Americanos* 17:183–300.

———. 1983–84. Los señoríos de Yaucha y Picoy en el abra del medio y alto Rímac (Siglos XV y XVI). *Revista Histórica* 34:157–279. Lima: Academia Nacional de la Historia.

———. 1992. Huarochirí y el estado inca. In *Huarochirí: Ocho mil años de historia.* Vladimiro Thatar Alvarez et al., eds. Vol. 1:115–94. Santa Eulalia de Acopaya, Provincia Huarochirí, Peru: Municipalidad de Santa Eulalia de Acopaya.

Estenssoro, Juan Carlos. 1997. ¿Historia de un fraude o fraude histórico? *Revista de Indias* 57 (210): 566–78.

Fane, Diana, et al. 1996. *Converging Cultures: Art and Identity in Spanish America.* Diana Fane, ed. New York: Harry N. Abrams.

Farr, Cheryl Ann. 1994. Metallic Yarns: A Technological and Cultural Perspective for the Development of a Morphological Classification System. *Ars Textrina* 22:65–86.

Feltham, J. 1984. The Lurín Valley Project: Some Results for the Latin Intermediate and Late Horizon. In *Current Archaeological Projects in the Central Andes: Some Approaches and Results.* 45–73. British Archaeological Reports International Series, 210. Oxford: B.A.R.

Flores Galindo, Alberto. 1987. *Buscando un inca: Identidad y utopía en los Andes.* Lima, Perú: Instituto de Apoyo Agrario.

Fonseca, César. 1983. Control Comunal del agua en la cuenca del Río Cañete. *Allpanchis* 19 (22):61–74.

Fossa, Lydia. 2000. Two Khipu, One Narrative: Answering Urton's Questions. *Ethnohistory* 47 (2):453–68.

Fuenzalida Vollmar, Fernando. 1979. Los gentiles y el origen de la muerte. *Revista de la Universidad Católica* (Lima) 5:213–22.

Gandz, Solomon. 1931. The Knot in Hebrew Literature, or, from the Knot to the Alphabet. *Isis* 14 (43):189–214.

García Cabrera, Juan Carlos, ed. 1994. *Ofensas a Dios, pleitos e injurias: Causas de idolatrías y hechicerías, Cajatambo, Siglos XVII–XIX.* Cuzco: Centro de Estudios Regionales Andinos "Bartolomé de Las Casas."

Garcilaso Inca de la Vega. 1966 [1609]. *The Royal Commentaries of the Incas.* Harold Livermore, trans. 2 vols. Austin: University of Texas Press.

———. 1991 [1609]. *Comentarios Reales de los Incas*. Carlos Araníbar, ed. 2 tomos. Mexico City: Fondo de Cultura Económica.

Gartner, William Gustav. 1999. Mapmaking in the Central Andes. In *The History of Cartography*. Vol. 2.3. Cartography in Traditional African, American, Australian, and Pacific Island Societies. David A. Woodward and Malcolm Lewis, eds. 257–300. New York: Cambridge University Press.

Gaur, Albertine. 1984. *A History of Writing*. London: British Library.

Gelb, Ignace J. 1952. *A Study of Writing: The Foundations of Grammatology*. London: Routledge.

Gelles, Paul H. 1984. Agua, faenas y organización comunal en los Andes: El caso de San Pedro de Casta. Master's thesis, Departamento de Antropología, Pontificia Universidad Católica del Perú.

———. 2000. *Water and Power in Highland Peru: The Cultural Politics of Irrigation and Development*. New Brunswick, N.J.: Rutgers University Press.

Gellner, Ernest. 1988. *Plough, Sword, and Book: The Structure of Human History*. London: Collins Harvill.

Gentile Lafaille, Margarita. 1998. La *pichca*: Oráculo y juego de fortuna (su persistencia en el espacio y tiempo andinos). *Bulletin de l'Institut Français d'Études Andines* 27(1):75–131.

Gilmer, Nancy C. 1952. Huarochirí in the Seventeenth Century: The Persistence of Native Religion in Colonial Peru. Master's thesis, Department of Anthropology, University of California, Berkeley.

Girault, Louis. 1984. *Kallawaya: Guérisseurs itinérants des Andes. Recherches sur les pratiques médicinales et magiques*. Collection Mémoires no. 107. Paris: Éditions de l'ORSTOM.

Gisbert, Teresa, and José de Mesa. 1966. Los chipayas. *Anuario de Estudios Americanos* 23:479–506.

Golte, Jürgen. 1980. *La racionalidad de la organización andina*. Lima: Instituto de Estudios Peruanos.

Goodman, Nelson. 1976 [1968]. *Languages of Art: An Approach to a Theory of Symbols*. 2nd ed. Indianapolis: Hackett Publishing.

Goody, Jack. 1986. *The Logic of Writing and the Organization of Society*. Cambridge: Cambridge University Press.

———. 2000. *The Power of the Written Tradition*. Washington: Smithsonian Institution Press.

Gordon, Cyrus H. 1982. *Forgotten Scripts: Their Ongoing Discovery and Decipherment*. Rev. ed. New York: Basic Books, 1982.

Gose, Peter. 1994. *Deathly Waters and Hungry Mountains: Agrarian Ritual and Class Formation in an Andean Town*. Toronto: University of Toronto Press.

———. 1996. Oracles, Divine Kingship, and Political Representation in the Inka State. *Ethnohistory* 43(1):1–32.

Gow, Peter. 1990. Could Sangama Read? The Origin of Writing among the Piro of Eastern Peru. *History and Anthropology* 5 (1):87–104.

Griffiths, Nicholas. 1996. *The Cross and the Serpent: Religious Repression and Resurgence in Colonial Peru*. Norman: University of Oklahoma Press.

Guaman Poma de Ayala, Felipe. 1980 [1615]. *Nueva corónica y buen gobierno del Perú*. John V. Murra and Rolena Adorno, eds., with translations by Jorge L. Urioste. 3 vols. Mexico City: Siglo XXI.

Guillén de Boluarte, Teresa. 1958. Las comunidades de Huarochirí. In *Las actuales comunidades indígenas: Huarochirí en 1955*. José Matos Mar et al., eds. 47–109. Lima: Universidad Nacional Mayor de San Marcos.

Gushiken, José. 1993. *Extirpación de la idolatría en la sierra de Lima*. Lima: Universidad Nacional Mayor de San Marcos, Seminario de Historia Rural Andina.

Hanks, William F. 1996. *Language and Communicative Practices*. Boulder, Colo.: Westview Press.

Harris, Roy. 1986. *The Origin of Writing*. LaSalle, Ill.: Open Court.

———. 1995. *Signs of Writing*. London: Routledge.

Herrmann, Bernd, and Roelf-Dietrich Meyer. 1993. *Südamerikanische Mumien aus vorspanischer Zeit: Eine radiologische Untersuchung*. Berlin: Staatliche Museen zu Berlin–Preussischer Kulturbesitz.

Holm, Olaf. 1968. Quipu o sapan: Un recurso mnemónico en el campo ecuatoriano. *Cuadernos de Historia y Arqueología* (Guayaquil, Ecuador) 18 (34/35):85–90.

Houston, Stephen, John Baines, and Jerrold Cooper. 2003. Last Writing: Script Obsolescence in Egypt, Mesopotamia, and Mesoamerica. *Comparative Studies in Society and History* 45 (3):430–79.

Hrdlička, Aleš. 1914. *Anthropological Work in Peru in 1913, with Notes on The Pathology of The Ancient Peruvians.* Smithsonian Miscellaneous Collections. Vol. 61 no. 18. Publication no. 2246. Washington: Smithsonian Institution.

Huertas Vallejos, Lorenzo. 1981. *La religión en una sociedad rural andina, Siglo XVII.* Ayacucho, Peru: Universidad Nacional de San Cristóbal de Huamanga.

Hugh-Jones, Stephen. 1989. Wāribi and the White Men: History and Myth in Northwest Amazonia. In *History and Ethnicity.* Elizabeth Tonkin, Maryon McDonald, and Malcolm Chapman, eds. 53–70. Association for Social Anthropology Monographs, No. 27. London: Routledge.

Hyland, Sabine P. 2002. Woven Words: The Royal Khipu of Blas Valera. In *Narrative Threads: Accounting and Recounting in Andean Khipu.* Jeffrey Quilter and Gary Urton, eds. 151–70. Austin: University of Texas Press.

Innis, Harold Adams. 1950. *Empire and Communications.* Oxford: Clarendon Press.

Isbell, Billie Jean. 1971–72. No servimos más: Un estudio de los efectos de disipar un sistema de la autoridad tradicional en un pueblo ayacuchano. *Revista del Museo Nacional* 37:285–98.

———. 1997. De inmaduro a duro: Lo simbólico femenino y los esquemas andinos de género. In *Más allá del silencio: Las fronteras de género en los andes.* Denise Arnold, ed. 253–301. La Paz: Instituto de Lengua y Cultura Aymara.

Isbell, William H. 1988. City and State in Middle Horizon Huari. In *Peruvian Prehistory: An Overview of Pre-Inca and Inca Society.* Richard W. Keatinge, ed. 164–89. New York: Cambridge University Press.

———. 1997. *Mummies and Mortuary Monuments: A Postprocessual Prehistory of Central Andean Social Organization.* Austin: University of Texas Press.

Julien, Catherine J. 1988. How Inka Decimal Administration Worked. *Ethnohistory* 35 (3):257–79.

———. 2000. *Reading Inca History.* Iowa City: University of Iowa Press.

Kahane, Henry, and Renée Kahane. 1979. Decline and Survival of Western Prestige Languages. *Language* 55 (1):183–98.

Langdon, Jean. 1992. A cultura Siona e a experiência alucinógena. In *Grafismo Indígena: Estudos de antropologia estética.* Lux Vidal, ed. 67–87. São Paulo: Livros Studio Nobel.

Larsen, Mogens Trolle. 1988. Introduction: Literacy and Social Complexity. In *State and Society. The Emergence and Development of Social Hierarchy and Political Centralization.* John Gledhill, Barbara Bender, and Mogens Trolle Larsen, eds. 173–91. London: Unwin Hyman.

Laurencich Minelli, Laura. 1996. *La scrittura dell'antico Perù: Un mondo da scoprire.* Bologna: Cooperativa Libraria Universitaria Editrice Bologna.

Lee, Vincent R. 1996. *Design by Numbers: Architectural Order among the Incas.* Wilson, Wyo.: printed by the author.

LeVine, Terry Y., ed. 1993. *Inka Storage Systems.* Norman: University of Oklahoma Press.

Lienhard, Martin. 1991. *La voz y su huella: Escritura y conflicto étnico-social en América Latina 1492–1988.* Hanover, N.H.: Ediciones del Norte.

Lira, Jorge. 1982 [1941]. *Diccionario kkechuwa-español.* 2nd ed. *Cuadernos Culturales Andinos,* No. 5. Bogotá: Secretarío Ejecutiva del Convenio "Andrés Bello."

Llanos P., Oliverio, and Jorge P. Osterling. 1982. Ritual de la fiesta del agua en San Pedro de Casta, Perú. *Journal of Latin American Lore* 8 (1):115–50.

Locke, Leland L. 1923. *The Ancient Quipu, or Peruvian Knot Record.* New York: American Museum of Natural History, 1923.

———. 1928. *Supplementary Notes on the Quipus in the American Museum of Natural History.* Anthropological Papers of the American Museum of Natural History 30. 30–73. New York: American Museum of Natural History.

Loza, Carmen Beatriz. 1998. Du bon usage des *quipus* face à l'administration coloniale espagnole (1500–1600). *Population* 1–2:139–60.

MacCormack, Sabine G. 1988. Atahualpa y el libro. *Revista de Indias* 48 (184):693–714.

Mackey, Carol. 1970. Knot Records in Ancient and Modern Peru. PhD diss., Department of Anthropology, University of California, Berkeley.

———. 1990. Nieves Yucra Huatta y la continuidad en la tradición del uso del quipu. In *Quipu y yupana: Colección de escritos.* Carol Mackey, Hugo Pereyra et al., eds. 157–64. Lima: Consejo Nacional de Ciencia y Tecnología.

Mackey, Carol, Hugo Pereyra et al., eds. 1990. *Quipu y yupana: Colección de escritos.* Lima: Consejo Nacional de Ciencia y Tecnología.

Mannheim, Bruce. 1986. Popular Song and Popular Grammar, Poetry, and Metalanguage. *Word: Journal of the International Linguistic Association* 37 (1–2):45–75.

Marcus, Joyce. 1992. *Mesoamerican Writing Systems: Propaganda, Myth, and History in Four Ancient Civilizations.* Princeton, N.J.: Princeton University Press.

Marshack, Alexander. 1972. *The Roots of Civilization.* New York: McGraw-Hill.

Martínez Chuquizana, T. Alejandro. 1996. Descripción Geográfica del Distrito de San Andrés de Tupicocha. Tesis de licenciatura, campus not specified, Lima.

Martínez Compañón y Bujalda, Baltasar Jaime. 1985. [c. 1779–89] *Trujillo del Perú.* Vol. 2. Madrid: Instituto de Cooperación Iberoamericana.

Mateos, Fernando. 1944. *Historia general de la Compañía de Jesús en la Provincia del Perú.* Madrid: Consejo Superior de Investigaciones Científicas.

Matienzo, Juan de. 1967 [1567]. *Gobierno del Perú.* Guillermo Lohmann Villena, ed. Paris-Lima: Travaux de l'Institut Français d'Études Andines.

Matos Mar, José, et al. 1958. *Las actuales comunidades indígenas: Huarochirí en 1955.* Lima: Departamento de Antropología, Facultad de Letras, Universidad Nacional Mayor de San Marcos.

Mayer, Enrique. 2002. *The Articulated Peasant: Household Economies in the Andes.* Boulder, Colo.: Westview Press.

Meisch, Lynn A. 1998. Qumpi and Khipucamayuks: New Perspectives on Textiles in Colonial Ecuador. Paper presented at the 38th Meeting of the Institute of Andean Studies, Berkeley, Calif., 10 January 1998.

Mejía Xesspe, M. Toribio. 1947. *Historia de la antigua provincia de Anan Yauyo.* Lima: n.p.

Michalowski, Piotr. 1993. Tokenism. *American Anthropologist* 95 (4):996–99.

———. 1996. Mesopotamian Cuneiform — Origin. In *The World's Writing Systems.* Peter T. Daniels and William Bright, eds. 33–36. New York: Oxford University Press.

Mills, Kenneth. 1997. *Idolatry and Its Enemies: Colonial Andean Religion and Extirpation, 1640–1750.* Princeton, N.J.: Princeton University Press.

Mishkin, Bernard. 1946. The Contemporary Quechua. In *Handbook of South American Indians.* Julian Steward, ed. Vol. 2:411–70. Washington: Bureau of American Ethnology, Smithsonian Institution.

Mitchell, William P., and David Guillet, eds. 1994. *Irrigation at High Altitudes: The Social Organization of Water Control Systems in the Andes.* Society for Latin American Anthropology Publication Series, 12. Arlington, Va.: American Anthropological Association.

Molina, Cristóbal de, "el cuzqueño." 1959 [1573]. *Relación de las fábulas y ritos de los Incas.* Ernesto Morales, ed. Buenos Aires: Editorial Futuro.

Morris, Craig, and Donald E. Thompson. 1985. *Huánuco Pampa: An Inca City and Its Hinterland.* New York, London: Thames and Hudson.

Moseley, Michael. 1992. *The Incas and their Ancestors: The Archaeology of Peru.* New York: Thames and Hudson.

Mróz, Marcin. 1984. Una interpretación numérica de la crónica de Guaman Poma de Ayala. *Anthropologica* (Lima) 2:67–103.

Murra, John V. 1968. An Aymara Kingdom in 1567. *Ethnohistory: Journal of the American Society for Ethnohistory* 15 (2):115–51.

———. 1975a. El control vertical de un máximo de pisos ecológicos en la economía de las sociedades andinas. In *Formaciones económicas y políticas del mundo andino*. 59–116. Lima: Instituto de Estudios Peruanos.

———. 1975b. Las etno-categorías de un *khipu* estatal. In *Formaciones económicas y políticas en el mundo andino*. 243–54. Lima: Instituto de Estudios Peruanos.

———. 1978 [1956]. *La organización económica del estado inca*. Mexico City: Siglo XXI.

Murúa, Martín de. 1946 [1590]. *Historia del origen y genealogía real de los Reyes Incas del Perú*. Constantino Bayle, ed. Madrid. Consejo Superior de Investigaciones Científicas, Instituto Santo Toribio de Mogrovejo.

Niles, Susan A. 1999. *The Shape of Inca History: Narrative and Architecture in an Andean Empire*. Iowa City: University of Iowa Press.

Nordenskiöld, Erland von. 1925. Calculations with Years and Months in the Peruvian Quipus. *Comparative Ethnological Studies* (Göteborg, Sweden) 6 (Pts. 1 and 2).

———. 1979 [1925]. *The Secret of the Peruvian Quipus*. New York: AMS Press.

Noriega, Maritza. 1997. Tupicocha: Viva la fiesta de los quipus. *El Comercio*, 29 December, p. F3.

Núñez del Prado, Oscar. 1990 [1950]. El kipu moderno. In *Quipu y yupana: Colección de escritos*. Carol Mackey, Hugo Pereyra et al., eds. 165–82. Lima: Consejo Nacional de Ciencia y Tecnología.

Ochoa Berreteaga, Roberto. 2000. Enigmas de Cinco Cerros. *Andares* [Supplement to La República (Lima)] 2 (96):4–15.

———. 2001. Tras las huellas del apu Pariacaca. *Andares* [Supplement to La República (Lima),] 2 (96): 4–15.

———, Roberto, and Lissette Herrera Casas. 2001. La Huayrona de Tupicocha. *Andares* [Supplement to La República (Lima),] 3(158):10–15.

Odriozola, Manuel de. 1877. *Documentos literarios del Perú colectados y arreglados por el Coronel de Caballería de Ejército Fundador de la Independencia y Director de la Biblioteca Nacional*. Vol. 11. Lima: Imprenta del Estado.

Olivas Weston, Rosario. 1983. *Marcahuasi: Mito y realidad*. Lima: Litografía Multicolor.

Olson, David R. 1994. *The World on Paper: The Conceptual and Cognitive Implications of Writing and Reading*. Cambridge: Cambridge University Press.

O'Phelan Godoy, Scarlett. 1997. *Kurakas sin sucesiones: Del cacique al alcalde de indios, Perú y Bolivia 1750–1835*. Cuzco: Centro Bartolomé de Las Casas.

Oppenheim, A. Leo. 1959. On an Operational Device in Mesopotamian Bureaucracy. *Journal of Near Eastern Studies* 18:121–28.

Ordóñez, Pastor. 1919. Los Varayocc. *Revista Universitaria [de la] Universidad del Cuzco* 27:27–40, 28:41–48.

Ortiz Rescaniere, Alejandro. 1973. *De Adaneva a Inkarrí: Una visión indígena del Perú*. Lima: Retablo de Papel.

———. 1980. *Huarochirí: 400 años después*. Lima: Pontificia Universidad Católica del Perú, Fondo Editorial.

Parmentier, Richard J. 1985. Diagrammatic Icons and Historical Processes in Belau. *American Anthropologist* 87 (4):840–52.

Pärssinen, Martti. 1992. *Tawantinsuyu: The Inca State and Its Political Organization*. Helsinki: Societas Historica Finlandiae.

Pease, Franklin. 1990. Utilización de quipus en los primeros tiempos coloniales. In *Quipu y yupana: Colección de escritos*. Carol Mackey, Hugo Pereyra et al., eds. 67–72. Lima: Consejo Nacional de Ciencia y Tecnología.

Pereyra Sánchez, Hugo. 1996. Acerca de dos quipus con características numéricas excepcionales. *Bulletin de l'Institut Français d'Études Andines* 25 (2)187–202.

———. 1997. Los quipus con cuerdas entorchadas. In *Arqueología, antropología e historia en los Andes: Homenaje a María Rostworowski*. Rafael Varón Gabai and Javier Flores Espinoza, eds. 187–98. Lima: Instituto de Estudios Peruanos.

Perri, Antonio. 2001. Writing. In *Key Terms in Language and Culture*. Alessandro Duranti, ed. 272–74. London: Blackwell.

Perrin, Michel. 1986. "Savage" Points of View on Writing. In *Myth and the Imaginary in the New World*. Edmundo Magaña and Peter Mason, eds. 211–31. Dordrecht, Netherlands: Foris.

Peru, Dirección Nacional de Estadística y Censos. 1994. *Censo Nacional, 11 julio 1993: Resultados definitivos*. Departamento de Lima Vol. 1, Pt. 2, Aspectos generales. Lima: Dirección Nacional de Estadística y Censos.

Pizarro, Hernando. 1920 [1533]. A los Señores Oydores de la Audiencia Real de Su Magestad. In *Informaciones sobre el antiguo Perú*. Horacio H. Urteaga, ed. 16–180. Colección de libros y documentos referentes a la historia del Perú, 2nd ser., 3. Lima: Imprenta y Librería Sanmartí.

Platt, Tristan. 1982. *Estado boliviano y ayllu andino: Tierra y tributo en el norte de Potosí*. Lima: Instituto de Estudios Peruanos.

———. 1986 [1978]. Mirrors and Maize: The Concept of *Yanantin* Among the Macha of Bolivia. In *Anthropological History of Andean Polities*. John V. Murra, Jacques Revel, and Nathan Wachtel, eds. 228–59. New York: Cambridge University Press.

———. 1992. Writing, Shamanism, and Identity, or, Voices from Abya-Yala. *History Workshop* 34:132–47.

———. 2002. "Without Deceit or Lies": Variable *Chinu* Readings during a Sixteenth-Century Tribute-Restitution Trial. In *Narrative Threads: Accounting and Recounting in Andean Khipu*. Jeffrey Quilter and Gary Urton, eds. 225–65. Austin: University of Texas Press.

Polia Meconi, Mario, ed. 1999. *La cosmovisión religiosa andina en los documentos inéditos del Archivo Romano de la Compañía de Jesús, 1581–1752*. Lima: Pontificia Universidad Católica del Perú.

Powell, Barry. 2002. *Writing and the Origins of Greek Literature*. New York: Cambridge University Press.

Prochaska, Rita Gertrud. 1983. Ethnography and Enculturation of Weaving on Taquile Island, Peru. Master's thesis, Department of Anthropology, University of California at Los Angeles.

Quilter, Jeffrey. 2002. Yncap Cimin Quipococ's Knots. In *Narrative Threads: Accounting and Recounting in Andean Khipu*. Jeffrey Quilter and Gary Urton, eds. 197–222. Austin: University of Texas Press.

———, and Gary Urton, eds. 2002. *Narrative Threads: Accounting and Recounting in Andean Khipu*. Austin: University of Texas Press.

Radicati di Primeglio, Carlos. 1965. La "seriación" como posible clave para descifrar los quipus extra-numerales. *Documenta, Revista de la Biblioteca Nacional* (Lima) 4:112–96 + illus.

———. 1979(?). El sistema contable de los Incas: Yupana y quipu. Lima: Librería Studium.

———. 1990a [1987]. Hacia una tipificación de los quipus. In *Quipu y yupana: Colección de escritos*. Carol Mackey, Hugo Pereyra et al., eds. 89–95. Lima: Consejo Nacional de Ciencia y Tecnología.

———. 1990b. El cromatismo de los quipus: Significado del quipu de canutos. In *Quipu y yupana: Colección de escritos*. Carol Mackey, Hugo Pereyra et al., eds. 39–50. Lima: Consejo Nacional de Ciencia y Tecnología.

Rama, Angel. 1996 [1984]. *The Lettered City*. John Charles Chasteen, trans. Durham, N.C.: Duke University Press.

Rivero y Ustáriz, Mariano Eduardo. 1857. Quipus. In *Colección de memorias científicas, agrícolas e industriales*. Vol. 2. Brussels, n.p.

Rivero, Mariano Eduardo, and Johann Jakob Tschudi. 1858. *Peruvian Antiquities*. Francis L. Hawks, trans. New York: A. S. Barnes and Company. Repr. Kraus Reprint, New York, 1971.

Robles Mendoza, Román. 1990 [1982]. El kipu alfabético de Mangas. In *Quipu y yupana: Colección de escritos*. Carol Mackey, Hugo Pereyra et al., eds. 195–202. Lima: Consejo Nacional de Ciencia y Tecnología.

Rostworowski, María. 1978a. El avance de los Yauyos hacia la costa en tiempos míticos. In *Señoríos indígenas de Lima y Canta*. 31–44. Lima: Instituto de Estudios Peruanos. Historia Andina, No. 7.

———. 1978b. Los Yauyos coloniales y el nexo con el mito. In *Señoríos indígenas de Lima y Canta*. 109–22. Lima: Instituto de Estudios Peruanos. Historia Andina, No. 7.

———. 1990. La visita de Urcos de 1652: Un kipu pueblerino. *Historia y Cultura* 20:295–317.

Rowe, John H. 1946. Inca Culture at the Time of the Spanish Conquest. In *Handbook of South American Indians.* Julian Steward, ed. Vol. 2, *The Andean Civilizations,* 183–330. Bureau of American Ethnology. Report no. 143. Washington: Smithsonian Institution.

———. 1985. Probanza de los Incas nietos de conquistadores. *Histórica* (Lima) 9(2):193–245.

Ruiz Estrada, Arturo. 1981. *Los quipus de Rapaz.* Huacho (Peru): Centro de investigación de ciencia y tecnología.

———. 1990. Notas sobre un quipu de la costa nor-central del Perú. In *Quipu y yupana: Colección de escritos.* Carol Mackey, Hugo Pereyra et al., eds. 191–94. Lima: Consejo Nacional de Ciencia y Tecnología.

Sala i Vila, Núria. 1996. La rebelión de Huarochirí en 1783: Entre la retórica y la insurgencia. In *Las ideas y los movimientos sociales en los Andes, Siglo XVIII.* Charles Walker, ed. 273–308. Cuzco: Centro Bartolomé de Las Casas.

Salomon, Frank. 1980. Don Pedro de Zámbiza, un varáyuj del Siglo XVI. *Cuadernos de Historia y Arqueología* (Guayaquil, Ecuador) 42:285–315.

———. 1995. The Beautiful Grandparents. In *Tombs for the Living: Andean Mortuary Practices.* Tom Dillehay, ed. 247–81. Washington: Dumbarton Oaks.

———. 1997. "Conjunto de nacimiento" y "línea de esperma" en el manuscrito quechua de Huarochirí (1608?). In *Más allá del silencio: Las fronteras de género en los andes.* Denise Arnold, ed. 302–22. La Paz: Instituto de Lengua y Cultura Aymara.

———. 1998a. Collquiri's Dam: The Colonial Re-voicing of an Appeal to the Archaic. In *Native Traditions in the Postconquest World.* Elizabeth Hill Boone and Tom Cummings, eds. 265–93. Washington: Dumbarton Oaks.

———. 1998b. The Half-Burned Priest: Native "Faith" in the Making. *Latin American Indian Literatures Journal* 14 (1):1–25.

———. 2001. How an Andean "Writing without Words" Works. *Current Anthropology* 42 (1):1–27.

———. 2002a. "¡Huayra huayra pichcamanta!": Augurio, risa y regeneración en la política tradicional. *Bulletin de l'Institut Français d'Études Andines* 31 (1):1–22, 2002.

———. 2002b. Un-ethnic Ethnohistory: On Peruvian Peasant Historiography and Ideas of Autochthony. *Ethnohistory* 49 (3):475–506.

———. 2002c. Patrimonial Khipu in a Modern Peruvian Village: An Introduction to the "Quipocamayos" of Tupicocha, Huarochirí. In *Narrative Threads: Accounting and Recounting in Andean Khipu.* Jeffrey Quilter and Gary Urton, eds. 293–319. Austin: University of Texas Press.

———, and George Urioste, eds. and trans. 1991. *The Huarochirí Manuscript: A Testament of Ancient and Colonial Andean Religion.* Austin: University of Texas Press.

Sampson, Geoffrey. 1985. *Writing Systems: A Linguistic Introduction.* Stanford, Calif.: Stanford University Press.

Sansevero di Sangro, Raimondo. 1750. Lettera Apologetica dell'Esercitato Accademico della Crusca contenente la difesa del libro intitolato "Lettere d'una Peruana per rispetto alla supposizione de 'Quipu' scritta alla duchessa d'S** e dalla medessima fata pubblicare." Naples: n.p.

Sarmiento de Gamboa, Pedro. 1942 [1572]. *Historia de los incas.* Buenos Aires: Emecé Editores.

Schmandt-Besserat, Denise. 1980. The Envelopes that Bear the First Writing. *Technology and Culture* 21 (3):357–75.

———. 1988. From Accounting to Written Language: The Role of Abstract Counting in the Invention of Writing. In *The Social Construction of Written Communication.* Bennett A. Raforth and Donald L. Rubin, eds. 119–30. Norwood, N.J.: Ablex Publishing.

Seed, Patricia. 1991. "Failing to Marvel": Atahualpa's Encounter with the Word. *Latin American Research Review* 26 (1):7–32.

Sempat Assadourian, Carlos. 2002. String Registries: Native Accounting and Memory According to the

Colonial Sources. In *Narrative Threads: Accounting and Recounting in Andean Khipu.* Jeffrey Quilter and Gary Urton, eds. 119–50. Austin: University of Texas Press.

Senner, Wayne M. 1989. Theories and Myths on the Origins of Writing: An Overview. In *The Origins of Writing.* Wayne M. Senner, ed. 1–26. Lincoln: University of Nebraska Press.

Sherbondy, Janet. 1982. The Canal Systems of Hanan Cuzco. PhD diss., Department of Anthropology, University of Illinois at Urbana-Champaign.

Silverman-Proust, Gail P. 1988. Weaving Technique and the Registration of Knowledge in the Cuzco Area of Peru. *Journal of Latin American Lore* 14 (2):207–41.

Smith, Richard C. 2002. Pueblos Indígenas de América Latina: Retos para el nuevo milenio. Compact Disc. Lima and Boston: Oxfam America. (Also published in summary on paper, imprint Oxfam America).

Sotelo, Hildebrando R. 1942. *Las insurrecciones y levantamientos en Huarochirí y sus factores determinantes.* Tesis de doctorado, Facultad de Letras de la Universidad Nacional Mayor de San Marcos. Lima: Empresa Periodística S.A. "La Prensa."

Soto Flores, Froilán. 1990 [1950–51]. Los kipus modernos de la localidad de Laramarca. In *Quipu y yupana: Colección de escritos.* Carol Mackey, Hugo Pereyra et al., eds. 183–90. Lima: Consejo Nacional de Ciencia y Tecnología.

Spalding, Karen. 1974. *De indio a campesino: Cambios en la estructura social del Perú colonial.* Lima: Instituto de Estudios Peruanos.

———. 1984. *Huarochirí: An Andean Society under Inca and Spanish Rule.* Stanford, Calif.: Stanford University Press.

Splitstoser, Jeffrey C., Dwight T. Wallace, and Mercedes Delgado Agurto. 2003. Bound to be Important: Wrapped Sticks and Cords in a Late Paracas Burial at Cerrillos, Ica Valley, Peru. Paper presented at 22nd Northeast Conference on Andean Archaeology, Cambridge, Mass., 2 November 2003.

Stavig, Ward A. 1988. Ethnic Conflict, Moral Economy, and Population in Rural Cuzco on the Eve of the Thupa Amaro II Rebellion. *Hispanic American Historical Review* 68 (4):737–70.

Steensberg, Axel. 1989. *Hard Grains, Irrigation, Numerals, and Script in the Rise of Civilisation.* Copenhagen: Velux fonden.

Stiglich, Germán. 1922. *Diccionario geográfico del Perú.* Vol. 2. Lima: Imprenta Torres Aguirre.

Taylor, Gerald. 1974–76. *Camay, camac* et *camasca* dans le manuscrit quechua de Huarochirí. *Journal de la Société des Américanistes* 63:231–43.

———. 1985. Un documento de Huarochirí, 1607. *Revista Andina* 3 (1):157–85.

———. 1986. Nota sobre un documento quechua de Huarochirí—1607. *Revista Andina* 7:211–12.

Taylor, Gerald, ed. and trans. 1987. *Ritos y tradiciones de Huarochirí del Siglo XVII. [With biographical material by] Antonio Acosta.* Historia Andina, no. 12. Lima: Instituto de Estudios Peruanos.

Taylor, Isaac. 1899 [1883]. *The Alphabet: An Account of the Origin and Development of Letters.* 2 vols. New York: Charles Scribner's Sons.

Tello, Julio C., and Próspero Miranda. 1923. Wallallo: Ceremonias gentílicas realizadas en la región cisandina del Perú central. Inca. *Revista Trimestral de Estudios Antropológicos* (Lima) 1 (2):475–549.

Titu Cusi Yupanqui, Diego. 1973. *Relación de la conquista del Perú [1570].* Lima: Ediciones de la Biblioteca Universitaria.

Toledo, Francisco de. 1986–89. *Disposiciones gubernativas para el virreinato del Perú.* Guillermo Lohmann Villena, ed. Seville: Escuela de Estudios Hispanoamericanos.

Topic, John R., and Coreen E. Chiswell. 1993. Inka Storage in Huamachuco. In Inka Storage Systems. Terry Y. LeVine, ed. 206–33. Norman: University of Oklahoma Press.

Treitler, Leo. 1981. Oral, Written, and Literate Process in the Transmission of Medieval Music. *Speculum* 56 (3):471–91.

Tufte, Edward R. 1983. *The Visual Display of Quantitative Information.* Cheshire, Conn.: Graphics Press.

Uhle, Max. 1990 [1897]. Un kipu moderno procedente de Cutusuma, Bolivia. In *Quipu y yupana: Colec-*

ción de escritos. Carol Mackey, Hugo Pereyra et al., eds. 127–34. Lima: Consejo Nacional de Ciencia y Tecnología.

Urioste, George. 1981. Sickness and Death in Preconquest Andean Cosmology: The Huarochirí Oral Tradition. In *Health in the Andes.* Joseph W. Bastien and John M. Donahue, eds. 9–18. Washington: American Anthropological Association.

Urton, Gary. 1984. Chuta: El espacio de la práctica social en Pacariqtambo, Perú. *Revista Andina* 2 (1):7–56.

——. 1994. A New Twist in an Old Yarn: Variation in Knot Directionality in the Inka Khipus. *Baessler-Archiv,* new ser., 42:271–305.

——. 1998. From Knots to Narratives: Reconstructing the Art of Historical Record-Keeping in the Andes from Spanish Transcriptions of Inka *Khipus. Ethnohistory* 45(3):409–38.

——. 2001. A Calendrical and Demographic Tomb Text from Northern Peru. *Latin American Antiquity* 12 (2):127–47.

——. 2003. *Signs of the Inka Khipu: Binary Coding in the Andean Knotted-String Records.* Austin: University of Texas Press.

——. In press. A History of Studies of Andean Knotted String Records. In *Historiographic Guide to Andean Sources.* Joanne Pillsbury, ed. Norman: University of Oklahoma Press.

Valderrama Fernández, Ricardo, and Carmen Escalante Gutiérrez, eds. and trans. 1977. *Gregorio Condori Mamani: Autobiografía.* Cuzco: Centro de Estudios Rurales Andinos Bartolomé de Las Casas.

——. 1988. *Del Tata Mallku a la Mama Pacha: Riego, sociedad y ritos en los Andes peruanos.* Lima: Centro de Estudios y Promoción del Desarrollo.

Valderrama Fernández, Ricardo, Carmen Escalante Gutiérrez, Paul Gelles, and Gabriela Martínez Escobar, eds. and trans. 1996. *Andean Lives: Gregorio Condori Mamani and Asunta Quispe Huamán.* Austin: University of Texas Press.

Vargas Salgado, Humberto. 1990. La comunidad campesina de Laraos y el rito de la champería. *Anthropologica* (Lima) 8(8):193–214.

Vázquez, Mario C., and Allan R. Holmberg. 1966. The Castas: Unilineal Kin Groups in Vicos, Peru. *Ethnology* 5:284–303.

Vidal, Lux, ed. 1992. *Grafismo Indígena: Estudos de antropologia estética.* São Paulo: Livros Studio Nobel.

Vilcayauri Medina, Eugenio. 1983–91. *Tupicochanos a tupicochanizarse.* Chosica, Peru(?): n.p.

Villavicencio Ubillús, Martha, et al. 1983. *Numeración, algoritmos y aplicación de relaciones numéricas y geométricas en las comunidades rurales de Puno.* Lima: Dirección de Investigaciones Educacionales, Ministerio de Educación.

Von Bischoffshausen, Gustavo. 1976. Algunos aportes sobre las denominaciones quechuas de color. Tesis de bachillerato, Departamento de Antropología, Universidad Nacional Mayor de San Marcos.

Von Hagen, Adriana, and Sonia Guillén. 2000. Nueva iconografía Chachapoyas. *Iconos: Revista Peruana de Conservación, Arte, y Arqueología* 4:8–17.

Von Tschudi, Johann Jakob. [1846] 1963. *Reiseskizzen aus den Jahren 1838–1842.* Graz, Austria: Akadeische Druck and Verlagsanstalt. Klassiker der Ethnographie Sudamerikas, Band 1.

Wachtel, Nathan. 1977. *The Vision of the Vanquished: The Spanish Conquest of Peru through Indian Eyes, 1530–70.* Ben and Siân Reynolds, trans. New York: Barnes and Noble.

Wassén, Henry. 1990. [1931]. El antiguo abaco peruano según el manuscrito de Guaman Poma. In *Quipu y yupana: Colección de escritos.* Carol Mackey, Hugo Pereyra et al., eds. 205–18. Lima: Consejo Nacional de Ciencia y Tecnología.

Wiener, Charles. 1993. [1880]. *Perú y Bolivia: Relato de viaje.* Edgardo Rivera Martínez, trans. Lima: Instituto Francés de Estudios Andinos.

Wood, Robert D. 1986. *"Teach Them Good Customs": Colonial Indian Education and Acculturation in the Andes.* Culver City, Calif.: Labyrinthos.

Zárate, Agustín de. 1995 [1555]. *Historia del descubrimiento y conquista del Perú*. Franklin Pease and Teodoro Hampe, eds. Lima: Pontificia Universidad Católica del Perú, Fondo Editorial.

Zuidema, R. Tom. 1980. El ushnu. *Revista de la Universidad Complutense* 28 (117):317–62.

——. 1989. A Quipu Calendar from Ica, Peru with a Comparison to the Ceque Calendar from Cuzco. In *World Archaeoastronomy*. Anthony F. Aveni, ed. 341–51. Cambridge: Cambridge University Press.

INDEX

Numbers in *italics* indicate illustrative material.

Camilo, Martín, 163–64, 265
Campesinos, 11, 102–3, 230
Canal systems: access to, 50; cleaning of, 47, 49, 75, 102, 198, 221, 224, 250; khipus compared to, 62; llanchas and, 218–19, 229; Willcapampa Canal, 41, 49–50
Cantito. *See* Threads run through
Cartomancy, 227, 236
Casa de Costumbre. *See* Collca
Casta Community, 47, 267
Castelli, Amalia, 57
Catholicism, 50–51
Caytus. *See* Quipocamayos
Centro Huangre, *61, 74*, 130, *187*
Cereceda, Verónica, 177
Chachapoyas khipu, 19
Chamacha, 68
Champería. *See* Canal systems
Chaucacolca: membership of, *74*; modernization and, 212; quipocamayos of, 71, 131, 152, 159, *193–94*, 212, 251, 294 n.9
Chaupi Ñamca, 194, 241–42
Checa, 4, 43, 57, 59, *61*, 122, *193–94*, 241–43, 285 n.3
Chinchano, María Micaela, 122–25
Choque Casa, Cristóbal, 118
Choquehuanca, Natalio, 243
Chorrillos, 122
Ch pendants: characteristics of, 254, 256; knots on, 256–57, 261; O pendants, 253, 261; redoubling on, 263
Chroniclers, Spanish. *See* Acosta, José de; Betanzos, Juan de; Calancha, Antonio de; Cieza de Leon, Pedro; Dávila Brizeño, Diego; Molina, Cristóbal de; Pizarro, Hernando; Polo de Ondegardo, Juan
Chronotopography, 19, 37
Chulla/chullantin (code variable), 15, 34, 106, 216, 236
Chunchos, 72
Chuquimamani, Rufino, 243
Cieza de Leon, Pedro, 110
Classen, Constance, 24
Cobo, Bernabe, 16, 113
Coca, 48, 60, 65, 70, 75, 199, 241, 249
Collapiña y Supño, 110
Collca, 69, 137–*38*, *14–42*, 199, 275
Color-cycle quipocamayos, 241, 245–46, 251–52, 255, 265, 272, *plate 15*

Colors: bichrome design and, *150, 157, 167*; black, 17, 24, 214, 218, 220, 238, 255, 259–60, *plate 16*; blue, 152; brown, 238, 250, 255; coded to subjects, 217; dyes and, 146, 152, 155, 161; gray, 217, 255, 261, *plate 15*; Munsell Soil Chart and, 160, 169–70; non-numerical meanings of, 17; oque (silvery gray), 187, 261; of pachacamantas, 156, 265; patterns of, 159, 229, 255, 258, 262, *plate 9*; of pendants, *150*, 153, 156, 159–60, 167; in reassembled quipocamayos, 264; red, 17, 152, 170, 215, 234, 250, 259–60, 263, 265, 274, 283; sorting of, 160–*61*, 169, 216; white, 24, 214, 218, 220, 255, 265; yellow, 170, 215, 234, 249–50, 259–60, 274. *See also* Thread run through
Community authority: alcades campos in, 84, *88*, 89–90, 95, 101–2; District Gobernacíon relations with, 83–84, *85*, 87–88, 94; dualism in, 192–95; investiture of officers and, 79–83, *88*, 90, 146–48; jefe de plaza (center) and, 84, 89; of officers, 88–*89*, 98, 100–102, 147; president in, 81, *82*, 146–47, 192–93; quorum for, 55; regidor (regulator) and, 79–81, 90, 93–94; six-month scheduling system of, 195–96, 292 n.13 (ch.7). *See also* Huayrona; New Year's Night; Vara inscriptions; Varas
Compañías (subsidiary cords), 153, 214, 229, 245, 259, 272
Concha, 47, 69, 114, 194, 201
Condorchagua, 116
Condori Mamani, Gregorio, 24–25
Confessional khipus, 3, 111, 117, 120, 152, 273
Conklin, William, 11, 36, 78, 142, 216, 223–24
Constancias: attendance at, 270; for festival scheduling, 195, 292 n.13 (ch. 7); importance of, 67, 188–89; performativity and, 276–77; as political affirmation of shared work, 279; of productivity, 49; quipocamayo presentation as, 216; tokens as, 292 n.13 (ch. 7); visibility and, 43. *See also* Ayllu books; Schedules
Cooper, Jerrold, 210
Cords: attachment loops, 131, 146, *150*, 171–72, 217, 221; compañías (subsidiary cords), 153, 214, 229, 245, 259, 272; dangle end, 222–23; diameter of, *150*, 169, 216, 219, 277, *plate 9*; directionality of, 146, *150*, 157, 159, 216, 223–24, 234; finishes on, 157, 170, 277, *plate 9*; hitos (ornaments), *150*, 155–56, *plate 8*; huayrona date fixed on, 220; in khipumancy, 225–

Cords (*continued*)

29; knotless, 215, 249, *plate 14*; lengths of, 153; markers on, 150, 156, 191–90, 223–24; overknotting of, 216; plying of, 159, 216, 219, 223–24, 234; redoubled, 256, 260–63, 274; as removable, 171; threads, spinning of, 157, 159; tightness of twist, 216; tools represented on, 219–20, 259–60; tronco (main cords), 6, 146, 153, 156, 217–18, 222–24, 250–52, 260, 270, 274; unknotted, 206, 215, 249–50, 259–60, 262, 264, 270. *See also* Khipus; Knobs; Knots; Markers; Pendants; Plies; Quipocamayos; Singleton cords; Vara inscriptions

Cosanche Reservoir, 69

Costales de Oviedo, Ximena, 113, 118

Coulmas, Florian, 26, 28

Council of the Indies, 110, 111

Crops, 46, 205, 218–19, 228–29, 234, 236

Cunow, Heinrich, 57

Curandero (folk healer), 164

Curcuches, 7, 49–50, 147, 194, *plate 1*

Cusichaca, Francisco, 110

Customary law. *See* Collca

Cuzco, 7–10, 19, 133–34, 152, 196, 216

Damerow, Peter, 29–30, 37, 39, 280–81

Dance: audits and, 206, 270; ayllu family re-unions and, 290 n.4; benefactors acknowl-edged by, 140, 142; huaris and, 9, 45, 49, 72, 283 n.4; huayrona and, 66–67, 286 n.9; improvisations in, 181; pre-Christian deities impersonated in, 241; women and, 290 n.4

Daniels, Peter T., 26, 29, 176, 279

Dávila Brizeño, Diego, 19, 56, 115

Day, Cyrus Lawrence, 11

Dearborn, David S. P., 34

Death, 71–72, 232–33, 271, 275–76

Decimal system, Inka: pachaka (hundreds), 56, 154–55, 240–41, 274; pichcamanta (fives), 148, 290 n.6; waranka (thousand), 18, 56, 115, 274, 285 n.3

DeFrancis, John, 26

De la Cadena, Marisol, 133

De la Cruz, José, 45

Del Río, Mercedes, 111

De Mesa, José, 12, 51

Derrida, Jacques, 26

Díaz Pinto, Leopoldo, 78

Dorian, Nancy C., 210

Doyle, Mary Eileen, 8

Draping of quipocamayos: as body politic, 18, 271; cotton cords and, 152; demonstration of, 6; fulfilled commitments indicated by, 224; investiture at huayrona and, 146–47; Mújica president and, 251; mummies and, 134–35; successors and, 76, 146–47, *plate 4*

Drinks and drinking, 48, 60, 66, 70, 142, 249

Dual quipocamayos. *See* Paired quipocamayos

Durkheim, Emil, 183

Duviols, Pierre, 8–9, 45, 192

Dynastic khipus, 168

Echeandía Valladres, J. M., 10

Echenique, Alfredo Bryce, 10

Edwards, Melanie, 128

Ehlich, Konrad, 28

Elkins, James, 15–16

Emblematic frames, 32, 36, 175–79, 277

Enfloro (enflowerment), 48, 202, *204*, 238, 248, 275

Equipocamayos. *See* Quipocamayos

Equipos. *See* Quipocamayos

Escalante Gutiérrez, Carmen, 24, 49, 152

Espinoza Soriano, Waldemar, 10, 78

Estenssoro, Juan Carlos, 287 n.5

Ethnographic khipus, 12, 127, 148

Ethnography, 3, 6, 12, 127, 148, 216, 276

Ethnologisches Museum, 16, 252

Extirpation era, 8, 10, 243

Faenas: agricultural, 69, 258, 272; announcement of, 260, 265; armadas at, 48; attendance records of, 48, 199, 270; in ayllu books, 197, 258–59; debt payments and, 262; dual-officer responsibilities in, 192–93, 244; enfloro (enflowerment) at, *48*, 202, *204*, 238, 275; fulfillment of obligations recorded and, 273; irrigation and, 45, 49–50, 248, 264, 284 n.6; labor for, 47, 70, 72, 74, 197, 199–200, 247, 261; labor reciprocity and, 47, 70, 72, 197; levies for, 198, 248; person carrying and, 70, 264, 265; rituals during, 48–49, 249; rounds (vuel-tas) of, 197–98, 246–47, 256–58, 261, 271–72, 292 n.17 (ch. 7); scheduling of, 47, 181, 195–96, 218, 271–72; space demarcations in, 62; supra-ayllu duties and, 197–98, 205, 271; thread run through designation of, 234, 250; tools for, 260, 265; women and, 203; work crosses and,

47–48, 75, 87, 95, 202, 238, 275. *See also* Agropastoralism; Canal systems; Festivals; Land
use; Schedules; Water resources

Families: in ayllu books, 190–91; as cuadrillas
(work squads), 64; in membership sequences
(orden de familias), 189–90; in Mújica ayllu,
247; patrilineage in, 57, 63–64, 67, 69, 190–
91, 213–14; reunions of, 64–65, 147, 290 n.4;
signature clusters in ayllu books, 191; spouses
in, 220, 235; suprahousehold functions of, 74–
75, 246–48, 265; surname groups (familias)
and, 62–64, 190–91, 257; women and, 203,
283, 290 n.4; yumay (sperm) and, 63, 69, 191,
291 n.5

Fane, Diana, 133

Farr, Cheryl Ann, 155

Feltham, Jane, 9

Festivals: of Catholicsm, 50–51; in Concha Sica,
194; faena obligations and, 263; of the Crosses
(May 3), 60, 72, 221; of Holy Week, 50; of
Machua Yunca fertility, 194; markers of, 156;
of patron saints, 44, 50–51, 75, 194, 199, 250,
263; scheduling of, 195, 292 n.13; of Virgin
of the Assumption feast day, 263. *See also*
Rituals

Fibers: alpaca, 129, 216, 269; binarisms in working with, 15; camelid wool, 24, 129, 157, 216,
269; cotton, 6, 152, 220; cow's tail hair (C-01),
217; dyes in, 146, 152, 155, 161; human hair, 16–
17, 152; sheep and wool, 6, 24, 114, 152–53, 157,
216, 251, 253, 274, *plate 6*

Flores Galindo, Alberto, 124

Flowers: as ayllu symbol, 60, 75; azul tiñi-tiñi,
152; constancies and, 65; enfloro (enflowerment) and, 48, 202, 204, 238, 248, 275

Folk-legal system: alcaldes in, 84, 88, 89–90, 95,
101–2; ayllus as llahta in, 56, 274; customary
mayors in, 56, 193, *plate 1*; documentation
in, 45–46; Huaranga de Checa (Thousand
of Checa) in, 56; quipocamayos in, 212, 268;
Spaniards and, 118. *See also* Community
authority; Varayos

Fonseca, César, 49, 201

Ford Foundation, 10

Fossa, Lydia, 110

Franco de Melo, Sebastían, 121–25

Fuenzalida Vollmar, Fernando, 247

Fujimori regime, 10, 41, 45, 52, 83, 103

Function-band hypothesis, 244–48, 271–72

Gandz, Solomon, 11

García Cabrera, Juan Carlos, 8

Garcilaso Inca de la Vega, 110, 113, 169, 173

Gartner, William Gustav, 19

Gateway God at Tiwanaku, 78

Gaur, Albertine, 26

Gelb, Ignace J., 25–26, 279

Gelles, Paul, 24, 47, 49, 78, 248

Gellner, Ernest, 212

Gentile Lafaille, Margarita, 148

Gilmer, Nancy, 8

Gisbert, Teresa, 12, 51, 152

Glottography. *See* Lexigraphy

Gobernacíon: community board, relations with,
83–84, 85, 87–88, 94; deputyships in, 101;
inspection of staffs by, 80; staff inscriptions
of, 79, 83, 86, 87–88, 89–90; staffs arrayed by,
93–94

Golte, Jürgen, 47, 189

Goodman, Nelson: canon of formal coherence
and, 36–37; on diagrams, 278; holistic models
and, 270; on notation, 33–34, 179–83, 277–78;
semiology of, 178

Goody, Jack, 26, 29, 175

Gordon, Cyrus H., 37

Gose, Peter, 49, 189

Gow, Peter, 23

Grammatology, 6, 23, 26, 174–75

Grass arrangements, 66, 140, 146–47, *plate 3*

Griffiths, Nicholas, 8

Guaman Poma de Ayala, Felipe: Collca drawing
by, *139*; function brackets in census, and, 191,
244–45; on khipu storage, 142, *144*; knobs,
154; on Paria Caca cult, 8; ritual and relief
fund (comunidad y sapçi) and, 140–41, 270

Guamansica, 119

Guangre, 247

Guillén, Sonia, 12, 232

Guillén de Boluarte, Teresa, 45

Gushiken, José, 78

Half-life, traditions of, 210–11, 222, 231, 234–35

Hanks, William, 35–36, 38

Harris, Roy: on emblematic frames, 32, 36, 175–
76, 178–79, 277; on integrationalism, 31, 36,
103, 277; on relation between signifier and
signified, 31; on signary as primary code, 31;
on writing, 170, 178

Harvard University, 282

Javier, Julio, 167, 215, 219
Javier, Tobías, 213–14, 216
Javier, Toribio, 217, 219, 222
Javier Medina, Vicenta, 160
Javier Rojas, Nery, 164, 171, 212–15, 260, *plate 10*
Jesuits: José de Acosta, 30, 111; on confessional khipus, 120; on fifteen-day cycle of cultic service, 242; on jhanca augury, 290 n.4; on Paria Caca cult, 241; Juan Sebastián de la Parra and, 120, 241; schools of, 8; Blas Valera and, 8, 112–13, 173. *See also* Avila, Francisco de
Julca Rirpo, Francisco, 78
Julien, Catherine J., 19, 110, 278
Junta Directiva Comunal, 42–43

Kahane, Henry, 210
Kahane, Renée, 210
Kauki, 167
Khipu Data Base Project, 282
Khipukamayuq, 3, 146, 206
Khipumancy: Andean death ideology and, 271; as augury, 147, 225–28; black and white mottled cords and, 229; grafismo and, 273; huayra huayra pichcamanta and, 148–49, 195, 290 n.4; names in, 226, *plate 11*; odd-even patterns in, 236, 270; terminology in, 230
Khipus, 2; accounting methods of, 110, 112–17, 168–69, 214, 268; alphabetic characters and, 6–7, 111–12, 125, 128; in Bolivia, 111, 148, 231; burial with, 134–35, 232–32, 275–76; canal system compared to, 62; as chronotopography, 19; clandestinity and, 113, 118, 129, 135, 243; coiling of, 142, 143–47 (*144–45*), *plate 2*; in repressive campaigns, 268; cross-referencing of, 221–22; as data collection systems, 11, 118–19, 221–22; demise of, 130–31; destruction of, 113, 117–18; display of, 139, 142–48 (*145–46*), 155, 269, *plates 2, 5, 10*; double-entry recording on, 200–201; as economic records, 119, 288 n. 26; handling of, 6, 146–47, 216, 290 n.2; as labor records, 117, 199–200; in legal depositions, 110–11, 118–19; as maps, 182, *219*, 236, 246, 278; paper records and, 118, 121–26, 128–29, 131, 288 n.20; proto-writing and, 29–30, 37, 276, 279–82; radiocarbon dating of, 127–29, 132–33, 186, 243, 251, 268, 272; Rebellion of 1750 and, 121–26, 131–32, 268; semasiography and, 27–28, 30; speech segments and, 6, 15, 17–18, 279; staffs compared

with, 78, 106–7; storage of, 142–48 (*145–46*), 222–23, *plates 2–3*; tablet-khipus hybrids and, 127; women and, 111, 122–25, 130, 214. *See also* Colors; Cords; Fibers; Huayrona; Knobs; Knots; Lockean conventions; Pendants; Varas
Kinship, 279; in ayllus, 57, 59, 187–88; Checa and, 43, 57, 59, 61, 241–43, 285 n.3; family reunion at huayrona, 64–65; patrilineages in, 57, 63–64, 69, 190–91, 213–14; surname groups (familias), 62–64, 190–91, 257; symbols of, *58*, 60; virilocality in, 63; yumay (sperm) and, 63, 69, 191, 291 n.5; yuriy (birth) and, 63
Kinship corporations. *See* Ayllus; Families; Parcialidades
Knobs, *150*, 154–55, 156, 222–24, 228, 234, *plate 7*; as end-points of main cords, 153; colors of, 156, 265; construction of, *154–55*; in draping, 147; of individual ayllus, 187; of Mújica quipocamayos, *154*, 251–52, 265; pachaka (hundreds) and, 56, 154–55, 240–41, 274; Santa valley khipus, 274; terminology, 145–46,155–56
Knots: cursive writing compared to, 165–66; directionality of, 15, 214; distance between, 218–19, 220–21; E-knot (figure-eight) 14, 214–15, *219–20*; hitolos, 230; I-knot (Inka long knot), *14, 150,* 162–64, 214–15, 249; internodes and, 218–19, 229, 234; in khipumancy, 230; knotlessness and, 215, 236, 249, *plate 14*; labor absentees registered by, 201; M-knots (Mújica, multiple figure-eight), *150,* 164–65, *166,* 187, 253; numerical values of, 13, 190, 262; objects inserted in, 16, 156–58; overhand, *145,* 214, 251; overknotting and, 216; on pendants, *150,* 162, 206, 221; placement standardized in, *173,* 271; reknotting and, 221; signatures and, 39, 165–66, 272; s-knot (single overhand or simple knot), 214–15, 220, 229, 259; straw knotting and, 120; T-knots (Tupicocha knots), *150,* 162–66 (*163, 165*), 214, 236, 249, 253, 258–59, 262; turns in, 165, 167, 220, 229; unknotting and changeability of, 169, 206, 215, 249, 264, 273; zero values of, 249, 262, 270
Koth de Paredes, Marcia, 57
Kurakas, 132, 190, 196–97

Laguna de los Cóndores, 12, 232
Lahuaytambo, 122, 289 n.33
Land control, 42–43, 45–46, 68–69, 285 n.3

Land use: under agropastoralism, 45; ayllu audits of, 205; chacra (cultivated field), 218–19, 229, 234; folk-legal documentation of, 45–46; puna, 43, 45, 140; tabla, 218; terracing, 218–19, 229–30, 234, 246

Langa, 122, 289 n.33

Langdon, Jean, 23

Language: extinction of, 210; metalanguage, 90–93, 95–96, 147; natural language, 32–33, 37

Larsen, Mogens Trolle, 29

Laurencich Minelli, Laura, 287 n.5

Lee, Vincent R., 19

Leguía, Augusto, 131, 134, 192, 198, 268

LeVine, Terry Y., 138

Lexigraphy, 25, 175, 273, 276, 279–80, 284 n.3

Lienhard, Martin, 19

Lima, 4, 7, 43; documentation of road construction and, 117; Gobernación at, 83–84, 85, 87–88, 94, 101; indigenisms in, 133; migration to, 10, 45, 101, 286 n.12

Limandas, 198, 201

Lira, Jorge, 25

Livermore, Harold, 173

Llacsa Tampo, 59. *See also* Llaquistambo

Llanchas, 218–19, 229, 270, 272

Llanos, Oliverio, 10, 49

Llaquistambo, 194. *See also* Llacsa Tampo

Lockean conventions (Leland Locke): arithmetic structure of khipus, 13–15 (*14*), 190; cord accountancy, 110; decimal formation in khipus, 56, 216, 277; harvest warehousing and, 246; I-knot (Inka long knot), *14*, *150*, 162–64, 214–15, 249; khipus as calculating devices, 168; mathematical syntax of, 37; in Santa valley khipus, 274; Tupicochan quipocamayos and, 148, 216, 255, 270; vara codes and, 105–6; zero, 13, 206, 249, 262, 270

Logograms, 273, 279

Long knots, 221; construction of, 163–64; I-knot (Inka long knot), *14*, *150*, 162–64, 214–15, 249; single, 229; T-knots (Tupicocha knots), *150*, 162–66 (*163*, *165*), 214, 236, 249, 253, 258–59, 262; in Tupicochan quipocamayos, *150*, 162, 164, 214–15; turns of (vueltas), 165, 167, 220

Lopéz, Francisco, 117

Lower Yauyos. *See* Huarochirí

Loza, Carmen Beatriz, 109, 110–11, 113, 115, 117–18, 146

Lurín River, *4*, 43, 57, 68

Lurin Yauyos. *See* Huarochirí

M-01 quipocamayo: color cycle structure of, 240, 251–52, *255*, 272, *plate 15*; dating of, 251; as household database, 256–57; knots in, 162, 164–65, *166*, 214–15, 219, 251; main cord of, 251–52; Musée de l'Homme quipocamayo compared with, 252, 254, 294 n.11; M-0X lost quipocamayo elements in, *155*, 251, 265, 272; pachacamantas of, *154*, 251–52, 265; pendant-quipocamayo ratio of, 240; as postnegotiation khipu, 256–57; quartets in, 252–54, *255*, 257, 260, 262, 272, *plate 15*; reconstruction of, 251, 252; wool in, 152, 251–52. *See also* Colors; V1 pendants; V2 pendants

M-02 quipocamayo, 157, *187*, 251–52, *255*, 272

M-0X quipocamayo, *155*, 251, 265, 272

Maca Huisa, 242–43

MacCormack, Sabine G., 24

Mackey, Carol, 12–13, 45, 148, 152, 169, 216, 232, 251

Magical khipus, 228

Mala River, *4*, 21

Mama María, 49

Mangas, 127

Mannheim, Bruce, 90

Marcus, Joyce, 105

Markers: on cords, 131, *150*, 155–56, 191–90, 223–24; of festivals, 156, 224, 250; hitos, *150*, 155–56, *plate 8*; knobs, 60, 146, *150*, 153–55 (*154*); motas, 131, *150*, 155–56, 218, *223*, *plate 8*; plumed bulbs, 146; pontoladores, 223–24; singleton cords as, 222; surface texture of, 224; tufts, 16, 156, *158*, 191, 218, *223*, 248–49, 274, *plate 8*

Marshack, Alexander, 34

Martínez Compañón y Bujalda, Baltasar, 127

Martínez Escobar, Gabriela, 24

Masllaulli, 69

Mateos, Fernando, 8

Matienzo, Juan de, 111

Matos Mar, José, 9, 64

Matucana, 52

Mayans, 38

Mayer, Enrique, 45, 185, 201

Mayors: ambassadorial role of, 244; customary law mayors (alcade de costumbre), 56, 193; duties of, *150*, 196, 244; president, dual leadership with, 192–93, 269–70; quipocamayos, 195

McJunkin, David, 128

Meisch, Lynn A., 113, 118

Mejía Xesspe, Toribio, 9

Mesa, José de, 12, 152

Mesopotamia, 28–30, 174, 280–81

Messianism, 121

Metalanguage, 90–96, 147

Meyer, Roelf-Dietrich, 78

Miccinelli, Clara, 134, 287 n.5

Michalowski, Piotr, 29, 174, 280

Middle Horizon era, 78

Mignolo, Walter, 20

Mills, Kenneth, 8

Minka. *See* Faenas

Minutes. *See* Constancias

Miranda, Próspero, 8, 12, 78, 127, 267

Mishkin, Bernard, 78–79

Mitas (forced labor), 117, 186, 196, 200

M-knots (Mújica), *150*, 164–66, 187, 253, 261

Molina, Cristóbal de, 111, 152

Monkey's fist knot. *See* T-knots

Morris, Craig, 138

Moseley, Michael, 77

Motas. *See* Markers

Mould de Pease, Mariana, 57

Mróz, Marcin, 19

Mújica, *61*; banded quipocamayos of, 265; curandero (folk healer) in, 164; families in, 247; khipus in, 133, 152, 159; land holdings of, 68; mayors in, 192; membership of, *74*, 192; M-02 quipocamayo, 157, *187*, 251, 252, 255, 272; quipocamayo ownership, *193*; seed bank, 71; surnames in, *257*; written inventories of, 128–29. *See also* M-01 quipocamayo

Mummies: Christian burial and, 232; khipus and, 134–35, 232, 271, 275–76; Laguna de los Cóndores, 232; mallki (mummified ancestor), 78, 232–33; of Ñan Sapa, 78; New Year festivities compared with, 271; Tutay Quiri, 57; wrapped staffs, 78; Ynga Topa, 115

Mural, 41–43 (*42*)

Murillo de la Cerda, Doctor, 112–13, 125, 287 n.4

Murra, John V.: detects ethno-categories in khipus, 19; on ethnocategories of economy, 119, 288 n.26; on household accountability, 189; on moiety lords of non-Inka polities, 192; vertical archipelago model of, 9, 43–46

Murúa, Martín de, 120

Musée de l'Homme, 252, 254, 260, 294 n.11

Museum khipus: colonial khipus, 12; display of, 143–44; Ethnologisches Musem, 16, 252; Musée de l'Homme, 252, 254, 260, 294 n.11; Tupicochan v. Inka quipocamayos, 273–74

Music: audits and, 202, 270; ayllus and, 60; of chicha, 10, 283 n.6; notation system in, 26, 31, 33, 277; song in cords, 225

New Year's Night: benefactors at, 140; elections, 79–83, 140; grass symbols at, 140; rites of succession at, 88, 146–47; review of staffs at, 79–80, *81–82*, 90, 93–94. *See also* Huayrona; Vara inscriptions; Varas; Varayos

Niles, Susan, 230

Ninavilca, Sebastián, 112, 119

Nongovernmental organizations (NGOs), 47, 52, 73, 205

Noriega, Maritza, 10

Notation systems, 26, 31, 33–34, 175, 179–83, 277

Numbers: fifteen, 241–43, 247, 271; hundreds, 56, 154–55, 240–41, 274; in khipumancy, 226; odd-even, 236, 270; thousands, 56–57, 154–55, 285 n.3; of turns counted in long knots, 167

Núñez del Prado, Oscar, 12

Ochoa Berreteaga, Roberto, 10

Olivas Weston, Rosario, 10

Olleros, Santiago de los, parish, 122

Olson, David R., 25, 28

1A-01 quipocamayo, *173*, *187*, *193*, 244, *plate 12*

1G-01 quipocamayo (Primer Huangre), 157, *193*, *plate 14*

1SF-01 quipocamayo: 2SF-01 quipocamayo and, *145*, 159, *163*, 170, *172*, *187*, 238, *plate 13*; colors of, 170; cord directionality of, 159, 234; delimiters of, 222–24 (*223*), *plate 7*; fibers in, 216; in khipumancy, 229; ownership of, *187*, *193*; pairing of, 244, *plate 13*; paper records and, 131; reading of, 216–21; simulacrum quipocamayo and, 214; tuft in knot of, *158*

O pendants. *See* I-knot; M-knots; T-knots

O'Phelan Godoy, Scarlett, 197

Oppenheim, A. L., 174

Oracles, 225–26. *See also* Huayra huayra pichcamanta

Ordóñez, Pastor, 78

Ortiz Rescaniere, Alejandro, 9, 24

Osterling, Jorge P., 10, 49

Oxfam America, 10

Pachacamantas. *See* Knobs

Pacha Kamaq, 56, 114, 115

Pacota, 140, 148–49

Paired quipocamayos: 1A-01/2A-01, *187, 193,* 244, *plates 12–13;* 1SF-01/2SF-01, *187,* 244, *plate 13;* Allauca and, 240; ayllu books and, 192–93, 234; ayllu fission and, 130–31, 192, 222; bands on, 246, 248, 265, 271; color-cycled quipocamayos as, 265; dismemberment of, 222; distribution of information between, 270; dual leadership and, 192, 269–70; Paria Caca/Chaupi Ñamca corresponding to, 242; pendants on, 271; polycyclical systems and, 47, 188–89, 194–95, 199; Santa valley quipocamayos, 274; singletons in, 240, 271; supra-ayllu functions and, 246; UCH-01/UCH-02, *187,* 244, *plate 13. See also* M-01 quipocamayo

Paper khipus, 19

Paramonga, 157

Parcialidades: camachico of, 60, 76, 131; chapel (cross/pasión) of, 60, 67; community face of the ayllu, 57; consensus among, 73–74; family information of, 220; field (chacra) use by, 218–19, 229, 234; khipus as corporate policy document of, 217; mural of, *42–43;* nicknames of, 60, 65, 283 n.5; social dances of, 72; space and, 62; staff-holders (varayos) of, 79; symbols of, *58;* use of term of, 57, 284 n.1; water policy of, 69–70; welfare and ritual funds of, 220, 246, 270. *See also* Ayllus

Paria Caca cult: 15/30-fold organization in ritual of, 242; Chaupi Ñamca and, 194, 241–42; chronology of ritual of, 241; descendents of, 57, 59, 194; huacsa priesthood of, 241; Hua-ranga de Checa (Thousand of Checa) and, 57, 190; road construction and, 117; thirty-man teams in, 242; Tutay Quiri and, *43,* 57, 59, 285 n.3; yanca, priesthood of, 241, 293 n.2

Parmentier, Richard J., 32, 177

Parra, Juan Sebastián de la, 120, 241

Pärssinen, Martti, 17

Patrimonial khipus, 11–12, 16, 20, 156–57

Peañas: as base for cross, 60, 87, 287 n.8; cerro and, 146; at huayrona, *84,* 140; in khipu han-dling, 146; p-spaces and, *86–87,* 102; sanctity of, 103; on varas, 79, *86–87*

Peasant Community (communidad campesina), 41–44 (*42*), 56

Pease, Franklin, 118

Peirce, Charles Sanders, 16, 35, 283 n.8

Pencollo, 49

Pendants, 155; attachment loops of, 131, 146, 150, 171–72, 217, 221; bands and, 238, 240–41, 245, 248; chronological sequence of, 217–18, 234; colors of, *150,* 153, 156, 159–60, 167, 229; combing of (peinado), 6, 146; function-band hypothesis concerning, 244; grouping of, 167–68; immobilization of, *145,* 260, 273; in khipumancy, 225; knots in, *150,* 162, 206, 221; in M-01 quipocamayos, 251; in paired quipocamayos, 271; as removable, *150,* 171; in Santa valley khipus, 274; single-tons, *150,* 238; spaces and, 218, 229; as table of contents for khipu, 146; tuft of wool in, *158;* unraveling of, *159. See also* Bands; Colors; M-01 quipocamayo; Threads run through

Pereya Sánchez, Hugo, 11, 16–17, 152

Performance recording, 188, 245–46, 269, 273

Perri, Antonio, 279

Perrin, Michel, 23

Phonography. *See* Lexigraphy

Pizarro, Hernando, 110, 116, *166,* 169

Planning quipocamayos, 264

Platt, Tristan, 23, 152, 197

Pledges, 51, 72–73, *150,* 198, 201, 206, 220–21

Plies: directionality of, 159, 223–24, 234; in reassembled quipocamayos, 264; S-plied, 15, 157, 159, 216, 253, 260, 263; unraveling of, 216, 219; Z-plied, 15, 159, 216, 253, 256, 260

Polia Meconi, Mario, 120, 241

Polo de Ondegardo, Juan, 110, 134

Polycyclical systems: agropastoralism, 34, 188; alternating ritual cycles, 49, 147, 194–95; paired quipocamayos and, 47, 188–89, 194–95, 199; scheduling in, 47, 188–89, 273

Pomachahua, 115–16

Pontoladores. *See* Markers

Powell, Barry, 36

Pre-Christian deities, 4, 9, 113, 230, 241, 267

Presidents: of ayllus, 60, 76, 192–93, 213, 225; duties of, *150,* 196; executive duties of, 244; faenas and, 244; mayors and, 192–93, 269–70; of parcialidad, 60, 76, 131; of Primera Sarafasca, 213; quipocamayos and, 131, 195, 260. *See also* Mayors

Priesthood: of Concha village, 63–64, 69; huacsa, 241–43, 247, 271; of post-Inka Maca

Huisa cult, 243; Tupicochan quotas required by, 271; yanca, 241, 293 n.2

Primera Allauca, *61*, *74*, 132, *187*, 240

Primer Huangre, *61*, *73–74*, *154–55*, 157, 249, *plate 14*

Primera Satafasca, *61*; artisans supported by, 71; paired quipocamayos and, 240; Lanzasa canals and, 198; membership of, *74*, 191; 1SF-01 quipocamayo and, 131, 158–59 (*158*), 170, *187*, 212–13, 216, 222–23, 229, 244, *plates 8*, *13*; patrilineages in, 213–14; president of, 213; work categories in, 246. *See also* Javier Rojas, Nery

Privatization (parcelación), 45

Prochaska, Rita Gertrud, 12, 17, 152, 157

Proto-cuneiform, 29–30, 37, 280–82

Proto-Elamite, 280–81

Puna, 43, 45, 140

Puno, 133, 216

Puruchuco, 232

Purun huacas, 68

Puyporocsi, Martín, 118

Quartet structure of quipocamayos. *See* Ch pendants; M-01 quipocamayo; v pendants; vV2 pendants

Quechua: dialect diversification in, 275; orthography of, 22; Spanish and, 18, 275; syllabography of, 113, 287 n.5. *See also* Huarochirí Quechua Manuscript

Quilter, Jeffrey, 12–13, 18

Quipocamayos: accounting with, 112–13, 214; audit records in, 203–4; ayllu fission and, 130–32, 222; ayllu membership indicated by, 191–90; band frequency in, 240; binomial nomenclature for, 22; as collaborative work, 269, 273, 276; colonial institutions recorded in, 186; combing of (peinado), 6, 146; competence in, 130–31, 210–11, 216, 222, 231, 234, 235, 243, 268; curation of, 135, 251, 267; data combined between, 221; as emblematic frames, 32, 178–79, 277; folk interpretations of, 211, 231, 235; geography of, 156; handling of, 6, 145–47, 170, 216, 269, 290 n.2; head-of-household status and, 63; hitos, *150*, 155, 156, *plate 8*; household sequencing in, 269; of Huaranga de Checa (Thousand of Checa), 57; moving parts in, 168–71, *172–73*, 178–79, 264, 273, *plate 9*; quartet structure in, 252–54, *255*,

257, 260, 262, 272, *plate 15*; simulacrum of, 211, 213–14, 217, 220, *plate 10*; wearing of, 3, 6, 18, 146–47, 195, 224, 251, 271, 292 n.14 (ch. 7), *plates 1*, *4*; women and, 192, 195, 214. *See also* Festivals; Huayrona; Paired quipocamayos; Radiocarbon dating; Rituals; Tupicochan quipocamayos

Qullka. *See* Collca

Racism, 10

Radicati de Primeglio, Carlos, 11, 16, 146, 148; on changeable parts of khipus, 169; on khipus in 18th century, 120; on knob as end of khipu, 224; on knotlessness as significant data, 249; on magical khipus, 228; on pendant groupings, 167; on seriation (seriación) in pre-Hispanic khipus, 274

Radiocarbon dating: of extirpation era, 243; interpretation of, 127–30, 186; of M-01 quipocamayo, 251, 272; of Tupicochan quipocamayos, 127–28, 132–33, 186, 196, 243, 268

Raimondi stela at Chavín, 77

Rama, Angel, 21

Rapaz, 17, 127, 267

Rayas: community offices represented by, 88–90 (*89*); in huayrona grass arrangements, 140; staff inscriptions and, *85–86*, *88–89*, *94–95*, *97–98*, 100–101

Rebellion of 1750, 121–26, 131–32, 268

Rebuses, 27, 174–76

Rescaniere, Ortiz, 9

Rímac River, *4*, 21, 45, 57, 68, 115–16, 194

Rituals, 34, 36; audits as, 202; ayllu gatherings as, 67; body contact in, 66–67, 286 n.9; chapel (cross/pasión) and, 60, 67; for Chaupi Ñamca, 194, 241–42; coca use in, 60, 65, 75, 199, 241, 249; Collca, 69, *137–38*, *141–42*, 199, 275; curcuches, 7, 49, 72, 147, 194; enfloro (enflowerment), *48*, 202, *204*, 238, 275; fundraising, 51, 66, 67, 72; huayra huayra oracle, 148, *149*, 195, 290 n.4; investiture of officers at huayrona, 79–83, 90, 146–48; offerings, 48–49, 114; peañas and, 103; of reciprocity, 70; silence in staff decipherment, 100; of water rights, 114; Willcapampa Canal and, 49. *See also* Dance; Varas; Varayos

Rivero, Mariano, 127

Rivero y Ustáriz, Mariano Eduardo, 11–12

Robles Mendoza, Román, 11, 127

Rojas, Silvano, 130
Rojas Alberco, León Modesto, 92, *98*
Rosetta stone, 3, 35
Rossi, Paolo A., 134, 287 n.5
Rostworowski, María, 9, 19, 186
Rowe, John H., 110
Rueda, Justo, 91–92, *98*, 100, 160
Ruíz Estrada, Arturo, 12, 17, 127, 156–57, 267
Runa yn[di]o ñiscap. See Huarochirí Quechua
   Manuscript

Sacred clowns, 7, 49, 72, 147, 194, *plate 1*
Sala i Villa, Nuria, 132
Salazar, José Antonio de, 121
Salomon, Frank, 57, 63–64, 69; 15/30-fold orga-
   nization in Huarochirí Quechua Manuscript,
   242; on movement of water, 229–30; water
   rights ritual and, 114
Sampson, Geoffrey, 25–28, 31, 93, 96
San Andrés de Tupicocha, 43, 50–51
San Damián de los Checa. *See* Checa; Huaranga
   de Checa (Thousand of Checa); Huarochirí
   Quechua Manuscript
Sansevero di Sangro, Raimondo, 211, 287 n.5
Santa Clara, 140
Santa Inés de Chíchima, 117
Santa María Jesús de Huarochirí, 119. *See also*
   Huarochirí
Santa valley khipus, 274
Santiago de Tuna, *61*; alternating ritual cycles of,
   49, 147, 194; Collca of, 140; family signature
   clusters in, 191; khipus used in, 118–19; land
   ownership and, 285 n.3; Rebellion of 1750 in,
   122; teamwork in, 75
Santos Atahualpa, Juan, 121, 128
Sapçi (community welfare deposit), 140–41, 270
Sarmiento de Gamboa, Pedro, 111
Satafasca, 130–31, 152, 159, *193*, 195–96, 240, 247.
   See also Primera Satafasca; Segunda Satafasca
Saussure, Ferdinand de, 25, 27, 30, 35, 170, 182,
   277
Schedules: in Ch pendants, 260–61, 272; of
   faenas, 46–47, 181, 195, 246–47, 272; of huacsa
   priesthood, 241–43, 247, 271; of meetings, 50,
   60, 218, 224, 260, 264, 272; in Paria Caca cult,
   241–42; of polycyclical systems, 47, 188–89,
   273; of rounds (vueltas) of faenas, 197–98,
   246–47, 256–58, 261, 271–72, 292 n.17 (ch. 7);
   of el seis-meis (six-month planning meeting),

   195–96, 292 n.13 (ch. 7); of semester system,
   195–96, 271–72
Schmandt-Besserat, Denise, 28–29, 174
Seed, Patricia, 24
Segunda Allauca, *61*, *193*; champerías (canal-
   cleanings), 198; collective obligations recorded by, 248; faena rounds (vueltas) in,
   197–98, 261, 292 n.17; labor registry of, 197,
   200; membership of, *74*, 191; quipocamayo of,
   130–131, *159*, 238, *plate 6*
Segunda Satafasca, *61*; 2SF-01 quipocamayo and,
   145, 159, *163*, 170, *172*, 187, 238, 294 n.9, *plate 13*;
   audits of, 195, 202, *204*; census in, 191; collective property of, 68; election meeting of, *65*;
   as junior ayllu, 130–31
Semasiography: khipumantic readings as, 231,
   273; khipus and, 27–28, 30, 168; notation systems and, 26, 31, 33–34, 175, 179, 180–83, 277;
   two full languages and, 27–28, 93, 96; vara
   inscriptions as, 103–7
Semester system, 195–96, 271–72
Sempat Assadourian, Carlos, 109, 110, 112, 127
Seniority, 50, 62, 189–90, 245, 256, 262, 272
Senner, Wayne M., 279
Sherbondy, Janet, 49
Shining Path, 10, 41, 52
Signatures, 165–66, 190–91, 272
Signs, 15, 31, 35–36, 103, 277
Silence: in examination of staffs (vara), 80, 100;
   in khipu display, 117–18, 146–47; in nego-
   tiations, 264; in quipocamayo presentation,
   265–66
Silverman-Proust, Gail, 177
Singleton cords: in banded quipocamayos, 241;
   colors of, *150*, 238; as cross-reference markers,
   222; as interrupters, 238; lone cords, 238;
   near pachacamanta knobs, 238; in paired
   quipocamayos, 240, 271; pendants, *150*, 238; as
   separators, 238
Sisicaya, 68, 117
Smith, Richard C., 10
Social audits, 199, 201–2, *204*, 250, 270
Sotelo, Hildebrando, 121, 127
Soto Flores, Froilán, 12
Spaces: architecture of ceremonial spaces,
   275; boundaries of, 60, 68, 79, 86–87, 285
   n.3, 287 n.8; chapel (pasión), 60, 67; grass
   arrangements, 66, 140, 146–47, *plate 3*; of parcialidades, 60, 62, 67; on pendants, 218, 229;

ritual space, 47–48, 75, 87, 95; Santa valley khipus, 274; in vara inscriptions, 92, 102; work cross, 47–48, 75, 87, 95. *See also* Canal systems

Spalding, Karen, 9, 19, 45, 56, 121

Spaniards: encomienda of, 283 n. 5; government by, 121–26, 131–32; Huarochirí rebellion against, 268; Indo-Arabic numerals and, 113, 287 n.4; on khipu accounting methods, 110–17, 268; on khipus, 30, 275; on language, 5, 24, 121–22; legal uses of khipus under, 110–11, 118–19; love of letters of, 268; Pacha Kamaq and, 56, 114–15; Rebellion of 1750, 121–26, 131–32, 268; reductions in establishments of, 43; regulation of khipus by, 111; viceroyalty of, 43, 111, 113, 117, 268; visitas (tribute inspections) of, 68, 117, 186, 291 n.2

Speech: habitual patterns of, 38–39; khipus and, 6, 17–18, 279; quipocamayos verbalized, 265–66; representation of, 28; staffs (vara) and, 93, 95–96; writing and, 25, 28–29

Splitstoser, Jeffrey C., 11

Staff God/Goddess, 77–78

Staff-holders. *See* Varayos

Staffs. *See* Varas

State government: community authority and, 55, 88; Gobernacíon, 83–84, 85, 87–88, 94, 101; 1890 system of, 193–94; Peasant Community recognized by, 56; quipocamayos and, 52–53; Tupicocha and, 193. *See also* Parcialidades

Stavig, Ward A., 124

Steensberg, Axel, 28

Sterling, Bruce, 209

Straw khipus (quipos de paja), 120

Sunicancha, 47, 122

Surco, 285 n.3

Surnames, 62–64, 190–91, 257

Tablet khipus, 127

Tally books (libros de rayas), 113

Tambiah, Stanley, 189

Tampocaya, 68

Taquile Island, 17, 152

Tawantinsuyu, 133, 274

Taylor, Gerald, 60, 118, 242

Taylor, Isaac, 26

Tello, Julio C., 9, 12, 78, 127, 133–34, 212, 267

Third Council of Lima, 113, 117

Thompson, Donald E., 138

Threads run through: Ch pendants lacking, 256; cords, 156–57, 199, 234, 238, 250; in M-01 quipocamayo, 260, *plate 16*; in reassembled quipocamayos, 264; in V1 pendant, 260

Titu Cusi Yupanqui, 24

T-knots (Tupicocha knots), 150, 162–66 (163, 165), 214, 236, 249, 253, 258–59, 262

Tobacco, 48, 65, 70, 249

Tokens, 28–29, 174, 176, 179, 193, 264, 292 n.13

Toledo, Francisco de, 43, 111, 113, 117, 268

Tools, 71, 202, 215, 219–20, 235, 259–60

Tourism, 10, 147, 225

Treitler, Leo, 33, 180

Tronco (main cords), 6, 146, 153, 156, 217–18, 222–24, 250–52, 260, 270, 274

Tschudi, Johann Jakob, 12

Tufte, Edward, 182, 281

Tufts, 16, 158, 191, 218, 248–49, 274

Tupicocha, 3; annex settlements (anexos) without khipus, 44; bullring of, 57–58; consensus among ayllus, 73; demography of, 44, 51–52, 284 n.1; documentation in, 19; governmental structure of, 43–44; indigenism in, 133–34; knots as initials, 257; Peasant Community (communidad campesina) of, 41–44 (42), 56; Rebellion of 1750 in, 121–26, 131–32, 268; scheduling system in, 194–96, 292 n.13; varayos (staff holders), 78; yunka ayllus, 194. *See also* Huarochirí Quechua Manuscript; *and individual ayllus (e.g., Mújica)*

Tupicochan quipocamayos: I-knot (Inka long knot) in, 14, 150, 162–64, 214–15, 249; knobs of, 274; knots on, 150, 162, 164, 206, 214–16; Lockean arithmetical regularities and, 148, 216, 255, 270; markers on, 150, 153, 156, 191–90; modern view of, 147–48; multiple hands on, 145–46, 170, 269; ownership of, 187; pendant groupings, 150, 167; radiocarbon dating of, 127–28, 196, 268; reinterpretation of, 212; reinvention of, 133–35; Santa valley khipus compared with, 274; sign deployment, 279–80; structure of, 148, 150; T-knots (Tupicocha knots) in, 150, 162–66 (163, 165), 214, 236, 249, 253, 258–59, 262; top cords lacking in, 270; tufts inserted in, 17, 249. *See also* Colors; Huayrona; New Year's Night; Rituals

Tutay Quiri, 43, 57, 59, 285 n.3

2A-01 quipocamayo, 130–131, 159, 187, 193, 238, 244, *plate 6*

tamia, 27–29, 280–81; non-phonetic scripts, 27; paper and, 24–26; performative force of, 269, 276; proto-cuneiform, 29–30, 37, 280–82; proto-writing, 29–30, 37, 276, 279–82; rebuses and, 27, 174–76; speech and, 25, 28–29; tokens and, 28–29, 174, 176, 179, 193, 264, 292 n.13; writing proper, 6, 25, 96, 273, 276. *See also* Semasiography

Ximénez Inga, Francisco, 121–23, 126, 133

Yapita, Juan de Dios, 231

Zárate de, Agustín, 110
Zero, 13, 206, 249, 262, 270
Zuidema, R. Tom, 19

Frank Salomon is a professor of anthropology at the University of Wisconsin, Madison. He is the author of a number of books, including *Native Lords of Quito in the Age of the Incas: The Political Economy of North-Andean Chiefdoms* (1986), and translator (from Quechua, with George L. Urioste) of *The Huarochirí Manuscript: A Testament of Ancient and Colonial Andean Religion* (1991). With Stuart Schwartz, he edited the two South American volumes of the *Cambridge History of the Native Peoples of the Americas* (1999).

Library of Congress Cataloging-in-Publication Data
Salomon, Frank.
The cord keepers : khipus and cultural life in a Peruvian village / Frank Salomon.
p. cm. — (Latin America otherwise)
Includes bibliographical references and index.
ISBN 0-8223-3379-1 (cloth : alk. paper) — ISBN 0-8223-3390-2 (pbk. : alk. paper)
1. Quipu—Peru—Huarochirí (Province)—History. 2. Quechua Indians—Peru—Huarochirí (Province)—History. 3. Quechua philosophy—Peru—Huarochirí (Province). 4. Quechua Indians—Peru—Huarochirí (Province)—Social life and customs. 5. Huarochirí (Peru : Province)—History. 6. Huarochirí (Peru : Province)—Social life and customs. I. Title. II. Series.
F3429.3.Q6S35 2004   985'.00498323—dc22   2004007975